AFRICAN WOMEN
SOUTH OF THE SAHARA

AFRICAN WOMEN SOUTH OF THE SAHARA

edited by
Margaret Jean Hay and Sharon Stichter

Longman
Scientific &
Technical

Copublished in the United States with
John Wiley & Sons, Inc., New York

Longman Group Limited,
Longman House, Burnt Mill,
Harlow, Essex CM20 2JE, England
and Associated Companies throughout the world.

Published in the United States of America
by Longman Publishing, New York

First published 1984
Seventh impression 1992
Second edition 1995

First published 1995

ISBN 0 582 21241 3 PPR

British Library Cataloguing-in-Publication Data

A catalogue record for this book is
available from the British Library

Library of Congress Cataloging-in-Publication Data

A catalog record for this book is available from the Library of Congress

Set by 5 in 10/11 Pt Palatino
Produced by Longman Singapore Publishers (Pte) Ltd.
Printed in Singapore

Contents

Preface to the Second Edition

Academic interest in the study of women in Africa has grown enormously since the first edition of this book appeared in 1984. Among scholars and policy-makers, there has been increased recognition of the importance of women's past and present contributions to African development, coupled with a sobering realization of the many obstacles to further economic and social progress. During the past decade, an even larger body of scholarly literature on African women has emerged. University courses in African history, society and development, and in black studies and women's studies, now routinely incorporate material on African women.

It remains a challenge, however, to make the fruits of this extensive scholarship available to undergraduates and to the general reader. Much of the best work on African women is now in edited collections focussed on a single theme, such as class, politics, agriculture, or literature. It is difficult to choose from the myriad of richly detailed and specific case studies those which might qualify as illustrative of the general African situation. Thus there continues to be a need for a general work on sub-Saharan women, one that provides an overview of the subject, incorporates and synthesizes the best insights of the new scholarship, and is at the same time accessible to undergraduate and nonspecialist readers.

This book is designed to fill that need. It is an introductory, interdisciplinary text, written from the perspective of a number of disciplines but set in a historical context. Each chapter is written by a specialist familiar with the issues in that particular field. Each introduces a topic in clear and straightforward terms, and attempts to point the way towards deeper study of the area discussed.

All chapters in the second edition have been revised and updated by their authors, in order to integrate new research and changing theoretical perspectives. New developments over the past decade are fully discussed, such as the adverse impacts on women of food shortages, debt crises, and structural adjustment policies, as well as the many efforts made during the United Nations Decade for Women.

Two contributors to the first edition, Barbara Lewis and Luise White, were unable to participate in the revision; Kathleen Staudt and Betty Potash kindly stepped forward to write the chapters on development policy and on the family. In addition, we are pleased to be able to include three completely new contributions, a chapter on health issues by Meredeth Turshen and case studies on family planning by Tola Pearce, and on inheritance laws affecting women by Margaret Munalula and Winnie Mwenda.

As in the previous edition, the book emphasizes present-day conditions, but also gives a comprehensive review of African women in precolonial society and of the major changes that occurred during the colonial era. The geographical focus on sub-Saharan Africa remains as before, and material on women in South Africa has been integrated throughout the discussion.

The work reflects a combination of group effort and individual expertise. We think that the combination is a fruitful one. Although each chapter remains the individual creation of its author, each was written within editorial guidelines that attempted to ensure continuity and comprehensiveness. The circulation of outlines and drafts among contributors facilitated discussion and interchange and contributed greatly to the book's internal cohesion.

Editorially, the work has been a joint effort in the fullest sense, both of us having worked together on all phases of the project. As editors, we would like to thank all the contributors for their hard work, patience, and good-humored willingness to accommodate revisions. Our appreciation also goes to Chris Harrison at Longman Publishers, who encouraged us to prepare this revised edition.

Margaret Jean Hay
Boston University

Sharon Stichter
University of Massachusetts, Boston

List of Tables

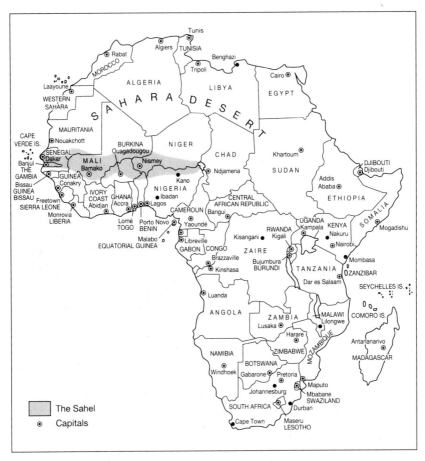

Contemporary Africa

Introduction

As one of the world's major cultural regions, sub-Saharan Africa has
been distinguished by a tradition of shifting hoe agriculture and lineage-
based societies. Here, in contrast to societies in some other parts of the
world, women have played and continue to play a major role in food
cultivation and trade, in addition to food preparation and child-rearing.
In some, though not all, African societies, women enjoyed control over
the fruits of their labor and wielded substantial political power.

Even in Africa, however, women's power and status were always in
some major ways less than those of men. In this book we will explore
the range of variations in women's social position in Africa, taking into
account not only the great diversity of traditional social arrangements,
but also the overlay of outside influences, from European colonial
conquest in the late nineteenth and early twentieth centuries to the
Arab/Islamic penetration of earlier eras. The contemporary situation of
women has been shaped by all of these historical forces.

The first three chapters of the book look at the role of women largely
from the point of view of their economic position and roles. Conceiving
of 'the economic' in a broad sense, these chapters describe the work
women do in production, distribution and reproduction, as well as their
degree of access to economic resources such as land, livestock and trade
items, and to education, skills and wage employment.

Chapter 1 opens with the observation, also underlined in later
chapters, that African women do the bulk of subsistence labor in
agriculture, yet do not control much of the surplus generated from
this labor. To explain this situation, Jeanne Koopman elaborates a
view of the traditional African household as embodying the control of
labor of women and junior males by senior men. Women are economic
and social dependents of males; yet they are expected somehow to
provide all the food for their family's daily consumption. The many
modifications which are introduced into these relationships in state and
stateless societies, slave-holding societies, matrilineal and patrilineal
kinship systems, and pastoral and hunting and gathering societies are
also delineated.

This account of the traditional African household as a patriarchal economic unit differs from earlier formulations which had emphasized only the functional complementarity between women's and men's work roles. Instead, this approach calls attention to who controls productive and reproductive labor and who benefits from it. It also provides a starting point for the analysis of women's position in the society as a whole, since in most cases household and lineage were the most important political and economic units. Yet there is a danger in this view of representing African women as mere pawns in the hands of 'patriarchs'. That such a conclusion would be erroneous is amply demonstrated in the material in subsequent chapters, particularly those on the family, religion, women's associations and women in politics. These chapters stress African women's many areas of enterprise, autonomy and independence, both traditionally and in modern times.

A second theme, introduced in Chapter 1 and elaborated in subsequent chapters, is the complex and contradictory effects of colonial rule on African women's economic position. On the one hand, women's workload increased in many areas as men migrated to towns and mines for wage employment. Women's legal and use-rights to the land were undermined in the change-over to Western systems of individual land tenure. Men controlled the proceeds from the new and lucrative cash crops such as coffee, cocoa, and cotton. The strength of patriarchal households was broken down in some ways and reinforced in others. Chapter 1 notes, however, that in some areas of personal rights and freedoms, women's position improved as a result of colonial changes.

In Chapter 2, Jane Guyer points out that, with some exceptions, most rural women today have access to some productive resource or market which gives them a small income. This chapter provides a detailed look at contemporary variations in women's rural economic role, variations that are linked to the differential impact of the world economic system on varying local structures. Three rural economies are described, each attached to the world economy in different ways: (1) through limited participation in regional economic relationships, (2) through cash-crop production for the world market, and (3) through men's wage work for industrial and agricultural enterprises. A fourth case, illustrating female wage work in large-scale plantation agriculture, is also discussed.

The first case is the West African system of savannah agriculture among the Senufo, where the complex balance of men's and women's roles has not been much affected by outside forces. The important role of men in growing staple food crops here constitutes an exception to the more general situation in Africa of female predominance in subsistence agriculture. The Senufo also illustrate the case of matrilineal kinship, in which women inherit limited but secure access to land and incomes.

The second case examined is the well-developed cash-crop economy of the Ewe in Ghana, where cocoa growing resulted in a male monopoly of the proceeds from that export crop and the transfer of nearly all food-producing functions to the women. But not all export-oriented economies have followed this pattern, and some sources of variation in women's position in other cash-crop producing areas are ably analyzed.

The third case examined is the labor reserve economy of southern Africa, where the majority of men migrate to wage jobs elsewhere. Agriculture stagnates, and women remain heavily dependent on male remittances if they do not migrate themselves.

In a new section on changes in the 1980s, Guyer points out that amid the bleak general picture of food shortages and rural stagnation there are a few areas – notably in Nigeria and Zimbabwe – where food production has been growing and rural women's lot has, paradoxically, begun to look brighter.

African towns of colonial origin were previously the temporary homes of male labor migrants; today they are witnessing a more rapid immigration of African women. Towns of indigenous origin always had a more balanced sex ratio. Facing job discrimination and generally high unemployment in towns, women often join the 'informal sector', where their activities range from small-scale trading of all sorts to semi-legal activities such as beer brewing and prostitution. In Chapter 3 Claire Robertson describes the various occupations of urban women, making effective use of the life histories of a market trader in Accra, a domestic servant in Johannesburg, a prostitute in Nairobi, a leader of the women's movement in Nigeria, and a secretary in Lusaka. The chapter is revised to include some of the latest available employment and census figures for African cities, and includes new observations about women in the informal sector, drawn from the author's own research.

The picture of urban women presented in Chapter 3 is supplemented by a statistical Appendix, compiled by Sharon Stichter; the Appendix also coordinates closely with Chapter 12 on development impacts and Chapter 13 on health. The Appendix is completely revised and updated, containing tables on women's economic activity rates 1970–1990, women's employment and unemployment 1980–1990, occupational distribution in selected countries, and estimated fertility and maternal mortality rates for the majority of countries. These facilitate comparison and contrast between different parts of the continent. The Appendix also introduces the changing definitions of 'labor force' or 'economically active population', and comments on their limitations as descriptions of women's work.

Chapter 4 on women in the African family, by Betty Potash, is entirely new. It stresses the differences between customary family and kin organization in Africa and the independent nuclear family idealized in contemporary Western society. Colonial and present-day development policies have too often been predicated on the assumption that African families are conjugally structured, whereas in fact they are consanguineal. Men's, and in some cases women's, primary loyalties and support may be given to their natal kin groups rather than to their spouses. Women are customarily assigned the main responsibility for feeding themselves and their children. Pooled incomes and joint decision-making are still the exception rather than the rule. Institutions such as polygyny and bridewealth are common.

Chapter 4 describes women's complex roles within extended family structures, such as relations among co-wives and between wives and their mothers-in-law, and the position of widows. Patrilineal and matrilineal variants are detailed. Social change benefitting men during colonial rule and since has led to the increased dependence of many women on their conjugal relationships, and pressures for men to give increased support to their wives and children. It has also led to family separation, the prevalence of 'outside wives', and growth in the numbers of single women and female-headed households.

A companion case study, Chapter 5 on widow inheritance in Zambia, illustrates how a traditional custom in a new context can disadvantage women. Margaret Munalula and Winnie Mwenda, two Zambian lawyers, explain that in all Zambian descent systems, whether matrilineal or patrilineal, affinal ties take precedence over conjugal ties in determining property inheritance. Therefore widows were not defined as heirs; on the contrary, they themselves were often inherited by their husband's kin, or might be required to make a death payment to them. Twenty years of pressure and protest by Zambian women have led to some legal reform. Statutory law, which supersedes customary law, now guarantees a widow 20 per cent of her husband's property.

The portrayal of women in religion, ideology and the arts, as well as women's own expressions in these spheres, are the concerns of Chapters 6, 7 and 8. In Chapter 6, Margaret Strobel gives a full and incisive account of women's roles in African traditional religions, in Christianity and in Islam, and of the gender ideology expressed through those religions. She observes that the traditional female rites of passage, so prevalent throughout Africa, transmit the ideology of female inferiority to the initiates and socialize them to their proper roles as wives, while at the same time giving them a sense of the value and importance of womanhood. The rites often express or mediate the contradiction between autonomy and submission inherent in women's roles. The widespread participation of women as ritual specialists, spirit mediums, and members of spirit possession cults in traditional Africa is related to the struggle to compensate for inferior status, as well as to the real physiological problems encountered by women. Such roles illustrate another avenue through which some women could acquire influence and wealth in traditional societies.

The advent of Christianity, with its own version of the proper spheres for men and women, initiated conflicts between African beliefs and imported ones; many conflicts revolved around women's roles. Christianity condemned such practices as polygyny and clitoridectomy; many African separatist churches defended them. Islam, too, brought its own tenets regarding women, including specific legal rights for women in marriage and divorce, 'purdah' or the seclusion of women, and the exclusion of women from formal religious office. It mingled perhaps more successfully than did Christianity with indigenous cultures, but not without many internal tensions. The updated version of Chapter 6 includes a new section on activism among Islamic women who seek to raise women's status through the reinterpretation of

Islamic law. There is also a new discussion of groups speaking out against clitoridectomy.

A special feature of this text is the inclusion of chapters on women and the arts, areas that are too often omitted from discussions of social change. The plastic and verbal arts both express and illustrate many of the themes that emerge from the other chapters. In Chapter 7 Lisa Aronson notes the separateness yet complementarity of women's and men's arts, a reflection of the complex interrelationship of men's and women's work. Similarly, the domestic orientation of many women's arts reflects the large proportion of labor time spent in domestic activities. Nonetheless, some women's arts, such as pottery and weaving, can be highly professionalized and have considerable religious significance and economic worth in the 'public' domain. Groups of potters and weavers protect their craft skills and marketing channels, much as do the other sorts of women's occupational associations discussed in Chapter 9. As might be expected, changes in marketing opportunities can promote changes in women's arts. In Chapter 8 Deirdre LaPin contrasts the 'sweetness' of traditional women's narratives with the 'sharper edge' found in contemporary writings by women. Narratives, songs, and praise poems reveal much about social life, and women are as important as creators and practitioners of these arts as they are as subjects.

The many varieties of African women's cooperative actions and solidarity groups are described by Audrey Wipper in Chapter 9. The prevalence of such groups in the past and today in Africa confirms that a division of men's and women's roles in which women are confined to a 'domestic' sphere and men monopolize a 'public' sphere, while common in Western culture, is not an accurate characterization of Africa. This theme is further pursued in Chapter 10 on politics. Women's community participation today ranges from rural work groups and secret societies to modern cooperatives, from urban associations of women traders and professional women to those of beer brewers and prostitutes. Chapter 9 provides an overview of these groups, contrasting the indigenous associations, in which membership was largely ascribed, to the modern ones, which are based on voluntary membership.

The variety and power of women's groups in some traditional societies suggest that in these cases women had considerable autonomy in the areas of special concern to them, such as farming, trading, female rites of passage, childbirth and the education of young girls. Some modern associations have also exerted considerable power. However, the updated version of Chapter 9 stresses the recent growth in the number of women's groups, and the extent to which many of them have become government- or donor-sponsored. As the groups gain power and resources, they often neglect the interests of their grassroots membership and become co-opted by male politicians and political parties.

Chapters 10, 11, and 12 concern women as political actors and as objects of public policy. Chapter 10, by Jean O'Barr and Kathryn Firmin-Sellers, returns to the question of women's status and power raised in

Chapter 1, looking at it from the new perspective of recent feminist scholarship. The authors highlight the ideologies of gender embodied in the cultural, social and political institutions imposed on Africa by the West, particularly the assumption of a public/private dichotomy between men's and women's activities, and the nuclear family model. A review of women's political roles in precolonial hunting and gathering, horticultural and centralized African societies illustrates the inadequacy of the first assumption. The accounts of the 'Aba Riots', the Anlu rebellion, and the Pare tax revolt show how women's indigenous collective institutions, described in Chapter 9, were used as vehicles for wider political protest during the colonial era.

Women played critical roles in many of the anticolonial nationalist movements. Chapter 10 recounts the differing styles of participation and varying outcomes in several types of nationalist movements: Nigeria, where the movement was early and relatively nonviolent and where market women were an important pressure group; Guinea, where the movement adopted a more socialist ideology and where women were rewarded for their participation with substantial gains; and South Africa, where the struggle has been long and success is only now in sight.

These cases show both parallels and contrasts to women's roles in the armed liberation struggles in Mozambique, Guinea-Bissau, Angola, Zimbabwe and Namibia, described by Stephanie Urdang in Chapter 11. What distinguished these movements was their ideological commitment to a more equitable society, which included the liberation of women. The chapter describes the movements' strong emphasis on the political mobilization of women, women's important roles in the armed resistance, and their new roles in production in communal villages and state farms. Sadly, the visions of a just society, the high hopes for peaceful economic progress, were cruelly dashed after independence. Caught up in external and internal conflicts and world economic stagnation, most of these countries still have far to go in addressing the problems of women. In vivid vignettes from Mozambique, Chapter 11 shows the contrast between the beginnings of development and the destruction of war.

In most African nations today, women have been largely excluded from state resources and denied access to state power. Chapter 10 brings the account of women's political participation up to date, emphasizing their under-representation and even 'withdrawal' from national-level politics, and their somewhat greater success in areas outside formal state control. A new section on the United Nations Decade for Women 1975–1985 presents its three goals of institutional reform, such as the creation of new ministries for women's affairs; legal reform, primarily in family law; and economic initiatives for women. Under the third head, examples of successful development projects such as the Green Belt movement in Kenya are described. But the authors conclude, as does Wipper in Chapter 9 and Staudt in Chapter 12, that the great majority of development efforts focussing on women have not fulfilled their goals.

'Gendered development' is the term Kathleen Staudt coins in Chapter 12 to describe the complex of male-dominated political institutions implementing policies of male preference in development underwritten by misguided gender ideologies. This chapter, which is entirely new to this edition, describes the World Bank policies of 'structural adjustment' imposed on African economies in the 1980s, and their mostly negative impacts on women. Three development case studies are included: irrigated rice projects in Gambia, program reforms in agricultural extension services in Kenya, and structural adjustment impacts on market women in Ghana. None of these have benefitted women. Chapter 12 concludes that the lack of a women's voice in the design and implementation of these projects is the key factor leading to their failure.

Chapter 13 and its companion case study in Chapter 14 are new to this edition, and draw attention to women's health issues, an area of increasing concern in the effort to improve women's quality of life. Meredeth Turshen introduces the topics of famine and nutrition, environmental degradation, birth control, female circumcision, and AIDS. She calls for more preventive health services for women as the chief need in Africa today. The chapter argues that maternal and child health, rather than population control, should be the focus of family planning programs. It does not, however, deal with the problem of Africa's very rapid rate of population growth; this is discussed in the Appendix. The continuing controversy over female circumcision is discussed in both Chapters 13 and Chapter 10, as well as Chapter 6, which covers traditional meanings and the colonial mission conflicts. With reference to AIDS, Chapter 13 argues that efforts should focus on prevention of its spread rather than cure, and that a coordinated health policy, that combats AIDS along with other widespread diseases such as malaria and tuberculosis, is what is needed.

The theme of the importance of women's health is expanded in Chapter 14 by Tola Olu Pearce. This new case study stresses the importance of monitoring the health effects of contraceptive use. Drawing on data she gathered at rural health centers in Ondo and Oyo states in Nigeria, the author shows that information given to clients about possible side effects is inadequate, and that due to technical limitations, initial and follow-up medical examinations are cursory. Since women's fears of adverse health effects are one important deterrent to greater contraceptive use, Pearce concludes that family planning programs should give much more attention to this matter.

Chapter 14 ends the textbook on African women on a practical note, giving an example of just one among the many specific problems confronting African women today. African women themselves are well aware of these problems, since they experience them daily. They have shown great strength and resourcefulness in devising solutions appropriate to their situation and culture. Yet many areas of exclusion and subordination remain. It is to be hoped that recent trends toward democratization in African politics will give women's voices greater impact. To a large extent, the future progress of Africa is in their hands.

xvii

Part One

African Women in the Economy

Women in the rural economy: past, present, and future

Jeanne Koopman

In the 1990s, as in the past, the great majority of African women are farmers. Today, more than ever, it is women who feed the continent. Most spend four to eight hours a day in their fields, aided only by a simple hoe. Feeding the family, however, requires more than food production: it takes another five to six hours to collect water and firewood and to harvest, process, and cook food products, even if there is only one hot meal per day.

The tasks and technology of the rural woman's labor day have changed surprisingly little since the precolonial era. High-yielding plant varieties, fertilizers, and pesticides are rarely used on women's fields. Separate budgets, modest incomes, and major responsibilities to provide purchased food and to meet children's needs effectively preclude investment in labor-saving mechanized or animal-drawn agricultural implements. Technological progress has largely passed women by, in large part because the social and economic constraints that shaped women's agricultural and domestic responsibilities in the precolonial era have been intensified by the colonial integration of African economies into international circuits of trade and investment.

This chapter summarizes the impact of precolonial socioeconomic structures, colonial changes, and postcolonial trends on contemporary women's work and welfare. Given the problematic nature of historical sources, the cultural, economic, and ecological variety of African societies, and the salience of active debates about the nature of gender relations in the past, any such broad summary must be approached with caution.

Source materials on the precolonial era are relatively scarce. Most written records are the products of 'outsiders', mainly European and Middle Eastern travellers, traders, missionaries, and anthropologists (Musisi 1991). Even when relatively free of ethnocentric distortion, these records capture only a fragment of the changing tapestry of social systems that were continually adapting to a millennium of periodic migration, cultural and economic interpenetration, and the violence fostered by the international slave trade.

Source materials on the colonial period are more numerous, but those written by outsiders are often even more distorted by the racism and sexism so frequently relied upon to 'justify' the colonial enterprise. Both African and foreign scholars are increasingly turning to the tools of oral history, particularly to interviews with old people who can recall the traditions, myths, and events enshrined in the collective memory of a family, clan, or people. But even these sources have their limitations. The 'collective memory' is itself a means of reinterpreting 'tradition' in support of the informant's position in contemporary social struggles, not least those between women and men (Chanock 1982, Stamp 1991).

These caveats aside, the historical literature is increasingly rich. Over the past two decades, historians have made explicit efforts to understand how class and gender affected people's experience of the past. Both oral and written sources have been reworked in ways that have substantially enhanced our ability to understand the past from the perspective of rural African women (Hunt 1989).

Precolonial period

Economic systems

Food farming in precolonial Africa was almost everywhere based on an extensive form of hoe culture. A new field of one to two acres was cleared in forest or bush land once or twice a year. After three to six seasons of cultivation, the field was either abandoned or left to fallow for 10 to 20 years. This type of farming system required either low population density and plenty of virgin land or the periodic migration of the farming community to new areas. The perpetual need for new land and the episodic dangers posed to small stateless societies by expanding or slaving states made migration a perennial feature of most people's lives.

Men's role in extensive hoe agriculture was commonly limited to land clearing. Men also played a military role in defending and acquiring land – a relatively frequent requirement with shifting agriculture. Women usually carried out all the major farming tasks – breaking up the soil, planting, weeding, harvesting, and carrying the harvest home – with little or no male help. This pattern was so widespread that African shifting agriculture is sometimes referred to as a 'woman's farming system' (Boserup 1970).

In contrast, a smaller number of African societies practiced a more intensive form of hoe agriculture, fertilizing their land or fallowing for very short periods. Intensive agriculture was often found in mountainous areas where volcanic soils had high natural fertility and in areas where invaders or aggressive neighbors had pushed smaller groups into limited spaces. The use of organic fertilizers, the terracing of slopes and the maintenance of water control systems tended to require more labor than women alone could supply. Thus intensive farming systems often combined men's and women's labor.

Mixed sex farming was also prevalent in the Sahel, where men and women worked collective plots of millet and sorghum as well as individual plots where women often cultivated groundnuts and men grew cotton. In some cases, like the Senufo (described in Chapter 2), men did the bulk of the work on staple foods while women cultivated individual plots of rice and groundnuts. When the ox-drawn plow was introduced in Lesotho in the late nineteenth century, men took a greater role in preparation of the sorghum fields and young men in threshing the harvest, but women's work in all phases of cultivation increased enormously as men's fields increased in size, and because women still had to prepare the smaller family fields by hand (Eldredge 1991).

Farming systems in which men performed the bulk of the work with little or no female help were quite rare in precolonial Africa. They were found among the Hausa (who also used slave labor), the Yoruba of southwestern Nigeria (where women specialized in food processing and trading), and in Ethiopian societies (where animal traction was used).

An article published by Hermann Baumann in 1928 gives a good indication of the relative importance of women's, men's, and mixed sex farming systems. Baumann studied the sexual division of labor in 140 African societies that had been described in anthropological studies and travellers' reports from the late precolonial and early colonial periods. He found that women did all the field work except clearing in 40 per cent of the cases, men did most of the work in 15 per cent, and mixed sex labor patterns prevailed in 45 per cent (Baumann 1928: 308–16).

When agriculture was combined with cattle keeping, as in many societies of eastern and southern Africa, women usually took responsibility for food farming while men and boys herded the livestock. In pastoral and nomadic societies, such as the Maasai of East Africa and the Fulani of the West African Sahel, men herded and women milked the cows and produced butter. In hunting and gathering societies such as the Pygmy peoples of the central African forests and the San peoples of the Kalahari Desert in southern Africa, men hunted and women supplied the daily diet of roots, berries, and fruit.

The household and the state

African political systems ranged in structure from small stateless communities to vast hierarchial empires. There was, however, a strong element of continuity in that all were based on the extended family as the fundamental socioeconomic unit. The polygynous household, headed by one man with several wives and unmarried male dependents or, alternatively, a larger household comprised of several married brothers with their wives and dependents (with the eldest brother as household head), was the basic production and consumption unit in almost all societies. Within the extended family household, each wife and her children formed an economic sub-unit with a separate kitchen and fields for food production (Guyer 1981).

Each extended family was embedded in a sociopolitical structure characterized by networks of wider economic and political obligations, some based on kinship ties (lineages and clans),[1] and others on relations of military dominance and subordination (Coquery-Vidrovitch 1988). Nonetheless, most households were economically autonomous, producing their own food, housing, and most other necessities.

Roles, rights, and responsibilities within the household were defined by gender, age, and seniority. Three categories were basic to all households: the top position of household head or patriarch, the middle position of temporary dependents (younger men who would one day become household heads), and the base position of permanent dependents. Permanent dependents were people who could never become heads of their own households, including almost all women and male slaves or clients who joined a household seeking the protection of its head.

The division of labor and the control of resources in the precolonial household reflected this tripartite structure. The household head, sometimes in collaboration with the lineage or clan chief, controlled the use of land, tools, livestock and, most critically, the labor of his dependents. He was primarily an owner/manager, and worked in the fields himself only if young or relatively poor. He allocated food fields to his wives (and perhaps to his sons) for the production of household food supplies, and he managed the labor of his male dependents. Temporary dependents (sons and nephews) and clients were usually responsible for male functions such as field clearing and military raiding or defense, while male slaves might be assigned either male or female tasks. Women slaves and pawns often became helpers for free women and many were also integrated into the household as slave wives of the patriarch or of his male dependents (Robertson and Klein 1983).

'Men's work' most often included land clearing, house building, cloth weaving, herding, hunting, and military functions. 'Women's work' included food production, storage, processing, and preparation; the manufacture of pottery, baskets, mats, and clothing; care of children and the sick; and personal services, especially for their husbands. Centuries of practice have enshrined this sexual division of labor in cultural ideologies and contemporary ideas of appropriate gender roles. One of its most salient legacies is the widespread belief that women are responsible for feeding their families. This responsibility sets the parameters, and the constraints, of women's economic life.

During the precolonial era women also had important roles in the social and political reproduction of their households and lineages. These roles, however, were shaped by the agency of men and grew out of women's status as dependents. Women were, for example, exchanged among men as wives, thereby providing their fathers and husbands with social, economic, and military links to other lineages and clans. Alliances created by marriage ties buttressed the political prestige and increased the military strength of household heads. It was, however, the men who became the partners in these relationships. Women were but the means to male-defined ends.

As wives and mothers, women provided their husbands with the most valuable of their 'possessions' – children. A large progeny was the key determinant of a man's social prestige, political power, and economic prosperity. The basic measure of a man's wealth was the number of dependents in his household. The association of wealth with persons is explained by the conditions of production: in precolonial Africa, labor was by far the most critical factor of production. Control of land depended on control of labor, specifically on the ability to mobilize the military strength to obtain and defend new, fertile land and on the capacity to deploy male and especially female labor to produce the food required to support a large dependent household.

With control over people as the key to political power and economic accumulation, control over marriage was a vigorously defended patriarchal privilege. Marriage was the turning point in a free male's life, the beginning of his social and economic emancipation. Until he was married, a young man remained a dependent who owed total obedience and economic service to his patriarch. No man could arrange his first marriage on his own: he had to wait for his father to 'give' him a wife. A man's first marriage was the first phase of his own transformation into a patriarch. He could now control the labor and output of his wife and begin the accumulation of his own dependents by exchanging his daughters for additional wives. For men, therefore, marriage initiated a critical change in social status. For women, marriage simply marked the transfer of their dependence from father to husband.

States and stateless societies

Many precolonial African societies had no permanent political structures above the household level. Sociopolitical linkages were formed on the basis of kinship and marriage alliances, but positions of leadership and political power were rarely vested in a single person or group. In stateless societies the ideology of equality among all household heads was widely proclaimed, and even though differences in wealth and prestige inevitably emerged as certain elders and lineage groups strove to become 'first among equals', the basic rules of political and social organization tended to diffuse rather than concentrate political power.

Decisions on important social and military matters requiring inter-household cooperation were made in a council of elders. It was extremely rare for women to be recognized as heads of households, much less to participate in councils of elders or other male-constituted political structures.[2] Women did, however, often form similar, albeit less powerful, social and ritual organizations.

The line between states and stateless societies in precolonial Africa cannot be clearly drawn. Some societies described as stateless routinely violated the principle of equality among heads of households. When certain elders or lineage chiefs were able to exact both military allegiance and economic tribute from subordinate households and lineages, it no longer seems appropriate to term the society stateless.

State societies ranged from those borderline hierarchical lineage systems to complex empires grouping several ethnic groups under a single political center. Expanding states absorbed and exploited subjugated societies by several means: tribute systems in which ivory, slaves, and women were periodically given to the ruler or ruling group; feudalistic labor service systems in which conquered peoples worked for the ruling family or for all prominent households of the dominant clan or ethnic group; and systems of direct slavery. In all state societies there was a clear economic differentiation among households: the vast majority of families provided an economic surplus that was expropriated by the dominant strata.

The study of women's economic roles is more complex in state societies because intra-household relations intersect with class and tribute relations. Ethel Albert's fascinating discussion of women's roles in the kingdom of Burundi provides an excellent example of the interaction of patriarchal and feudal relations (Albert 1971).

The conquering Tutsi king distributed land and cattle among his male kin. These 'nobles' had the right to demand tribute and labor service from Tutsi and Hutu 'commoners'. The pastoralist Tutsi looked after the cattle of the king and the nobility, while the agricultural Hutu worked as serfs on the farms of the Tutsi.

Women's economic roles depended on the class position of their husbands. The 'noble' Tutsi wife merely supervised the agricultural labor of male Hutu serfs. The 'commoner' Tutsi wife had to clean the cattle kraal, churn butter, and do a great deal of farming herself. The Hutu wife, whose husband was most often absent farming for the Tutsi, was obliged to provide essentially all the food required for the survival of her family.

These feudal relations were most fully developed in the precolonial period, but they still have an impact on contemporary socioeconomic relations. In 1971 Albert observed that 'most of the women of Burundi . . . must work to the limit of their strength so that they will not die of hunger. This is because most Rundi are of the inferior castes where men and women share the wretchedness of the poor' (Albert 1971: 181). But even though a Hutu man is clearly economically subjugated and impoverished, he is nonetheless a patriarch within his own household where his wife must 'kneel before him when she offers him his gourd of beer' (1971: 187). While the practice of kneeling before one's husband is dying out, rural Hutu women are still at the bottom of the social and economic hierarchy (Fikry and Ward 1992).

Slavery

Slave relations existed in both stateless and state societies. In most cases slaves were integrated into the household social structure. Female slaves often became slave wives of the household head, who claimed all their children as his own. To become the wife of the patriarch did not necessarily give a female slave any greater security than a male slave: both were 'kinless' with no relatives to defend them, and both could be given to others as gifts or as collateral and payment on a debt (as could 'free' wives and children in many societies) (Grier 1992). In some societies, slaves of either sex were liable to serve as human sacrifices, especially at the funeral of an important elder (Keim 1983).

In most cases, African slavery was of the 'domestic' type, limited to a few slaves per household who were integrated into productive and domestic work on a gender-specific basis (Miers and Kopytoff 1977). But in some state societies such as the Muslim sultanates of the West African Sahel, the eighteenth-century Bakongo kingdom of present-day Zaire, and the Arab-dominated Swahili coast of East Africa, the wealthiest families might own hundreds of slaves who were settled in agricultural villages or on plantations and/or were integrated into the ruler's household as concubines or servants (Fisher and Fisher 1971, Cooper 1977, Broadhead 1983).

Two generalizations from recent research on slavery in Africa are particularly pertinent to this chapter's historical overview of women in the African rural economy. First, in both highly centralized slaving societies and in systems of domestic slavery, the majority of slaves were women. Most researchers cite several factors to explain the African preference for women slaves: the fear that male slaves could be hard to control if retained in great numbers, and the fact that women's traditional roles made them highly useful as agricultural laborers, household servants, and producers of children for their masters (Robertson and Klein 1983, Wright 1984). Men were more likely to be killed in raids and wars than women, and, when taken captive, were more often sold in the international slave trade (Manning 1981).

Second, the Atlantic slave trade of the sixteenth to nineteenth centuries fostered the growth of highly militarized African states against whose slave raids traditionally stateless societies had little protection. The forms of slavery seemed to shift during this period. Household or domestic slavery continued to dominate among less hierarchical peoples, but large-scale slavery controlled by the wealthy ruling classes grew in response to new opportunities to sell both slaves and commodities on international markets. As the international slave trade declined, slaves were sent into the Sahel to produce grain, cotton, and cloth for sale to nomads bringing salt from the desert and also to the coastal areas that produced peanuts and palm oil for European markets. Many farming systems producing export crops, such as the 'male farming system' of the Hausa of northern Nigeria, made extensive use of both male and female slave labor.

Kinship systems

A person's gender and position in the kinship structure largely determined his or her economic role. This section discusses the impact of kinship on work and socioeconomic rights and responsibilities by examining differences between patrilineal and matrilineal societies.

The majority of agricultural societies and all pastoral societies in nineteenth-century Africa were patrilineal – societies in which the most important kinship relations are traced through the male line. At marriage (or sometimes as a betrothed child), a woman moved to her husband's village where she was expected to remain for the rest of her life. Marriage established or reinforced an alliance between the households and lineages of bride and groom. Nevertheless, for a long period the young bride was considered a 'stranger' by her husband's kin. Women had to prove their fidelity to their husbands' patrikin by bearing several children, especially sons, and producing many good harvests.

Because a woman in a patrilineal society always farmed her husband's land, her basic economic security could be severely threatened by divorce. If the marriage were harmonious, a woman farmer normally had adequate access to land. But if the marriage were unsatisfactory and a woman fled from her husband's village or was divorced, she would always lose her fields and in many cases her children as well (Davison 1988). In most patrilineal societies a divorced woman could activate land rights in her natal village, but if her father or brothers opposed her actions, a woman who left her husband could find herself landless and destitute (Albert 1971, Goheen 1988). Many women farmers still face this dilemma today.

When a male elder or household head died in a patrilineal society, his eldest son usually inherited his social position, while his land rights, cattle, slaves, and other possessions would be divided among his other male heirs. Daughters inherited little or nothing from their fathers; wives inherited nothing from their husbands. In fact, the wives and unmarried daughters were often themselves inherited by the sons of the deceased (Goody and Buckley 1973). Thus, even after the death of her husband, a woman was considered to 'belong' to the patrilineage that had paid her bridewealth.

A widow was under considerable pressure to accept the role of wife to her husband's heir. Acquiescence brought both social acceptance and the continuity of her own and her sons' land rights, whereas refusal meant that she would have to leave her husband's village, an option that put her children in danger of losing their land rights. Furthermore, children beyond a certain age (often seven or even younger) were rarely allowed to accompany a departing mother: in patrilineal societies, children always belonged to their father's lineage.

Matrilineality refers to the practice of tracing kinship and inheritance rights through the mother's family. In matrilineal societies, men inherited land and social position from their maternal uncles rather than from their fathers. Uncles also arranged the marriages of their sisters' children, requiring and benefitting from the brideservice labor of their nieces' fiancés and husbands.

Almost all matrilineal societies still followed the basic tenets of patriarchal rule: men controlled the allocation of land, the arrangement of marriage, and the lives of dependents (Muntemba 1982). The basic difference is that young men and women were dependent on their uncles, rather than their fathers. A woman was not consulted about arrangements for her marriage, and marriage still involved an obligation to work her husband's fields, in addition to or in place of her own fields in her natal village.

On the other hand, several aspects of matrilineal customs tended to improve women's economic and social security. Most basic was the fact that a woman did not normally move away from her natal village when she first married. If her husband had not yet inherited land from his maternal uncle, he would establish a household and farm on land controlled by his wife's uncle. Even when a man obtained his own land, the matrilineal custom of marrying between nearby villages sometimes meant that a wife did not need to move to her husband's village in order to farm his land. She might also receive small personal fields in her husband's village.

Finally, when a woman was divorced or widowed, she could reactivate land rights in her maternal village much more easily than divorced or widowed women from patrilineal societies. Furthermore, her children remained with her because they 'belonged' to their maternal rather than to their paternal kin. One matrilineal society, the Senufo, is discussed in the next chapter.

Pastoral societies

African pastoral societies were both patrilineal and patrilocal. Five or six extended family households usually lived together in small hamlets. Most pastoral communities moved twice a year between wet and dry season pastures. Each household head, most often the husband of several wives, was considered the social equal of his fellow patriarchs. Each wife had her own one-room house in the village compound. In contrast to the practice in agricultural societies, women were the housebuilders; men constructed the thorn fences that surrounded the village and formed a protective kraal for the cattle at night.

The need to manage and share far-flung and delicately balanced ecological resources prompted pastoral societies to develop wide-ranging sociopolitical institutions within and between distinct ethnic groups. For men, economic and political rights were determined by membership in clan-wide age groups. Men whose groups had junior dependent status during their twenties and thirties became elders in their forties and fifties. Younger men were the primary herders and warriors, while elders directed the herd movements, negotiated water rights with other groups, controlled raiding and military activities, and arranged marriages (Hedlund 1979, Reisman 1980).

As in agricultural societies, women were social and economic dependents first of fathers, then of husbands (Kapteijns 1991). Women's access to cattle, the primary means of subsistence, was based on the fulfillment of their obligations as wives and mothers. A woman always used her 'marriage cattle' to feed her family. The milk and butter she produced were shared among a wide network of kin and friends, because the socially regulated use and sharing of food were vital to the reinforcement of communal relations and territorial cooperation with respect to land and water rights. A woman's cattle could also be used to provide bridewealth for her sons. A woman could not sell or independently dispose of 'her cattle' because she had to hold them in trust for her sons.

On the other hand, pastoral women often had considerably more choice than women in agricultural societies on matters concerning sexual partners and residence (Dupire 1971). Nonetheless, like their agricultural counterparts, today's pastoral women work harder and longer than their husbands and sons in order to complete the tasks socially considered as the obligations of their sex.

Hunting and gathering societies

While most agricultural societies engaged in hunting and gathering, only a very small number of African peoples relied on hunting and gathering for their entire subsistence. These were primarily the Pygmy peoples of the dense tropical rain forests north of the Congo (Zaire) River and the San people of the Kalahari Desert. Because hunters and gatherers depended entirely on food supplied by nature, communities were small and highly mobile. Research among the !Kung San of the Kalahari found that groups averaged 35 people (Draper 1975). Both men and women ranged far from the camp when seeking food. The camps themselves were moved at intervals of several days to several weeks.

In the precolonial period, and even to this day, hunting and gathering societies had no apparent hierarchical domestic structure. Patriarchal rule was not a feature of extended family relationships. Marriage tended to be relatively impermanent: wives could leave husbands or even the community itself with little difficulty, taking their children and simply joining another group. It was generally accepted that children 'belonged' to their mothers, although neither boys nor girls were controlled in their economic and social behavior in a manner comparable to prevailing customs in agricultural and pastoral societies. It is important to note, however, that women's rights in children among the !Kung peoples seemed to diminish when some groups began to settle in villages in the 1960s and 1970s.

The Mbuti Pygmies of northeast Zaire are nomadic hunters and gatherers who, during the nineteenth century, developed trade relationships with the agriculturalists entering their dense forest (Sacks 1979). Pygmies killed the elephants whose ivory was the basis of extensive trade between powerful African kingdoms and foreigners. They supplied agriculturalists with meat in exchange for metal knives and axes. Colonialism intensified the patron–client stratification, as villagers induced the Pygmies to work on colonial crops. Still, hunting and gathering skills tended to limit exploitation since, as long as a band remained strong and cohesive, it could always fulfill its subsistence needs by withdrawing into the forest.

Mbuti women enjoyed an autonomy similar to that of !Kung women. Responsible for gathering wild vegetables, slow game, and grubs, women also helped in periodic net hunts in which men extended some 1,000 meters of nets while women and children drove the game into the trap. Men, in turn, could help with gathering. Age was more important than sex in defining tasks. There was no gender hierarchy. Women had an equal voice in group decision-making, built and owned the houses, distributed food, and developed individual relationships with agricultural patrons.

The egalitarian relationships among men and women in all types of hunting and gathering societies contrasts strikingly with the subordinate position of women in most other African societies. Karen Sacks (1979) and other scholars attribute this gender equality to the fact that the labor of women and youth was not mobilized by men to produce a surplus product. Each individual owned and disposed of the fruits of his or her own labor.

Colonial period

The process of linking African rural economies with non-African markets began long before the colonial era. Africans exported gold, ivory, and slaves from the early Middle Ages on, but prior to the colonial period, European and Arab merchants were largely confined to the coasts while the interior circuits of Africa's long-distance trade were controlled by African patriarchs and rulers.

During the nineteenth century increasing trade in natural rubber, palm oil, groundnuts, and other raw materials heightened the interest of European capitalists in Africa as a source of raw materials and a market for cheap industrial and consumer goods. Soon factory owners joined merchants in calling for colonial conquest. By the late 1880s, Britain, France, Germany, Portugal, and Belgium had established claims to nearly the entire continent.

Colonial conquest fundamentally changed precolonial economies. Under colonial rule Africans were forced to produce the agricultural raw materials Europeans wanted: peanuts, cocoa, palm kernels, cotton, coffee, and so forth. For the most part, the new crops were grown by women and dependent males in traditional agricultural households under the supervision of the household head who was responsible for meeting colonial production targets, paying taxes, and receiving whatever cash income these 'export crops' might earn. In some areas, however, especially in eastern, central, and southern Africa, agricultural households were systematically deprived of access to inputs and markets in order to force men to emigrate to European-controlled mines or plantations and to work as extremely low paid or even forced laborers.

To impose such sweeping economic changes, colonists first had to break widespread and tenacious resistance to foreign rule. Only after decades of warfare could the various colonists consolidate their political dominance over traditional rulers and the elders of stateless societies.

The contradictory effects of colonial change on women

The processes of conflict and accommodation involved in the colonial restructuring of traditional economies had a significant impact on women's economic activities and social options. On this all observers agree. Nevertheless, to categorize the effects of colonialism on African women is to enter a still unsettled debate.[3] Some scholars (Boserup 1970, Sacks 1979) suggest that the combination of capitalist exploitation and European ideas about appropriate economic and domestic roles for women all but destroyed the economic independence and traditional forms of social authority exercised by African women in the precolonial era.[4] Others question the idea that women had significant independence in the precolonial era (Huntington 1975). They point out that in many societies colonial intervention gradually weakened patriarchal control over women, lessened the possibility of torture, slavery, or death as punishment for rebellion, and for the first time made divorce available to women caught in an intolerable personal or social situation.

During a discussion on the topic, 'which life was better for women, that of the past or that of today', Cameroonian women emphasized the importance of greater personal security in the current period:

(Marguerite-Marie) In the past women were terribly mistreated, especially widows. Some were killed and others severely beaten. They were subjected to very painful insect bites. Really, one cannot see that it was better in the past for women.

(Micheline) There was no means to unite among women. And if you ran away, they caught you and beat you. (Vincent 1976: 74–75)

Evidence from other societies, however, shows that not all women were without defense against such harsh treatment (Obbo 1976). Igbo women, for example, developed effective women's self-help and mutual protection associations during the precolonial era. These women's associations could subject men who mistreated women to public ridicule and even to group punishment (see Chapters 9 and 10 below).

The debate about the effects of colonialism on women still simmers. Generalizing across diverse societies is inevitably controversial given the incredible variety in African precolonial societies. And even before colonialism, the 'traditions' of most societies had been shifting for centuries in response to internal tension as well as external influence. Colonialism sped up the pace of change as it intensified the process of economic exploitation. Thus on one issue, at least, researchers all agree: during the colonial period, African women's workload increased substantially.

The colonial extraction of economic surplus (via high taxes, forced production and sale of export crops, food levies, and forced labor on railways, plantations, and mines) was the underlying cause of women's (and men's) rising labor burden. In order to extract a significant surplus from the rural population, colonial powers had to make fundamental changes in the context in which African household and kinship relations took place.

A basic principle of the colonial strategy was co-optation. Thus, elders and chiefs who could be compelled to 'produce' what the colonial powers wanted – export crops, taxes, and cheap labor – were often rewarded with colonial backing of their traditional 'rights' to command the labor of the population under their authority. At the same time, by acquiescing to colonial demands to provide forced laborers, taxes, and other forms of surplus, African leaders were obviously submitting to the rule of foreign conquerors, thereby forfeiting much of their traditional legitimacy. Lineage or village chiefs, in particular, were in a highly ambiguous and contradictory situation, politically and ideologically weakened in African terms, but sometimes substantially strengthened economically if they were willing to use the power of their alliance with the conqueror (Coquery-Vidrovitch 1988).

Colonial rule forced changes that shifted the balance of power within the traditional African household. As male dependents (sons and clients) were drawn away from the village into forced labor or work on colonial enterprises, as household slaves were freed, and as the power of elders to sanction disobedient dependents and to prey upon weaker clans was curbed, extended family households began to break up into man-wife-children units. As a result, traditional forms of intra-household cooperation broke down: women food farmers lost the field-clearing labor of absent men, and everyone's labor time was diverted from food and local crafts production to work on colonial export crops, colonist-controlled plantations, or other colonial enterprises.

Certain colonially favored headmen and chiefs were able to reconstruct past social hierarchies in a changed context. African allies of the colonial state were rewarded with extensive powers of tax collection as well as unofficial but virtually unchecked authority to mobilize less-favored villagers to carry out unpaid work on their own private farms. As property rights became individualized under the influence of colonial legal changes and with the planting of tree crops, men who either retained traditional bases of influence or who successfully converted colonial favor into local power were sometimes able to accumulate much of the best land.

At the other end of the social hierarchy, precolonial clients and slaves were still denied access to adequate land and labor time to enable them to become self-sufficient. Former slaves and people from small or weak lineages tended to become the forced laborers, poorest peasants, and, in a few areas, the landless rural proletariat of the colonial era.

The effects of increasing socioeconomic differentiation were not as predictable for women as for men. While women from the less privileged groups were obviously in a highly disadvantaged situation, wives and daughters of the emerging colonial African elite were rarely as privileged as their husbands. Neither colonial predisposition nor African custom favored women's production of newly introduced export crops, whereas the expansion of these crops under male control both encroached upon women's access to good land for food production and forced them to work long hours on their husbands' fields.

Colonial policy also had contradictory effects on women's personal rights. Occasionally colonial administrators were pressured by missionaries to intervene against child marriage, the killing of widows, or the pawning of women and children to pay men's debts. But these episodic interventions were rarely sustained, especially as women's own attempts to escape the bonds of patriarchy by migrating to towns or mining compounds made colonial authorities increasingly aware of the importance of patriarchal power in mobilizing the labor of women and youth for the production of export crops and food supplies (Parpart 1988). When conflicts arose between the need to increase colonial taxes, foreign exchange, and profits by intensifying women's labor and the desire to protect women from excessive oppression, the basic economic logic of colonialism prevailed: patriarchal power over women was upheld in the interests of colonial profits (Schmidt 1991, Grier 1992). In the end, contradictory colonial interventions produced relatively little change in women's status as social and economic dependents of their fathers and husbands (Lovett 1989).

To state that women were economic dependents does not mean that they were incapable of supporting themselves and their children in a material sense. On the contrary, virtually every investigation of African women's economic contributions demonstrates their impressive physical and technological capacity to make a living for themselves and their families. The constraints on women's economic independence were not biological or intellectual, they were social: male control of land and export crops precluded women's production of the most lucrative crops; male rights to mobilize women's labor deprived them of time to engage in productive activities on their own account; and male control of cash incomes and new technology marginalized women from the means of increasing their productivity. As one researcher points out for nineteenth-century Lesotho, 'men made decisions about whether to adopt innovative technology, and as a rule they invested only in those technologies that benefited themselves' (Eldredge 1991: 724). Similar constraints on a woman's ability to make economic choices and to invest in improved technology remain a fundamental frustration to millions of African women farmers today.

African production of colonial export crops

At the beginning of the colonial period and again during the great depression of the 1930s, prices for export crops were so low that there was almost no incentive for self-sufficient African households to produce them. Colonial authorities therefore imposed heavy taxes in order to force production of colonially demanded raw materials. In many areas most peasants could only acquire the cash needed to pay taxes by producing specific export crops and by selling them at official prices. During the 1920s and again in the 1950s, prices for export crops improved significantly. This induced many household heads to divert increasing amounts of family labor to colonial crops even though it meant that women had to neglect some types of subsistence food crops and/or abandon certain types of craft production (such as weaving and pottery). These developments made African villagers increasingly dependent on cash incomes to purchase basic necessities, forcing them to continue producing export crops even when their prices fell drastically, as they did during the 1930s and 1940s.

The colonial transformation of the African household from a self-sufficient unit into a peasant household obliged to produce some crop or commodity demanded in external markets marked a profound change in the African rural economy. A type of international dominance over the rural household was established under colonial rule that has not been lifted to this day.

The production of export crops altered the sexual division of labor and significantly increased the total labor time of *all* members of the rural household, but the increased workload fell hardest on women. Men commonly withdrew from food production tasks when they began to produce export crops; women not only took up the slack in food production, but also helped with colonially imposed export crops (Bukh 1979, Carney and Watts 1991). Among the Beti peoples of southern Cameroon, during the depression year of 1934 when cash crop prices were extremely low and taxes high, women worked over 70 hours a week. The corresponding labor times for men were 25 hours a week for household heads and 55 hours for their sons and other male dependents (Koopman Henn 1978). Chapter 2 discusses similar changes among the Ewe of Ghana.

In order to meet colonial demands, most heads of households tightened their control over household resources and dependents' labor. In the Ivory Coast, for example, cotton had been grown by women in the precolonial era to meet family clothing needs; when it became a cash crop, male household heads began to require that the portion of the crop to be sold must be grown on their personal fields, thereby establishing claim to ownership of the harvest (Etienne 1980).

As cash transactions expanded during the colonial period, household heads attempted to maintain tight control over family cash resources in order to minimize the economic independence of both male and female dependents. Young men often managed to escape patriarchal dominance by seeking wage work outside the village, but their fathers could still prevent them from growing cash crops on their own account. Patriarchs were even more anxious to prevent their wives from controlling cash incomes, fearing that a woman might try to initiate a divorce by repaying her own bridewealth (Kaberry 1952).

Colonial officials recognized that the power of the household head to control the labor of his dependents was essential to increasing the production of export crops. To help heads of households maintain the power to mobilize the labor of their wives and children, colonial policy supported firm patriarchal control of land and cash. It was therefore very difficult for women to challenge the economic changes that so drastically increased their working days while eroding their control over the product of their labor.

African wage labor in colonial enterprises

African employment in colonial factories, mines, and plantations was everywhere extremely low paid. Earnings were rarely adequate to allow a full-time worker to provide for his own consumption needs, much less to support a family. Men's wages had to be supplemented with food and other goods and services from the peasant household (Hay 1976, Guyer 1978). It was the unpaid labor of rural women that subsidized the colonial wage.

When inadequate wages were exacerbated by harsh working conditions (whippings, dangerous environments, long hours), people often resisted work on European plantations and colonial construction projects. When Africans would not willingly 'offer' their labor, the state was quick to resort to force, sometimes kidnapping villagers for forced labor sites, but more often simply requiring that the village chief supply the required numbers of workers. Forced labor was used by the colonial state right through the Second World War, first to provide men and women to serve as head-loaded porters for colonial trade goods, then to build roads, railways, factories, mines, and government buildings. The colonial state also provided forced laborers to private European enterprises.

The hierarchical structure of the African household and the sexual division of labor determined who was sent when the colonial demand for forced labor could not be avoided. The slaves, clients, nephews, and, if necessary, the sons of household heads were sent to colonial labor sites, while wives and daughters were required to produce food and to transport it by headload to the laborers. Women were also obliged to supply food to colonial administrative centers and to feed the large gangs of merchants' porters who regularly passed through their villages.

In addition to mobilizing forced labor, the colonial state helped recruit wage laborers for private European agricultural and mining enterprises in what came to be known as the migrant labor system (Stichter 1985). African men would be recruited for six-month to two-year contracts. The wages paid could barely keep the worker alive, but to keep the worker from leaving a small bonus was often provided after the contract was completed. A migrant laborer often worked hundreds of miles from his home, hoping that at the end of his contract the bonus would be sufficient to pay his bridewealth and start him on the road to economic independence. Unfortunately, in many areas where the migrant labor system was widely established, such as eastern and southern Africa, a single labor contract was usually not enough either to pay bridewealth or to meet the cash needs of a rural household. Married men were therefore forced to leave their households many times over in search of wage work, especially men from villages in which colonial governments discouraged the production of cash crops in order to assure a large supply of migrant labor.

Wives of migrant laborers were often obliged to manage the family farm and livestock with little or no male help and often without the authority to make decisions regarding sales of output, purchases of inputs, or hiring of labor. These women had neither access to credit nor adequate monetary income to purchase tools, fertilizer or seeds. Some women, among the Luo of western Kenya, for example, coped fairly well with male absence by adopting new trading strategies and new agricultural techniques, but the more common result of the continual absence of working-age males was a gradual and significant deterioration of rural family welfare. The extremely impoverished female-headed households of South Africa, Botswana, Lesotho, Swaziland, Zambia, and Mozambique are the contemporary result of more than a century of South African capitalist 'growth' based on migrant labor (Sibisi 1977). The situations in Botswana and the Transkei of South Africa are described in Chapter 2.

Few jobs were open to women in the colonial period. European plantations sometimes employed women on a seasonal basis, especially for crop processing, but these positions were normally limited to women living in the immediate vicinity (Bryceson 1980). In some areas a wealthy class of export crop-producing peasants provided seasonal 'wage work' for women, but more often than not this work brought only a small payment in food or land-clearing services, or the promise of a gift when the harvest was sold. In all cases a woman's return for wage work was considerably lower than the meagre amounts paid to men.

The gradual development of urban labor markets during the colonial period provided very limited economic opportunities for women (see Chapter 3). Urban wage jobs were almost entirely restricted to men, especially in government and industrial enterprises. A rural woman who accompanied her husband to town could attempt to fulfill her traditional obligation to feed the family by trading in food, brewing beer, or producing cooked food to be sold on the roadside, but a woman's earnings from these so-called informal sector activities, even when combined with a man's wage, were nearly always too low to allow her family to survive in the city (Stichter 1985). Thus, the great majority of workers' wives remained in the villages where they could protect their husbands' land rights, feed their children, and provide a refuge for the wage workers of their family in times of sickness, unemployment, and old age. In this way, rural women's agricultural products and domestic labor subsidized the extremely low wages paid to the African working class.

The past, present, and future

The past is still evident in the contemporary working lives of rural African women. Patriarchal dominance in the household economy combined with the forces of external exploitation (as expressed in worsening terms of trade between rural output, on the one hand, and purchased commodities and agricultural inputs, on the other) constrain rural women's economic options and confine the great majority of African women to a life of heavy labor and limited welfare.

Two decades of intermittent or chronic food shortages, over a decade of debt crises, and the imposition of structural adjustment policies forced on African governments by their huge external debts offer scant evidence and little prospect that rural women's economic situation is changing for the better. Recent research has clearly demonstrated that the structural adjustment policies being pursued to restore macroeconomic balances and to provide adequate amounts of foreign exchange to service foreign debts are having particularly negative effects on the poorer segments of the population, among whom the majority are women and children (Gladwin 1991, Elabor-Idemudia 1991).

Change is needed on two fronts. First, the policies and international economic relations that have tended to privilege industrial and urban development over agricultural investment and rural modernization must be refocussed. The rural economy has been weakened by at least a century of 'surplus extraction' to the point that rural areas are no longer capable of providing the cheap labor and cheap export crops that have financed urban and industrial growth as well as substantial profits for foreign-owned enterprises. There must now be serious attention to providing the types of rural infrastructure and agricultural investment that can raise both agricultural productivity and rural living standards for the overwhelming majority of smallholder house-holds. Thus far, structural adjustment policies have not achieved this essential objective. Second, in order to have a positive impact on women farmers, policies to improve the productivity of agricultural enterprises and the profitability of food and export crop production must be targeted at women as well as men. They cannot simply be targeted at households. Women's specific problems of low yields, low productivity, lack of cash to invest in modern technology, lack of time for income-generating activities, and extreme overwork are related both to macroeconomic policies and to long-standing patriarchal traditions operating at the household, village, and state level. Women farmers' gender-specific problems are only beginning to be recognized by policy-makers. To improve rural living standards, however, they must be directly addressed.

Patriarchal relations still govern the economic behavior of most rural households. Men control and manage most agricultural resources: land, livestock, export crops, tools, means of transport, purchased inputs, credit, and so forth. Men keep the proceeds of the most lucrative crops and off-farm activities under their own control, but still expect that their wives' food crops and small cash earnings will be sufficient to meet most of the family's daily consumption needs. However, both national evidence on levels of aggregate production, food imports, and child nutrition as well as village-level case studies demonstrate that women's food output and incomes are rarely adequate to permit women to fulfill their heavy responsibilities.

A woman's attempts to increase her earning capacity by engaging in independent agricultural or off-farm activities are severely limited by her lack of time (subsistence agricultural and domestic labor tasks take up eight hours of each day) and by customary social constraints on women's independent access to economic resources. Traditional practices, especially the belief that land must be controlled by the men of a local lineage group, continue to limit women farmers' ability to make efficient market-oriented choices in deciding what to plant, what to sell, and what inputs to invest in. Women may enjoy a legal 'right' to own and control land, but there are few women with sufficient income and family backing actually to be able to purchase and cultivate a plot of land on their own account.

Contemporary state institutions, such as producers' cooperatives and export crop marketing agencies, reinforce patriarchal dominance over women farmers' labor and earnings. Often only heads of households are accepted as members of cooperatives. This excludes most women from access to the improved seeds, agricultural advice, fertilizer, pesticides, tools, credit, and crop payments that are commonly dispensed only through cooperatives.

These tenacious remnants of precolonial and colonial discrimination against women work directly against the need to increase Africa's agricultural output, especially in the food sector. What makes this situation alarming is the fact that the decline of the agricultural sector has literally driven many men off the farm even while their families continue to live on the land. Women thus make up an ever-increasing share of full-time farmers, 70 per cent in Malawi, for example. This feminization of smallholder agricultural is increasing throughout the continent but appropriate policy response is lagging far behind.

If Africa's agriculture is to become more productive in a manner that will benefit the 60–80 per cent of the population still living in the rural areas, women farmers must gain much greater access to improved technology and resources. For this to happen on a significant scale, rural development programs, agricultural research, and credit for productive investments must be targeted at women as well as men.[5] Targeting women will be more effective if the delicate process of dismantling patriarchal constraints is undertaken at the same time.

Notes

1. Lineages are groupings of several extended families all directly related to a single ancestor three to five generations back. Clans are similar groupings of lineages related to an ancestor further removed, where all the intervening steps in the genealogy may not be directly remembered and may even be invented.
2. For a different opinion and counter-examples, see Hoffer (1972).
3. Mullings (1976) and Tiffany (1978) provide reviews of this debate.
4. For sympathetic critiques of Boserup's highly influential work, see Huntington (1975) and Beneria and Sen (1981).
5. Contemporary development policies and their intended and unintended effects on women are discussed further in Chapter 12.

CHAPTER 2

Women in the rural economy: contemporary variations

Jane I. Guyer

Two themes recur in analyses of women's positions in the rural areas of Africa: enterprise and autonomy on the one hand, and poverty and overwork on the other. In almost every region women have access to some kind of productive resource or a particular market which provides them with an income of their own. And yet almost everywhere that income seems limited, and earning it absorbs time and effort that has to be integrated with housekeeping and child care. This situation is clearly not simply 'tradition'. Every rural economy has been affected in a more or less profound way by production for national and international markets, the migration of its people as wage workers to areas of high labor demand, or integration into regional market systems. And yet in many cases it is still versions of indigenous customary law that define the access of each sex to productive resources. In order to understand women's present position, one therefore must understand the way in which the demands of the wider economy and the possibilities and constraints of local systems interact.

During the past three decades a wealth of basic research has been done that documents the main components of women's economic lives: what women are responsible for in any particular ethnic group; what land rights they may hold; how they spend their time; what they do with their income; what they can expect from fathers, husbands, brothers, sons; and the whole range of ethnographic questions that illuminate how women make a living and contribute to the livelihood of others. In its detail each ethnography can be highly particular. The purpose of comparative work is to explore major themes which may lie behind the particularity and variability, in order to go beyond *what* is happening and suggest possible reasons *why*.

The criterion used here to group cases for comparison will be the nature of the links between the local and the wider economic systems. During the last hundred years, the commodity economy penetrated into African agriculture in three major ways: (1) through the growth of export crop production by smallholder farmers, (2) through expansion of employment outside the smallholder sector, and (3) through the more diffuse effects of the extension of trade. For most of the colonial period these modes of domination tended to be pursued in different geographical regions. For example, in southern Ghana, Nigeria, and Senegal, smallholder farmers expanded production to include crops for the export market, but wage employment was very little developed and in some cases was deliberately limited by the colonial governments, eager to maintain high levels of agricultural output. By contrast, the mines of South Africa and Northern Rhodesia (now Zambia), and the plantations of Kenya withdrew labor from the rural areas, whose own production for the market was constrained by a battery of discriminatory legislation. Finally, throughout the colonial period there remained areas that were more remote or less strategically important, from which people and goods were occasionally requisitioned, and on whom taxes were levied, but whose local economies were infiltrated rather than transformed. One might characterize the attachment of these communities to the world economy as (1) through commodity production for international trade, (2) through wage work for national industrial and agricultural enterprise, or (3) through regionally specific economic relationships.

This chapter is an ethnographic exploration of women's position in ethnic groups falling into each of these three broad categories. This initial division provides a useful starting place. However, one modification needs to be made at the outset, and that is to include historical change. Since the end of the colonial period African economies have become far more complex. Some of the colonial states which depended on export agriculture (Nigeria for example), have since developed substantial mineral resources, leaving agriculture far behind as a source of revenue for the government or income for the individual. In others, like Ghana, Senegal and Tanzania, small-holder agriculture remains the basic resource of the national economy but serious concern has developed on the part of the government about stagnant levels of production, and on the part of the farmers about low prices and high levels of government control. In yet other nations, like the Ivory Coast (on a large scale) and Cameroon (on a much smaller scale), plantation agriculture has been expanded with the partial aim of bypassing the small-holder sector. Some rural economies have continued to supply workers to other sectors but under changed conditions of demand, because industry and mining now require a more highly skilled, permanent labor force. Others, as in parts of Kenya and Tanzania, have been converted into cash crop regions. In all cases there has been expansion of nonfarm employment, particularly in the public sector, and with this has come a heightened appreciation of the importance of regional production and marketing systems, to supply the urban areas with food. As a result the constraints and possibilities for particular rural economies and the people working in them have become more complicated, and in many places local balances of labor and resources have been seriously affected by political crises, price fluctuations, demographic pressures on the land, and natural disasters.

In this situation it is hardly realistic to cling to three stereotypic cases and compare them in a static framework. Instead, each selection will describe women's position in a particular case, trace its direction of change, and then briefly compare and contrast this case with others falling roughly into the same category as the sun set on imperial rule. Because of the element of change, a fourth case has been added to represent a very small, but possibly growing area of female employment, namely full-time wage work in large-scale plantation agriculture. A final section following the case studies will discuss more broadly the challenges facing rural African women as a result of economic and political change during the 1980s.

Each case study will include a general description of what women do, and will pay close attention to a set of particular issues: first, the sex ratio in the rural areas and the forces that determine it; second, the proportion of women who are managing the day-to-day requirements of their families single-handed; third, the kind and amount of resources women control relative to men; and finally, the value of women's work by comparison with the value of men's work.   Having described these local, or 'micro'-level questions, it is now necessary to return to the broader 'macro' issue of how they fit into a wider economic system.

Case 1 – A peripheral economy: the Senufo of the northern Ivory Coast (Source: SEDES 1965)

The Senufo people are known for their skillful farming and out-standing wood-carving. They grow a variety of staple food crops (yams, rice, maize, millet, and some cassava) in a complex and productive farming system. Maize and cassava are crops imported from the New World in the centuries before colonial rule, and they have been successfully integrated with the indigenous staple foods. Export crops, however, were resisted and finally rejected. The French colonial government made great efforts to introduce cotton and groundnut (peanut) production, without long-term success. Senufo men were also recruited in forced labor for the privately owned plantations of the coastal region, and many young men still migrate in search of paid employment. A detailed study done in 1962 presents the picture of a population still primarily concerned with the provision of its own needs: two-thirds of the total value of goods consumed was provided directly from subsistence production (SEDES 1965 5: 57), and only about one-third of total production was sold on the market (SEDES 1965 5: 27). The sex breakdown of the population was 48 per cent male and 52 per cent female, indicating a limited amount of out-migration by men.

The Senufo live in large villages, in open savannah countryside.

The farming system is still relatively intensive hoe agriculture, as described in Chapter 1, with fields being left to fallow one year out of three if possible. Both men and women farm, but the staple food crops are primarily managed by men. The villages are composed of several 'quarters', many of whose inhabitants trace their descent from a common ancestor in the female line. In the past the members of each quarter farmed collectively and the quarter chief administered the food supplies for the whole group. The farming unit today is the compound, a smaller group composed of a set of brothers, their sisters and/or wives, and their children.

In the matrilineal kinship system of the Senufo, women retain the right to live in their natal compounds throughout their lives, and many of them do stay, even after marriage. If husband and wife come from the same village, they can keep up the obligations of marriage without living together in the same compound. The women who live in a compound, therefore, include wives who have moved in and sisters who have chosen not to move out. The compound members grow the main staple, millet, in a collective field, and every adult has his or her own personal plot to cultivate and a personal granary. Thus each woman has rights in land either through her natal kin or her husband's kin, and she has the right to be provided for from the collective plot.

In whichever compound they live, brother's or husband's, women take care of the children, cook the food, and fetch wood for fuel and water for washing and cooking. Domestic work accounts for almost half of their total work time (SEDES 1965 3: 125), which is a very similar proportion to findings of time-allocation studies in many African rural societies. For Senufo women, water and fuel provision are particularly time-consuming because of the relatively dry climate and savannah vegetation.

The remainder of women's work time is divided between farming, associated tasks of porterage and storage, processing farm goods for sale, and marketing. One form of processing that gives Senufo women a regular income is brewing beer from millet, which they can sell either within the village or at a local market. All small-scale marketing is done by women, although any large transactions are handled by middlemen from a neighboring ethnic group, the Dioula. The goods women sell in the market consist of produce from their individual farms or crops sold on behalf of their menfolk. Some 41 per cent of women's work time is spent on the farm, and 9 per cent in processing and marketing.

How does this compare with men's work? First of all, men spend a greater proportion of their time in farming and related tasks (72 per cent), which in absolute amounts of time, is about twice the time which women devote to agriculture. Their next most important time-consumer is house building. By comparison with women, men spend much more time on schooling, religion, and rest. This last category accounts for 28 per cent of men's days, and 17 per cent of women's (SEDES 1965 3: 125). Findings very similar to these emerge from studies of men's and women's work the world over because of women's primary responsibility for what is generally called 'domestic work'.

Many of men's and women's tasks are complementary and contribute to collective welfare, but there are some areas of separate responsibility. In the Senufo case, men and women are responsible for different crops in the farming system. The traditional staples, millet, yams, and now maize also, are assigned to the men. Women help only with weeding, harvesting, and transport of the crop from field to village. The women's personal fields are devoted mainly to rice and groundnuts. The important question then becomes: are rice and groundnuts mainly subsistence crops contributed to the compound for its food supply, or are women free to sell them? And how does this compare with the use to which men put their own crops?

The data are striking. Among the Senufo it is rice and groundnuts that are commercialized and men's crops which are devoted in the higher proportions to subsistence (SEDES 1965 5: 28, 38–39). Women also earn cash incomes by doing agricultural labor for others. The study does not tell us how men's and women's total cash incomes differ. Probably men still earn more because they sell livestock, wood carvings, and a small proportion of their farm products. What is important to note is the freedom of women to earn their own incomes, separate from the joint endeavors of their compound.

Their involvement in day wage work points up the final critical comparison to make between men's and women's economic positions: the value of their work. At the time of this study, the daily wage for men was 150 francs; for women it was 75 francs. Looking back at the value of the crops produced by men and women, a similar discrepancy is apparent. A day's work in yam, maize, or millet cultivation is worth three times as much in the value of the final harvest as a day's work in rice or groundnut production (SEDES 1965 3: 197). Women's activities are confined to products whose returns to labor are low.

Comment and comparison

In much of Equatorial and East Africa women supply by far the greater labor input into agriculture. They are the mainstay of the subsistence food supply system, in contrast to the Senufo, where the men have a larger role. The Senufo system is particular, but it does show very clearly some of the potential strengths and weaknesses of women's position. Women have control of certain resources, and they have access to personal incomes, but the value of their labor time is lower. For the moment, compound organization and staple food farming by men protect women from having to support themselves completely from this disadvantageous position. In many cash-crop and labor-reserve areas elsewhere in Africa, the protection afforded by this kind of system has begun to break down without significant improvement in the terms of which women earn an income.

Case 2 – An old cash-crop economy: the Ewe of southern Ghana (Source: Bukh 1979)

The old cocoa region of southern Ghana in the 1930s was one of the richest areas in West Africa. Vast cocoa groves provided incomes high enough to finance schooling, housing, and investment funds for other endeavours. People live in large villages, set in wooded countryside, accessible by motor transport, and with some modern amenities and services. Almost all of their children attend school, and many people travel to the cities and hold jobs in the nonagricultural sectors of the economy. But in the long run the rural areas have ceased to be an important source of high personal incomes. By the second generation, land suitable for cocoa was less available and cocoa prices began a long, slow decline to a trough in 1964–65. Under these circumstances men began to leave the countryside to search for better paying work, but the rapid inflation of the 1970s left many of them without an income adequate to support a family in an urban area.

To deal with this situation, Ewe people relied on the ability of women to keep the food supply system functioning without much help from men. During the cocoa boom they had reorganized family work in a way that is echoed in many other export-crop areas: men turned all their attention to cocoa, while women took over the cultivation of basic food for the family. In the economic crisis of the 1970s, women and children remained in the countryside because it was the only place where they could be sure of food supplies. Many women are now forced to do what Senufo women do not – that is, provide for themselves and their children. According to Bukh's study, 65 per cent of women over 18 are solely responsible for their children's daily nutrition. Women form 58 per cent of the rural population, and are the heads of 40 per cent of the households (Bukh 1979: 37, 111). Men do contribute to certain aspects of the economy, but under the circumstances women have to be prepared to support their dependents on a day-to-day basis.

Although expressed in different terms than the Senufo study, the advantages and disadvantages of women's position to achieve this are brought out clearly. By comparison with their own menfolk, women are at a clear disadvantage in providing for a family. Cocoa is still the best source of cash income, but women own only 4 per cent of the total cocoa acreage. Women's food farms are smaller and on poorer land than men's because women working alone find it difficult to do the heavy work.

The advantages seem few, but they are striking by comparison with other cases. As in other patrilineal societies, Ewe women do have rights to land, and the local market for the goods they sell is strong enough to provide a cash income. Sixty per cent of women over 15 years old are farmers, but half of them combine farming with petty retail trade, processing, wage labor, and artisan work to bring in the money necessary to cover personal and household expenses.

Like other women, they devote large proportions of time to domestic duties, including two hours per day cooking. The total workload adds up quickly when it includes three occupations. Bukh gives an example of a widow supporting her aged father and seven children by working from 4:00 a.m. to 10:00 p.m..

One of the most important resources that women have to draw on in meeting these demands is the help of their children. Children look after each other, run messages, take care of small livestock, fetch water, wash dishes, and later take part in the more difficult work that contributes to income more directly. Luo women in western Kenya, who also combine farming with small-scale trade, depend heavily on children to cover many of the daily duties (Okeyo 1979). In West Africa, children are often fostered in order to provide women with help or an apprentice in their craft.

Bukh does not calculate the value of women's labor relative to men's; in fact, this is extremely difficult data to collect. But their control of resources is poorer, and in particular the low fertility of the land they cultivate is bound to mean that their work is relatively poorly rewarded.

Comment and comparison

Certain aspects of the situation Bukh describes are very common results of the integration of export crops into rural economies. As described in Chapter 1, many peoples have intensified the old gender division of labor so that food production has become primarily a female responsibility. Margaret Haswell shows a similar pattern in a groundnut-producing village in the Gambia. The men have entirely given up cultivation of millet, the traditional staple, in favor of groundnuts, and the women cultivate rice almost exclusively for the family diet (Haswell 1975).

But again, there are marked variations. In another old groundnut-producing area, northern Nigeria, women do not work on the farm at all because of the Muslim observance of seclusion (Hill 1969). Men farmers have to provide both the food and the export crop, or buy food from cash incomes from the sale of other crops in the market. A similar pattern, but without the influence of women's seclusion, has developed in the cocoa-producing areas of southern Nigeria. Women are not, on the whole, responsible for much farm labor either on their own or on a family farm. In both these areas women's niche in the economy has become, to a far more extreme degree than any of the other cases discussed so far, the processing of agricultural goods and small-scale trade, the sale of cooked food, or the production of groundnut oil and other ingredients of the local diet. Yoruba women more or less monopolize their regional food marketing and distribution systems. Some are wholesale traders on a large scale, while others practice much more marginal and intermittent businesses.

For these women, their primary income is in cash, and not in farm

29

products for direct family use. It is possible but rare for women to earn higher cash incomes than their husbands. They earn enough to take care of many expenses for their children, and may have to support the family during the season when men have no incomes from their farms. But again, the economic survey data suggest that women's occupations give low returns to labor input, relative to men's within the same system.

Women's work in the cash-crop economies tends to cluster around two occupations: food farming for the family with small amounts sold on the market, and entirely market-oriented activities in processing and trade. The question then arises of whether there are any systematic differences between these two kinds of situations, whether in the systems themselves or in women's level of welfare. The response of different rural areas to the stagnation of export-crop incomes may give a partial answer.

Southern Ghana is an area where export crop production brought relatively high incomes at one time. Women's subsistence food production was one element in the ability of male farmers to take the risks of expansion. As prices fall men search for other alternatives, again using women's food production as a cushion against the volatility of national and international economies.

Women who have access to land cling to food production as a source of security. Men's occupations become differentiated and women's remain relatively uniform. By contrast, in economies where women are primarily involved in trade, when they need to take over greater responsibility for the family income, they have to exploit the regional market, become more enterprising and more mobile. The active marketing system that already exists provides this possibility, and with it, all the risks and potential rewards of the cash sector.

Women farmers may also prefer to specialize or diversify their activities, but there are major constraints: the tradition of subsistence maintenance by each domestic group, the intensification of subsistence values by the export-crop economy, and the unavailability of non-family labor to supplement on the food farm. Their problem is compounded because in economies where women did little trading in the past, the successive governments have encouraged the development of other kinds of marketing systems: shops owned by foreigners, cooperatives, or marketing authorities. In some areas no significant internal market system for peasants to trade with each other has ever developed because of low peasant incomes, government policy, domination of a single cash crop, and the commitment of female labor to subsistence farming. For example, an authoritative study of the Senegalese rural economy states that the 'primordial place occupied by groundnuts in the rural economy . . . has prevented the organization of an internal market, turned peasants away from seeing each other as potential consumers . . .' (Pélissier 1966: 897). In this situation it can be difficult to create local marketing institutions strong enough to compete with entrenched interests in the more lucrative wholesale sectors.

The whole issue of economic differentiation in Africa's rural areas is complicated and understudied, and women's position within it is even less clear. The straightforward occupational differentiation discussed so far is just part of the more profound issue of income differentiation. The old cash-crop areas have been in the commodity economy long enough to begin to develop and consolidate class differences, which makes it somewhat misleading to discuss women's economic role in terms of the average man and the average woman. Where some farmers of cash crops are able to cross the critical Rubicon from use of family labor to extensive use of wage labor, the position of women may be quite fundamentally altered.

A 1973 study of Ganda cotton and coffee farmers shows how critical the farm owner's wife may be to the management of the entire farm (Richards *et al.* 1973). In this part of Africa women can be successful managers of agricultural enterprises as long as they have access to the same resources as men. It appears, however, that they rarely own and manage land in their own right. What happens to these farm-wife-managers in case of divorce or widowhood is not clear, whether they can continue to work the farm, or have to move out and possibly down in the class hierarchy. To get a complete picture of the relationship between class and gender, one would also need to know about the status of the kinswomen of wage laborers. The economic life histories of men and women may be quite different from one another if women cannot accumulate productive resources on their account.

To summarize briefly, women's activities are primarily geared to local demand for locally produced goods and can expand when the possibility of occupational differentiation does exist. Although theories of economic growth expect local markets to grow as producers become more involved with export-crop production, this has happened in some areas to a much greater degree than others. The growth of the internal market appears to have been particularly slow where women are committed to subsistence food production, not because of women's 'motives' but because of the constraints on their range of choices.

Case 3 – Labor reserve economies: Botswana and the Transkei (Sources: Brown 1980, Lucas 1979, Leeuwenberg 1977)

Botswana and the Transkei were brought within the orbit of South African industry during the last years of the nineteenth century. Their rural areas consist of open range land where the local populations once herded cattle and kept farms for their staple food. The cattle economy went into dramatic decline in the 1890s as a result of an epidemic that killed off large proportions of the herds. Since then, the reconstruction of rural life has been directly influenced by South Africa's needs for migrant workers in the gold and diamond mines and in industry.

31

In areas treated as 'labor reserves', cash cropping was deliberately limited by colonial governments and subsistence production was maintained; the need for a cash income would force out the employable members of the population, and the subsistence farming would feed the rest at no cost to the wage-earner. In this way wages could be kept as low as possible. The implicit assumption behind such policies was that the mutual obligations between kin could be activated at intermittent points during a worker's life without being reinforced by the day-to-day reciprocity implied in coresidence.

In the long run this policy has left the rural areas extremely vulnerable, subject to many demands and very few inputs. Subsistence farming on limited land is simply not flexible, and the farmers in these systems have no other alternatives: little possibility to expand production for the market, little access to the (low) wages of distant migrants, and few resources to cope with ecological problems, production fluctuations, or population changes. As a result the last 30 years have witnessed a steady decline in subsistence maintenance. In a rural survey of Botswana (reported in Brown 1980: 5), the poorest 50 per cent of households depended on cash transfers and employment as their primary sources of income. The situation in the Transkei is much worse. Only 10 per cent of the households in the survey produced enough from their farms to feed themselves, and two-thirds of all food consumed was imported from outside. But sources of cash income within the Transkei were almost nonexistent. Cattle ownership is very unequal, there are virtually no cash crops and only 10 per cent of the adult population, mainly men, is employed for wages. In both these cases rural households need wage remittances from their kin in order to hire labor and ox-teams to plough the land, and just to buy the food they need to live on. Almost by definition, this kind of system leaves the women and children disproportionately in the rural areas. At least 25 per cent of all adult men are absent in both of these regions. In the Transkei 67 per cent of households are headed by women, a far higher proportion than any of the other cases (Leeuwenberg 1977: 2–8).

So far these two cases have been discussed together, but in the last 20 years their situations have diverged. Jobs for unskilled migrants are less available, as South Africa's industry becomes increasingly capital-intensive. Brown's survey in 1978 suggests that 48 per cent of men from a rural area in Botswana are employed but only one-third of them now work in South Africa (Brown 1980: 4). Burdened with most of the agricultural work, but suffering from the level of poverty which keeps land and equipment ownership for female-headed households much lower than for males, women are exercising another option, which is to give up farming altogether. Brown found that 25 per cent of women from the rural area in which she worked were employed, a far higher proportion than in any of the other economies discussed here (Brown 1980: 4). The out-migration of women has the effect of redressing somewhat the sex ratio in the rural areas.

Women in the Transkei, however, cannot leave the rural areas.

As the farming system declines further, the male migration rate rises and the ratio of men to women falls still further. How these women manage is a tribute to human stamina and ingenuity, but the costs in declining standards of nutrition and climbing child mortality are very high. As in the cash-crop areas, children's work is a significant addition to the family labor force, especially in female-headed households (Lucas 1979: 37). On the other hand, one fact stands out in studies of both countries, and that is the determination of women to educate their children to make them employable outside the rural areas. Even at the low levels of living in the Transkei, families spend anything from 20 per cent to 70 per cent of their cash incomes on education (Leeuwenberg 1977: 15; see Alverson 1978).

Comment and comparison

Studies in other areas of southern Africa give the same impression: 60 per cent of households headed by women, heavy dependence on remittances, lack of income-generating activities for women within the reserves and limited avenues to leave them. However difficult women's lives seem in the rural areas further north there are always some mitigating factors. Land may be scarce, but there are trading opportunities; employment is limited, but the land is still fertile enough to provide the basic necessities; women are less often faced with making a living alone, and some kind of money-earning work can be pursued year round to offset the relatively poor returns per day.

Case 4 – Female plantation workers in Cameroon
(Sources: DeLancey 1977, Koenig 1977)

In a very few areas of Africa, women are full-time employed agricultural workers. The cases discussed here are very large, partly state-run enterprises which have been in existence for a long time. The rubber and palm plantation at Dizangué was founded in the 1920s and worked by forced laborers as late as the Second World War. The vast plantations of the Cameroon Development Corporation (CDC) on the slopes of Mount Cameroon occupy some of the most fertile soil in Africa and have been producing tropical products for the world market for almost a hundred years.

The workers for both these plantation systems were imported from other regions of the country, first by force and then by recruitment. The CDC workers in particular are now an established proletariat through two or more generations. Since they are not local by origin, they have less access to land and less opportunity for developing 'peasant' farming than the local populations. The workers are organized and work under the protection of the national labor code. Since the two cases are a little different, they will be discussed separately.

The women working at Dizangué turned to wage labor 'in times of extreme need', as a way of supporting their children (Koenig 1977: 258). The average age is a little over 40, but only 28 per cent of these women are currently married. For the most part, they are rural women who have migrated to the plantation as an alternative to trying to manage alone in subsistence farming. Once at the plantation, they form a small sector of the total labor force (20 per cent) and tend to cluster in jobs with lower pay and no productivity bonuses (Koenig 1977, 94). However, when the daily wage is computed, it appears that women earn about three-fourths of the average male salary. As noted earlier, this differential is considerably smaller than the differential in returns to labor in the peasant sector.

The workers on the CDC tea plantation appear to be even better off. Although the data are not precisely comparable, DeLancey shows that the employed women had double the cash income of a sample of married women working in the peasant farming and marketing sectors. They had higher savings levels and, significantly, invested heavily in their children's education.

Comment and comparison

The Cameroonian plantation workers, as an example of rural wage workers, benefit from certain advantageous conditions. In large enterprises the conditions of work are public knowledge and government-regulated. By contrast, employment conditions and wages can be highly variable in the smallholder sector, depending on local and seasonal levels of demand for laborers. In addition, the work on tea and forest crops is not as distinctly seasonal as, for example, coffee or sugar, so that workers have some degree of job security. Many of the women in both samples had been employed continuously for over five years. One hesitates to generalize from this kind of employment to seasonal farm labor in South Africa or the whole range of work arrangements with local farmers. It is not wage work by itself that makes the difference, but the conditions of year-round commitment to wage work, visibility, and organization.

Conclusions from case studies

Table 2.1 summarizes findings from the cases studied, with respect to the four criteria set up in the beginning.

In Africa women account for a high proportion of the work involved in food supply: in the farming itself; in processing, drying, and storage; and in both retail and wholesale marketing for local and regional trade. In the poorest areas this is a supportive, subsistence farm work to supply food to their own households. But in many countries large urban populations depend on this female labor force for the regular supply of their daily food through complex marketing systems.

Table 2.1 Women's position in four African economies: summary

	Senufo	Ewe	Xhosa (Transkei)	Dizangué plantation
Sector	Food: farming and sales	Food: farming and sales	Food: subsistence farming (insufficient)	wage work
Rural sex ratio (women per 100 men)	108	143	144	20
Female-headed households (%)	0(?)	42	67	n.d.
Resources	Land: market sales	Land: small, no cocoa market sales	Land: insufficient, little capital, no employment	Employment
Ratio of returns to labor (m:t)	2:1	4:1 (Nigeria 1952) 2:1 (Cameroon 1964)	1.8:1 (Botswana 1976)	1.3:1

Sources: SEDES 1965, Leeuwenberg 1977, DeLancey 1977, Guyer 1980, Lucas 1979. In the absence of data from Bukh, data from comparable West African cocoa economies has been used.

Women's access to resources appears to be inferior to men's, in one way or another, in all cases: smaller farms, less fertile land, less opportunity for occupational mobility, less wage employment. On the other hand, women's access to income can, in the short run, sometimes be more secure than men's. In many cash-cropping areas men's incomes from agriculture are seasonal, whereas women can earn small incomes from local trade year round. Men's crops may be more subject to the volatility of world markets or state pricing policy than women's food crops. In areas where high population density has affected access to land, the poorest men may be unable to get the resources to put themselves to work, whereas their wives may find ready markets for the bean cakes they make, the groundnut oil, or the baskets. Until agriculture becomes a more productive occupation than it is at present, the existence of other options may make the difference between managing or not. For women who have little or no access to a man's income, the ability to put themselves to remunerative work on a regular basis is critical, even if they are forced to do it on disadvantageous terms.

The evidence suggests that women's work is everywhere valued less than men's. But is women's labor really less productive than men's? The evidence is ambiguous, at best, because in most areas the kind of work done by each sex is different. In places where certain tasks are common to both sexes, one finds either narrower gaps than one might expect, or further factors to explain the differential. Women farmers in western Kenya, for example, had significantly poorer access to advice and credit from the agricultural extension system (Staudt 1978). Lucas's analysis of men's and women's farming in Botswana shows that production *per acre* differed hardly at all, even though women's resources were significantly poorer (Lucas 1979: 4, 47). Finally, Dunstan Spencer's (1976) discussion of rural wage rates in Sierra Leone suggests that productivity differences between the sexes are mainly task-specific, and therefore not constant across the board. In his case the daily wage rate reflects this: women receive even a slightly higher wage than men for rice harvesting but only two-thirds of the men's wage for land preparation and planting, and even less for 'other farm work'.

The data are too locally specific to allow one to draw major conclusions. But they suggest the possibility that differentials between men and women in returns to labor are highest in the smallholder, cash-crop economies and lowest in the fully proletarianized populations. Over and above the likelihood of women's marginally lower physical productivity and the established fact of their poorer control of resources, there appears to be a further determining factor that derives from the system of labor control and labor valuation in the wider economy.

The wider system

In examining women's economic position in the context of national and international economies, it is necessary to go beyond the fact that much of rural women's work provides security, inexpensive food, and the next generation of workers. On the basis of slender evidence, there seem to be some characteristic sets of contradictions for women that differ according to the dominant source of wealth in the economy. In the case of peripheral market involvement, the possibility of more equal access to resources between men and women may exist in certain indigenous social systems, but that possibility is purchased at the cost of a static level of living. Production of cash crops for the market appears to intensify the disparity between the value of men's and women's labor and their access to productive resources. On the other hand, the concomitant growth of market trade and general occupational complexity often provides regular employment opportunities for women under conditions that can be integrated with domestic duties. Women in these systems are anything but underemployed. Where the labor force is proletarianized, the wage disparity between men and women may narrow; the critical problem for women then becomes differential access to limited wage employment.

For the moment, the majority of women in rural Africa live and work in the peasant sector, involved with the wider system to a greater or lesser degree depending on the region. Their work will continue to be the backbone of the food supply system, but under shifting conditions. The urban areas are growing extremely quickly, while agricultural productivity remains stagnant. At a time when policy-makers are slowly and painfully becoming aware of women's key position in food supply, many of those women are trying to educate their daughters for occupations other than agriculture. A literate female farming population is one possibility for the future, but so is a female rural exodus to match the male migration of the past two generations.

Changes in the 1980s

The 1980s have been an extraordinarily challenging and complicated decade for rural Africa. Over the course of that decade the image of Africa held in the West has changed. Where once Africa was seen as generally self-supporting, with intermittent problems of disease and drought, it became a continent seen as chronically vulnerable to food shortages. One main reason for this shift in perspective was the dire effect on production and distribution of continuing civil disorder in areas that are otherwise well-endowed with resources, such as Uganda, Ethiopia, Angola, and Mozambique, and political disaffection in many others. In addition to political instability, the prices of traditional export crops on the world market plummeted precipitously because of currency devaluation. The provision of services by governments declined, and rural people had to manage with poorer health services, schools, roads, and water supplies. Inevitably, rural women living in all areas of the continent and practicing a whole range of occupations found themselves struggling with old issues at a new level of intensity (see Gladwin 1991), and any aspirations of formal sector employment for women or their daughters have dramatically diminished due to cut-backs in education and lay-offs in the civil service.

There are, however, some new dynamics in the rural areas that are worth focussing on. The realization that food security was threatened has brought the food economy – where most women are employed – into the limelight with much greater urgency than in the past, when research, funding, and policy concerns were devoted disproportionately to export crops. In some countries, such as Ghana, agriculture has been vigorously promoted in the 1980s and in others, such as Nigeria, production of some home-grown crops for the local market has been stimulated by protecting them from international competition. Internationally supported agriculture projects have been promoted under the two banners of 'food security', on the one hand, and 'sustainability' – in deference to Africa's fragile soils – on the other. The urban food market is growing everywhere, offering new possibilities for women in the peripheral economies to be drawn into market production and for those in the old cash-crop economies to expand their processing and trade. In some areas large-farm agriculture has expanded to meet the needs of breweries, feed mills, and industrial processing plants, thus drawing more rural women into wage labor. The only regions where this dynamic has little relevance are the labor reserves of southern Africa, where all production possibilities have been severely limited and where rising unemployment levels in the nonfarm formal sector simply put the rural areas under greater pressure.

A further influence on rural dynamics everywhere in Africa is the simple fact that most farming communities change slowly. As long as people have resources, they do not go out of business except in case of disaster. Rather they continue to manage, improvise, try new ideas without threatening the old, even under stress (see Barker 1989). The poorer the resources (as in the labor reserves), the greater the difficulties. One should never forget, however, that political activism can also be an economic response: witness the emergence all over the continent of women's organizations with agendas bearing on women's property rights, credit access, rights under family law, political representation, and so on. These slowly developing forms of organization may in the end be among the more important influences on women's economic roles in the future.

The current picture of women's position in rural Africa, then, is one that should emphasize the areas of growth in the food economy and the slow processes by which people in different relationships to that market reformulate and redirect their activities. One of the key new questions this picture raises is whether small-scale women's endeavors can hold their own in the food economy and expand along with it. With the somewhat higher levels of education women achieved up to the mid-1980s and with the radically diminished chance of formal sector employment, there is reason to expect that some women will be innovative at work and more militant in protection of their interests.

It is, perhaps, highly selective to concentrate on areas of growth when women in so many regions of Africa are struggling with the effects of war, repression, and radical instability. But the shape of a possible future for rural women can perhaps be glimpsed in those growing agricultural economies where the dynamics discussed separately under 'peripheral', 'export', and 'wage labor' economies are no longer regionally distinct but increasingly interact with one another. Here, in the hinterlands of growing cities, and in other areas of expanding production, women are finding niches in a more complex and more competitive food sector. Zimbabwe and Nigeria are two examples where these conditions are emerging, and these changes are examined briefly below.

The Zimbabwean agricultural economy was dominated by white settler farms and black labor reserves until independence in 1980. After 1980, some black farmers were resettled on abandoned, formerly white farms, but the main thrust of agricultural policy was to maintain the large-farm sector while vigorously developing services and a price policy for the small farms. The proportion of commercialized output coming from small farms has risen dramatically in consequence. The development in Nigeria is almost exactly the reverse. There was little plantation farming until very recently in Nigeria, and the vast majority of agricultural output came from smallholders in 'old export crop regions'. In the late 1970s an effort was made to expand the large farm sector and link it up to agroindustry in the way that resembled the long-term patterns of Zimbabwean agriculture. As a result, large farming raised its profile considerably. In both countries, the farm sector was diversified and differentiated by social class at one and the same time.

One major finding in both these areas is the pervasiveness of women's wage labor in agriculture, if only for a short season of the year (Cheater 1981, 1984, Guyer 1991, Idowu and Guyer 1993; also Mbilinyi 1986, 1988 for Tanzania). The whole issue of agricultural wage labor has been investigated by relatively few scholars (Swindell 1985: 91–128), and women's work has been given even less attention. This issue becomes increasingly urgent as the old plantations and the new agribusiness ventures have been joined by mid-scale and even smallholder farms in their demand for workers. Only where farming is mechanized can the mid-scale farmer manage without hiring peak period labor (Cheater 1984). And a significant proportion of that hired labor is female.

There is not yet enough information available to know what this means for women's own enterprise in the rural areas. The conditions of work vary. In Zimbabwe, women have been part of a commercialized, permanent, year-round labor force for the settler farms since the 1930s. By the 1960s there was an increasing use of casual laborers, who were disproportionately women, earning very low wages by comparison with men. There is a great deal of female hired labor on small-scale African farms as well. These women do not have other opportunities for earning an income within the same area and do not appear to think of their farm work as a seasonal activity. Where women are landless or without alternative income-earning possibilities in their home areas, they may have to accept the poor working conditions that have been described for the workers on a Libby's pineapple plantation in Swaziland (McFadden 1982): 'The majority of the workers . . . live in slums bordering the pineapple plantation . . . there are no water or sanitation facilities. . . . These women work . . . without any protective clothing to keep the prickly pineapples from injuring their legs and arms. . . . After the pineapples have been cleared from the fields, the women are laid off until the next season. . . . And so on' (McFadden 1982: 149–57). Vulnerability to these kinds of working conditions rises with the constriction of realistic alternative sources for women to earn a year-round, living income.

In southern Nigeria, women's wage employment in agriculture is markedly different; it is strictly seasonal, and is combined by the women with a variety of other work. Women are hired mainly for the harvest of maize, egusi-melon, and cow-peas. Women agricultural workers are hired to work on corporate agribusinesses, the farms of middle-class retirees and prominent individuals, the mid-scale farms of local men, and smallholder farms owned by both men and women. Within the hinterlands of the large cities, all these types of farm exist side by side, with the newer large farms having to compete for land and labor with the established small producers of the old peripheral and export crop economies (Idowu and Guyer 1993, Guyer 1991). The seasonal and competitive nature of labor demand means that the large farmers cannot impose conditions such as those described at Libby's and still recruit a labor force.

Our own study in Yoruba-speaking Ibarapa Local Government Area suggested that women who work for the larger enterprises are generally in a poorer position than women who work for their male kin in the smallholder sector, and they are paid somewhat less in real terms. Since wage labor is only one of the activities that women engage in to make a year-round income, however, they tend to recognize the value of the employment opportunity offered by agribusiness. If the wages go too low, the women simply take up another activity – such as marketing or working for a smallholder – leaving the farmer high and dry. Men and women earned the same wages for the same task in 1988, but the tasks that men and women did often differed, with the lower-paid tasks being assigned to women.

For much of the year, when they are not employed as labor, Yoruba women are engaged in the trade and processing of agricultural goods. Their proximity to urban markets offers them new opportunities but also new competitors. Men from the urban area have entered the food economy as transporters and as packers for the drivers who routinely pick up goods at the villages or even harvest the crops in the field and transport them quickly to semi-mechanized processing centers. Unless rural women make careful arrangements for access to the farmers' crops that they are accustomed to harvesting and processing, they can begin to feel the competition: first in sheer access to enough of the crop, then in the decreased prices of goods that they are preparing by hand and others are preparing by machine. Only those women with capital, a strong business sense, and urban networks can get into mechanized processing unless they organize themselves into groups.

Two lines of development have opened up for rural women: greater differentiation among women traders and processors, according to their access to capital and their ability to deal in bulk, and greater involvement in farming itself, on their own account. Farming gives women access to a living, it ensures their provisions as processors, and helps them stand aside from the sharp competition in trade and processing. The expansion of women's own-account farming in response to the urban market, albeit on very small plots with a mean size of just under two acres, is one of the most striking changes of the late 1970s and 1980s. Women's ability to move so decisively in this direction rests firmly in the Yoruba tenet that a woman should have her own occupation, her own income, and her own 'purse', and that she is eligible for land allocation by virtue of membership in her natal compound or through marriage. No woman is expected to work on her husband's farm without return, but concomitantly every woman contributes to her own and her children's expenses in life.

What, by comparison, is the larger context of women's wage work in Zimbabwe? In the Mzengezi area, family farms predominate but rather few women own their own farms, compared with Yoruba women (Cheater 1981, 1984). These lands are purchased, not granted for use according to lineage allocations. The farms are much larger than the smallholder farms of western Nigeria, and the majority are worked by the whole family: men, their wife (or wives), and children of both sexes. In this situation farmers see advantages to polygamous marriage, because it gives them a complex, diversified, and obedient labor force, and it is often the wives who effectively manage the entire farm. Wives are remunerated by their husbands with a land allocation to grow crops on their own account, but only after they have completed the work on the main farm. When calculated in terms of returns to labor, the male owners benefit from their wives' input at a level far higher than the gains to the women themselves (Cheater 1981: 363).

In Zimbabwe, casual workers still have to find a year-round living, and have far fewer possibilities for doing so than the women of Western Nigeria because of the greater hierarchy in the agricultural economy and the greater numbers of landless peasants. Landlessness is still a political issue in Zimbabwe. The wives of mid-scale farmers have other concerns, namely a customary family law that does not allow women to inherit land from their husbands, thereby putting wives in danger – as eventual widows – of losing the farm they may have managed for their entire adult lives. The whole issue of women's status in property law has been better documented, more keenly debated, and more vigorously advocated in Zimbabwe than elsewhere as a result (May 1982; see also Chapter 5 below). A very recent development achieved through legal advocacy has been a measure allowing a year's grace period between a husband's death and the acquisition of his property by the husband's customary heirs; it is hoped that the grace period will allow negotiations to take place and women to make their own plans. It is not as bold a measure as women wanted, but it is a wedge in the door of a very difficult problem. Access to resources, and particularly land, is the key determining factor in rural women's lives in Zimbabwe.

For the women of western Nigeria, where processing and market trade offer a living outside farming, the key concern is to maintain or extend the diversity of income-earning opportunities in the rural economy so they can have access to a year-round income. Women are actively experimenting with new niches in the economy, of which farming itself is one. For them, the question of the legal framework of land access will arise only slowly and indirectly, if women find that they cannot extend their farms as much as men. Even then, women's land access is likely to remain a struggle within compounds and communities rather than taking place in a national legal context, because 'custom' as it has been formalized in the Yoruba region is not so clearly negative with respect to women's rights as it appears in Zimbabwe. Nigerian women's organizations promote other interests to meet the needs of involvement in small-scale enterprise: credit facilities, cooperative use of processing machinery, resistance to increased market taxes (Eames 1988), fertilizer purchase and other supports for small-scale and highly diversified businesses (see Trager and Osinulu 1991).

Throughout Africa, women continue to be very active in the rural economy and potentially very vocal in regional affairs. External support for African rural women is also greater than in 1980 (Spring and Wilde 1991), even if in many places women's situations have deteriorated (Gladwin 1991). The priorities vary with women's position in the economy: family farm workers are concerned with secure land access; full-time wage workers are concerned with the availability and conditions of jobs; workers in diverse rural economies such as that of southern Nigeria are concerned with year-round income sources. Everywhere, the existence of realistic alternative ways of making a living provides the foundation for improvement. The problems and achievements of the 1980s – profound political unrest aside – have not, on the whole, stifled or further marginalized rural women in their search for more secure and diverse spaces in economic life, but this is largely because their experiences have prompted African women to participate in a higher level of activism and debate. As African political and economic life struggles with the adverse conditions of the 1990s, this is likely to be a difficult and tiring, though indispensable, course forward.

CHAPTER 3

Women in the urban economy

Claire Robertson

Cities in sub-Saharan Africa occur in many types, reflecting the diversity of a huge area. Some are primarily mercantile in origin, some administrative, and a few are industrial. There are old cities whose founding dates preceded the beginning of continuous European contact in the fifteenth century. For instance, some towns along the East African coast like Mombasa and Malindi grew up as part of the vital Arab trading world, while in West Africa towns on the edge of the desert, like Timbuktu, functioned as the hubs of ancient empires. Some West African coastal towns also predated European contact. Cape Town in South Africa was founded in the seventeenth century by Dutch settlers. There are also relatively new towns, however, whose formation was a product of changes wrought by the colonial powers; these include most of the big cities of central, inland East, and southern Africa.

A common way of analyzing African cities has been to divide them up according to their indigenous or foreign mode of origin (Southall 1961). This division has been extended to their inhabitants, so that those who are migrant and those who are indigenous are thought to have significantly different characteristics. In the 1950s and 1960s analysts often concentrated on the social dislocation experienced by the migrants, while later scholars went on to talk of the reintegrative functions of ethnicity and voluntary associations in an urban context. Because most cities were viewed as being relatively new, and because the majority of the inhabitants of even the old cities are migrants, these studies did not show much about the effects of long-term urban residence on indigenous city-dwellers.

It is becoming evident now that, whatever the presumed differences are between migrant and indigenous city-dwellers (for example, that the latter would be in a more stable socioeconomic situation), they do not apply to women. Whatever their origins, urban African women are experiencing the same sorts of changes, many of which are detrimental to their well-being. The fact that most women share similar pressures and crises raises questions concerning not only the

44

impact of sexism on their fate, but also the impact of class formation. This chapter will explore some of these ramifications.

Class formation is progressing rapidly in sub-Saharan Africa, with African elites occupying the niches formerly reserved for colonial administrators. The persistence of white minority rule in South Africa long made that country an exception. This differentiation by economic status is graphically expressed in the physical aspect of many cities. For instance, in Accra, the capital of Ghana, there is an old, very densely populated precolonial central city composed of mud and cement houses with corrugated zinc roofs. Further inland from the shore is a colonial elite neighborhood now mainly occupied by upper-class Ghanaians. Further north still are some extremely exclusive suburbs where large houses are surrounded by compound walls and shaded by palm, mango, and frangipani trees. Near these villas are the packed squatter settlements so characteristic of Third World cities, where electricity, running water, and toilet facilities are scarce. These differences are mirrored on the roads where, behind slick new Mercedes, *tro-tros* (open-backed trucks) and minivans bump along, carrying as many people as can fit inside and cling to the outside. In Lagos, Nigeria, the same situation exists on a bigger scale because of the influx of oil wealth, and in Abidjan, Ivory Coast, there is even a luxury hotel with an ice-skating rink (as well as a swimming pool) – a surrealistic phenomenon in a tropical climate.

In South Africa the class differences are even more dramatic: laws in effect until quite recently prescribed that blacks live in dreary, poverty-stricken, government-owned developments outside the cities, while whites enjoy a luxurious urban lifestyle maintained by the cheap labor of blacks. In parts of Central and East Africa, the situation is similar, although the contrasts are perhaps not so stark.

In discussing urban women and class formation, a first requirement is to rid ourselves of the tendency to submerge the women's identity in that of the men. That is, in too much of the literature, women's socioeconomic status is presumed to be the same as that of their husbands or fathers. Under certain conditions this may be a per-missible assumption, especially when women are wholly dependent on men for their support, as in some Western situations. Even in the West, however, this assumption ignores power relations within families and differential access to family resources. In sub-Saharan Africa women often have property, and rights to property, quite distinct from that of their husbands, and women perform work outside the home that is vital to the economy. In most rural areas, women provide at least 70 per cent of subsistence needs by growing or gathering food, and in cities this function often continues as women are responsible for feeding their families. It becomes important, therefore, to distinguish women's money from men's in determining socioeconomic status, as well as in discussing economic change.

A second pitfall best avoided is the use of the traditional/modern dichotomy in analyzing socioeconomic change. This model is ahistorical, because change is continuous in all societies, making it impossible to fix on one (usually apocryphal) point as having been 'traditional', and another as being 'modern'. The underlying goal of change is usually assumed to be Westernization – that is, patterns of change that duplicate the Euro-American experience. Here, rather than assuming that socioeconomic change necessarily involves only the imposition of Western-type structures from above, I will consider it to be a continuing series of fundamental changes within indigenous African social structures, for which outside forces can act as catalyst but not as instigator. Economic forces, especially the integration into a capitalist world economy that accelerated in the nineteenth century, have been a primary agent of change, but modified in major ways by different cultures.

A third problem frequently encountered in the literature is the routine undervaluation of women's work. The official statistics on women's economic roles, presented in the Appendix and in Tables 3.1 and 3.2, frequently reflect this limitation. As shown in the Appendix, a woman who works 18 hours a day trading, housecleaning, and child-rearing may be classified as 'underemployed'. The importance of earning wages may be stressed, and self-employment ignored or deprecated. Gross domestic product statistics are compiled that omit the value of domestic or unpaid labor; women's work is sometimes assumed to be valueless because it is done by women. Fortunately, we now know better. This chapter is a brief introduction to the knowledge about the work of urban African women that has been gained in the past several decades.

Women's occupations

Women in sub-Saharan African cities work inside and outside the home in a variety of occupations. Whatever the origins of the women, the occupations they pursue tend to fall into certain categories because of women's differential access to education and the constraints imposed by the gender division of labor, both colonialist and indigenous. Although most African nations have enacted laws that forbid discrimination on the basis of sex, only very few women have been able to overcome the socioeconomic constraints which keep women illiterate, poorly paid, or marginally self-employed.

Whatever the causes of female inequality, the results can be seen in Table 3.1, which describes the occupations of female and male residents in 10 black African cities. (For the statistical sources of Tables 3.1 through 3.3 see page 65). Analysis of Table 3.1 makes a good beginning for the explanation of women's economic roles in urban Africa. First, the paucity of the data shows just how little is known about the exact situation. The Nigerian censuses are difficult to obtain and unreliable. For Khartoum and Abidjan, 1955 was the most recent date for which detailed information was readily available. In Bamako in 1960 the census-takers assumed that most women were exclusively housewives. Housework was not considered to be work

Table 3.1 Occupations of adult[1] African urban dwellers by sex, 1955–1976 (percentages)

Town	Year	Professional, technical, and related workers		Administrative, managerial, clerical workers		Sales workers		Service workers		Agricultural, forestry, and related workers		Production, manufacturing and maintenance workers		Homemakers		Other workers		Unemployed		Total	
		F	M	F	M	F	M	F	M	F	M	F	M	F	M	F	M	F	M	F	M
Abidjan,[2] Ivory Coast	1955	0.0	1.3	7.5	8.5	70.0	21.4	5.0	15.2	0.0	3.1	7.5	38.8	–	–	7.5	5.9	2.5	5.6	100.0	99.8
Accra, Ghana	1960	2.3	4.4	2.3	16.8	35.3	12.9	3.0	11.5	0.5	4.4	6.0	24.4	32.1	0.2	9.6	14.8	8.9	10.5	100.0	99.9
Bamako, Mali	1960	0.0	1.0	0.0	3.1	1.9	20.4	0.6	23.3	1.0	9.8	1.5	5.0	–	–	2.0	30.7	93.9[3]	6.7	100.0	100.0
Mali – all urban	1976	1.4	5.6	1.0	3.3	1.9	8.9	1.3	5.0	2.4	26.9	1.5	26.1	88.7[4]	20.9[4]	1.3	1.1	0.8	3.9	100.3	101.7[5]
Cape Town, South Africa	1970	1.2	0.3	0.1	1.0	0.3	1.6	22.3	5.6	0.1	4.9	0.6	58.3	–	–	9.9	3.9	65.5[3]	24.3	100.0	99.9
Dar-es-Salaam, Tanzania	1967	2.0	4.2	3.5	13.6	1.0	9.0	7.6	26.7	2.2	3.2	2.1	22.2	76.7	0.4	1.7	22.0	2.6	4.3	99.4	105.6[5]
Fort Lamy, Chad[2]	1962	0.3	10.2	0.0	1.8	11.1	13.3	0.2	39.0	4.3	11.4	0.3	15.5	76.5	0.0	6.2	0.3	8.2	99.5	99.7	–
Khartoum, Sudan	1955/1956	1.6	4.8	1.4	12.3	2.6	8.0	2.6	17.8	0.1	2.9	1.7	21.5	81.9	–	22.3	7.2	10.4	99.9	100.0	–
Lusaka,[2] Zambia	1970	1.1	3.1	0.1	0.7	2.9	10.4	1.5	5.6	1.1	9.8	0.4	4.8	67.6[6]	13.7[6]	1.8	29.4	23.6	22.4	100.1	99.9
Tananarive, Malagasy Republic	1960	- -	. -	1.6	17.9	3.3	13.4	7.8	10.5	0.1	5.3	2.1	16.5	–	–	0.1	7.8	84.8[3]	31.6	99.8	103.0[5]
Yaoundé, Cameroon	1976	4.0	8.0	5.1	11.6	2.9	9.1	2.8	9.8	1.3	1.5	5.3	38.4	66.0	0.6	6.8	7.7	5.8	13.1	100.0	99.8

Notes:
[1]Aged 14–15 or older.
[2]Bantu population only, or African population only. Lusaka figures differ from Hansen's because of the inclusion of homemakers.
[3]Housewives included.
[4]The Mali 1976 census differentiated economically inactive from unemployed, putting most women in the former category under homemakers. I have put their inactive category under homemakers, but it probably also includes retired persons.
[5]Percentages may add up to more than 100 because some categories overlap; people may have multiple occupations, or different censuses used different categories, that is, sales workers in one census may have included some clerical workers but not in another census.
[6]Included also students and disabled.
— – Not given, or impossible to discern.
. - Included under administrative, managerial, and clerical workers.

47

and was lumped together with 'unemployment' in Bamako and Cape Town. Most tellingly, in attempting to update these statistics in 1991, I could find nothing more recent that had sufficient detail. The 1990 ILO *African Employment Report* found that only nine African countries broke down statistics by sex out of only 19 that had collected statistics on employment (p. 65n).

Second, the data in Table 3.1 sometimes include only wage-earning workers and omit the self-employed. Most women are self-employed, since discriminatory hiring policies and the lack of training often bar them from available wage-paid jobs. For instance, only the 1960 Ghana census inquired about self-employment in detail and made a thorough attempt to count the self-employed in each type of occupation. In that census, 79.8 per cent of the working women were self-employed, compared to 24.5 per cent of the working men (Republic of Ghana 1960: 72, 115). Similarly, in Nigeria in 1966/67, some 81.4 per cent of the employed women in urban areas were self-employed, compared to 59.2 per cent of the men. In addition, 12.4 per cent of the women were unpaid household workers or apprentices, compared to 8.6 per cent of the men. The remainder earned formal wages (Republic of Nigeria 1966/67: 20–21). Self-employment is sometimes not mentioned even if the census-takers ask about it; sometimes it is illegal. In South Africa and in Kenya illegal beer-brewing provides employment for many urban women. Prostitution is usually illegal. When governments insist on licenses for traders, women who cannot afford them, or who wish to avoid paying for the licenses, will say that they are housewives. Because of the prestige occasionally attached to being a housewife (a luxury few families can afford), some women will report that they are housewives, not mentioning their hairdressing or vegetable-selling businesses.

Third, the data are inconsistent. This table should be used with caution, because the census takers' categories were often different. I have tried to make them comparable, but it was not always possible to ascertain the definitions used. The figures are therefore more reliable for making comparisons of labor force participation by sex within a city than across nationalities.

Despite all these reservations, Table 3.1 still shows us something about female labor force participation, an impression reinforced by the statistics in Table 3.2, which gives the percentage of females of all waged workers in various sectors of employment in 10 countries. (Except for those in agriculture and mining, most wage workers are urban.) It is clear that there is a far greater percentage of men than women in professional, technical, administrative, and clerical jobs. Although women sometimes do slightly better in the 'professional' category, because of their roles as teachers and nurses, the male/female difference is particularly striking for the administrative, managerial, and clerical workers. In Table 3.2 the concentration of women in service jobs is noticeable. The variations between African countries in women's access to professional, managerial, and clerical work are treated more fully in Table A.4 of the Appendix.

Table 3.2 Female wage employment in selected countries, 1980s (% female in various sectors of employment)

Sector	Kenya	Zambia	Tanzania	Botswana	Gambia	Malawi	Mauritius	Niger	Swaziland	Zimbabwe
Agric/Forestry	23.5	7.1	9.0	13.4	18.7	15.5	26.6	3.1	21.8	17.6
Mining/quarry	2.2	5.4	11.2	7.0	—	—	49.4	2.6	4.3	2.2
Manufacturing	10.0	5.7	10.0	24.1	18.0	24.2	57.4	4.5	31.1	6.8
Electricity/water	8.9	1.5	8.7	6.5	5.8	8.5	3.5	2.0	7.9	3.9
Construction	8.4	1.9	6.8	4.7	1.9	1.0	1.6	1.5	3.0	1.6
Wholesale/retail and restaurants/hotel	16.4	8.4	6.8	45.8	18.1	7.4	21.8	7.6	41.9	15.4
Transport and communications	10.0	5.8	5.0	14.2	7.5	5.6	8.2	6.7	12.6	6.2
Finance, insurance, real estate business, and services	21.6	11.9	29.5	32.1	15.8	9.9	29.3	22.9	35.5	34.0
Community/social and personal services	28.9	11.0	26.4	37.9	21.2	18.0	20.9	17.3	45.0	24.8
All industries	21.7	7.3	16.0	29.9	15.2	14.8	34.5	7.1	27.7	16.6

Source: ILO JASPA *African Employment Report*, 1990: 72.

High-ranking urban white-collar workers are, of course, the most powerful group in African countries today, and they are as overwhelmingly male in sub-Saharan African countries as they are elsewhere. In Table 3.1, where the figures most approach equity in Abidjan, the women's figures are artificially inflated by the omission of homemakers as a category. Certainly, one can find a female high court justice or UN ambassador here, and a female senator there, but these are exceptional cases. As described in Chapter 10 below, precolonial African societies had women rulers with real political power, but during the colonial era women's status in indigenous political systems was undermined, and the situation has not improved in the contemporary wage sector or in political activities.

One area of women's precolonial authority was in market trading, which has a long history in West Africa. The results for 'sales workers' in Accra and in Abidjan in Table 3.1, and in urban Nigeria where 59.7 per cent of the employed women were in sales in 1966/67 (Republic of Nigeria, 1966/67: 20–21) show the dominance of coastal West African women in trade. (Regional variations in women's role in trade in the 1980s are shown in the Appendix, Table A.4.) In inland East and Central Africa, where few towns existed before colonial rule, women's participation in market trading dates back to the nineteenth century, rather than the fifteenth. That occupation is growing very rapidly, however, absorbing many women with little capital or education. Where Islam prevails, men are most likely to dominate trade, as they do in Bamako, Dar es Salaam, and Khartoum. In Kano, Northern Nigeria, on the other hand, Muslim women are still active as traders despite their tradition of seclusion – they use intermediaries, like their children, to sell for them. Even in this area, women's trade has generally been concentrated in the preparation and sale of foodstuffs; the more valuable precolonial long-distance trade in gold, ivory, kola nuts, and slaves was usually, but not always, dominated by men. Big business now is dominated by multinational corporations (MNCs) which got their start with the help of colonialism; after independence most of their management positions were filled by African men. In Nairobi the first Kenyan woman managing director of a multinational corporation was appointed in 1988.

Because of their restricted access to credit and capital, as well as management problems and family obligations, few women have been able to develop large-scale businesses. Getting start-up capital is becoming more difficult as kin-based women's work groups break down in the urban setting, and also partly as a result of universal primary education. Family obligations such as paying school fees often absorb women's capital, so that the scale of their businesses is related to the age of their children. The unequal gender division of labor in the home reduces women's hours spent in the market and therefore their profits. Also the introduction of intermediate technology, as described in Chapter 12, may deprive women of the means of acquiring capital without substituting alternative employment. In some areas, for instance, hand corn-grinding was carried out on a piecework basis, with poorer women working for women with large food-preparation businesses. The introduction of male-owned and -operated gas-powered corn mills helped the large traders, who could afford to pay for machine-ground corn, and deprived the smaller ones of the means of getting capital. The profits from corn-grinding then went into the male sector. The case of Naadey, whom I encountered in Accra, illustrates some of the problems faced by traders.

> Naadey was a vigorous 41-year-old woman living in the center of Accra in 1978. She, her grandmother, and her mother were all involved in selling fish; she was teaching her daughters the trade. Her eldest daughter was 20 and in the process of taking over some of the business. But her younger daughters did not want to do it. They went to school and were unsuccessfully looking for clerical positions. Meanwhile, the business was not prospering because the fish supply was becoming concentrated in a very few hands, due to the mechanization of the fishing industry and discriminatory policies by the government and large foreign-owned corporations. A few women, aided by their powerful male governmental connections, were making things extremely difficult for most fish traders.
>   Naadey found that her alternatives for employment were extremely limited, since monopolistic conditions are increasingly prevalent in other commodities as well. Her clerk husband, who was supposed to be paying for the education of her four youngest children (three boys and a girl), had taken another wife who was young, attractive, and educated. He had a house in a suburb and had stopped visiting downtown or asking Naadey to visit him, although on occasion he grudgingly gave her some money to buy food for the children. The young wife objected to his associating with Naadey at all (partly because he had told her he had no wife before they got married), and wanted all of his resources to go to her own two children, aged one and three. Naadey was finding life increasingly difficult, despite putting in more time selling fish than ever before. She could not afford to buy meat or eggs to eat, and their diet consisted largely of a starchy cassava product (*gari*) with little nutritional value. She particularly worried about the future of her sons, 'as for my daughters, they can always trade, but my sons, what can they do without a good education? I cannot pay the school fees'.

In earlier years, men usually dominated among waged service workers except in South Africa, as shown in Table 3.1. Domestic service, in particular, developed under colonial rule, and it was a distinct advantage for a domestic servant to speak the colonialist language. Since boys were more often educated than girls, and since it was often not acceptable for women to work in the houses of unattached white men (who left their wives in Europe), domestic service came to be dominated by men in many places (Schmidt 1993, Hansen 1993).

In the postindependence era the trend in service work as a whole has been reversed, as shown in Table 3.2. New types of service jobs for men emerged, often in the public sector, leaving lower-status domestic work to women. South Africa is an exception in that women there have strongly dominated domestic work for a very long time. This work absorbs more female wage laborers there (37 per cent) than any other field. In 1980 their average work week was 61 hours in length, and their average wage 11 cents an hour (Lapchick and Urdang 1982, see also Cock 1980).

Matilda Smith was a domestic servant for a white family in Johannesburg in 1980. She was in her mid-thirties, a small sturdy woman whose experiences had left her bitter. She lived in a tiny, flimsily constructed torrid room on top of a modern high-rise, one of a row of cells occupied by the servants employed by the white residents. It was furnished with whatever odds and ends she could find; she could not afford to buy furniture. Her pay was $30 a month, plus room and board. Any meager savings went to her mother, who lived in an African 'location' with Matilda's two children, and her younger sister, also a servant.

Matilda's job was to care for the three small children of her employers. Servants until recently were not allowed to have their families with them in white areas, so she only saw her own two children on her day off. If by chance a family member was caught visiting by the police in their periodic raids, stiff fines were imposed on both employees and employers. Local accommodation was still not available for most servants' families.

Matilda was on call 24 hours a day, six days a week, was fed poorly ('kaffir food'), and treated disrespectfully by her employers. One of her children was the son of a former employer, who raped her several times; her pregnancy resulted in her dismissal. She preferred not to do domestic work, but found her employment opportunities severely limited. She disliked the low pay, the humiliation, and the boredom, but her training and experience, as well as the laws limiting black pay and job opportunities, gave her few alternatives.

When Matilda was not too tired to think, she wondered what would come of all this misery. She was only with her husband two years before he lost his job as a mechanic and got caught picking pockets. She had hardly seen him since he got out of jail. Her 16-year-old daughter left school and became a prostitute. On the rare occasions Matilda saw her, they would argue about her future. In her mature years, Matilda had become a devout Christian, a member of a fundamentalist sect popular in the location. On her day off, she went to church and talked to the minister about her daughter. Her eight-year-old son was a better student than her daughter, but Matilda worried that the lack of opportunities would discourage him and that he would begin running around with one of the youth gangs in the location. Many people had been killed by government-backed forces opposing the ANC and she feared his involvement there. Despite the excitement of possible political changes, Matilda worried that her mother would be arrested for illegal brewing and that they would lose their house (two rooms with no indoor plumbing or electricity). In case such an arrest took place Matilda was afraid her mother and children would be sent to live on the reserves, where her mother had never lived. The family was a third-generation urban one, far removed from farming skills. But beneath everything Matilda felt the corrosion of her self-respect. She held her employer's 18-month-old daughter and said, 'I love this child, though she'll grow up and treat me just like her mother does. Now she is innocent' (adapted from Cole 1967).

Migration to towns

In many southern African countries and in the Congo, restrictions were placed by colonial governments on women coming to town. The idea was that Africans were by nature rural dwellers, that only male labor was needed for the mines and other industries, and that African men should return to their rural homes after completing their work contracts. The provision of urban employment for men but not women, even in places where restrictions were not imposed on female urban migration, led to severely unbalanced sex ratios in some cities, especially in the period between the two world wars. Table 3.3 shows that the imbalance prevailed even well after the Second World War; it was particularly characteristic of Central, East, and southern African towns populated mainly by migrants, such as Nairobi and Cape Town, and mining towns like Lubumbashi (Zaire) and Johannesburg.

In Table 3.3, Maseru shows the results of intensive male labor migration to South Africa, for which Lesotho serves as a labor reservoir just as the South African reserves do. The European presence, as in Abidjan, exacerbated the surplus of men, as did the successful South African effort to restrict the influx of women to Cape Town. In most countries policies to control urbanization failed; in South Africa they succeeded only because of rigid apartheid policies. Apartheid removed black South Africans from the white towns and resettled them in segregated areas such as Soweto, from which blacks required passes to leave.

In Table 3.3 in the few cases where more current sex ratios, as well as population, were available, it is clear that the urban population has grown considerably. This growth is from both natural increase and migration. Dar es Salaam more than doubled in size from 1967 to 1978; Bamako grew by almost a factor of six from 1960 to 1984. This huge growth rate, also evident in Abidjan, was largely at the expense of the countryside. The urban proportion of the total population also grew considerably in the 1970s and 1980s in all of the countries listed in Table 3.3: Ivory Coast and Zambia are rapidly becoming heavily urbanized countries, to give just two examples. At the same time the sex ratios are becoming more even – because of the development of long-settled urban populations in newer cities, and because more women are migrating to towns. For example, in Kenya and Tanzania, women's migration to towns has increased during the postwar years, and female migrants now are more often coming independently, for economic and educational reasons, rather than as dependents of males (Shields 1980: 17–27). In fact, some rural women are migrating to town now to escape the hard farm labor that is their usual lot, posing another threat to African agricultural production and making change imperative in the skewed gender division of labor whereby women do most of the farmwork. In other cases, however, the differential employment opportunities for men and women still leave an imbalance in town. Population imbalances and differential employment opportunities in

Table 3.3 African cities: population, sex ratios, and proportion of country population in urban areas, 1955–1984

City	Country	Year	Total City Population	Ratio men:women	Proportion of country population/urban 1978	Proportion of country population/urban 1987
Abidjan	Ivory Coast	1955	120,051	100:72	35.14	43.8
		1980	1,596,965	100:90.8		
Accra	Ghana	1970	564,194	100:97	30.3	32.1
Bamako	Mali	1960	125,300	100:99	16.8	18
		1984	739,975	100:98.8		
Cape Town	South Africa Bantus only	1970	1,107,763	100:100	n.a.	n.a.
		1970	108,827	100:52		
Dakar[1]	Senegal	1955	230,887	100:89	34.6	37.2
Dar-es-Salaam	Tanzania	1967	272,821	100:81	13.9	25.1
		1978	769,445	100:88.7		
Fort Lamy	Chad	1962	88,162	100:91	13.5	29.5
Khartoum	Sudan	1955/6	69,006	100:75	19.4	21.2
Lusaka	Zambia	1969	184,895	100:91	40.2	51.9
Maseru[2]	Lesotho	1966	171,226	100:127	12.5	18.1
Mombasa	Kenya	1969	247,073	100:72	14.8	21.3
Nairobi	Kenya	1969	509,286	100:68		
Tananarive	Malagasy Republic	1960	247,917	100:102.4	17.9	23.1
Yaoundé	Cameroon	1976	291,071	100:88	31.6	45.2

Notes:
[1] African population only
[2] District

54

turn encourage the employment of women in services such as the provision of prepared foods and prostitution. The case of Wambui Murithi illustrates how prostitution can be an advantageous strategy for some women.

> Wambui Murithi, an elderly Nairobi woman in the 1970s, had been a prostitute in her youth. In 1922, when she was still in her home area, she married a part-Indian, part-Kikuyu man after her initiation. After a few years, she left him because of repeated beatings and returned to her parents for several years. In the late 1920s, she went to Nairobi along with a friend who had also recently divorced an Indian man. In Nairobi, Murithi added English to her vocabulary (she already knew Swahili) by attending night classes given for Christian converts by the Church Missionary Society.
>
> She and her friend rented a room downtown and began streetwalking. Streetwalking, known locally as *watembezi*, offered more adventure and higher profits than the form of prostitution practiced in Nairobi's African location; she had a clientele composed of Europeans, Indians, and better-off Africans. Her profits allowed her to begin assuming some family obligations. By 1930, Murithi was regularly paying the hut tax for both her father's wives and also the hut tax for her brother on occasion. She built a stone house for her parents on their farm in about 1933. She made the marriage payment for two of her brothers' wives. Between 1933 and 1936, her sister was widowed and left with three children. After her sister returned to their parents' land, Murithi promised to support her and the children. She paid for their education, and eventually made the marriage payments for her nephews.
>
> In 1937/38, Murithi built a six-room house in Nairobi's African location. She moved into one room and rented out the others, mainly to teenage Kikuyu girls who were beginning to dominate *watembezi* prostitution in Nairobi. By this time, Murithi had given up that form of prostitution but maintained close relations with several men who had been her lovers over the years. She never had any children, probably due to gonorrhea. She helped socialize her teenage tenants into the norms of Nairobi prostitution during the Second World War, and recalled warning them not to accept gifts in kind from soldiers, since they then would be liable to arrest for receiving stolen goods. Between 1937 and 1946, Murithi's earnings from prostitution were only slightly more than those from rent.
>
> At the end of the war, she bought her parents two cows. In 1948, when restrictions on African coffee production were lifted, she bought coffee trees for her parents' farm. One of her reasons for subsidizing the family farm was to give her sister's children a place to live. In the 1950s both of Murithi's parents died, but her brother and sister still worked the family farm, where she visited them. She was able to live on the income from her Nairobi house, which she shared with the 17-year-old grandson of her sister, who was in Nairobi looking for work (adapted from Luise White, private communication, January 1981).

Both Naadey the trader and Wambui Murithi were employed in what is often called the 'informal sector'. This term usually refers to the labor-intensive, nonwage employment that absorbs over half the population of both sexes in most Third World countries, but especially the women. The characteristics of the 'informal sector' are usually described as underemployment, labor intensity, low productivity, and lack of capital formation. In the past analysts using the term often measured economic progress according to how far the population of a country had been absorbed into capital-intensive, large-scale enterprise – the 'formal sector' – and deplored the continued existence of the 'informal sector'. More recently the more positive aspects of the informal sector have been stressed with the realization that small-scale enterprises are efficient and can lead to capital formation, especially if they receive help in the form of the types of government loans and credit that the 'formal sector' enterprises routinely obtain (ILO 1978, Liedholm and Chuta 1976). In a situation where management skills are scarce and transport and supply problems persistent, small-scale enterprises often have the advantage over larger ones. Here it can be seen that Naadey's enterprise contributed to human capital in paying for education and Murithi's to education and agriculture, where she invested her profits.

Most urban women's employment is in the informal sector, and yet both women's paid and unpaid labor there tends not to be measured as part of the GDP. For instance, the 1988 ILO *African Employment Report* had apparently absorbed the newer point of view requiring that important attention be given to the informal sector; one-fourth of its contents were devoted to the subject. The point about the importance of women's economic activities, however, had been missed – the statistics given for informal sector labor participation in 10 countries stated that, on the average 94 per cent of the participants were male (p. 76). Their own research apparently ignored the statistics provided by African governments; in 1978 in Kenya 30.3 per cent of the participants in the informal sector were female (*Kenya, an Official Handbook*, 1988: 155). In 1988 two-thirds of the retail sellers in Nairobi's open air markets were female, according to my own research. The average size of the informal sector enterprises covered by the ILO surveys was three employees; most women traders have no employees. What happened here seems to be that statistics were mainly gathered about manufacturing enterprises in the informal sector, or skilled occupations such as shoe repair that are dominated by men. Again women were nearly invisible. By 1990, however, the ILO had upgraded their assessment of women's work, and one-quarter of that year's *African Employment Report* was devoted to them.

In the economy there is a continuous gradation of enterprises in terms of size, and an interpenetration of wage earners and self-employed that makes the arbitrary classification of the terms 'informal' and 'formal' sectors of questionable value. Nowhere is this more evident than in considering the role of women in manufacturing. Male dominance in urban occupations is most overwhelmingly evident among the production and manufacturing workers in Table 3.1. It is still evident in the 1980s in such categories as manufacturing and construction (Table 3.2; see also Appendix, Table A.4). In some countries, however – such as Malawi, Botswana, and Swaziland –

substantial numbers of women are employed in manufacturing. The heavy investment by MNCs on the island of Mauritius has resulted in over 50 per cent of the workforce in manufacturing being women.

There are several reasons for continued male dominance in manufacturing in most African countries. First, because of the bias in the statistics toward wage workers in large-scale enterprises, many small industries conducted by women do not get counted. Second, men were considered by the colonialists to be more suited than women for work involving the use of machines. Thus, vocational schools were established most often only for boys, or male workers only were recruited for wage labor, whether agricultural or industrial. Sometimes women's agricultural labor on plantations was hidden as family labor, and payment made only to the male head of the household. Third, these policies occasionally reinforced an indigenous gender division of labor which did not encourage women to obtain formal education or to work for wages outside the home. This was particularly true in Islamic areas where women were secluded (not common in sub-Saharan Africa). Home production was important for those women, since outside work was forbidden. The legacy of these policies continues today, due to the lack of investment in Africa by large multinational corporations, which elsewhere in the developing world rely on cheap female labor (Bujra 1986). Only in South Africa is there a large industrial work force that includes a substantial number of women (Berger 1992: 252–53).

Fourth, women craft-workers in precolonial Africa made soap, pottery, medicines, cloth, baskets, and other things. In some areas putting-out systems similar to those in early industrial England were operated by women. However, women's products incurred competition from European manufactured items and often lost out. European items had more status as imports and often were of more uniform quality. Such imports were encouraged and protected by the colonial governments, who wanted not only raw materials, but also markets for their manufactured goods. Local African businesses, whether male- or female-owned, often suffered from lack of credit, tariff protection, and other resources enjoyed by the large foreign firms. They often failed. But whereas the men were often offered education and alternative employment, the women were not. It is no wonder, then, that in Accra (Ghana), Nairobi (Kenya), Lusaka (Zambia), Kisangani (Zaire), Kampala (Uganda), Ibadan (Nigeria), and many other cities, women turned in large numbers to small-scale trading in local commodities (Schuster 1979, Pons 1969, Southall and Gutkind 1957, Robertson forthcoming, MacGaffey 1986).

Before discussing the influence of education on women's employ-ment, a comment is needed on women's urban agricultural activities. Many cities have urban farming on small plots of vacant land in widely dispersed locations, with women supplementing their income by farming. Agricultural work is, however, not common in an urban situation for either sex. One reason it appears in the statistics is that fishing and related activities are still pursued in coastal or riverine towns. Women's work in this regard is probably underrecorded because men more often own the land or land rights. One of the significant changes for many women who come to town is that they may lose their rights to agricultural land. Migrant women often accompany their husbands to town. In many African societies a woman's access to farmland depends on her continued relation with the family of her husband, or with her family of origin. Long-term absences can jeopardize their rights to land. Even indigenous women city-dwellers are often in a similar situation; their lands were either lost or sold in the immense growth of towns during the colonial period, the proceeds going mainly to male lineage members. Women are nevertheless expected to feed their families. If they cannot grow the food, they must earn money to buy it or become dependent on their husbands for that money.

The impact of formal education

According to Table 3.1, more African women are homemakers than anything else. This, of course, is the census-takers' catchall term for women who do not do other things, and masks a lot of self-employed women. However, it does reflect the fact that women's industrial and agricultural opportunities are severely limited in the urban situation. Nor are there many professional, technical, administrative, managerial, or clerical opportunities for women. Their lack of education contributes substantially to this situation, as figures cited in the Appendix show. The Appendix also mentions some of the differences between African nations with respect to women's education.

There are several stages in the development of formal education for African women. In the colonial era, in the mid-1950s in Dakar and Abidjan, for instance, there was a large disparity between boys' and girls' literacy levels, because the colonialists were not usually concerned about providing education for girls. This situation is reflected in the statistics for older age groups in most ex-colonies: in Yaoundé in 1976, some 38.5 per cent of the men aged 65 and over had gone to school of some sort, compared to only 8.2 per cent of the women aged 65 and over. (All education statistics are derived from the sources listed at the end of this chapter.) It is common to find complete illiteracy among women over 65 in some areas.

In the 1970s there was a push for education in most of the newly independent countries, and primary and/or middle school education was often made compulsory. Facilities were expanded drastically to accommodate the influx of students of both sexes, and in some cases, the access of boys and girls to primary school was equalized. In Accra in 1970 more girls were in primary school than boys, because there were more girls in the population. Children in urban areas, of course, have had more access to schooling than those in rural areas because development spending has usually been concentrated there.

The third stage is reflected in the higher percentages of females than males having primary school as their highest level of education – in Accra, Maseru, Tananarive, and Yaoundé, for instance – because more schools have been provided, but more boys have gone on to middle and secondary school. The educational system is steeply pyramidal for everyone, with very few secondary schools compared to middle schools, but even fewer secondary places for girls than boys. Many secondary schools are private and/or costly, and enrollment is not compulsory. A few elite women, however, were able to complete secondary school or university and combined high education levels with an indigenous tradition favorable to influential female roles. The case of Funmilayo Anikulapo Kuti, a Yoruba woman, is outstanding in this respect.

Funmilayo Anikulapo Kuti was a lifelong resident of Abeokuta, a large older town in southwestern Nigeria. Her grandparents were taken by Portuguese slave dealers to Sierra Leone, having been captured by the British antislave trade patrols. They subsequently returned to Abeokuta. Her mother and father were both born in Abeokuta of Christian convert parents.

Kuti was christened Frances Funmilayo, but after encounters with racism while studying in England she dropped the Frances altogether. In England she studied general education, French, and domestic science, and in 1922 returned to Nigeria and began to teach at the Abeokuta Grammar School. It was there she met her husband, the Rev. Ransome-Kuti, and they were married in 1925. From 1925 to 1931 Kuti and her husband resided in Ijebu-Ode near Abeokuta, where Kuti became the principal of a girls' school and began literacy classes for adult women. Upon her return to Abeokuta in 1931, she founded a nursery school and became its headmistress. In 1942 she organized a club of educated women known as the Abeokuta Ladies' Club, which subsequently undertook to aid the market women who complained that their goods were being confiscated by the government to aid in the war effort. It was then that Kuti truly became involved with the market women, and by 1946 the Ladies' Club had become the Abeokuta Women's Union, which with Kuti at its head spearheaded the protests of the market women that culminated in the abolition of female taxation (for a time), the resignation of the Alake (king) of Abeokuta, and the total reorganization of the Native Authority System in Abeokuta. These were tremendous victories for the women, and Kuti became an international figure, travelling in eastern Europe, China, and Israel.

By 1950 the Abeokuta Women's Union had changed its name to the Nigerian Women's Union and was documented as having about 80,000 members. It began to inaugurate branches in other parts of Nigeria, and in Abeokuta operated a weaving corporation, ran a maternity and child welfare clinic, and conducted literacy classes for adult women.

In 1980 Kuti died; the news was front-page headlines throughout Nigeria. She had spent her life in active pursuit of basic human equality of the sexes, recognition of the rights of ordinary people to have their basic needs met, and the creation of a Nigeria where justice reigned (adapted from Cheryl Johnson, private communication, June 1982).

In general, however, it was not easy for women to translate educational credentials into an actual job. Accompanying the provision of primary schooling came a steady inflation in the amount of education required to get a job, and sometimes a lowering of the quality of the education provided. In addition, the generally worsening economic situation of the 1970s and 1980s meant that wage employment was not available for many primary or middle-school leavers, and especially not for girls, who had to compete with the better-educated boys. Even in Kenya, where in 1976 some 89 per cent of the secretarial workers were female, only approximately 16 per cent of the wage labor force was female, and 77 percent of self-employed women in the modern sector were in trade, restaurants, and hotels (Republic of Kenya 1978: 43, 45, 46). The primary refuge for the unemployed is self-employment in small, sometimes illegal, enterprises. Self-employment offers the advantage to young women of being able to watch their children while they are working. Even in areas where the self-employment of women was not previously important, it is becoming more common out of economic necessity.

The provision of formal education, then, has not so far remedied the economic inequalities between men and women, because that education has been provided unequally. Furthermore, it may be damaging to women's opportunities for self-employment where these are well developed. For instance, a girl who spends her time at school will not put in the same number of hours as an apprentice seamstress, market trader, or potter. Formal education could in theory teach skills valuable for self-employment – such as accounting, carpentry, or car repair – but too often it does not. Instead, girls may be taught home economics, which may concentrate on convincing girls that Western ways of housekeeping, table-setting, and child care are superior to indigenous ones, and, by implication, that housework should be done exclusively by women. In many cases schoolgirls, not boys, are assigned housekeeping tasks involved in school maintenance. At a few schools, apparently, the notion so prevalent in the Western media that female bodies are for male exploitation is taught, as a notorious Kenyan case of July 1991 suggested. In this incident, 20 secondary school girls were killed in a raid by boys intended, according to the assistant headmistress, 'only' to rape them, not to 'harm' them. Thus, Western-type education may reinforce or impose ideas of female inferiority and promote the ghettoization of women into underpaid 'female' occupations.

Formal education may also arouse expectations in girls that they will obtain a clerical job and a lifestyle similar to that depicted in the movies. Thus they may no longer be interested in pursuing self-employment as traders, for instance, because trading is too low in socioeconomic status for them. And because trading itself is less lucrative than previously, it is less attractive. In the end, many women will have to compromise and take up some sort of self-employment because other opportunities do not exist, are not open to them, or are not compatible with child-rearing. Inexpensive day care is hard to come by for many urban women, and they are less likely than rural women to have coresident relatives who will help.

The problem of child care is particularly acute for the women who have obtained jobs as secretaries or typists. Their wages do not usually allow payment for good quality day care; governments or businesses seldom provide it, yet their long hours require it. They often rely on the help of a poor relative, usually a young girl, living with them. They usually have fewer children than poorer women – four or five instead of six or seven, still a substantial burden. Some governments provide or require benefits such as day care, maternity leave, and hospital care; this has caused some employers to become even more reluctant to hire women. In addition, the tendency to maintain relatively high fertility, requiring many maternity leaves, has had a statistical impact in reducing upward mobility for white-collar workers (ILO *African Employment Report 1990*: 66). It is a common practice not to promote women who are pregnant.

There have been complaints from clerically employed women in many countries that men regard them as legitimate prey for sexual exploits. Sexual harassment may even cause some to leave their jobs for self-employment, which at least offers more control over the environment. Where self-employment is not attractive, some workers find they can supplement their pay with occasional prostitution or long-term liaisons with office superiors. In countries where the impact of the inflation of the 1970s and the structural adjustment of the 1980s and '90s was particularly severe, real wages fell, causing people to supplement their earnings by part-time self-employment. However, the interpenetration of the formal and informal sectors is such that damage to the formal sector has also harmed the informal sector. Whereas the informal sector in the past could easily absorb large growth, it has suffered from the greatly increased competition in the area of retail trade, in particular, while being asked to accommodate more women, who have borne more of the brunt of unemployment caused by structural adjustment (*African Employment Report 1990*: 69, 75–78; Appendix, Table A.3).

It has often been observed that the higher the stage of technological development, the more clerical jobs are given to women (Boserup 1970). This process has both good and bad aspects for women. In Africa, as in most of the world, very little is being done to avoid the gender stereotyping of women as secretaries, roles that may prevent their advancement into better-paying jobs. Other positions that are becoming typically female in Africa include nursing and lower-level teaching positions. The type of education offered is partly responsible for this trend; the denial of technological education to women is particularly important, and appears not only in Africa but also in most developing countries.

The case of Mary Chinubu is pertinent as a typical woman clerical worker.

Mary Chinubu was a young woman of 22 working as a clerk-typist in Lusaka in the late 1970s. She grew up in a village with her parents and siblings; when she showed promise as a student, she was sent to live with her older brother, who had become a successful small businessman selling auto parts. She finished her middle schooling while living in Lusaka with her brother and his wife, and helping to care for their three children. She was then fortunate to get a place at a secondary boarding school; her brother paid the fees, although it strained the budget. After a year or so she started slacking off in her work; at age 16 she was developing an interest in boys, whom she would meet secretly to go to the cinema. After a time she got pregnant and was forced to leave school; her brother was furious and reluctantly allowed her to return to his home. He was even more upset when she named one of her teachers as the father of the child. Under pressure from their mother, her brother agreed to keep the baby, a girl, while Mary went to a commercial school to get secretarial training and, with her brother's help, she got a job clerking for a mining firm.

After several years of work Mary took a flat that she shared with another woman in similar circumstances. She could afford it only because she had become, under much pressure, the mistress of an older man who was one of her bosses. She was more attracted to some of the younger men she and her friend occasionally met in bars, but they could not provide for her as lavishly. Also she wanted to keep her job. Her sister-in-law remonstrated with her, saying that at age 22 she had already ruined her life. Mary gave in to the pressure when her affair with the boss waned, partly because she had fallen in love with a younger man who had promised to marry her.

She married the 28 year old rising young engineer and everything went well for six months. Then her husband's sister came and told her that he had another wife, whom he had married in his village some time before; they had a child. Mary was unhappy that he had not told her this (although she had not told him about her daughter). But more important, she had suspicions that he was being unfaithful. (A single standard regarding marital fidelity is a relatively new expectation among urban Africans; older women are most likely to tolerate husbands' infidelity.) He had quit taking her out in the evenings several months after their marriage. Furthermore, he increasingly left the household expenses to her, even though he earned far more than she did. Eleven months after their marriage she had a child, a boy this time. By this time they were quarrelling a lot and he was spending most evenings out, giving no explanation for his absence. After another six months of deteriorating relations, he ceased paying household expenses altogether, and she moved out, taking the child and her belongings with her.

Mary was able to return to her former way of life. Through thick and thin she had held on to her job; by supplementing her pay with donations from boyfriends she could afford day care for her son. She seldom saw her daughter, although she occasionally contributed to her support, but she had great hopes for her son. She planned to send him to school, and expected him to be smarter and more successful than his father, and the support of her old age. She did not plan to remarry, unless it provided financial security. She enjoyed the freedom of being single and controlling her own finances. 'I wouldn't like to begin giving my salary to a man while my parents and family suffer. . . . I would not like to live under a hawk's eye every day . . . men are very jealous' (adapted from Schuster 1979).

Conclusions

For all of these reasons, most urban women find that they cannot grow what they need in town, so they must buy it, meaning that they must work outside the home. Wage work opportunities are severely limited, however, because of discrimination in education and hiring and the economic situation, so that women must be self-employed in a shrinking number of occupations. The skills imparted by home economics courses, baking cakes or bread, for instance, can help them to make a living selling prepared foods. This is one area where competition from foreign firms has not been a major factor, but selling prepared foods is not a lucrative occupation for most people. The result is that urban women are generally far more dependent on their husbands for support than are rural women. Husbands may resent this increased dependence and incessant demands from wives. As described in Chapter 4 on the family, men formerly were not expected to provide as much support as is now necessary. Urban living brings new demands and expectations in terms of the standard of living – children must go to school, rent must be paid, entertainment is costly. The husbands may demand that the women work harder, since the women's earnings are usually needed. Spouses do not usually pool their incomes, so that a woman without an income is in a difficult position with no say in household decisions. Her very dependence may make her hesitate to seek a way out of an intolerable marriage, but she may be forced to if the man stops providing adequate support. If he becomes abusive, which sometimes happens, she may have to divorce him.

In earlier times economic pressures on marriage were alleviated by substantial contributions from women for household expenses. Spouses often pooled their labor in communal enterprises. Even now in South Africa, some urban African men are subsidized by rural women sending them food, despite the desperate poverty of the reserves. In Ghana, children's nutrition is chiefly dependent upon their mothers earning enough through trade to feed them properly. In Nairobi thousands of women flock to sell in outdoor (often illegal) markets, many of them refugees from dysfunctional marriages and/or landlessness, seeking support for their children. Women, then, must still bear much responsibility for the economic well-being of their families, while they have access to fewer resources. Even working very hard for long hours, they may find themselves without sufficient income to support their children, and without a male partner or grown children to share the burden (in many towns the divorce rate is increasing along with the physical mobility of the population). My friend Nsuwa is a good example.

Nsuwa, an old woman living in central Accra in 1978, became partially blind before her death and was totally dependent for support on her two daughters, who live with her. Their children ran errands for her, and they gave her food. Nsuwa's two surviving sons lived elsewhere, one abroad and one in another town. Although both sons were educated and doing well, she rarely received anything from them. She surmised that they put their own children's needs first. She felt poorly used since in her youth she had worked hard at trading to pay for their secondary schooling. Her husband earned very little as a fisherman, and contributed nothing to school expenses. 'They were my investment,' she said, 'but I never expected this would come of it. My daughters help me and their father with food, even though they themselves are poor. My sons never come here, and only send money maybe once a year. It's not enough; I often go hungry but I don't like to deprive my grandchildren of food.'

Because more women than men are poor, the already high birth rate for sub-Saharan Africa is likely to remain high. Women look to their children for social security and help in their labor-intensive activities. Only under pressure from desperate poverty, or when their standard of living rises considerably will women limit their fertility, particularly if they go into more skilled occupations that are not labor-intensive. As long as the women's sector of the economy remains mostly poor, the cycle will be perpetuated of high fertility = low education = low skills = low income = high fertility. If development managers are serious about the long-term economic health of Africa, they will incorporate local women in development planning and execution. Non-elite women need equitable, well-paid employment and appropriate education to develop marketable skills inside and outside the home. Many development efforts have failed because they do not address women's needs. Despite their problems, urban women are forming a number of development-related organizations, as discussed in Chapter 9.

It can be concluded, then, that women's socioeconomic status can be very different from that of the men related to them. These differences must be considered in our attempts to understand social and economic processes and develop new ways to look at class formation. In economic terms, it is productive to look at money flows in separate men's and women's spheres, whose interactions can change over time. In the realm of society and politics, it is worthwhile analyzing change in the relative strength, functions, and power of male and female networks. These methods can help us to develop more refined ways of analyzing women and class formation.

Statistical sources for Tables 3.1, 3.2, 3.3

Cameroon, Statistics and National Accounts Department (1976) *Census*, Vol. I, book 2.
Chad, Bureau de la Statistique (1962) *Recensement de Fort Lamy*, 27–30, 1.
Côte d'Ivoire, Direction de la Statistique et des Etudes Economiques et Démographiques, *Recensement d'Abidjan, 1955*, 39; *Memento Chiffre de la Côte d'Ivoire 1985–86*.

Ghana, Census Office, *1960 Census, Special Report A; 1970 Census,* Vol. III.

International Labor Organization, JASPA (1988, 1990) *African Employment Report Yearbook of Labour Statistics 1989–90,* Addis Ababa.

Kenya, Central Bureau of Statistics, *Statistical Abstract 1989; Census 1969,* Vol. 1; (1978) *Women in Kenya;* Ministry of Information and Broadcasting, (1988) *Kenya, an Official Handbook.*

Lesotho, Bureau of Statistics, *Population Census, 1966,* Vol. 1; *Annual Statistical Bulletin, 1983.*

Malagasy Republic, Institut National de le Statistique et de la Recherche Economique, *Recensements Urbains 1960.*

Mali, Ministère du Plan, *Annuaire Statistique du Mali 1984;* Service de la Statistique, *Bamako Recensement 1958–1960;* Bureau Centrale de Recensement, *Recensement Général de la Population, Dec. 1976,* Vol. 2.

Senegal, Service de la Statistique et de la Mécanographie, *Recensement de Dakar 1955,* Vol. 2.

South Africa, Central Statistical Service, *South African Statistics 1988;* Department of Statistics, *Census 1970* Metropolitan Area, Cape Town, Vol. 23.

Tanzania, Bureau of Statistics, *Statistical Abstract 1987;* Economic Affairs and Development Planning Ministry, *Census 1967,* Vol. 2.

United Nations (1990) *African Statistical Yearbook 1987,* Parts 1–4.

Zambia, Central Statistical Office, *Country Profile 1985;* Ministry of Education (1974) *Annual Report;* Hansen, K.T. (1979) 'When sex becomes a critical variable: married women and extradomestic work in Lusaka', paper presented at African Studies Association Conference.

Part Two

African Women in Society and Culture

CHAPTER 4

Women in the changing African family

Betty Potash

An examination of women's family relationships must begin with an understanding of how African family and kinship organization differs from that of the independent nuclear family idealized in contemporary Western society. African families are based on the enduring, separate kinship ties of husbands and wives. Women and men always retain membership in their own kin groups, in which they have certain rights and responsibilities. In many places such loyalties take precedence over the bonds of marriage. The types of kinship claims that women have vary among societies and have important implications for their situations. In some areas kinship gives women access to land and housing, which provide both alternatives to dependence on husbands and leverage in marital relationships. In other societies women do not have such rights. Women may also turn to their kin for support in disputes, participate in kin group decision-making, and obtain labor assistance, although these rights are declining in some places.

Men's primary loyalties and responsibilities may be to their mothers, sisters, and other kin rather than to their wives or children. But, as explained in Chapter 10 of this volume, colonial and postindependence development policies have focussed on providing greater economic opportunities to men than to women on the unexamined assumption that African families are conjugally structured. Even groups seeking to promote women's interests focus only on wives. Thus, it is assumed that husbands and wives should pool income, share decision-making, and have their primary responsibilities to one another rather than to other kin, in the familiar patterns of Western societies. Such development policies have left women even more vulnerable and have contributed to marital conflicts, as wives need economic assistance in societies where men had no tradition of being the sole or primary provider and as men seek to control cash income. Where men do take on greater responsibilities for wives and children, other kin including mothers and sisters may be affected.

The organization of domestic life is usually different from that of the Western-style nuclear family. Although there are varied patterns of household organization in cities, most rural families are large units. Women or men marrying into such rural families are brought into daily interaction with a variety of people occupying distinct social positions in the household and community. These complex and varied relationships have implications for women's family life. The presence of polygyny is also important. These principles of organization affect urban household life as well, since kin may claim housing, or co-wives may take turns living with husbands. At the same time, it is important to remember that women's family roles are not static but change over the course of their life cycle. The constraints and powers that women have as wives and as the mothers of adult children are distinct. So, too, are their rights as daughters and as sisters. Women in these different positions may have competing needs rather than shared interests. Moreover, these roles are affected in different ways by social and economic transformation.

An extensive body of anthropological literature is available on African family structures and the cultural expectations associated with women's family roles. Less is known of women's behaviors in relationship to such cultural norms or of the emotional meaning of family life for women. For such insights we are better served by novels and films. In this chapter I shall describe some of the major features of African families as they relate to women. I shall also examine some of the transformations that have occurred since the onset of colonialism.

Family and household: conceptual issues

One of the most useful approaches to understanding family systems is that of Ralph Linton (1936) who focussed on the key principles by which families are organized. Linton distinguished *conjugal families*, where the central relationship holding the unit together is marriage, from *consanguineal families*, where domestic groups are based on descent. Most African societies reckon descent through either the male line (patrilineal descent) or the female line (matrilineal descent), although a few systems recognize bilateral descent in which both lines are given equal recognition. In patrilineal systems children belong to the father's group, where they have their primary rights and responsibilities. Ties to the mother's kin are recognized, but maternal kin are regarded as different kinds of relatives to whom one has different claims and obligations. In matrilineal systems the pattern is reversed. Marriages usually occur between members of different descent groups and couples reside with either the husband's or the wife's kin. (Other differences between patrilineal and matrilineal systems are discussed in Chapter 1 of this volume.)

In patrilocal extended family systems men live in or near their father's compound. The key ties on which the family is based are those of parents, sons, and brothers. Daughters move out and wives are brought in. In matrilocal extended families the key relationships are between mother, daughters, and sisters. In some societies ties between brother and sister or between maternal uncle and nephew determine community composition, although they do not necessarily reside in the same compound. In all of these systems, in-marrying spouses must adapt to such kin who have lived together throughout their lives. Should the marriage fail or dissolve through death, the larger family endures. By contrast, in conjugal families it is the marriage tie that is central. As children mature they leave their natal family to establish their own households. In consanguineal families, however, children remain and their labor replaces that of ageing parents for whom they now care. On the African continent consanguineal principles clearly predominated in the past, and they continue to influence household composition even today. In many rural areas such households are still found, sometimes in truncated form. Even urban household composition may be affected by these principles, as shall appear.

Despite their larger size, households based on consanguineal ties seldom comprise more than three generations. On the death of parents, or in some places even before, adult children leave to form separate households, usually on family land nearby. These new units, however, cooperate with one another for specific purposes such as ritual, economic support, or dispute settlement. Senior members may continue to exercise authority. This continuous cycle of development makes it difficult to establish firm boundaries that sharply distinguish the family, household or residential group from other kin. Some family members may reside in one place but take their meals or engage in productive activities elsewhere. There are societies where children live away from their parents with grandparents or other kin to whom they provide labor assistance. Sometimes children are fostered out to kin to be educated or for social advancement or discipline. Young unmarried men and women may live separately from their parents, formerly in bachelors' quarters or grandmothers' houses either within or outside the compound. Responsibilities also cut across residential groups when adult children support parents or form cooperative labor units comprising several households.

The internal organization of households also varies. Identifiable sub-units of a compound may consist of women with their children, each wife occupying her own house or room which the husband visits. In such systems the husband has his own quarters or takes turns visiting wives. In some societies co-wives in polygynous marriages may live in different compounds or even in different communities. Men may take their meals in their wife's house or all of the men may eat together. Frequently women are responsible for their own economic support and that of their children, but sometimes husbands and wives make separate contributions of particular goods and services. In a few societies spouses constitute a single production and consumption unit and work cooperatively. In some other places, the entire compound may be one economic unit under the authority of a family head who allocates goods and organizes labor.

Given this diversity of arrangements, what constitutes the family? As several anthropologists have noted, there is no satisfactory definition of either family or household (Yanagisako 1979, Guyer 1981). Rather, the significant relationships must be empirically determined, not presupposed. What is clear, however, is that African families are not nuclear units of spouses and children with conjugality as the central relationship. Nor can one treat the extended family as if it were simply a collection of nuclear families, since the organizational principles and key relationships are different. To understand women's family position these complex patterns must be examined.

Kinship and marital relations

Patterns of kinship organization, including women's rights in their own descent groups, are important in understanding women's situations and have implications for relationships between spouses. Women always retain membership in their own descent group but the claims that they can exercise and the manner in which they participate vary in different places. Where women have rights to land and housing and can call on kinsmen for support, they have greater leverage in marriage. Active participation in kin group affairs, including political or ritual office, improves women's overall social position. Since husbands and wives usually belong to different groups, participation in kin-based activities can provide a focus that competes with conjugal ties.

Common conjugal funds where spouses pool income and resources and have joint decision making over expenditures are not characteristic of African societies. Rather, wives and husbands have independent control over income and separate responsibilities, although income sharing is a new development among a few Westernized elites (Oppong 1974, Stichter 1988). It is kinsmen or children rather than spouses who inherit and who benefit from the wealth individual men acquire. Some of the problems these inheritance patterns can pose for women today are discussed in Chapter 5. Contrary to the older literature, which assumed that widows were supported by the husband's kin, more recent research shows that widows are primarily responsible for their own and their children's support and receive little assistance in most places (Potash 1986). Colonial marriage laws and missionary influence have sometimes modified these inheritance arrangements, but the claims of kin remain strong. In contemporary Africa there are reports of kinsmen not only claiming all resources of the deceased, including household effects, but even goods and income that widows have obtained through their own earnings. Anecdotal accounts suggest a worsening situation, particularly if the deceased was better off financially than his relatives. Widows are sometimes losing custodial rights over children to the husband's kinsmen, who obtain guardianship in order to control the property. Sometimes the children are neglected as well. Chapter 5 in this volume shows how women in Zambia today have struggled to change inheritance laws to guarantee widows some access to their husbands' property.

Given these patterns of rights and inheritance, as well as the existence of plural marriage, it is not surprising that spouses rely on their own kin or children rather than on one another for economic security. Indeed, the key relationships for many women and men are intergenerational, not conjugal. Women look to children for emotional and economic security; men to mothers and other kin.

In many societies a man's responsibility for providing assistance to his mother, father, brothers (or in matrilineal societies, to his sisters and sisters' sons) outweighs the claims of wives who are responsible for supporting themselves and their children. With the monetization of the economy and colonial and postindependence development policies that focussed on involving men in cash-earning activities, this pattern has posed particular problems for wives and children who have less access to cash and whose needs for support may not be met. In a cash economy women's subsistence activities tend to be devalued, resulting in a loss of prestige and increased dependence on men. Although wives seldom complain of the assistance that husbands give to mothers and sometimes siblings, which they regard as legitimate, they do complain about inadequate cash contributions that are necessary for survival. Some women consciously seek husbands from small families with few dependents. Men are sometimes torn between competing obligations, with only limited resources to meet these claims. Sometimes they simply ignore the demands of wives and children or use resources for their personal benefit, such as acquiring additional wives or girlfriends or entertaining. They expect wives to meet their own needs, as was customary in the precash economy. The growing impoverishment of women and children is partly related to such patterns and to development policies based on the assumption that male income is family or household income, ignoring women's needs.

Although precolonial productive patterns varied, even in those societies where men formerly made important subsistence contributions, their role has generally diminished as they adopted cash cropping or wage labor. Wives, by contrast, have had to take on increased subsistence as well as cash-earning activities to meet their productive and reproductive responsibilities. These developments have contributed to gender inequalities and have created tensions in marital relationships (Potash 1989). In some countries women's groups have campaigned for legislation requiring men to support children and for changes in inheritance laws (Kuria 1987, Vellenga 1986). What generally goes unrecognized in such campaigns is the impact that such changes might have on the support currently given to mothers and sisters.

Women in patrilocal extended families

In contrast to the large body of recent research on women and marriage, there are few accounts that focus specifically on women's lives in extended families (Sudarkasa 1981). There is, however, some ethnographic data on particular relationships, such as mother-in-law and daughter-in-law links or co-wife relationships, and an extensive older literature on family structure. I shall draw on this literature as well as data on life cycle changes and material from my own fieldwork to examine women's family relations. The initial focus will be on traditional patterns; later sections will deal with transformation and change.

Among the Yoruba of Nigeria, women marry into patrilocal extended family households, in which each wife is given her own room. Seniority is a key principle governing relationships within the compound. Juniors are expected to show deference to those who married in first. Not only are wives ranked with reference to one another, but daughters and sons born prior to the marriage are always senior to wives regardless of age (Sudarkasa 1981, Eades 1980). This ranking operates even when family members live apart. In Lagos, for example, I witnessed a man's visiting sister demand and receive items of clothing and household goods that belonged to the wife. I have also encountered situations where a man ordered his brother's wife to stop her activities and cook for him, even requiring her to get out of bed to do so. Women marrying into a Yoruba family thus assume a particular position within a hierarchy with culturally defined expectations of behavior.

While seniority as a principle of organization is also found in some other African societies, it does not necessarily take the Yoruba form. Among the Luo of Kenya I witnessed no deference behavior. However, seniority determines the order in which sons should marry and the placement of wives' houses within the compound. It also has ritual importance. There are various restrictions based on seniority and gender. Younger brothers of a husband, for example, may enter his wife's room or sleep in the same house; older brothers may not. Violations do occur, but failure to follow these rules is thought to result in the death of children or other misfortune. However, compound-wide ranking of wives does not generally operate except with reference to farming. The senior wife of the household head should initiate each stage of the farm cycle, with co-wives and sons' wives following in turn according to their position. The co-wives of a single man are terminologically distinguished as first, second, and third wife. A man can only be buried in front of his senior wife's house (or a replica, if she has predeceased him). Senior wives should also initiate the opening of a new homestead when men move out of their father's compound. Apart from these distinctions, seniority does not generally affect day-to-day behavior. Each wife operates autonomously, controlling her own house and lands. In the past there were some homes where a particularly competent senior wife was given authority by her husband to organize her co-wives into a cooperative farming unit. She could not do so on her own, however, but only as his agent. Even in these situations, each wife kept the produce from her own fields and had her own granary. A senior wife who was given such authority might also act as an intermediary between her co-wives and her husband, reporting on their needs for food and medical attention and informing the husband if a wife wished him to visit for sexual purposes. Labor migration and male absenteeism led to the decline of such arrangements; men living outside the community cannot delegate power or use their authority to enforce a senior wife's control. Today the senior wife has little power over others, although a few women try to press such claims, which junior wives often reject. Occasionally co-wives who get along particularly well may voluntarily cooperate in farming activities on an egalitarian basis.

Co-wife relationships have important implications for women. Many men continue to practice polygyny out of a desire for many wives and many children. Rivalry is characteristic of some but by no means all societies. This is sometimes reflected in language, where the terms for co-wife have their roots in words meaning jealousy, as among the Luo and Hausa. Competition for the husband's favor may be expressed through bearing many children, a practice that is sometimes used unsuccessfully to avert plural marriages. Wives may try to outdo one another in the performance of domestic and economic activities and in attractiveness. Co-wives also compete over land and resources and particularly over the advancement of children. In the past, political rivalry over succession to headmanships and chieftainships often involved mothers and their kin. Today the competition may center on education, land, and resources. The creation of a cash economy has exacerbated such conflicts. Although women produce most of the food for the household, they need cash to pay for educational and health care expenses and to buy some foods and clothing. Since men have better access to cash-earning activities than women, wives compete over the amount of cash the husband provides. Even in societies where the husband is expected to equalize contributions among his co-wives, they are often suspicious of favoritism. In large polygynous households where men cannot cover the cost of educating all of the children, women typically have to cover these expenses themselves.

In contrast to those polygynous systems in which jealousy is widespread, in other places senior wives are reported to welcome polygyny since they control the labor of junior wives. Prior to colonial rule, wealthy Igbo women took wives to whom they stood as husbands in order to obtain assistance with household and marketing activities, thereby increasing their wealth. Since female husbands were frowned upon by Christian missionaries, this practice changed. A new pattern emerged in which women pay bridewealth for additional wives for their husband whose labor they similarly control (Amadiume 1987). Among the Sherbro of Sierra Leone, polygyny helps women economically. Co-wives who live in different communities use this relationship to trade (MacCormack 1982). In Tombo village in Sierra Leone there is a different arrangement. Senior wives engaged in fish processing and trade depend on the labor of junior wives. It is the senior woman who owns the smoking oven and controls production and household activities. She is also responsible for maintenance. In such systems first wives do not resent a husband's subsequent marriage since they benefit, but junior wives may have different attitudes. In Tombo divorce is commonly initiated by junior wives seeking to become senior wives in other households. Eighty-five per cent of the women over 40 had been married at least twice (Steady 1987).

The organization of domestic activities under polygyny is also varied. In some places co-wives take turns cooking for the husband. This frees other wives to engage in trade when it is not their turn. Such institutions are particularly important in some parts of West Africa, as among the Ewe of Ghana. In other places, as among the Luo, arrangements differ. Each wife must cook daily. Rather than freeing women, cooking becomes an avenue of competition so that wives tend to work harder to produce superior meals. Co-wives generally do not care for each other's children, nor do they cooperate in the performance of other domestic tasks.

Another relationship of particular importance to women is that of mother-in-law and daughter-in-law. Daughters-in-law often provide labor assistance, and older women may exercise considerable authority over child-rearing and other matters. Among the Lovedu of South Africa, a woman has the right to claim a brother's daughter as her daughter-in-law even if she has no son. Her daughter will stand socially as a son and act as a female husband to the brother's daughter. This relationship is particularly important for labor assistance (Krige 1974).

Luo women begin their marriage working under their mother-in-law's supervision. Initially they farm and cook for her. As they have children of their own and as their husband's younger brothers marry, they are allocated their own fields and begin to work independently. Brothers' wives replace them as assistants to the husband's mother. However, the wife of the youngest son works for her mother-in-law throughout the older woman's life. It is only on her death that her remaining fields are passed on to the youngest son and allocated to his wives. Today the period of working for the mother-in-law is sometimes shortened, particularly if the women do not get along or if wives have been married for some time and live with their husbands in town. But mothers-in-law continue to exercise authority in other areas, such as child care. Luo wives are expected to consult the mother-in-law when a child is ill, particularly if the husband is working outside the community. They would be severely criticized for failing to do so. A woman may need her mother-in-law's or her husband's permission to obtain medical care for her children or herself (Potash 1985).

In other societies as well, the mother's influence has important implications. Among the Coniagui of Guinea, mothers sometimes arrange marriages. Even when this does not occur, the mother's consent is needed (Gessain 1963). Luo wives often blame a husband's decision to take an additional wife on his mother's influence. Whether this is an accurate reflection of reality or a psychological defense (or both) is not known.

Other relationships within patrilocal households are less well documented. There are respect and avoidance relationships in some places between a woman and her father-in-law. Sometimes relationships of privileged familiarity called 'joking relationships' operate between designated categories of kin. Relations between sisters-in-law or between a woman and other children of the compound have not been subject to much examination.

As in any large group with diverse personalities, relationships vary. Some households are harmonious; others are characterized by quarrels, competition, and suspicions of witchcraft. Some women conform to the norms; others do not. Sometimes women form cliques of mutual support with selected household members. Other women trust only their own children on whom they rely for emotional support, or they turn to friendships outside the compound.

Women in matrilineal and bilateral systems

Women do not always move to their husband's home after they marry. In some places they continue to reside with their own kin. Among the Yao of Malawi, for example, communities are organized around a group of sisters and their children; husbands marry in. It is brothers or maternal uncles, not husbands, who are responsible for the well-being of their sisters and sisters' children. They mediate quarrels, defend their sisters in disputes, act as marriage counsellors and marriage sureties, and obtain health care for sisters and sisters' children. Women can transfer allegiance from one brother to another or from a maternal uncle to a brother if they are dissatisfied with the manner in which their interests are looked after. Sisters can be quite demanding. However, neither the group of sisters nor the brother share a common household. Sisters live near one another. Sometimes they move as a group under the headmanship of a brother who establishes a new village. Brothers who want to compete for leadership must either marry a woman from another kin group within their sisters' community or obtain permission to bring their wives there. Otherwise they cannot be available when sisters call and consequently lose their support (Mitchell 1956).

A different arrangement is found among the bilateral Swahili of Tanzania. In this society first marriages are arranged with particular categories of kin. However, such marriages are often short-lived. On divorce or widowhood, a woman returns to her mother's home or to a household owned by female uterine kin, women to whom she is related through her mother. When women remarry, they choose spouses who will allow them to live near these households with whom they cooperate in farming. If a woman has children from an earlier marriage, these children are likely to reside in such households (Landberg 1986).

The Akan of Ghana have yet another pattern. Many women and men believe that coresidence of spouses is too difficult; each may prefer to remain with his or her own matrilineal kin. In such situations husbands visit their wives, and wives prepare meals that they send to their husband's home, but they do not live together. Sometimes women and men do live together during the early years of marriage, only to separate when they have had children. Katherine Abu found only 45 per cent of marriages characterized by coresidence in the Ghanaian town that she studied (Abu 1983). Such patterns point to two issues that need explication: the importance of kinship for women, a topic that shall be examined in more detail below, and the need to consider life cycle changes and the age-related differences in women's interests when examining their situations.

'Life cycle changes and older women

Family positions do not remain constant. In systems where women move into their husband's home or community, there is a marked difference between women at three stages: the young bride who must prove herself to her husband's kin and who is often expected to be shy, deferential, and hard-working; the mature woman competing with others for resources and trying to safeguard her children's interests; and the mother of adult sons who may wield considerable influence and power, becoming matriarch of the household. Indeed, in many African societies a man's primary loyalty and financial responsibility is to his mother, not to his wife and children. Sometimes the only woman a man trusts is his mother. The interests of mothers and wives are not identical. In some societies women who live with their husbands during their reproductive years leave when childbearing ceases. Sometimes mothers move in with adult sons, helping them to establish independent households. In other situations, as among the Ndembu or Baule, women may return to their own kin (Turner 1957, Etienne 1986). Sometimes women remain in their husband's compound after menopause, but sexual contact ceases. However, postmenopausal women often exercise considerable influence and are sometimes able to assume ritual or political roles that were formerly denied to them.

Widowhood similarly changes relationships. Given the age disparity, particularly in polygynous marriages, women may be widowed at a relatively young age. Where remarriage is prohibited, there is usually some provision for ongoing sex and procreation; consort relationships or the levirate, in which a kinsman of the husband becomes a sexual partner to the widow, are common but do not constitute marriage.

Rather, widows become the effective heads of their households and continue to reside on their husband's land. Although they have full responsibility for their children's support, typically receiving little or no assistance, they have more independence than wives. In other societies widows remarry or sometimes return to their own kin. A wide spectrum of arrangements is found (Potash 1986).

Where matrilocal residence prevails, there are also transitions, but many key relationships endure from childhood. Yao sisters, for example, do not have to adapt on a daily basis to husband's kin, but they may become more competitive with one another as they seek to advance their children's interests. Sometimes matrilocal residence occurs only during the early years of marriage, as in situations of bride service, which were formerly more widespread than today. Here men must prove themselves by working for their wife's family. But men may be permitted to remove their wives to their own community after the period of service is completed. Today bride service is often replaced by the payment of bridewealth.

Women in descent groups

Most of the African literature on descent group organization has focussed on its importance to men. As Karen Sacks has argued (1979), African women are not only wives but they are also 'sisters', members of families and descent groups into which they are born and in which they retain membership throughout their lives. The particular rights that women acquire through descent and their patterns of involvement in kin group affairs vary widely. Symbolically such differences may be expressed in funeral rites. Among the Igbo of Nigeria, for example, a woman's descent group always reclaims her body for burial. They inquire into the cause of her death and her treatment by the husband and his kin, and can levy fines and demand compensation as a condition for removing the body (Amadiume 1987). By contrast, Luo women in Kenya are so identified with their status as wives that they must be buried in their husband's compound. Should a woman die while visiting her natal home or while separated from her husband, she cannot be buried there but interment must occur outside the homestead fence.

Variations in women's kin group rights are not only symbolic. In some places women are active participants in descent group affairs, attend lineage meetings, contribute financially to ritual and other activities, and have a voice in political decision-making and/or in the selection of chiefs or headmen. This is the case among the Yoruba of Nigeria, for example. Ashanti queen mothers in Ghana are office holders selected by a matrilineal descent group to protect the group's interests and act as a check on the chiefs or the ruler whom they help to select (Aidoo 1981). Prior to colonial rule Igbo women were organized into two distinct types of groups responsible for women's affairs and for protecting their interests. One group comprised daughters of the lineage; the other wives married into the lineage. In this context the daughters had authority over the wives. Such women's groups successfully pressured men who mistreated women to modify their behavior (Amadiume 1987). These groups are discussed in greater detail in Chapters 9 and 10.

Such participatory patterns have implications for women's general social position and provide avenues for power and influence. Regular involvement in kin group affairs is, of course, affected by residence after marriage. If women move far away, they cannot participate on a regular basis. But geographic propinquity itself is not enough to insure involvement. Nandi women in Kenya, for example, often marry men of another lineage within their community, but are still not involved in the affairs of their own descent groups (Oboler 1985).

Property and descent

The degree of participation in kin group affairs is only one factor affecting women's situation in Africa. Rights to housing and to land in their natal community are perhaps even more important insofar as they provide alternatives to dependence on marriage and give women some leverage in conjugal relationships. Although men generally acquire rights to land through descent, the situation for women is more varied. In some places women have access to land and housing only through marriage; in others they, too, have claims on kin group property but the particular rights and the situations in which claims are exercised vary. Where matrilocal residence prevails, women remain in their own kin communities where they always have rights. They are not dependent on husbands for land or housing. Moreover, they can call on kin for support in marital disputes. Since women and men continue to have strong attachments to their natal groups, a high incidence of marital instability characterizes such systems. Indeed, divorce and separation are more common in societies with matrilineal descent where women either remain with their kin or can return home if marriages are dissolved.

In other types of descent systems marriages are sometimes highly stable, sometimes not. Attitudes towards divorce and its availability vary. Although husbands and wives have many reasons for wanting to please one another and to maintain harmony, marital stability does not always indicate a satisfactory relationship. In some places stable marriage may be the result of the limited options available to women. Where women have no access to land and housing outside of marriage and therefore no means of supporting themselves and their children, they may have to maintain even unsatisfactory unions. Custodial rights over children is another factor. Where women must leave children behind, they may be reluctant to terminate marriage. This is the situation among the Luo. Luo also frown on divorce, reducing the prospects for a satisfactory remarriage. In such systems husbands have considerable power over wives since women have no real alternatives (Potash 1978). But in some societies where women depend on marriage for land, there is no stigma attached to divorce. Kofyar women, who are always valued as wives, can readily find a new partner. These options give women leverage in marriage relationships, since husbands are reluctant to lose wives to other men (Netting 1969).

In other societies women can claim land in both their own and their husband's communities. Baule brothers compete with the husband and his kin in trying to attract women to reside in their communities. Since women accrue numerous dependent children, natural or adopted, they add to the size of the community and the importance of its leaders (Etienne 1979). In some places women have more limited natal group rights. Divorced or widowed women may be permitted to return to their natal community but cannot transmit rights to their children. Sometimes they must leave children behind and cannot remarry; Nandi women in Kenya can take children with them, but on maturity children return to their father's home (Oboler 1986). In these situations women do not contribute to the growth of their natal community. They may be regarded as dependents rather than assets. Returning women may be warmly welcomed as sisters but still regarded with suspicion since they did not have good relationships with their husband's kin.

Kinship and labor assistance

Kinship is not only important in giving women access to land; it is also a basis for obtaining labor assistance. The ability of women to combine productive and reproductive roles is partly based on the types of assistance that are available to them. Where such help is available through mothers or older children, women may be able to engage in more lucrative long-distance trade or modern sector employment. Otherwise, they are more likely to work closer to home. In a few places such as northern Nigeria, Muslim women in purdah depend on children to trade for them (Schildkrout 1978). In some societies women in their child-bearing years rely on junior relatives, such as nieces, nephews, and younger siblings, as well as their own children. Sometimes mothers help. Older women rely on daughters-in-law and grandchildren. Fosterage is a common pattern in many areas of Africa. Foster arrangements have generally been interpreted as a mechanism for strengthening kinship or for providing education and training for children (Goody 1982). I would argue that it is also a major means by which women recruit labor.

These patterns of kin-based assistance are currently undergoing change. With the increase in school attendance since independence, many children are no longer available to help. Today many women must either perform household and productive activities alone, adding to their workloads, or they recruit poorer relatives or non-kin whose families cannot afford school fees to act as hired servants. This development has implications for class formation.

Older women, too, are experiencing a decline in the assistance available to them. Not only are grandchildren often in school, but in some cases sons and daughters-in-law may be working outside the community and not available to help. Sometimes younger children are sent to grandmothers for rearing if the mother is working and has no access to domestic assistance. Fostering children was once used to assist older relatives among the Ewe of Ghana, for example; as the economy changed, it became a means of training children in new skills while they assisted relatives working in town. Nowadays young children are often sent to grandmothers for rearing while their mothers work outside the community (Brydon 1979). The AIDS epidemic has added further to grandparental responsibilities. Older women are now caring for the orphaned offspring of one or more children in Uganda and other places that have been devastated by AIDS.

Marriage

Although marriage is a universal or near-universal experience for African women and men, it is not necessarily the most central relationship in their lives. Women may rely more on children than on husbands for emotional and economic support, particularly in polygynous marriages; men, as has been noted, may have their strongest attachments to their mothers and other kin although they, too, depend on children for assistance in old age. Since women and men marry into existing families and communities, considerations governing marriage involve more than two individuals. The reputations of families and their agreement to the marriage often outweigh the personal predilections of the prospective bride and groom.

Many African marriages are still arranged today, although there is more self-selection of spouses than in the past. But even in situations where women and men meet on their own, the consent of parents and other kin is usually required. Sometimes intermediaries are sought to find suitable spouses and inquire into the family's reputation. Luo turn to a father's sister or mother's brother who reside in other communities to find a suitable mate. They either know the family personally and can vouch for them or they inquire into their reputation and family history. Such individuals are concerned with the future well-being of their nieces and nephews. Today in cities such as Nairobi, a man may turn to an urban friend from a different rural area rather than to a relative to perform such services.

In contrast to these patterns of arranged marriages, in some societies women and men are free to choose their own spouses, as among the Baule of Ivory Coast, for example (Etienne 1986). Sometimes both patterns coexist, and an earlier courtship is followed by an arranged marriage. In virtually all African societies, traditional marriage is confirmed by payment of 'bridewealth' from the husband (and his close relatives) to the bride's father (and his close relatives). Such payments establish the husband's right to his wife's labor, and sometimes also to the children she may bear. In the past, bridewealth was seen as an important confirmation of the woman's value; today, it is often criticized as having become commercialized.

The interpretations given to arranged marriages have been a source of contention. During the colonial era missionaries often advocated laws requiring a woman's consent to marriage. In contemporary Africa some women's organizations such as the Women and Law in Southern Africa Research Project are pressing for the enforcement of such laws (Armstrong 1990). Common to both cases is the implicit or explicit assumption that arranged marriages are forcing women into marriage against their will. The presumed beneficiaries are men; in some schema husbands, in others fathers. From my own experience, I would suggest the situation is more complex and women's attitudes need explication.

In many places the primary beneficiaries of arranged marriages are the couple themselves and their children, who will acquire two sets of kinsmen to whom they can turn for assistance. In-laws and maternal and paternal relatives can be called upon for particular types of help, such as economic help in emergencies and support or refuge in disputes. It is the couple and their offspring, rather than their parents or guardians, who generally receive such aid. In urban Africa such kin ties are used to obtain access to housing and help in finding employment. In many families the desire for a successful union is the major consideration governing marriage arrangements.

However, in some places and among some families marriage is used to benefit the marriage arranger. This is more likely to occur in hierarchical societies or in societies with emergent stratification, where marriage can be used to consolidate power. In precolonial African states and chiefdoms, rulers and other members of the elite received wives from subordinate chiefs and commoners, and patron–client ties were established or cemented by giving a daughter or a sister in marriage. Women received some benefits from these arrangements through residence in wealthy households, through higher status, and as mothers of sons who might succeed to high positions. In Dahomey, the ruler's wives became officeholders in their own right (Bay 1982). In other places, as among the Ashanti, women were used as pawns to secure loans; if the loan was not repaid the woman became a wife (Vellenga 1983). Senior women could also benefit from control over marriages. Aristocratic Kpelle women who are in charge of the women's secret society control the marriages of members (Bledsoe 1980), as will be discussed in Chapter 9.

As political and economic structures change, so too do the considerations governing marriage. Ethnohistorical research is beginning to document some of these changes. The expansion of the ivory trade led to a proliferation of polygyny among the Beti of Cameroon as marriage became a means of establishing relationships with trading partners in distant communities. Wives were also transformed into a labor force to raise food with which to feed retainers. With the shift from trade to cocoa farming, polygyny declined (Guyer 1986). The expansion of female slavery also affected marital relationships in some places. Slave wives were used as an alternative to free wives in parts of Zaire, thereby enabling men in matrilineal systems to obtain control over children and to avoid obligations to in-laws (Harms 1983). Where female slaves were taken as wives, husbands had greater control. The status of free wives was sometimes undermined as well. In contemporary Africa, fathers are sometimes accused in the press of selling daughters to obtain high bridewealth, a practice that is regarded unfavorably. One example that I encountered in my fieldwork involved a 13-year-old girl from a poor family, who was married before she reached puberty to a dying man in his sixties because her family needed the bridewealth.

Attitudes towards marriage and marital expectations are both culturally variable and idiosyncratic. Many women accept the legitimacy of arranged marriages, which also provide a built-in solution to problems of mate selection. Sometimes women are particularly desirous of a marriage that has been arranged, especially if the arrangement followed a prior courtship and understanding. Some women trust their parents, guardians, or marriage intermediaries to look after their interests. Sometimes women agree to unwanted marriages because of family or social pressure. Others may do so out of family loyalty and a wish to assist their brothers or other siblings with bridewealth or school fees.

But women are not merely pawns in marital transactions; they also employ their own strategies. Mkako women of Cameroon convince their fathers to delay acceptance of the final bridewealth payment until they are sure that they want the marriage. Women may enter a number of 'test marriages' until they find a man that pleases them (Copet-Rougier 1987). Women can also use other forms of resistance. In one negotiation that I witnessed, a reluctant woman finally agreed to a meeting with the prospective groom after much family pressure. However, her resistance was so apparent that the groom withdrew his suit. In some societies, although first marriages are arranged, these may be followed by subsequent marriages in which the woman has more choice. Swahili women often divorce and remarry, for example (Landberg 1986). Rukuba women in Nigeria are permitted multiple husbands. Although the first marriage must take place with a designated partner, women are free to take as many additional husbands as they wish. They decide with which husband they want to reside (Muller 1986). Elopements, adultery, and other violations of norms point to other forms of resistance. Virtually all bodies of customary law have procedures for dealing with such irregular unions.

But women are not always able to resist. The conflict between personal desires and cultural norms and the consequences of rebellion are themes in many African novels and films, such as Buchi

Emecheta's *The Bride Price.* Three of the Luo women whose life histories I collected were abducted after repeatedly refusing to marry the chosen man. They were then taken to the man's house, held down by his friends and family, and forced into sexual relations. In two of the cases a marriage ensued. One family refused to take their daughter back, since they feared that other men would be reluctant to marry her. The other woman agreed to remain and to accept the marriage. The issue was not the occurrence of premarital sex *per se*, which is common today. Rather, it is the public character of the event, which might affect a women's marital prospects. In the third case, the woman's family agreed to her return. She later met and married another man whom she loved. I should note that all of these women regard their marriages as satisfactory.

The Luo term for such abductions is translated by English speakers as 'ambush marriage', a category that also includes elopements occurring with the woman's consent. Both are strategies to overcome resistance to desired marriages. Armstrong finds similar forced unions in Zimbabwe. However, her emphasis is on the coercive sexual relations, which she equates with Western concepts of rape. For Zimbabweans, however, rape and consent had different meanings than in the West, according to her research. Informants focussed on parental agreement rather than on the consent of the woman herself. In Zimbabwe, as among the Luo, such coercion usually leads to marriage (Armstrong 1990).

Attraction and love are not unknown in African societies, as evidenced by rich oral traditions that include love poems and courting songs. But such emotions may not be considered a sufficient basis for marriage or a necessary condition. Some of the Luo women whose life histories I collected had loved one man but married another. Sometimes the man was a distant relative whom they had met at dances but could not marry because of the kinship connection. In other situations, the man or his family was deemed unsuitable because they were poor, came from a group with low social standing, or had a reputation for witchcraft, infertility, or other problems. Sometimes it was her family that objected; sometimes the woman herself decided against the marriage. When queried about desirable marriages, Luo women typically focussed on hard-working men from good families who would provide economic help, did not drink, and would not beat them. A number of women expressed hopes for a monogamous marriage, but were fatalistic about the prospects of a husband taking additional wives. Neither love nor companionship were mentioned.

Social transformation and rural families

Family systems are not static. Relationships change in response to economic transformations, new social arrangements, and new ideologies. Prior to colonialism, as has been seen, the shift in patterns of trade and the increase in female slavery altered the meaning of marriage and the position of wives. Other precolonial developments, such as the movement of populations into new areas, new modes of subsistence, and state expansion presumably affected family organization as well. But much of the historical research remains to be done. Although I have used the term 'customary family patterns' as a convenience to cover ethnographic data spanning several decades, it is necessary to recognize that the patterns so identified are only points in an ongoing process. Frequently it is not possible to know their history. Nor is there updated material available on subsequent changes for many of the societies that were studied decades ago.

The establishment of colonial rule and developments since independence have led to considerable transformations in family relationships and in women's roles. The conversion from a subsistence to a cash economy, labor migration and male absenteeism, new bases of status differentiation, and a general devaluation of women's subsistence activities are some of the developments that have affected women's family relationships. Urbanization, new legal codes of marriage, and new ideologies and religions are other factors associated with modifications in women's situations. Most of these transformations have left women more vulnerable; some have opened up new possibilities.

As explained in Chapter 1, colonial economic policies sought to promote the production of export crops and to create a migrant labor force by involving men through taxation, labor conscription, and forced cultivation. Women were expected to cultivate food. Postindependence policies have continued that trend. Since women have major family support responsibilities in much of Africa, the concentration of cash in men's hands has sometimes left women without adequate resources to acquire even those goods and services that were formerly available through barter. Few good income-earning opportunities exist in rural areas. Women have been resourceful in trying to cope by adding new activities to subsistence cultivation, such as trade in food and other items or raising small amounts of cash crops. As a result, women's workloads have increased while the availability of labor assistance has declined.

Despite their attempts to meet family support responsibilities through increased labor, women have often become increasingly dependent on cash remittances from their husbands, which may be inadequate or not forthcoming. In some places even plowing, seed, and fertilizer require cash outlays that women do not have. This situation has promoted gender inequality, as only cash-earning activities come to be regarded as work. As noted earlier, this has also added to family tensions and rivalry over resources among co-wives in polygynous households. The differential success that family members have in acquiring wealth has sometimes increased jealousy among brothers and brothers' wives and affected their willingness to defer to authority based on seniority. Wealthier women or those with good education or employment may be favored by mothers-in-law. Sometimes women are resented by others for being proud or acting arrogantly. Ideals of brotherly love and mutual aid, which were not always realized in the past, are increasingly contested by some, while followed by others. Women are sometimes blamed when brothers do not assist one another.

In some places where men adopted cash crops, women have had to add work on their husband's farms to their own activities. In other areas, women have had to increase food production to replace the crops that men formerly raised. Except in those places where they have been able to purchase, inherit, or receive a gift of farms, women generally do not receive the income from cash crops even when they do most of the work. Not surprisingly, women are resentful. Sometimes they show their resistance by withdrawing their labor or by using the labor department or legal system to sue their husbands. Sometimes women simply leave. Finally, land shortages and reduced fallowing have affected yields, adding further to the impoverishment of women.

In other parts of Africa, labor migration rather than farming has become men's major source of cash. Initially men left rural areas for limited periods of time to earn money for particular purposes, such as tax payments, bridewealth, or the purchase of clothing or other items. As the economy became more monetized, the recurrent need for cash led to situations in which men lived away from their rural homes for increasingly long periods of time. In the postindependence period, the worsening economy and high unemployment make men reluctant to leave jobs. Both mature men with families and younger men may now spend their entire productive lives away from their rural homes. In some cases wives accompany their husbands if the men have adequate resources for support and access to housing, or if the women are able to trade or find work. Some men may have a favored wife living with them in town while other wives are left in the countryside. In some polygynous households, wives take turns residing with the husband. But many women live without their husbands except for brief visits. Where women have the option of returning to their families, or where they can remarry or move to town on their own, marriages may dissolve. Ewe women see no point in staying married to an absent man who does not provide (Bukh 1979), but marital stability remains high in some places.

Older women's situations have also been affected by labor migration. As noted earlier, the absence of sons and daughters-in-law have left some elderly women alone and without labor assistance, even if children provide financial help. Some have taken on the responsibility of caring for the young children of absent parents. The expectations of a comfortable old age surrounded by children and grandchildren and commanding influence and respect is not realizable for many women today. In a few places widows are even being driven from the land by their husband's kin.

Women's situations have deteriorated in other respects as well. Where women could formerly turn to elders in cases of marital neglect or mistreatment, elders may have little influence over absent men, particularly if they depend on those men for cash remittances. Although organized ethnic associations wield influence in some urban areas, they deal largely with conflicts in the urban setting. In other places, the precolonial women's groups that formerly acted to protect their interests have largely disappeared. Today women may have little recourse if husbands fail to provide or otherwise neglect or mistreat them.

Although the family situation for many rural women has worsened, some husbands do provide adequate resources and some households have harmonious relationships. It is also important to recognize that African women take great pride in their work and in their ability to provide for their children's education and advancement. Women have adopted their own strategies to improve their situations, which range from self-help groups to cooperative organizations that allow them to safeguard income from their husbands (see Chapter 9). Some women have been able to benefit from new opportunities. There are rural women who are successful traders, shopkeepers, and beer brewers. Educated women may obtain work as teachers, nurses, or government officials. In some places, women have been able to use earnings from trade or other activities to purchase land, or they use cash crop earnings to hire labor to help with cultivation. Occasionally the wives of prosperous men are given sufficient cash to hire help. Such women are better off economically and may command high status and respect.

Women in urban families

Women's family life in urban areas is also varied. There are women living with husbands, unmarried women residing with parents or other kin, and a growing number of women who live alone or with children. Added to these variations are differences among women in socioeconomic position, education, and employment. Finally, religious beliefs, attitudes towards marriage, and the resourcefulness of the women themselves are other factors affecting their situations. This section can only touch on a few of these issues. It will distinguish the situations of women residing with husbands from women who live alone, and also consider some of the differences in social organization of different African cities.

Before the establishment of colonialism, there were urban centers in West Africa where people's homes were organized around neighborhoods or wards based on descent. Extended families were the residential or domestic groups – patrilocal among the Yoruba of Nigeria, matrilocal among the Ashanti of Ghana. Patterns of social organization were similar to those described for rural areas. Such compounds and wards are still found in such cities as Lagos, Accra, and Ibadan, but urban development has sometimes brought about the demolition of these older neighborhoods. The expansion of cities and the development of new housing estates has led to a scattering of family members, some of whom moved to newer residential areas. In addition, non-kin are now found in older neighborhoods as lodgers in indigenous family compounds. Despite such developments, indigenous inhabitants are often able to maintain a full range of family and kinship relations, although not necessarily on a daily basis. Women participate in descent group affairs and can claim rights to housing and support in domestic difficulties. Some of the tensions resulting from socioeconomic differences that were described for rural families also operate in town, where wealthy and successful men and women may exercise a disproportionate influence on family and kin group affairs.

For newcomer populations in both the older West African cities and the colonially created cities of eastern, central, and southern Africa, the situation is different. Even where families are long-established, neither family organization nor neighborhoods replicate the kin-based social organization of rural areas. Nor are the full range of kin present. Kinship norms are still operative, however, and many individuals provide temporary or long-term housing for relatives, as well as help in seeking employment and other types of assistance. The composition of urban households is therefore varied, including a variety of kin of both the husband and wife. It also fluctuates as some relatives return to the rural areas, others become established in their own homes, and others leave due to quarrels and overcrowding. Wives, too, may shift residence between rural and urban areas, although women who are in modern sector or other lucrative employment may be more permanently ensconced. Since neighborhoods are not kin-based, women find friendships and support outside the family circle, sometimes across ethnic lines (Obbo 1980).

It seems to me that one of the major characteristics distinguishing rural from urban women centers on rights to housing. Where rural women have well-established rights to their own houses, kitchens, and granaries, urban women do not. The Luo, for example, distinguish between the rights of the rural wife as the owner of her house and those of the husband or his father as the owner of the compound. In cities, by contrast, wives do not generally have their own homes; they are residents in their husband's quarters. A man may require one wife to leave if he wishes to bring another wife into the apartment. In some homes wives take turns residing with the husband. Sometimes women wish to return to the rural area to safeguard their land rights. Occasionally several wives may occupy the same quarters. Housing policies reinforce this dependence. Many positions in government, universities, and elsewhere provide low-cost housing as a job-related benefit. But these benefits are usually not available to married women. Even if they are in polygynous marriages and need separate quarters, or if their husbands have no housing benefits, wives are expected to depend on the men for housing.

Some married women are purchasing their own homes. This was the case among the Ewe women in Ghana whom I studied some years ago. In other places, men's ability to require wives to leave may contribute to family tensions, particularly when women refuse to go. Urban living arrangements that center on the married couple may bring husbands and wives closer together, but these new residential arrangements can also create strain due to new behavioral expectations and the loss of privacy formerly available in the gender-segregated domains of rural households.

Other developments associated with urbanization concern patterns of income control and men's attitudes towards women's work. While rural men do not object to wives working, in some urban areas, particularly in the eastern part of the continent, men fear losing control. In Lusaka, men are ambivalent. They regard nonworking housewives as parasites who live off their husbands, yet they object to wives coming into contact with strangers (Schuster 1982). Luo men in Nairobi also fear women's independence. Some men try to control women's income by requiring wives to deposit their earnings in a joint bank account, for which men hold the only passbook (Potash 1989). In Zambia and in Nairobi husbands may control wives' expenditures by doling out funds for particular purposes or giving women a limited allowance. Wives may be expected to use all of their earnings for household expenses; husbands are free to use some of their income for entertaining. Women are unhappy about this arrangement (Munachonga 1988, Stichter 1988). Sometimes women hide funds or deceive husbands about their real incomes, which can lead to quarrels.

In many West African cities, by contrast, men are more accepting of women's working and women and men have independent control over their own incomes. Husbands and wives often do not know each other's earnings. Joint budgeting and common conjugal funds are rare, except among a small elite (Oppong 1974, Fapohunda 1988). The differing conclusions in the literature on urban women's independence may reflect these cultural and regional differences. However, even in places where men seek to control women, resourceful women and those with good incomes may be able to achieve some autonomy.

Some urban women do not reside with their husbands; they live alone or with children. Since the colonial period, cities have been a place to which resourceful women or women fleeing unwanted marriages could come and survive, often independent of marriage. Colonial authorities and indigenous leaders both tried to prevent women from coming to the new colonial cities of East and Central Africa, yet women persisted. Fewer such barriers were reported in the older West African cities. Early female migrants to Nairobi survived by selling cooked food, brewing beer, and selling sexual and domestic services. Some were able to use earnings to assist rural kin, enhancing their positions in their natal families. A few prospered sufficiently to purchase their own land or houses (Bujra 1975, White 1988). Women continue to use such strategies today with varying degrees of success (Nelson 1979).

In modern times, African women from a variety of educational and socioeconomic backgrounds are also choosing not to marry. Some are mistresses or 'outside wives', who prefer such relationships to marriage for the greater independence and economic benefits such unions sometimes provide. Others see such relationships as temporary until 'Mr Right' comes along (Karanja 1987). Some women form more temporary liaisons, sometimes depending on men for gifts or hoping for marriage. The legal situation of women on consensual arrangements is quite complex. During the colonial period, marriage ordinances were enacted that promoted monogamy. Men who married under these laws were barred from taking additional wives. Many women today want civil or church marriages in order to, avoid polygyny. But such legal strictures do not alter men's behaviour. Men take girlfriends and mistresses and often desire to have children with these women. Sometimes the women are recognized as wives under customary law by the man and his family. Legal wives may or may not agree to the husband's providing for any children born to such outside wives, which they recognize as his responsibility (Obbo 1987). There is considerable controversy in contemporary African societies over whether or not men should be responsible for the support of the children that they sire, and over what rights, if any, outside wives are entitled to, including rights of inheritance. Many of these matters come before the courts and legislatures (Vellenga 1983, 1986, Kuria 1987, Armstrong 1990).

Conclusion

Women's relationships in African families are different from those that obtain in nuclear families where marriage is the key bond. In Africa, women are brought into regular interaction with numerous household members, which has important implications for women's lives. Household forms vary, as do expectations of behavior. Since the onset of colonialism, and earlier as well, family systems have been in a state of flux, which is related to the major economic, legal, ideological, and other transformations that have occurred. Most recently, the AIDS epidemic and the creation of large numbers of political and economic refugees have had devastating impacts on families, but detailed studies remain to be done. Many of these transformations have weakened the situation of rural women and contributed to their impoverishment. But some women have benefitted from new economic opportunities. Family life in urban areas is even more varied. Some women reside with husbands or parents; other women live alone.

Contrary to earlier modernization theorists who predicted that African families would become nuclear and monogamous, these changes have not occurred. Rather, a variety of new and old arrangements exist side by side, many of which represent adaptations in the use of kinship to fit new environments. Older norms persist, are reinterpreted, and are sometimes contested. The impact of these developments is not uniform for all women, nor are the interests of different categories of women identical. How women are affected depends in part on their age, marital status, residence, and socio-economic position, as well as on the resourcefulness of the women themselves.

CHAPTER 5

Case study: women and inheritance law in Zambia

Margaret Mulela Munalula and Winnie Sithole Mwenda

Inheritance in Zambia is governed by both customary and statutory law. For purposes of this chapter, inheritance will be defined as property, either real or personal, received by a person or persons from the estate of a deceased person. The person who inherits the property has the right to its possession as an heir or beneficiary.

Inheritance as it affects women is a timely subject in contemporary Zambia, for several reasons. First, women have become more conscious of their rights, among which is the right to the property of their deceased spouse, and are seeking to enforce those rights. Second, although women in Zambia constitute the demographic majority, customary laws and practices that affect the majority of women in Zambia have worked to perpetuate social injustices against women. Most notable of these injustices are the neglect of women's inheritance in favor of men and the proliferation of what is commonly known as the 'property-grabbing syndrome', a phenomenon that has left many widows and children destitute, with neither property nor home. Third, the existence of conflict between customary and statutory laws of inheritance has brought about a situation where statutory law, which has been more favorable to women, has often been disregarded in favor of customary law, which has often been less favorable. Penalties for breaches of statutory law, which is applicable to all property in Zambia except land acquired under customary law, property held under chieftainship, and family property, have not deterred further breaches of the law.

Customary law of inheritance

The customary law of inheritance may be defined as that body of customary rules determining the apportionment of land at the time of death of the intestate that was held under customary law, property held under chieftainship, and family property (or property held collectively).[1] Under Zambian customary law, succession includes the English ideas of both succession and inheritance (which refer to the passing of personal property and real property, respectively), and for that reason, the terms 'succession' and 'inheritance' are used interchangeably in as far as customary law is concerned (McClain 1970: 87).

Precolonial law in Zambia was essentially customary in character, having its source in the practices and customs of the people (Ndulo 1985). The British colonial regime recognized customary law, which was the law which applied to indigenous peoples, while received or statutory law applied to the white settlers. Throughout the colonial period, these two types of laws existed side by side. Customary law is still applicable in Zambia, provided such customary law is not repugnant to natural justice, morality, equity or good conscience, and is not incompatible with the provisions of any written law.

Among the 73 ethnic groups found in Zambia, there are three dominant modes of descent patterns and these are patrilineal, matrilineal and bilateral. A patrilineal community, such as that of the Ngoni of Eastern Zambia, traces descent through the father's line. Thus the only persons who can claim a share in the deceased's estate are those who are related to the deceased through a common male ancestor. Among the matrilineal ethnic groups such as the Bemba of Northern Zambia, on the other hand, descent is traced through the mother's line. Only persons related to the deceased through the deceased's mother or a more remote female ancestor are eligible to share in the estate (Mvunga 1979). A bilateral community, such as that of the Lozi of western Zambia, is one that practices both matrilineal and patrilineal rules of inheritance, in the sense that descent can be traced through both the father's and mother's line. In all of these societies, affinal ties (those created by birth) have precedence over conjugal ties (those created by marriage), and thus widows are not defined as primary inheritors.

It is difficult to categorize the inheritance systems of traditional societies in Zambia as strictly patrilineal, matrilineal, or bilateral. Different types of goods are distributed after death to different categories of relatives, and ownership of a title or office may pass to one kinsman or woman while property associated with that title may pass to another; the widow may be taken by yet another relative (Allot *et al* 1969: 51–52). Nevertheless, for convenience we shall refer to those three systems in terms of their dominant modes.

The Ngoni system of inheritance strongly resembles the English system of inheritance in that property passes to the successor of the deceased on the principle of primogeniture; in other words, the first-born son inherits as long as he generally demonstrates good character. However, this is subject to the requirement of good behavior and character on the part of the son. The case of *Re: Estate of Mekelani Mphanza* illustrates this principle (cited in Mvunga 1979: 643). In that case, the deceased was survived by a widow and nine children. The issue was who among these children qualified to be the heir. The family appointed the eldest son as heir and proceeded to obtain the sanction of the court. The court duly appointed him administrator of the deceased's estate. Further, under Ngoni customary law of succession, if no sons survive the deceased, the eldest daughter inherits; failing daughters, the deceased's eldest brother inherits. Failing brothers, the deceased's eldest surviving blood sister inherits; failing sisters, the deceased's father inherits; and failing all these, the deceased's mother inherits.[2] Failing the mother, the eldest surviving paternal relative inherits. It is clear from the above that the Ngoni widow is not among the list of possible heirs. However, the widow is allowed to continue occupying the house and land of the deceased husband for as long as she remains unmarried. If she is 'inherited' (remarried under customary law) by a relative of the deceased husband, the new husband is responsible for her and her children's welfare.

Although Mvunga refers to an 'heir', research done by the Women and Law in Southern Africa Research Trust Zambia Group (WLSA Zambia) between 1992 and 1993 shows that in Zambia the concept of 'heir' as understood in the English sense does not exist. We do, however, find 'successor' (WLSA Zambia forthcoming). Whereas under English law an heir is a person who inherits the property (whether real or personal) of a deceased person, he or she does not succeed to the social responsibilities of the deceased person. A successor on the other hand takes over the deceased's social responsibilities as well as the property. An heir's property is his or her's personally and can be disposed of as the heir wishes, whereas the successor holds most of the property on behalf of the family and has to consult them before disposing of it. A successor steps into the shoes of the deceased, so to say, and becomes head of the family.

Among the matrilineal Bemba, when a man dies, the relatives who have a share in his estate are his matrilineal kinship group – namely, his brothers, sisters, nephews, and nieces. Strictly speaking, the deceased's children belong to their mother's kinship group and are therefore not entitled to a share of their father's property. They can, however, be given a share of their late father's estate if that was the father's wish. The person who 'inherits' the widow, where this happens, gets a larger share of the deceased's property. The general position under the various customary laws in Zambia is, in fact, that the person who succeeds to the status of the deceased should not only take a larger share of the property of the deceased but should also assume the obligations of the deceased. When a widow is 'inherited', she remains in the husband's village, but otherwise she returns to her own village, where it is expected that she will be looked after by her own kinship group. In both cases a widow is not an heir, her only share in the estate being limited to clothing, cooking utensils, grain, and a portion of the growing crops.

Under the bilateral descent system of the Lozi, heirs are the children of the deceased, both male and female, who get equal shares of the property. Failing children, the deceased's brothers inherit the property equally. Since it is a bilateral system, descent among the Lozi can also be traced through the mother's line. The widow under Lozi customary law of inheritance is still not a possible heir of her husband's property, but she may be permitted to stay on in the village and till her late husband's land. Her automatic entitlements, however, are her clothing, cooking utensils, and a share of the crops. Widow inheritance is also practised among the Lozi.

The position of the widow is rather precarious among all the ethnic groups in Zambia; as a general rule, a wife has no right of inheritance in her husband's property since she is not a member of his kinship group. If the widow is not inherited by a male relative of the deceased and returns to her own village, it is often difficult for her to be reintegrated in the community she had left upon her marriage. However, inhuman treatment of the widow, such as forms of 'cleansing', which involve sexual intercourse and death payments, is generally frowned upon by courts. An example is the case of *Beluti Kaniki vs. Lot Jairus* (Zambian Republic 1967), in which a widow was required to make a death payment on the death of her husband, in accordance with the Lala custom called *akamutwe*. Here the family of the widow accepted that some payment was due, but felt that the amount demanded was too high. On appeal, the court held that payment of the death fee was contrary to natural justice. Despite cases of this nature, a great many cases of harassment and inhuman treatment of widows have gone unnoticed under the guise of custom, leaving widows at the mercy of their late husbands' relatives.

Statutory law of inheritance

We explained above how Zambia had applied a dual legal system under British colonial rule, using many English laws as well as accepting African customary law. After independence, indigenous Zambians were legally empowered to divest themselves from the application of customary law (which had applied to all indigenous Zambians) by adopting English law through two options: (1) they could write wills in conformity with the provisions of the English Wills Act of 1837, or (2) they could choose to marry under the Marriage Act, and thus be subject to the application of the Inheritance (Provision for Family and Dependents) Act if either spouse died intestate. Very few Zambians took the trouble to write their wills, however. In the period from 1976 to 1981, for example, 223 wills were registered, out of which only 19 were made by indigenous Zambians. In addition, although many educated people opted to get married under the Marriage Act, this ceremony was usually preceded by marriage under customary law, and therefore customary law was applicable upon the death of either spouse. The limited number of people to whom English law applied in practice meant that it played a peripheral role in comparison to customary law, which occupied center stage. Most women recognized the obvious disadvantages of customary law, but were unable to rebel against its application because of its stronghold on society (Himonga 1989).

Despite the availability of English law, therefore, grave injustices such as property grabbing continued against women and children in the name of custom. The resulting inconsistencies in a society that claimed to be civilized, led to a 20-year struggle to bring an end to the application of customary law (Longwe and Clarke 1990: 183). This struggle began in November 1970 at a Women's Rights Conference, where the need to consolidate and restate the Zambian law of inheritance was first formally recognized, and presumably ended in 1989 with the enactment of two Acts of Parliament intended to block the application of both English and customary law subject to the limitations already referred to. The struggle took place between various women's nongovernmental organizations and the lawmakers.

As early as 1976, the government had commissioned the Law Development Commission to review the inheritance problem in response to public concern. The resulting 'Working Paper on Customary Law of Succession' and the Commission's report and recommendations for legal reform were shelved until 1987, when as a result of persistent lobbying by the various women's organizations, a draft bill on Wills and Inheritance was finally tabled before Parliament (Acts Nos. 5 and 6 of 1989). However, following the first reading, the bill was shelved, ostensibly in order to enable members of the House to discuss the issue with their constituents. Once again the women's organizations led the campaign to raise awareness and conducted opinion polls to agitate for the passing of the bill. In many cases, widows were asked to come forward and recount their personal ordeals in order to shock the public. One such account delivered in the presence of the head of state in December 1988 had the desired effect, as it culminated in his announcing that the new inheritance laws would be passed by March 1989 (Longwe and Clarke 1990). Several important points that came out of this struggle include (1) the reluctance of the majority of the population to embrace a new law in place of accepted custom; (2) the reluctance of the lawmakers to set aside customary law (Longwe and Clarke 1990); and (3) the realization that the 'custom' of property grabbing was actually a distortion of the customary law of inheritance brought about by modernization, economic difficulties, and social change (Chona 1976).

The two Acts now governing the law of inheritance in Zambia are 'The Wills and Administration of Testate Estates Act' and 'The Intestate Succession Act' (Acts No. 5 and 6 respectively of 1989).

The Wills and Administration of Testate Estates Act

Act No. 6 of 1989 (for convenience referred to as the Wills Act) is based on the English Wills Act. It is an attempt to rationalize and simplify the law related to the making and administration of wills in Zambia and, where necessary, to ensure adequate financial and other provisions for dependents in a will.

Basically, the Wills Act of 1989 allows adults of sound mind to decide what will happen to all their property after their death by writing a will. They are given power to decide who will execute their estates and even, where necessary, to appoint a guardian for their young children. The wills themselves must be validated by their signatures, which they must acknowledge in the presence of two witnesses who are not blind, are of sound mind, and are not beneficiaries under the will. The witnesses must also append their signatures in the presence of each other and the testator. It must also be the testator's last will. In order to protect the person making the will, any beneficiary who intentionally causes the death of the maker of the will forfeits the right to inherit any part of the estate of the deceased (Section 59).

The power of people to dispose of their property is not absolute under the Wills Act. The court is empowered to alter the provisions of a will where it is of the opinion that these are unreasonable in their failure to make adequate provision for the maintenance of a dependent, thus causing hardship (Section 21). The court's power to interfere is justified by the basic needs of the dependents and does not extend to mere dissatisfaction expressed by a dependent as to the size of his or her inheritance. The court order is in fact governed by the rules relating to maintenance; for instance, maintenance will be terminated by the remarriage of the widow or widower. The execution of the estate does not take place until probate has been granted. Probate is only granted after the will has been proved as valid. The person named as executor is thereafter authorized by the court to deal with the estate. Where an executor was not named in the will, then the court may appoint an administrator or personal representative to administer the estate (Section 36). The job of the executor or administrator is to pay all debts, taxes, and funeral expenses, and then distribute the balance of the estate in accordance with the will. Executors are not entitled to derive any personal pecuniary benefits unless the will expressly provides them, and are personally accountable for the proper administration of the estate. The Act makes it an offense for them to deprive any minor beneficiary of his or her legal entitlement, and any meddling with the property by the executor or any other person is a crime that carries a maximum term of two years imprisonment upon conviction (Section 58).

The Intestate Succession Act

Act No. 5 of 1989, on the other hand, is a codification and restatement of the English intestacy law, greatly modified to fit Zambian society and obviously intended to circumvent the mischief arising from the 'custom' of property grabbing by making specific provision for the widow. The terminology of the Act is gender-neutral, but its effective application is undoubtedly biased in favor of widows, since they are often the ones negatively affected by property grabbing. Further, since customary law is only legally valid where it does not conflict with statutory law, the Act empowers women to revolt against any imposition of the 'custom' of property grabbing with the full knowledge that they will be protected by the legal system. This provision not withstanding, research by Women and Law in Southern Africa Research Trust has shown that most women do not take advantage of the law due to fear of witchcraft. Threats of witchcraft by relatives of the deceased husband have instilled fear in most widows. In one case studied in Kasama, a WLSA research site, the fact that a widow lost three children in a matter of hours after she had differed with her in-laws over her husband's estate seemed to validate the widows' fears.

Basically, under the Intestate Succession Act (Act No. 5 of 1989), when a man dies his property is shared out as follows (Section 5):

1   20 per cent of the property goes to the widow or widows;
2   50 per cent of the property goes to the children of the deceased, regardless of whether they were born in or out of marriage;
3   20 per cent of the property goes to the deceased's parents;
4   10 per cent of the property goes to the deceased's other dependents.

Property here refers to the personal possessions of the deceased and any monies to his credit, and it is distributed by a person appointed by the court, who is referred to as the administrator (Section 3). It does not include the family home, household appliances, and utensils, which legally pass on to the widow and children. Where the entire estate is valued at less than 30,000 kwacha (about US $50 as of May, 1994), then it goes to the widow and children in its entirety (Section 11).

Conclusion

Changes in the way of life of the Zambian people due to urbanization, the money economy, and the rise of the nuclear family have had a very great impact on the law, both customary and statutory. Customary law has been distorted to the disadvantage of the weaker sectors of society, manifested in the 'custom' of property grabbing. The resulting imbalance in society brought about by property grabbing could not be sustained indefinitely, hence the enactment of the new statutory law of inheritance, which is intended to rationalize the whole system of inheritance. Women can no longer be forced to submit to injustice under the guise of custom.

It is important to acknowedge that the full implementation of the new law has been delayed by several minor problems. For example, the implementation of Acts No. 5 and 6 of 1989 has been difficult due to the failure of the chief justice to prepare the rules for their application. Such problems will be ironed out in due course through litigation and a proposed review of the new law by the Law Development Commission of Zambia.

Notes

1. Family property is defined by Section 2 of the Intestate Succession Act of 1989 as 'any property, whether movable or immovable, which belongs to the members collectively of a particular family or is held for the benefit of such members and any receipt or proceeds from such property'.
2. Research done by the Women and Law in Southern Africa Research Trust, Zambia Group (WLSA Zambia) has shown that in practice women rarely inherit. Males are given preference over females and therefore a male relative will always be found who will inherit.

CHAPTER 6

Women in religious and secular ideology

Margaret Strobel

In the beginning of things the man Gikuyu, the founder of the tribe, found that the Mogai (The Divider of the Universe) had provided him with a beautiful wife whom Gikuyu named Moombi (creator or moulder). [Gikuyu had no male heirs, which situation Mogai rectified by providing nine strangers who married Gikuyu's nine daughters and thus set up nine matrilineages.] It is said that while holding superior position in the community, the women became domineering and ruthless. Through sexual jealousy, many men were put to death for committing adultery or other minor offences. The men were indignant at the way in which the women treated them, and planned to revolt. It was decided that the best time for a successful revolt would be the time when the majority of women, especially their leaders, were in pregnancy. [The men impregnated the women, and the revolt succeeded. Polygyny replaced polyandry.] The women frankly told the men that if they dared to eliminate the names which stood as a recognition that women were the original founders of the clan system, the women would refuse to bear any more children [hence the man agreed to let the nine main clans retain the names of the daughters of Gikuyu].

(Kikuyu creation myth, taken from Kenyatta 1938: 5–10)

In the beginning God created the heavens and the earth. . . . So God created man in his own image . . . and the rib which the Lord God had taken from the man he made into a woman. [Eve ate the fruit of the tree of knowledge, expressly forbidden by God. In punishment Adam and Eve were cast out of Eden, and God told Eve], 'I will greatly multiply your pain in childbearing . . . yet your desire shall be for your husband, and he shall rule over you.'

(the Bible, excerpts from Genesis 1 and 2)

God made us male and female, and in His wretchedness He filled women with weakness in body and weakness in thought. In His bounty He filled men with goodness in strength, great intelligence, and good thoughts, and for this reason He ordained men to be the ones to oversee women in their affairs, to take care of them. As He told us in the Koran: Men shall oversee women.

(a Muslim leader in 1930: Al-Amin bin Aly Mazrui, 1932: 1)

I am afraid that the young women who are today shouting for 'liberation' are using wrong arguments and are causing unnecessary breakups of marriages and murders in a country where there are no discriminations between the sexes. Again, our educated women, as usual, are aping arguments and activities of some ugly, disgruntled, lonely and derailed American and English women. Our values are definitely very different from their values. I can remember that there used to be a time when African women were very real women, and their menfolk were proud of them.

(a university lecturer on the occasion of International Women's Year 1975: Ochieng' 1975: iv)

Gender difference, ideology, and religion

Sexual differences are a fact of biology, but the particular significance societies attach to sexual differences is a human cultural creation. These differences in value and behavior assigned to men and women are embodied in gender roles. Thus, gender is a social construct, while sex is a biological condition. Various ideas, values, and beliefs about women and men are expressed through an ideology, that is, a coherent set of values and beliefs held by members of a particular society. Though coherent, an ideology may contain conflicting elements; for example, Western literature and thought have viewed women as both madonnas and whores. Nonetheless, the ideology forms the basis of what members of a society think is true and natural. The connection between gender and sex makes the ideology of gender seem all the more a fact of nature rather than a result of human culture. Furthermore, the apparent natural basis for attitudes about women reinforces the ethnocentrism of people, who find it hard to believe that alternative conceptions of gender roles or of women are valid.

The quotations above are part of the ideology of gender and of women expressed in religious and secular writings. The Gikuyu (Kikuyu) myth exemplifies African traditional religions. The second and third quotations reflect the Christian and Islamic beliefs shared by many Africans, although, of course, each society blended its own indigenous traditions with the Islamic or Christian ones. The Gikuyu and Christian examples express the primacy of patrilineal descent. Although respect is accorded women as givers of life in these myths, females are also associated with negative characteristics in all three religious selections: in the Muslim statement they are weak and in need of supervision; in the Bible Eve introduces evil into Paradise; in the Gikuyu myth women are unjust in running society and must be replaced. The fourth extract represents a secular ideology: a description of history and the present in which a previous golden age of harmony between men and women has been disturbed. In this view, women are causing disharmony by listening to another, foreign ideology: feminism.

An analysis of religious and secular belief provides an excellent insight into a society's attitudes about gender differences and women, although neither can, of course, be reduced to beliefs about gender. In addition, we must remember that neither religious beliefs nor secular ideology have created gender. Rather, they are an expression of the ideas concerning gender that have evolved out of the economic, political, and social organization of a particular society, and, as the other chapters in this book have shown, gender differentiation is a basic feature of the social organization of African societies, in the past as well as today.

Religion in Africa

Roughly 50 per cent of the African population follows traditional religious practices; some 25 per cent are Muslims who follow the way of Islam; and the remaining 25 per cent are Christians, including Roman Catholics, Protestants, and members of African independent churches (Middleton 1981: 410, 412). In reality, each category includes wide variations, and these religious systems and beliefs have inter-penetrated. Traditional boys' circumcision has become integrated into Christian and Islamic rituals. Prayers to Muhammad for intercession now preface puberty rites for girls that have no basis in Islam. In particular, Christians and Muslims have infused their beliefs with elements drawn from traditional African religions. Thus, the beliefs and activities described under traditional practices can be found in Muslim and Christian communities as well.

African traditional religions

Traditional religious activities are focussed on protecting the well-being of the lineage or society; dealing with routinely difficult or anomalous situations such as jealousy between co-wives or marriage partners, foreign invasions, or disease; and marking important changes of status such as birth, puberty, marriage, and death through rites of passage. Religious beliefs and rituals might embody conflicting gender ideologies, as in the tension in Igbo society between the worship of the female goddess Imedili and the more patriarchal ancestor cult (Amadiume 1987: Ch. 6). In societies that did not have highly developed political structures or states, religious authorities often performed political functions. Religious specialists would be called upon to adjudicate between complainants through divination, filling the role taken by a judge in a kingdom or nation-state. Sometimes religious heads became the leaders of anticolonial rebel-lions in the absence of a chief to lead the resistance, as in the case of the priestess Muhumusa described later. Thus it is rarely possible to draw a clear distinction between the religious and the political, or between the religious and the secular.

A range of religious roles is open to women. They often serve as ritual specialists for activities that pertain to women's affairs or concern fertility. For example, the *omu* among the Igbo of Nigeria controlled medicines and performed sacrifices to ensure the safety and success of the marketplace, where women were active traders (Okonjo 1976: 49). Among the Lovedu in South Africa, the queen was responsible for bringing needed rain and for guaranteeing the fertility of both the soil and the population (Lebeuf 1971: 97). The link between agricultural and human fertility is clear: since women give birth, they are thought to have special capacities related to fertility generally. Moreover, since most African women are active farmers, the link is not merely symbolic.

Often women act as mediums and members of spirit possession cults. These cults are found throughout African societies and are not limited to the traditional sphere. Members include people who feel themselves to be possessed by an external spirit; the spirit can be controlled only when the individual joins with other afflicted persons. Some scholars explain spirit possession by emphasizing the real physiological basis for some of the problems, particularly those relating to reproduction, the stressful situations to which possession is a response, and the creation of a community of women outside their shared domestic role (Spring 1978, Sibisi 1977, Middleton-Keirn 1978). Other anthropologists have explained women's predominance in spirit cults as an aspect of the 'war between the sexes'. In male-dominated societies, they argue, where women are excluded from political and religious positions of authority, spirit possession compensates for their otherwise low status (Lewis 1971: 79–80). While possessed, women are allowed to utter the unutterable, to be placated, and to receive gifts for the spirit, thus alleviating their misfortunes. More recently, scholars see spirit possession in a less instrumental way. Instead, *zar* possession in the Muslim Sudan, for example, is understood as a cultural text, that is, a representation of ambivalent and often contradictory meanings (including meanings about gender) that men and women appropriate and deploy in counterpoint to a more orthodox rendering of Islam that privileges men (Boddy 1989, Lewis 1986, Alpers 1984).

The following examples drawn from the lake regions of East Africa illustrate both the basis of the cults in women's experience and the way in which female mediums could exercise uncommon influence. Spirit cults were common among the peoples of Uganda, Burundi, Rwanda, and northeastern Tanzania. Many of these societies were and are hierarchically structured. Chiefs representing one group rule over others, and females are subordinate to the males of their own group. Women frequently participated in these cults and were conspicuous among the mediums. Often the cults dealt with female problems such as childbirth, agriculture, sterility, or marital problems. For the female mediums, their ritual role allowed greater physical mobility than was usual among women and made possible the accumulation of wealth through initiation fees. In some kingdoms female leaders functioned at the highest level of political authority. In Kitara, part of present-day Uganda, the female medium of Ndahura, the spirit of smallpox, controlled her own territory and wealth and played an important role in the ceremony acknowledging the new *mukama*, or king. To the south, the priestess Muhumusa, who claimed to be the wife of a nineteenth-century Rwandan king, led an anti-European attack in 1911 as the personification of Nyabingi, a female deity of the area (Berger 1976). Only a few women reached this level of influence, however. Average women benefitted from relief from low status and everyday problems or from increased influence and respect locally or within the lineage through their role as spirit mediums.

Spirit cults have been particularly important for women in South Africa. As a result of apartheid they were forced to live separately from their families and suffered a multitude of daily problems. For those lucky enough to have jobs, wages were low. They lived in fear that family members may be arrested and detained for political activity or for minor violations of apartheid laws. The reminders of their lack of citizenship in their own country were always present. In addition, they were often both separated from and subordinate to their husbands. Under these circumstances, many women have turned to spirit cults as relief from the tensions of daily living and to create a community of sister sufferers (Middleton-Keirn 1978). In this way they collectively dealt with the special problems they faced as a result of gender roles assigned to them under apartheid. Analyzing the Zulu in particular, one scholar sees in spirit possession the response of these people to conquest by alien whites, the separation of families and mixing of ethnic groups that are part of the migrant labor system, and the general insecurity of lives that marked the twentieth century. Spirit possession is a manifestation of mental disturbance; diviners diagnose and treat the disturbance (Sibisi 1977).

Even more than spirit cults, perhaps the most prevalent religious experience for females both as participants and as leaders has involved rites of passage that mark transitions from one socially significant stage in life to another. All societies mark birth and death, the most basic human experiences. Puberty, marriage, and childbirth are significant human experiences that provide societies with the opportunity to express ideologies regarding gender through ritual. At puberty and marriage, females and males are taught what is proper behavior for their gender, in particular sexual mores and marital roles. Childbirth, and particularly the birth of the first male child, often brings the acceptance of a woman as a full, adult member of the community and acknowledges her value in the role of mother.

Puberty rites vary widely across Africa, and traditional rites have changed over time with the introduction of new rituals from other societies, the coming of Christianity and Islam, and changing attitudes on the part of urban or educated Africans. Some rites, for example those of the secret Sande society of the Mende people of Sierra Leone, express fundamental notions of aesthetics and morality through their elaborate decoration (Boone 1986; Sande is also discussed in Chapter 9). The example described here is particular to the Bemba, a matrilineal group in Zambia studied in the 1930s (Richards 1956), but the structure and content of the rites are common to many societies.

Chisungu is the name given to the rites performed for an individual or a small number of girls prior to marriage. A brief ritual was performed at the onset of menstruation but the full *chisungu* took place only after the family had time to collect the necessary food and items. The *chisungu* rituals were led by the *nacimbusa*, a woman of talent and reputation whose special relationship with the initiate (the *nacisungu*) lasted through the birth of her first child.

During the month-long ritual the initiates were instructed in secret. Clay figures and drawings in red, white, and black colors illustrated the lessons: work hard, don't have intercourse too often, don't deceive your husband. Instruction entailed girls' learning the proper attitudes toward their gender role rather than domestic duties as such.

Acknowledging and reinforcing the community of women was a crucial function of *chisungu*. The young girls were initiated into a group of women beyond that of their immediate family. Many of the elements of the ritual in fact expressed the hierarchy of relations among females in the group, which suggests the importance of *chisungu* for adult women participants in addition to the initiates.

Finally, *chisungu* expressed the tensions between the importance of the matrilineal principle and the fact of female subordination. Matrilineality offers women the support of female kin, which strengthens their position within the conjugal unit. Yet men dominate in various ways: they can beat their wives, they receive the first and best food, they initiate sexual intercourse. The ritual expressed this contradiction between the 'masterful man and the submissive son-in-law, between the secure young married woman backed by her own relatives and the submissive kneeling wife' (Richards 1956: 10).

As with spirit possession, life cycle rituals are found beyond the sphere of traditional religion. Circumcision rites of boys became Muslim ceremonies, as in the case of the *jando* rituals in Eastern Africa. Female puberty rites coexisted alongside Islamic rituals. In Mombasa, on the Kenya coast, slaves brought rituals surrounding female puberty, and their descendants have continued to perform them. Now, after several generations of performance in an urban, patrilineal, Muslim environment, the functions of these rites have changed and the rituals are introduced by prayers to Muhammad, but the Muslim hierarchy has not attempted to forbid them. Criticism of the rituals from elites relate to their slave origins rather than their original, non-Muslim character (Strobel 1979: Ch. 8). However, as discussed below, life cycle rituals sometimes sparked conflict between Christian missions and their local followers.

Christianity and independent churches

The spread of Christianity was integral to the extension of European influence in Africa, although missionaries were often at odds with colonial governments over the treatment of 'the natives'. The first arrivals were Portuguese priests, who were encouraged by the positive reception of the faith by Alfonso, the 'king' of Kongo in the early

sixteenth century. They were later augmented by Protestant missionaries from the various colonial powers and from the United States,
who came from the late nineteenth century on with the establishment
of formal colonial rule. African converts found various attractions in
Christianity. For some, the failure of traditional spirits to protect them
from the disruptions of war and disease led to a crisis of faith, which
they resolved by adopting a more universal and cosmopolitan religion.
Others fled to mission stations in order to escape slave traders and
slave owners. There they recreated kin ties and a new community to
replace the lost lineage and home (Wright 1993, Alpers 1983). Access
to mission education and the new source of power in the colonial
situation drew some to join the mission. Christian marriage practices
appealed to Yoruba women in western Nigeria, who saw advantages
in the right of a Christian woman to share her husband's property
after his death. Not all aspects of Christian marriage were followed
or valued, however. Men routinely avoided monogamy by taking
mistresses; and Yoruba women, used to active and independent
business careers, chafed under the dependence embodied in the ideal
of the Christian wife (Mann 1982, 1985).

Gender differences permeated this process of the spread of Christianity, just as they did the other changes associated with colonialism.
Christian missionaries brought with them strong beliefs in the 'separate spheres' of male and female activity. (Africans also separated
male and female activities, but the content of the spheres was
different.) For nineteenth-century Victorians, the role of women
was that of mother and wife, critical in preserving the home as
a haven from the difficult world of capitalist competition in which
men operated. Politics belonged to the world of men, as did the
running of the church itself. Moreover, Victorian sexuality posited
that the normal female felt little sexual arousal and that sexual activity
that did not result in conception was a dangerous waste of precious
energy. Needless to say, such an ideology found much to criticize and
question in African societies where, for example, women were active
traders as well as homemakers, or where the conception of a child
was an essential proof of fertility prior to marriage, or where women
played an important role in decision-making for the entire group.

In the course of the development of Christianity in Africa, various
groups split off from the original mission churches. In some cases
they objected to European control of church governance. In others,
they sought to preserve particular practices such as polygyny that
missionaries opposed. These new religions represented a synthesis
of Christianity and traditional religions (Sundkler 1961), and some
(a minority) were founded by women (Hackett 1995, forthcoming).

The Harrist movement is one example of a syncretist religion, and
one in which women played a key role. In the early twentieth century
a Liberian named William Wade Harris began converting masses of
people to Christianity. He advocated giving up indigenous gods
and reformed some practices with regard to women, but he did

not renounce polygyny. As his movement spread, women became leaders. In southwestern Ghana, Maame Harris 'Grace' Tani joined with Papa Kwesi 'John' Nackabah to form a branch of the Harrist movement. Their roles balanced one another. Tani, a traditional priestess, conducted healing rituals primarily directed at alleviating women's problems; Nackabah's role was to preach (Breidenbach 1979).

In the Ivory Coast another woman, Marie Lalou, was inspired by a dream to found a cult in the Harrist tradition. Previously outcast because of her inability to conceive children and the death of her two husbands, Marie Lalou founded a cult that criticized indigenous practices towards women. As this cult became institutionalized, however, political control devolved to men, while women retained positions of ceremonial leadership (Walker 1979, Hackett 1993).

Since the 1960s, membership and participation in such 'independent' churches has grown dramatically, especially in Ghana, Nigeria, Sierra Leone, Zaire, and Zimbabwe; they now represent approximately 15 per cent of Christians in sub-Saharan Africa (Hackett 1995). Often urban, the new religious movements address both economic and spiritual concerns, providing supportive networks for immigrants who lack traditional family structures. In addition, they address women's needs in particular ways, often allowing greater spiritual freedom and activity than women found in mission-based religion. Participants give verbal testimony to the spirit; sing, compose, conduct choirs; and recruit new members. Women leaders in independent churches sometimes use new technology: Mary Atieno, a Kenyan evangelist, broadcasts her religious musical productions, for example, while Dorcas Olaniyi and Lady Evangelist Odeleke of Nigeria employ television. On the whole, however, participants in these independent churches need not have significant Western education or high social status (Hackett 1995, forthcoming). Overall, while missionaries and leaders of independent churches at times criticized traditional customs regarding women, in recent years both have articulated different roles for women, within the church and in society at large (Jules-Rosette 1979: 84–85, Hackett 1995).

Islam

Islam spread to most African regions centuries before Christian missionaries, moving into North Africa and along the East African coast following the life of the Prophet Muhammad in Saudi Arabia in the seventh century AD. Often Muslim traders brought Islam to an area, or a ruler converted, thereby gaining access to the highly developed administrative skills and literacy of Muslim advisors. In the colonial period, Islam became attractive for other reasons. Many Africans whose faith in the power of indigenous religion was challenged by the successful onslaught of colonialism turned to Islam as a universal religion, like Christianity, but one which was not the religion of the oppressor and which was not seen as racist. Thus some areas experienced mass conversion to Islam, such as southeast Tanzania after the unsuccessful Maji Maji rebellion against the Germans in 1905.

Like Christianity, Islam contains an ideology of gender and embodies particular assumptions about women. Wherever it spread, Islamic beliefs and practices intermingled with local custom, exhibiting perhaps a greater acceptance of indigenous culture than did Christianity, as long as certain basic precepts were followed. The most significant elements of this ideology of gender include the extension of basic legal rights in marriage, divorce, and property; the practice of *purdah*, or the seclusion and veiling of women; and the exclusion of women from formal office in the governing structures of the religious community.

Muslim law ensured basic rights, if not equality, for women. An adult woman had to consent to her marriage. Once married, a woman was entitled to be maintained at the level to which she was accustomed. She could obtain a divorce from the Muslim judge for breach of this maintenance, among other grounds. Finally, she could own and inherit property in her own right. Each of these rights was limited compared with those of men: a man could marry up to four women, while a woman could marry only one man; a man could divorce his wife on a whim, although a woman had to have specific grounds that qualified; a man inherited twice the share of a woman unless otherwise specified in the will. Furthermore, in the absence of significant power and influence, a woman's rights could be abrogated or ignored or manipulated by her male kin. Nonetheless, when upheld, these rights represented an advance for some African women from societies where women were always legal minors, unable to own property (Strobel 1979: 54–76). Indeed, Muslim women had greater legal rights than did married Western women in the nineteenth century, when a wife's legal identity was subsumed under her husband's.

The custom of *purdah* separates women from men who might be marriage partners. Spatially this is accomplished by segregating male and female areas within the home (since visitors and some kin are potential mates) or in public. Women are encouraged to remain at home or, if they go out, to cover themselves with a veil. One Muslim scholar has argued that the rationale for purdah is rooted in the Islamic ideology of female sexuality. In contrast to the Victorians who saw females as asexual, Islam sees women as very sexual creatures who, if not restrained, will distract men from the proper and loftier pursuit of religion. Control of female sexuality follows: virginity upon marriage is required, and its absence is an affront to family honor. Men are to be chaste also, but it is harder to find evidence of male sexual misadventures (Mernissi 1975).

The rigor with which purdah has been observed varies greatly. In rural areas where women must work outside the house, they are secluded less thoroughly than they are in urban centers. The same woman may wear her veil in her home village but remove it if she is visiting relatives in Nairobi. Older women, well past the age of sexual attractiveness and childbearing, may go to a market that their younger daughters avoid. Lower-class or rural women are less bound by (or able to afford) the propriety demanded by purdah than are upper-class women (Coles and Mack 1991). In the past, observing purdah brought a certain status to prosperous Muslim families. Today, with increased secular education and the adoption of Western practices, some women seldom wear the veil or have discarded it altogether. In other areas, the rise of Islamic fundamentalism has resulted in increased pressure on women to observe the rules of seclusion and veiling. For example, in 1991 the Islamic fundamentalist military junta in the Sudan decreed that henceforth 'all Sudanese women will wear long black dresses to their ankles and a black veil covering their head and face. . . . those who disobey to be instantly punished by whipping' (Hale 1992: 40, citing the *Sudan Democratic Gazette*, 19: 8).

Purdah is not necessarily experienced as restrictive by Muslim women. In rural areas of the Kenya coast of East Africa, women work in fields without wearing a *buibui*, the required covering (Bunger 1973: 97). Muslim Hausa women in northern Nigeria have continued their roles as active traders, working out of their houses with children as intermediaries (Hill 1969). Moreover, at the turn of the century both Swahili and Hausa women of low status eagerly adopted purdah as a way of elevating their status. Hausa ex-slaves, for example, began to demand that their husbands gather wood and water, tasks that might expose the women to inappropriate encounters with men (Smith 1981: 22). Nonetheless, where seclusion was strictly followed, it could inhibit a woman from actively pursuing her own economic interests and force her to depend on male relatives (Strobel 1979: 58–63, 73–76, Mirza and Strobel 1989).

Although certain formal offices are foreclosed to women under Islam, they nonetheless exert leadership. Among Hausa women in Kano, Nigeria, are found Islamic scholars such as Hajiya Maria Mai Tafsiri, who learned the specialized field of Qur'anic exegesis; mystics such as Hajiya Laraba Karaba, a leader in the Qadiriyya Muslim brotherhood; and social workers such as Hajiya Hauwa Adamu, who directs the 'assistance section' of the Society for the Support of Islam, a Muslim voluntary association.[1]

Organizations that articulate Muslim women's interests emerged in the 1980s, blending an Islamic fundamentalist view of women with the activism generated during the United Nations' Decade for Women. In Nigeria in the mid-1980s, for example, the Federation of Muslim Women Association (FOMWAN) was formed in order to 'reclaim [Muslim women's] self-esteem, which has been vastly damaged by stereotypic traditional and cultural values and negative Western influences', to provide for education in the areas of religion, family planning, literacy, and the like, and to ensure that Muslim women have an impact on national policy (Yusuf 1991: 192). In Sudan, Suad al-Fatih al-Badawi emerged as an activist and one of two female representatives in the People's Assembly and a member of the governing National Islamic Front. She and her colleagues articulated a program that emphasizes women's participation in nation building, employment for women if necessary and in appropriate jobs, support for Muslim families through Islamic child care institutions for working mothers (and for socializing the next generation properly) (Hale 1992). These and similar groups embrace the idea that women's rights and high status can be secured within Islamic law, properly interpreted.

Conflict between religious practices

Although Christianity and Islam have absorbed traditional practices and vice versa, it would be misleading to imply that there have been no conflicts between the missionaries' views of female sexuality and associated practices on the part of indigenous people. Such conflicts are illustrated in the following examples of the Masasi mission station in Tanzania and the various missions in the Kikuyu area of Kenya.

Missionaries in Masasi, southern Tanzania, responded differently to boys' and girls' initiation ceremonies. Briefly, in the second and third decades of the twentieth century the Universities Mission to Central Africa (UMCA) in Masasi successfully developed a Christian ritual to replace the indigenous boys' rites. Attempts at a similar substitution for female rituals failed; women consistently evaded the mission's directive not to participate in 'heathen' rituals. The explanation for the failure goes beyond the missionaries' sexual mores, although this was part of the problem, to structural features of the church and Masasi society. The decision to adapt local puberty rituals to a Christian form came at a time when the UMCA was also developing African clergy in intermediate positions of authority. The young African men who became teachers and clergy took over the running of the Christian boys' rites. They helped develop its content; they supervised the rituals; they received payments from the initiates' parents. Religiously, the symbolic content of the Christian ceremony was rich and meaningful. In contrast, virtually all aspects of successful adaptation of the boys' rites were lacking for the females. Women were not consulted in devising the content of the female rituals, which were symbolically impoverished. Moreover, an important part of the girls' puberty initiation was the elongation of their labia through massage and their instruction in sexual movements designed to heighten sexual pleasure. Such items were considered inappropriate to the Christian ritual. In addition, the patriarchal structure of the mission admitted no role for female leadership comparable to that for the male African clergy. In fact, there was often implicit conflict between the patriarchal assumptions of the mission and the matrilineal principles of its converts. Thus the interaction of African and mission ideology and practice exacerbated gender differences in the resulting Africanized church (Ranger 1972).

The complexity of the conflict between missionaries and their African followers on the one hand and supporters of indigenous customs on the other is vividly illuminated in the Gikuyu clitoridect-omy controversy of the late 1920s and early 1930s (Murray 1976). Clitoridectomy, or the removal of the clitoris (also known as 'female circumcision') was a key component of Gikuyu female puberty rites, as was circumcision for boys. As Jomo Kenyatta, later the first president of Kenya, wrote in his 1938 anthropological study *Facing Mount Kenya*, 'No proper Gikuyu would dream of marrying a girl who has not been circumcised, and vice versa. It is taboo for a Gikuyu man or women to have sexual relations with someone who has not undergone this operation' (Kenyatta 1938: 127). It was the cutting itself, rather than educational instruction, that formed the core of Gikuyu puberty rites.

The Kikuyu Central Association was formed in the 1920s specifically to defend the custom against missionary attacks; the missions focussed international attention on the custom and in some cases specifically organized against the KCA. Thus the issue of the alleged harm done to females through this custom became intertwined with Gikuyu complaints about white settlers taking their land. The antagonists on both sides, settlers/missionaries/government officials vs. the KCA, were playing for bigger stakes than the health and comfort of women. The clitoridectomy question represented an early part of the anticolonial struggle, which later developed into demands for schools independent of the missions, and finally for independence for the nation of Kenya. At this stage, however, the key expression of the anticolonial impulse was the KCA counter-attack on European cultural imperialism through the defense of indigenous culture. Within elite colonial circles, liberals such as MacGregor Ross, Leonard Woolf, and Norman Leys argued against suppressing local custom; those most adamant in their concern for the girls' health appeared to be insensitive to the integrity of African culture. Ideologically and politically, the issue pitted the oppression of women against the oppression of colonized Africans, including women. And, however correct it may be to criticize clitoridectomy on humanitarian and hygienic grounds, in this historical context the criticism became part of consolidating the exploitative system of colonialism within Kenya. In recent years there appears to have been a significant decline in the practice among the Gikuyu themselves; only about 40 per cent of Gikuyu schoolgirls were excised in 1974, whereas nearly all of their mothers had been (Murray 1974, 1976).

Conflict within religious groups

Not only did conflicts arise between Christian missionaries and traditional religious leaders, tensions at times emerged within a religious community over the role accorded to women. Islam provides several examples of this tension. First, women have been excluded from authoritative political and religious roles within Muslim com-munities because of purdah and the belief that men must 'oversee women'. This exclusion from formal power has resulted in women's active participation in unorthodox spirit cults, known as *zar* in the Sudan, *bori* among the Hausa, or *pepo* for the Swahili – all Muslim communities (Boddy 1989, Smith 1981, Strobel 1979). Similarly, women play a greater role in some tariqas, usually translated as 'brotherhoods', which are groups organized around charismatic leaders, often with greater mystical and emotional focus than orthodox Islam contains. For example, Qadiriyya communities in the 1930s in Bagamoyo and Tabora, Tanganyika, involved women in mosque activities (Strobel 1979: 77–78).

Second, in some cases the coming of Islam undercut women's ritual roles. Among the Pokomo, who live inland from the northern Kenya coast and have become Muslim in the past century, conflict arose between Muslim leaders and women over who would bury babies who died at birth. In demanding that the babies be washed and buried by Muslim custom, the local Muslim authority was intruding on the women's prerogative and duty under local custom to bury under the house any child who died within 30 days of birth. A compromise was arrived at in which the women collectively delivered the baby to the Muslim official, who performed a Muslim ceremony (Bunger 1973: 96).

Finally, where men utilize Islam to claim their control and superiority over women, women sometimes reassert pre-Islamic rituals to maintain their autonomy. Such a dynamic occurred in Upper Volta in the late 1960s. Men had given up an earlier form of dancing associated with the Dioula warrior ethos, yet women wished to continue dancing. When the male Muslim leader declared it inappropriate behavior for Muslims, the women countered by arguing that earlier religious authorities did not forbid the dancing. In so doing they appealed to a pre-Islamic religious authority to legitimate their actions, which local people themselves acknowledged to be linked to a struggle over domestic authority (Quimby 1979: 217).

Thus, even where the official structures and authorities of religion seek to restrict their roles, women pursue various strategies to assert alternative views. In some cases they may participate in less orthodox aspects of religious practice; elsewhere they may reaffirm their rights according to earlier traditional religious custom.

The transmission of religious ideologies regarding women

Ideas about the characteristics of and relationship between men and women are represented in various ways, sometimes symbolically and sometimes didactically. The idea of female inferiority can be conveyed through taboos. Certain foods, usually those high in protein, are reserved for men to eat: for example, Mbum women in Chad did not eat chicken, eggs, or game meat; Luo women in western Kenya were forbidden chicken, eggs, milk, sheep, rabbit and other game (O'Laughlin 1974, Hay 1976). In addition to seriously affecting women's health, such food taboos express a male/female hierarchy. Other taboos surround sexuality and purity. Muslims must purify themselves after sexual intercourse and before performing religious rituals such as prayer. Although sexual intercourse is seen as polluting for both sexes, females are at a biological disadvantage. Menstrual blood is thought to be polluting; a menstruating female therefore does not perform such religious duties as praying or fasting during the month of Ramadan. A man may avoid some pollution by avoiding a menstruating woman, but a woman cannot escape pollution; it is part of her nature.

Less subtly, the ideology of female subordination may be overtly stated or taught. Often female obedience is a lesson learned in female puberty rites. In other cases didactic literature directed to young women may preach wifely obedience. An example is the poem *The Advice of Mwana Kupona Upon Wifely Duty*, composed in the 1850s on the northern Swahili coast and transmitted orally from one generation to the next. The poem was written down in the 1930s. An aristocratic woman, Mwana Kupona, advised:

> She who obeys her husband, hers are honour and charm; Wherever she shall go, her charm is published abroad. Be gay with him that he be amused; do not oppose his authority. If he bring you ill God will defend you (Werner and Hichens 1943: verses 96, 36).

If Islam preached wifely obedience, mission Christianity concurred and elaborated an ideology of domesticity, envisioned in the model of Western society (Morrow 1986, Hansen 1992). In the 1920s in South Africa, the Christian youth movement sought, in the words of a local missionary, 'to make good servants, Housewives and Mothers who will understand how to take good care of their children' – not recognizing the contradiction that the domestic service in white homes for which African girls were trained took them away from their own families (Gaitskell 1983: 246). The Western domestic model was directed particularly at elite families. After the Second World War the missions and the colonial government of Ruanda-Urundi (present day Rwanda and Burundi) joined hands to socialize elite women to be appropriate wives: to instill 'devotion, unselfishness and discreet and intelligent collaboration in the profession of the husband'. Local women responded but did not passively absorb the projected ideology (Hunt 1990: 455). Similarly, in colonial Uganda, disagreement arose over the content of colonial and missionary girls' education between Europeans and Africans, men and women. Such educated women as Florence Lubega exceeded the rather constricted role envisioned for girls; during the colonial period she served as the first Ugandan woman on the Legislative Council and, with independence, joined the parliament (Musisi 1992).

As colonialism proceeded, secular voices joined religious ones in shaping people's values.

Secular ideology

Increasingly in the colonial period Western-derived gender norms were projected for African women through Western education and the media. Notions of domesticity dominated this secular expression of gender ideology, as seen in some of the voluntary associations in West African towns in the 1950s that taught women the 'proper' (that is, Western middle-class) way to dress or conduct dinner parties (Little 1966: 160). American and European movies conveyed powerful messages about romance, sexuality, and male–female relationships. Such films were a source of controversy in the *Mombasa Times* in the 1950s, where educated Muslim men debated whether or not Muslim women should be allowed to go to the movies. As one advocate of films stated:

> The Cinema . . . has revolutionized, at least in us men, our conception of love. I submit that to live with this new type of husband, a new type of wife is required. . . . Either the cinema is a good thing or it is bad. But it cannot be good to me and bad to Fatma. Yes, Clark Gable might 'impress' her. But since no one objects if Ava Gardner impresses me, I fail to see the potency of the argument! (quoted in Strobel 1979: 121)

Feminist film critics today see Gable–Gardner films as reinforcing the stereotypes of female subordination and seduction, male strength and domination. Yet for Mombasa's educated Muslim men, such films were one more example of 'sex equality, the West's "deadliest misfortune"' (cited in Strobel 1979: 118–23).

The contemporary picture of women in most secular media – films, magazines, newspapers, television, popular theater – represents an ambivalent portrait. Town women in Zambia, according to one scholar, are seen as both 'folk devils' and 'folk heroes'. In the first guise they are a threat to social values; in the second they act as a role model (Schuster 1979). Women in the media are sexier than before. Such women's magazines as *Viva* from Kenya or *Africa Woman* are filled with the appropriate commodities and fashions for maintaining the sexy image. (Some discussion of women's equality is broached as well, and *Viva* has run articles on clitoridectomy, but the predominant image is fashion.)

While town women can be an attractive model to some, their sexuality acts as a pole for negative images as well. Modern Yoruba drama, performed by male touring companies in western Nigeria, incorporates women in five predominant roles: the prostitute, the co-wife, the witch, the half-human/half-animal, and the transvestite. None of these roles is flattering, and the characterization represents the conflict between independent Yoruba women and otherwise dominant men (Hoch-Smith 1978).

The association of female equality and independence with fashion and sexiness has unfortunate consequences for feminism as an ideology that challenges the ideology of female subordination. Generally, feminists argue that society and women alike will benefit from women's equality with men. Some go further and state that gender difference inevitably leads to inequality, that 'complementarity' ultimately masks inequality. Thus while the issue of women's right to go into bars, get drunk, and lead sexually uninhibited lives is not peripheral to feminism, it is neither the form of sexual equality that most feminists would advocate nor the issue they see as most pressing. Yet the issue of sexual independence – 'loose women' – becomes linked in popular thought with the whole issue of equality between the sexes.

With the development of African nationalism came a systematic critique of cultural imperialism and pride in African traditions, reminiscent of the Gikuyu clitoridectomy controversy of the 1920s and 1930s. However, the critique of cultural imperialism easily lapses into a scapegoating attack on urban women, focussing on their dress, sexuality, greed, and parasitical nature. Government ministers joined the man on the street in attacking immoral fashions such as mini-skirts, urban prostitutes, and women who stepped away from the African/missionary tradition of homemaker (Wipper 1972, Schuster 1979: 165–79). An editorial in the *Malawi News* in 1968 regarding mini-skirts illustrates this trend:

> The move by the Government to ban mini-skirts and dresses has come at the most appropriate time. Mini-skirts and dresses are a diabolic fashion which must disappear from the country once and for all. Foreign women such as the one seen on Sunday by the President, Ngwazi Dr Kamuzu Banda, indecently dressed, are setting bad examples to our young girls and we will not tolerate anyone who wants to spoil our nation by importing these diabolic fashions (cited in Wipper 1972: 332).

As recently as 1991, a Malawian lawyer was briefly jailed for questioning in print the law banning mini-skirts (*Chicago Tribune*, 15 September 1991).

Fashion has been seen as a foreign import; feminism has taken on the same taint. In the 1970s some African women began articulating ideas similar to those of Western feminists, although the evolution of an African feminism has followed a rocky road at both international and local levels. The 1975 conference in Mexico City that inaugurated the United Nations' Decade for Women witnessed angry confrontations. Third World women criticized European and American feminists for their perceived preoccupation with issues of sexuality, especially lesbianism, and their avoidance of issues of imperialism and development. Moreover, African female scholars and government officials, witnessing a wave of Western feminist researchers, accused the latter of misrepresenting and misunderstanding the African reality and of disproportionately obtaining research funds that should have been available to African women themselves – that is, of cultural imperialism. More recently at the 1985 Nairobi conference marking the end of the Decade, Western and African women were able to meet and deliberate with improved understanding, as each group had come to appreciate the political viewpoints and agendas of the other (Cagaty et al. 1986).

The struggle to challenge the ideology of female subordination has been long and difficult. Some progress has been made, as is mentioned in several other chapters of this book. The 1970s saw an increase in at least rhetorical support for women's equality among government officials: President Samora Machel of Mozambique declared in 1973, for example, that 'the liberation of women is a fundamental necessity for the revolution' (Machel n.d.), and President Jomo Kenyatta proclaimed the same year the 'equality of women's rights' in Kenya (*East African Standard*, 12 October 1973).

The content of what constitutes equal treatment is vigorously debated. Hence in parliamentary debates over a marriage bill in Kenya, one member of parliament, Kimunai Soi, stated that it was 'very African to teach women manners' by beating them and bemoaned, 'If this legislation is passed, even slapping your wife is ruled out' (*Los Angeles Times*, 27 July 1979: part 1, p. 10). Wambui Otieno's campaign to bury her husband's body in Nairobi and to inherit part of his estate became a media circus; the government sided with patrilineal custom and Kenya's women's organizations were left in disarray, although Wambui's struggle focussed attention on women's legal inequalities (Stamp 1991). Her supporters were maligned for their presumed association with foreign feminists.

Still, African women are increasingly challenging the ideology and reality of women's inequality, whether or not they choose to call themselves feminists and their activity feminist. Women's groups in various African countries are publishing their own journals, for example, in order to escape the sexist representations of mainstream journalism and reach non-elite women. *Sauti ya Siti* (Women's Voice) is published quarterly by the Tanzania Women's Media Association. In explaining its purpose and origin, the editors note 'it is important that women stop being mute and start having their own voice'. The special issue on women and law, for example, discusses problems of inheritance, child custody, rape, and domestic violence, as well as the organization of self-employed women in India and abuses of female political prisoners worldwide. The contents of *Speak*, published by a women's collective in Durban, South Africa, are similar. Some articles discuss such issues as women's health, menstruation, women's work, organizing domestic workers, sharing housework, demands for child care, and bridewealth. Other articles deal with detention and South Africa's prisons, South African women's organizations, women's resistance in Chile, and Philippine women.

In various countries, organizations have formed to promote research and action to improve women's lives, to challenge the ideological, economic, political, and social structures that limit women's potential. Emang Basadi (meaning 'stand up, women') was formed in 1986 in Botswana to advance women's legal and economic position (Molokomme 1991). The Women's Research and Documentation Project at the

117

University of Dar es Salaam in Tanzania, the Women's Research and Documentation Center at the University of Ibadan in Nigeria, and the Women's Studies Program at Makerere University in Uganda all represent new developments in the 1980s (Meena and Mbilinyi 1991, Awe and Mba 1991, Ankrah and Bizimana 1991). In addition to formal efforts to challenge women's inequality, women are using popular culture to express their disagreement with social norms that privilege men and punish women. In Mombasa in the 1980s, female composers and singers employed the traditional Swahili musical form known as *tarab* to chastise men for mistreating them, projecting a message quite different from the ideal of Swahili womanhood described earlier·by Mwana Kupona (Ntarangwi 1993).

Because belief systems influence behavior, religious ideology plays an important role in reinforcing the social norms that articulate appropriate gender roles. Religious ideologies can be used to suppress women and support gender hierarchy; alternatively, women may use the rubric of religious law and belief to critique society and expand women's options. At times secular ideologies, such as feminism, challenge gender roles that limit women's options. Other secular ideologies, often associated with consumer culture, reinforce restricted gender roles by projecting women as sexual objects.

Various factors impede the general acceptance of an ideology of male and female equality in place of an ideology of female subordination. At the most abstract level, people feel that their beliefs in gender difference and inequality are natural rather than created or variable. In addition, men benefit in real ways from a system of gender difference that reinforces female subordination. Challenges to custom, even when 'progressive', are experienced as cultural imperialism; conversely, defense of customs, even 'reactionary' practices, can be interpreted as politically progressive. Finally, the ideology of inequality is rooted in economic and political structures. To challenge the ideology effectively, those structures must be changed.

Notes

1. The honorific title Hajiya indicates that these women have made the pilgrimage to Mecca.

CHAPTER 7

Women in the arts

Lisa Aronson

African women play a major role in art production. In nearly every ethnic group south of the Sahara, some women work as artists, in addition to carrying out their other activities. The arts women produce demonstrate an extremely broad range, including pottery, weaving, embroidery, cloth dyeing, basketry, calabash carving, wall painting, beadwork, leather work, and body decoration.

Women's and men's arts often constitute very separate spheres of activity, however. Two art forms generally not practiced by women are wood-carving and metalsmithing, the exclusive domain of men. Through boundaries that female (and male) artists impose, these spheres are kept divided. Nevertheless, women's arts can complement those of men; women can have an impact on the arts that men practice and, occasionally, they can enter art professions traditionally dominated by men.

The domestic orientation characteristic of women's arts must also be emphasized. Unlike men, women most often produce their arts within a domestic context, around other domestic activities and, at times, as part of their interaction with other women. This would explain why certain arts, such as the painting of compound walls, tend to be exclusively female. However, although produced in the context of their domestic work, many women's arts can have considerable economic value and serve important functions in social, religious, and political segments of society, therefore assuming a major role in the public domain.

Changes in these various spheres of society are among the many factors that account for innovations and change in women's arts. When these changes occur, women may find the need to establish new boundaries in their effort to protect their own social and economic interests.

It is on these main issues concerning women's arts that this chapter is focussed. The first section examines the issue of boundaries dividing women's arts from men's, reasons for the existence of these boundaries, and circumstances where they become blurred or redefined. This is followed by a discussion of women's arts within the domestic sphere, using the examples of weaving, wall-painting, and calabash decoration to illustrate the various dynamics of such compound-centred media. The next section looks at the socioeconomic importance of women's arts, and pottery production in particular, because of its highly professional nature, economic worth, and importance in serving household, religious, and political needs for the society. The concluding section addresses the impact that change can have on women's arts. Here considerable discussion is given to my own research on Igbo weavers of Akwete, Nigeria, and how they adapted to shifts in their economy brought about by new trading patterns.[1]

Boundaries separating women's and men's arts

The introductory paragraphs have already suggested that women's arts differ very much in type from the arts that men perform. Women dominate pottery production[2] and do wall painting, while men do wood-carving and metalsmithing. Although both men and women weave and do cloth dyeing, embroidery, beadwork, and basketry, it is rarely the case that both sexes engage in these activities in the same geographical area. If they do, the types of objects each makes and the tools and techniques of production differ, suggesting that the same art is either rooted in separate, gender-based traditions or is for exclusive use by one or the other sex. For example, in West Africa (mainly Nigeria) women usually weave on an upright frame loom, a type presumably of indigenous origin (see this type illustrated in Fig. 7.1). It is more common for men to use a horizontal, foot-operated loom producing narrow strips, a portable variety possibly introduced via nomadic groups from the north. North Africa may also be the source of one indigo dyeing technique in which men utilize pots sunk into the ground, in contrast to the placement of dye pots above the ground that characterizes women's methods. Among the Gurensi of northern Ghana, both men and women weave baskets. However, men exclusively make bags and hats while women weave the flat-bottomed cane basket (*piou*). Men claim they never make the flat-bottomed variety because it is only women who use it to carry goods to market; thus from their perspective it is 'part of the woman's world' (Smith 1978a: 78).

Women and men often desire to keep their artistic domains separate, and it is through taboos and other means of social avoidances that the lines of division are kept intact. One frequently hears of taboos that prevent women from doing men's wood-carving and iron-work, but taboos also prevent men from entering arts dominated by women. Thus, weaving in the Yoruba town of Oyo and the Igbo village of Akwete is strictly a woman's domain, and it is believed that men who attempt weaving will become impotent (Poyner 1980: 49, Aronson 1989a, 1989b). Taboos such as these also prevail among

Figure 7.1   Anoke Lawal, a Yoruba weaver from Ijebu-Ode. She is
weaving an *itagbe* cloth worn over the shoulder as insignia
by members of the Oshugbo (Ogboni) Society and traditional
Yoruba chiefs.

women dyers of Liberia who believe that the dye vats are sacred to
them and therefore are off limits to men. Such attitudes, also prevalent
among women potters throughout Africa, are a conscious effort on the
part of women to keep the lines of division intact and thus protect
their own professions.

The exclusion of men from women's arts and vice versa can also
be a function of the rules that artists must follow to ensure skill
and precision in art production. Zulu blacksmiths, like blacksmiths in
other parts of Africa, adhere to certain dress codes, food and speech
restrictions, and sexual and social taboos, the latter involving the

exclusion of women from the area where men are doing their work. If a Zulu blacksmith does not abide by the prescribed codes of behavior, 'his work would come to naught', he would become mad, or he would be wounded 'by iron' or killed for disregarding the taboos of iron work (Raum 1973: 216). Women artists and their arts can also be subject to similar kinds of controls, aimed at guaranteeing mastery over their art. Women potters will often prohibit menstruating, pregnant, or uninitiated women (who are perceived as potentially dangerous) from entering the area where the more crucial stages of pottery production, such as firing, are in progress.

While boundaries exist, men and women can cooperate in the production and use of certain types of art. Among the Baule, women spin and dye the cotton that men use to weave cloth strips on horizontal foot-treadle looms (Etienne 1980). Similarly, among the Kuba, men weave the plain woven raphia cloth to which women then apply elaborate brush-pile embroidered designs (Adams 1978). The social context in which men's and women's arts are used can also coincide; an example are the paraphernalia used by members of the Yoruba Ogboni (Oshugbo) society, a secret judicial body whose power is derived from its link with spirits of the earth. As their insignia, Ogboni members use brass cast figurative staffs (*edan ogboni*) and intricately patterned shoulder cloths (*itagbe*), the former produced by men, the latter by women.

Women can also influence and affect the arts traditionally done by men. Recent research reveals interesting information about the vital role that women diviners can have in the utilization of shrine sculpture, which men carve. Because of their close ties with spirits, gods, and ancestors, women are thought to have easy access to their requirements for shrines erected in their name. They can thus play a crucial role in commissioning shrine sculpture and in determining the configuration of artifacts placed in the shrines. Among the Ijo of Nigeria, Anderson has noted that women diviners (*buroyara*) are told by the spirits which items (such as sculpture or cloth) must be placed in a shrine. Men are commissioned to carve only if sculpture is requested by the spirits. The *buroyara* are also instrumental in the arrangement of the shrine objects (a key factor in the efficacy of each object), because only they receive that type of knowledge from the spirits (Anderson 1983). Similarly, among the Senufo of the Ivory Coast, the aesthetic of placing the figures on the shrine enhances the prestige of the owner. And there, too, it is only the Sando diviners (mainly women) who learn from the spirits what the appropriate configuration should be (Glaze 1975: 65). Women also have considerable decision-making power in the Poro society, ostensibly male-dominated, and the arts associated with it, because of their close link with the spirit world (Glaze 1975; 1981).

There are also instances where women enter into arts traditionally dominated by men, including those involving metal. With the introduction of foreign jewelry into Yoruba society, the number of men involved in jewelry production has decreased. Women, who traditionally were excluded from the profession, are now becoming bronze and gold metal-smiths (Awe 1975: 66). Similarly, the Hausa aluminum spoon industry, once rooted in the traditionally male art of silver-smithing, now includes women as well as men. Norma Wolff (1986) cites three reasons: the lessening of traditional sanctions on metal-working; technological change, such as the introduction of a new metal (aluminum); and the availability of secluded Hausa women as a labor force. But again, men's and women's technologies and designs remain separate. The men stipple the background while women stipple the design itself. Moreover, men tend to adhere to traditional Muslim designs, while women, not limited by traditions, are freer to select from a broader range of patterns, including, despite their seclusion, public and topical themes (for example, the emir's walking stick).[3]

Even in the case of blacksmithing in iron, a profession traditionally restricted to men, it has been possible for women (especially family members) to assist in the process and even smelt the iron itself. Among the Oyo Yoruba, for example, the blacksmith's wives and daughters will pound the ore, wash it in the river, and burn it in the furnace (Williams 1973: 146). They can even describe the design of the furnace and the process of smelting. Among the Bamana (Bambara), blacksmiths known as *namu* are both men and women of a particular lineage. All *namu* have access to the supernatural powers associated with blacksmithing, including knowledge of the smelting process itself. As a rule, a division of labor exists among *namu* such that men work with metal and wood while women are confined to clay, as potters. While women rarely smelt the iron, McNaughton notes that they occasionally do so (personal communication 1982).

Women's arts and domestic work

For the most part, women's arts remain distinct from those of men, a tradition consistent with the separation of other areas of labor common to men and women in Africa. One principal role for African women is the domestic one, that is, raising children, preparing meals, and supervising activity within the compound. Peculiar to women, this role can explain certain differences their arts can exhibit, both in type and in organization, from the arts of men. Women's domestic responsibilities often govern where their artistic production is to be confined within the village, how the arts are organized economically and socially, and how younger women are taught the traditions. It also determines what types of arts women perform.

Certain arts grow out of women's social relations with other women. For example, women among the Tera and neighboring groups along the Benue Valley region of Nigeria decorate calabashes which they circulate among themselves as part of their dowry and for use as domestic ware (Rubin 1970). Ndebele women make and wear beaded garments bearing designs that communicate their own social status

(Priebatsch and Knight 1978). Hair plaiting and body decoration are also done within the women's social spheres, at times when they are free from other work.

The remainder of this section looks at three specific women's arts (weaving, wall painting, and calabash decoration) to see the different ways in which women's arts are structured around their domestic sphere or draw on it for their meaning.

Weaving

A comparison of women's and men's weaving in the Yoruba town of Ilorin illustrates differences that are explained in part by women's domestic roles. Weaving for men is generally a full-time activity and takes place in centralized areas of the village. Drawn from disparate regions of the town, the men work under the organization of a guild headed by one person, who receives the commissions and pays the younger weavers to make the cloth. He also apprentices the young boys wishing to learn the craft. By way of contrast, young girls learn to weave by observing their mothers from early childhood. Ilorin women weavers, unlike men, most often confine their work to their living quarters, where weaving can be done as a part-time activity along with domestic responsibilities. Consistent with this, they avoid working in public arenas of the village, within centralized guild structures that require them to work away from their domestic domain. Regardless of the number of women weaving within a compound, each tends to work independently, earning her own wages. Much of their weaving is for domestic use. Other cloths are woven on commissions the women receive directly from the patron. There is an arrangement to sell surplus cloths in the market through intermediary traders.

Like Ilorin weavers, those of the Igbo village of Akwete, Nigeria, also work in their compound, and this factor seems to have hindered the success of a weavers' cooperative begun in their village in 1950. At that time, male chiefs wishing to centralize weaving production organized a cooperative and built a center, illustrated in Fig. 7.2, where women wove one month out of the year. Forced to close during the Biafran War, it was officially reopened in 1977. At that time, I noted that the project was only marginally successful because the women, preferring to weave in their compounds, rarely used the center. Excuses for avoiding responsibilities as coop members often hinged on their need to be near the family. When approached to pay fines for not appearing at the weaving center, they explained: 'My daughter is about to give birth and I need to be close to her', or 'An ailing family member requires my close attention'. Clearly the demands of domestic work governed where they wished to weave. Similar motivation underlies the fact that pottery production, basketry, embroidery, and calabash carving are done near women's living quarters, where they can be easily integrated with their domestic activities. The domestic orientation of Shai potters in Ghana is discussed below.

Figure 7.2   Akwete Cooperative Weaving Society Center, Nigeria. The
cooperative center was built in 1958–59. It was shut down in
the late 1960s during the Biafran War. This photograph was
taken in July 1977 on the day it was officially reopened.

Wall painting

The art of wall painting, like those arts mentioned above, is an activity
that a woman integrates with her other areas of productive labor and
her social interactions with other women. In addition, it is confined
to her own compound. The motifs themselves often refer to objects
and events familiar to her daily experience or to information about
her social identity. By virtue of public visibility, the images applied
to the walls communicate information to others in the village. Thus,
while done within a domestic area, wall painting can be an important
public concern.

Most domestic architecture in sub-Saharan Africa is made up of
mud wall construction. While men are mainly responsible for laying
the foundation and building up the mud walls, it is the women's task
to finish the wall surface, an extension of which can be the application
of decorative painted motifs.

Two regions of Africa are known for wall painting. The first region
includes a number of Voltaic-speaking groups along the Sudanic
stretch of West Africa, and the second is found among the Zulu,
Sotho, Ndebele, and related groups of Southern Africa.[4] In both
regions, wall painting is something women do when they have leisure

125

time from agricultural work. Among the Gurensi of northern Ghana, women paint the compound wall during the dry season, when the weather is suitable for such work and when work in the fields is at a minimum. It is also only done when the walls are in need of refurbishing, every four or five years (Smith 1978b, 1986).

Among the Gurensi, when wall painting is needed, the senior wife of the compound organizes her co-wives and the wives of her husband's brothers to work collectively at resurfacing and painting the walls (as seen in Fig. 7.3). Young girls participate and, in so doing, learn the patterns and how they are to be applied. No formal training is required. While the senior wife usually decides on the pattern and the compositional layout, the final decisions are made through collaboration and cooperation with the other women. Thus, wall painting, for the Gurensi, constitutes a collective effort recognized by the women as a vehicle for their group identity. An exception occurs when the senior wife paints her own room. Here, the choice of designs and execution on the walls is her work alone, as a statement about herself (Smith 1978b: 80).

While women's wall embellishments are contained within the compound, the designs have considerable public impact by virtue of their visibility to individuals beyond the compound walls. Recognizing

Figure 7.3   Wall painting being done by Gurensi co-wives of the Atia Compound in the town of Zuarungu in the Fra Fra region of northern Ghana. (Photograph courtesy of Fred Smith.)

this potential, women use the medium to communicate information about their social status and the status of the owner of the compound. Gurensi wall painting, when done well, can reflect positively on the male owner of the compound (Smith 1978b: 40), a fact that may explain the incorporation of male-prestige objects as decorative motifs, such as the cloth strips (*tana*) which men wear. But more often the patterns women paint are oriented towards their own social sphere. Coupled with the cloth strip motif, Gurensi designs refer to items such as the broken calabash piece (*wanyagese*), or fiber nets used to hold calabashes in their living quarters (*zanlengu*). In other regions of Africa, wall designs can derive from various forms of female body decorations, which enhance the beauty and communication information about the social status of women. Among the Sotho women of South Africa, wall designs relate to patterns on their beaded garments; the colors used to paint them correspond to those painted on women's bodies during initiation (Matthews 1977: 31, Rohrmann 1974: 18). For unmarried women of the Transvaal area of South Africa, the aim is to attract male suitors. The same may be true for Igbo women, whose wall designs often relate to body designs that communicate their social status as uninitiated women (Aniakor 1979).

Gurensi women regard any negative criticism of other women's work as 'antisocial and disruptive behavior' (Smith 1978b). While no explanation was given for this attitude, it could be viewed as a function of the very personal kind of referencing that wall painting can have for the women. Because Gurensi women regard the medium as a statement about other women, they feel inhibited from passing judgement on the designs, tantamount to making a value judgement about the individual who painted it.

Calabash decoration

At times women's art can become a significant symbol of power derived precisely from their female associations. This has been noted in two studies of calabash decoration among the Fulani, Ga'anda, and other groups of the Benue Valley of Nigeria, one by T. J. H. Chappel (1977) and the other by Marla Berns and Barbara Hudson. In particular, Berns and Hudson (1986) write a lengthy and vivid account of the techniques and designs employed in calabash decoration and their domestic and ritual uses (Fig. 7.4). Data from both studies point to the power and gender-laden meaning that calabashes can have in the culture. Not only do they function in both domestic and sacred contexts, but it is the gourds' domestic associations that warrant their use in the sacred realm. Chappel notes that decorated gourds for the cattle-keeping Fulani are both domestic, in their use as containers, and ritual in the ways they symbolically mark important stages in the life cycle, often through their ritual exchange at marriages and during childbirth. The decorative gourds used in these contexts can have a 'generalized expressive significance deriving from their direct

Figure 7.4   Waja women from the village of Talasse in Nigeria use decorated gourd bonnets to shield their babies from the sun when going to a well to fetch water. February 1982. (Photograph courtesy of Marla Berns.)

association with ideas about femininity and motherhood, and the values attaching to these concepts' (Chappel 1977: 16). By virtue of their maternal and household associations, they symbolize increase and order within the family. In this capacity, they can even serve as charms to ensure the health and fecundity of the cattle herd.

In other contexts, the gourd, as a female nurturing symbol, is combined with male symbolic forms to express the complementary value of the two spheres. Berns and Hudson note that Didiya women give young male initiates gourds decorated with iron rattles with which they dance to celebrate their coming of age (Berns and Hudson 1986: 60). These rattles combine the female symbol of the gourd (women's nurturing, domestic role) with the male symbol of iron (referring to the iron tools the boy uses in his capacity as cultivator). In this and many other ways, women's gourd arts are shown to contribute significantly to the moulding of culture.[5]

The socioeconomic importance of women's arts

Women's wall painting, while confined to the compound, can function as a network through which social status is communicated. In this manner and through other media as well, women's art performed in a context with domestic work serves significantly in the society's principal nondomestic realms – the economic, political, and religious spheres.

Most arts that women perform are economically valuable as a means through which they earn an independent income. At times that income can be quite substantial. Akwete weavers, for example, earn a subsistence wage which they use to support themselves and their children. They only give a portion of their earnings to their husbands if they so choose. The economic value can influence how the arts are performed. Sometimes it motivates artists to achieve a high level of skill at their craft, as noted among calabash carvers of numerous groups along the Benue Valley area of Nigeria (Rubin 1970). The economic value can also explain the boundaries that women establish to maintain domination and control of their art. Such boundaries often involve the exclusion of other women, thus permitting artists to keep the profession within their economic domain. These protective strategies are similar to those followed in the more specialized occupational associations described in Chapter 9.

In addition to their economic value, women's arts can be of political and religious importance. Many serve as emblems to validate the power of individuals of rank. An example is the cloth woven by the Ijebu Yoruba women for use by traditional chiefs and members of the Oshugbo (Ogboni) cult. Figure 7.1 illustrates such a cloth being woven. In Zaire, Kuba women embroider raphia cloths that serve as important emblems of traditional wealth and status in Kuba society in their use in bridewealth payments, divorce settlements, and ceremonies legitimizing the power of the king (Darish 1989, Adams

1978). Another important leadership art is the terracotta portrait head that Akan-speaking women make for deceased chiefs and elders. The terracotta heads also serve important religious functions, because these leaders are often divine in nature.

Ceramic pottery, the technique used for making such heads, is the most pervasive and perhaps the most important of art forms performed by African women. In addition to serving important religious and political purposes, it is economically vital as is indicated by the degree to which women impose rigid boundaries and controls to protect their profession and the processes with which it is associated. And yet, despite its economic importance, most stages of pottery production are confined to the women's domestic areas of the compound.

Pottery production involves five important stages of activity: the gathering of clay from clay reserves, the building of the pots, the predrying of them in the sun, firing, and marketing. While some women trade pots from a home base, most must travel to distant markets to sell their wares. Clay reserves are also frequently situated beyond the village boundaries, and in order for women to gather the clay, they must often go some distance from their compound. All other phases of pottery production, the building of the pots, and firing are activities the women do at home within the domestic realm.

It is here, for example, that learning takes place through observation and imitation, starting in early childhood. Girls begin before the age of five beating lumps of clay, a first step in acquiring the necessary familiarity with the medium. Pots are hand-built; the wheel is not used in Africa. Learning to build pots, done either by the coiled or pulled method (the latter illustrated in Fig. 7.5), takes considerable skill acquired gradually through persistent trial and error and positive instruction. Young Marghi girls of northeastern Nigeria are neither ridiculed nor admonished by the older women when their newly formed vessels crack while drying in the sun. Instead they are encouraged positively to try again (Vaughn 1973: 184).

Most potters in Africa do not master the art of building clay and decorating the pot until they have reached adulthood. Among the Ikombe Kisi of Tanzania, women potters claim to continue learning into motherhood and middle age, even though they began before the age of 10 (Waane 1977: 265). Skill in the production of sophisticated, sculptured wares created among the Akan-speaking groups of Ghana or the Yoruba of Nigeria may not be acquired until very late in a woman's life. Abatan, a woman potter from the Egbado region of Yorubaland, admits that it was not until she had reached middle age (30 to 40) that she became skilled at creating sculptured pots for the Eyinle deity, the most sophisticated and religiously complex of the many types with which she is familiar (Thompson 1969).

The majority of pots Abatan and other women potters make are for domestic use, a fact that may explain why the craft is predominantly women's work. Pots made by the Yoruba of Moro serve the following functions: cooking, dyeing cloth, smoking meats, frying foods, and

Figure 7.5   Mo potter of west-central Ghana making a large water pot
by the 'pulled method' of working the clay – pulling the
clay up to form the walls of the pot. (Photograph courtesy of
Roy Sieber.)

storing ashes, charcoal, firewood, water, food, or clothing. Another
type is used as a brazier to hold other pots for cooking (Wahlmann
1972: 325). Similarly, Spindel documents 29 pots in the Senufo potter's
repertoire, of which 20 are intended for domestic purposes and the
remaining nine for ritual use by both men and women (Spindel
1989).

Whatever the pots are used for, the methods of producing them
can be complex. The most difficult stage is firing, always done in

the open air, without a kiln. It is often done collectively with other women, since the larger the quantities of unfired pots placed in the fire arena, the more effective the firing will be (Fig. 7.6). When a sufficient quantity of pots have been predried in the sun, they are carefully stacked one on top of another and then covered with broken pot shards, palm fronds, and leafy twigs to help retain the heat while being fired.

Careful preparation is necessary to ensure that the temperature is kept under control, thus preventing pots from cracking or exploding, disasters that could cause the loss of many hours of productive work and thus considerable revenue. It is therefore at this crucial stage of production that taboos and rituals are observed and strictly enforced. It is taboo for menstruating, pregnant, or uninitiated women to approach the area where Shai women are firing pottery (Quarcoo and Johnson 1968: 68). Among the Mossi of Upper Volta, sacrifices are made before firing to ensure that the ancestors will not interfere in a harmful way (Roy 1975).

The clay reserves, the source for their materials, are also an important focus for women potters. Often the reserves are located near riverbeds, beyond the village boundaries. Thus, the women must travel a considerable distance from home to gather quantities of clay, which they keep stored in their huts. Shai potters of Ghana trek an arduous trail up and down a steep hill to acquire their clay. When queried as to why they prefer carrying the clay over such a distance to building pots close to the clay source, they responded that they would prefer working close to their families. Such a response reinforces the notion that women's domestic responsibilities determine where their artistic activity occurs.

The clay reserve is also an area where women come in close contact with the spirits and ancestors residing in the earth. Thus it, like firing, is an important focus for ritual activity. Among the Shai potters of Ghana, a priestess is placed in charge of each clay pit to ensure that the pit is kept 'healthy' and free from danger. The Barikiwa of East Africa have a similar practice (Cross-Upcott 1955: 25).

Even though women produce pots within the compound, such activity can be highly professional, lucrative, and prestigious. Like most potters in Africa, Gwari women of Ushafa market their own pots, travelling as far as 25 miles from the home to do so (Bandler and Bandler 1977: 31). Men may assist women potters in the transport. Among the Ikombe Kisi of Tanzania, pots made in the village must be carried to a market some distance away. While pots will be carried overland by women, they can also be transported by canoe, which only men navigate (Waane 1977).

Ikombe potters are the only potters in the region, and thus exchange their wares for foods or implements produced in other villages. Women carry on this exchange among themselves, traditionally not using cash in these transactions. When cash is received for the sale of a pot, the money often becomes the property of the men. In

Figure 7.6   Senufo women from the village of Dagbarakaha, Ivory Coast, arranging their pots for a firing.

most cases, women potters benefit from the sale of their pots, often substantially.

A song that Shai potters sing indicates their own awareness of the economic necessity of their profession:

> Hear, oh hear, we continue in the work so we shall lack nothing. The work of the great grand-ones, that is our heritage. Good omens we ask. Come ye mothers and drink. Come and eat. Drive bad luck from us. Teach us pottery. Flourish the work of our hands (Quarcoo and Johnson 1968: 68).

Because of the lucrativeness of the pottery market, it is not uncommon for women to establish boundaries that prevent outsiders from learning the profession. Non-Shai women are not permitted to learn the potter's craft, and men, in general, will not participate in it for fear of impotency. Ikombe Kisi potters of Tanzania also claim complete ownership of their art and thus exclude others from capitalizing on it. In such instances, exclusivity is aimed at protecting economic interests and a sense of identity in relation to their art.

Even the designs and forms can be economically motivated. When Fred Smith asked Gurensi women of Ghana why they apply designs to their pots, their response was that they do it to make them more marketable (Smith 1978b). Margot Gill's ethno-archaeological study of Kamba women's pottery in Kenya shows that the desire to ensure excellence motivates Kamba artists to sign their pots with individualized identity markers – geometric figures or dots and lines – as a kind of trademark and guarantee of the vessel's quality (Gill 1981).

In addition to its economic value, women's pottery can also have religious significance in the society, and because of this, its production is given special attention. Ritual pots made by the Yoruba of Moro must be treated carefully because of their close association with the gods. Clay used to make Shango pots is pounded separately from that used for domestic ware and the pots are never left in the sun to dry (Wahlmann 1972: 329). Because sacrifices must be made during the production of ritual pots, they are generally more expensive. As a rule, they are also made on commission and thus are not produced in large quantities.

A highly sophisticated sculptural form of pottery used in funerary rites is produced among Akan-speaking groups of West Africa (such as the Krinjabo, Attie, Anyi, and Baule). While men are known to make such figurative pots, it is also an important artistic tradition for women. Figure 7.7 shows such a head made by a Krinjabo woman potter in 1964 (Sieber 1972). Such clay modelled figures represent idealized portraits of deceased chiefs or important elders in their society. When an important individual dies, these ceramic portrait heads are commissioned and then carried in procession and used in ceremonies to honor the deceased. Similar ceremonial uses of these heads for royalty were noted by European merchants in the seventeenth century, thus dating this tradition as at least 300 years

Figure 7.7   A terracotta funerary portrait head hand built by a Krinjabo woman, Krinjabo, Ghana. The head would be used to commemorate a deceased elder in the village. (Photograph courtesy of Roy Sieber.)

old. Given the continued importance of Ashanti royalty, there is every reason to suspect that this centuries-old tradition continues to be as vital today as it was when documented in the seventeenth century and more recently in the early 1960s, when research was conducted.

Women's arts and change

While women's art traditions may persist over centuries, their artistic styles and roles can undergo change. Changes can often be linked

135

to the preferences of patrons. In response to the newer demands of urbanized upper classes for European pots, several pottery centers are now adapting traditional hand-built pottery methods to European pot designs and finishes. One noted Gwari potter, Ladi Kwali, now makes hand-built pots bearing traditional shapes and designs but using stoneware clay and transparent glazes (Wahlmann 1974).

Change need not be the result of external influence. The Yoruba potter Abatan introduced numerous innovations in design to her pots, stemming in part from inspiration she received from the god, Eyinle, for whom the pot is made (Thompson 1969). Among the Kuba, women embroider patterns on raphia cloths; while relating structurally to the traditional royal designs on men's wood-carved objects, these embroidery patterns also show a propensity for innovation. Kuba legends telling of Kashasi, the legendary inventor of the embroidery technique, suggest that it was her desire to please the king that prompted her to devise new ways for executing royal designs (Adams 1978).

Economic changes through trade or a fluctuating market can precipitate changes in the artist's role. Among the Mo of Ghana and the Gwari of Nigeria, pottery production had once been widespread, but over time became localized in one group who took control of the craft and began practicing it on a full-time basis (Bandler and Bandler 1977, Sieber personal communication 1981). Benetta Jules-Rosette notes that the demands of urbanization caused Bemba women of Zambia to reduce their vast repertoire to the making of only traditional beer pots and to carve out for themselves a new profession of making and selling beer associated with them. Moreover, Bemba men were permitted to take up the female art so that both women and men now do it. But unlike the women's wares, the men's pots are done in nontraditional, representational designs that convey nostalgic scenarios of traditional village life (Jules-Rosette 1984).

Akwete weaving

It was an economic shift due to the increase in trade that caused weaving in the Igbo village of Akwete in southeastern Nigeria to undergo change. In the process, Akwete weavers set up boundaries through which they could claim ownership of a craft once the prerogative of women throughout their clan. Amidst heavy trading with the coastal Ijo in the nineteenth century, innovations and changes were introduced into Akwete weaving. Weaving evolved into an elaborately decorated type, mainly woven by Akwete women within the clan. In spite of a history of weaving throughout the clan, Akwete women now believe that they invented weaving and are sole owners of their craft. This belief is reinforced by a legend telling of an Akwete-born woman who invented weaving in her dreams. Boundaries are also kept intact by the rigid rules Akwete women follow regarding who is permitted to learn the craft. Their need to establish such boundaries stems from their desire to take control of the weaving in its newly emerged form. The remainder of this chapter will be devoted to a discussion of the changes in Akwete weaving, how they occurred, and how the women adjusted to them.[6]

Akwete is one of 25 villages within the Igbo-speaking Ndoki clan. It is situated on the bend of the Imo River in southeastern Nigeria, approximately 50 miles from the coast. While some weaving exists in other Ndoki villages, it is in the village of Akwete that the craft is most dominant. There Akwete women are expected to weave cloth on a full-time basis. Before the age of five, Akwete girls begin imitating their mothers by playing at weaving on upturned stools (see Fig. 7.8). At that age they are already demonstrating some knowledge of the craft in the way they model their mothers' gestures and movements. Girls, such as the one shown in Fig. 7.9, begin weaving on an upright

Figure 7.8 Child playing at weaving on an upturned stool in the Igbo village of Akwete, Ndoki clan, southeastern Nigeria.

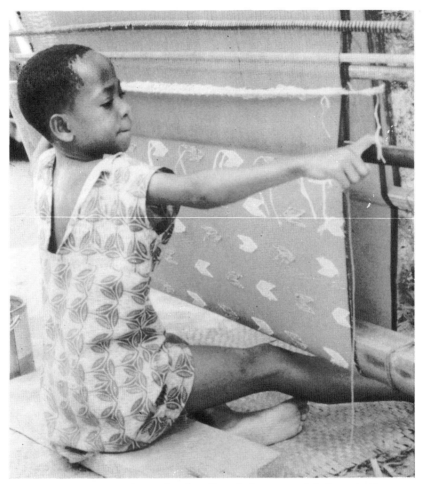

Figure 7.9   Young girl weaving her first cloth on an adult loom in the Igbo village of Akwete, Ndoki clan, southeastern Nigeria.

loom as soon as they are physically able and will continue to do so as long as they remain in Akwete.

At this early stage, girls are also told of a legendary figure, Dada Nwakwata, who invented weaving in her dreams. It is through Dada Nwakwata that weaving purportedly began in Akwete; no women before her had woven cloth. The following is a shortened version of the legend told to me on 11 August 1977:

> Dada Nwakwata was from the Uhuobu compound in Akwete . . . of the Egbe family. Nobody taught Dada Nwakwata how to weave. She learned the designs in her dreams; she said the ancestors taught her. She did not allow anyone into her back yard where she was weaving her cloth

except one deaf mute slave who therefore could not teach the weaving art to other women. But by carefully studying Dada Nwakwata's art, [this slave] learned the craft and started to teach other women secretly after Dada Nwakwata's death. Dada was not aware that she could teach Ngbokwo to weave.

Other versions of the legend state that Ijo traders so preferred Dada Nwakwata's cloths that they would pay twice as much to buy them. (With such profits, Dada Nwakwata could purchase two slaves instead of one, a monetary incentive that prompted other women to learn her weaving secrets.) Such legends, told time and time again in Akwete, serve as an historical document about change in weaving in the mid-nineteenth century when Akwete and other Ndoki villages were involved in active palm-oil trading with the coastal Ijo.

The palm-oil trade, which gradually replaced that of slaves after 1807, required both the use of intermediary markets situated near channels of water and greater numbers of individuals, including women, for the manufacture and distribution of the oil. Women from Ndoki and particularly Akwete, situated close to the Imo River, assumed an important intermediary function in the trade. They sold palm-oil products, brought down from northern Igbo areas where they were made, directly to Ijo traders who sold them to European merchants on the coast. Coastal Ijo traders, wishing to maintain control of the channels between Ndoki and the coast, frequently travelled up-river to purchase the goods from Ndoki women. At that time, they also began buying the women's cloths and influencing how they should be woven. While weaving throughout Ndoki changed in the process, the Dada Nwakwata legend informs us that it was cloths from Akwete that underwent the most significant changes.

Prior to this time, cloths throughout Ndoki were said to have been plain woven or of simple stripes, woven with handspun cotton. They were also narrow in width, approximately 8 inches (20 cms), occasionally sewn together in twos or in threes. In response to Ijo demands, Akwete cloths were widened, making them the widest variety of women's weave produced in West Africa (see example of such cloth in Fig. 7.10). Imported cotton threads were also introduced to Akwete women, presumably through the Ijo, who were in direct contact with the Europeans through trade. The greatest impact was on the patterns themselves. One pattern in particular, *ikaki*, an Ijo word for tortoise, is the most important design the Ijo introduced to Akwete's repertoire. *Ikaki*, illustrated on the cloth in Fig. 7.11, constitutes one of a hundred or more patterns familiar to Akwete women. Many of these are copied from cloths owned by the Ijo. Scores of others are derived from such designs. Still others stem from the weaver's own imagination, for Akwete women place a strong emphasis on innovation and change, an artistic accomplishment of which they are exceptionally proud.

Akwete weavers were able to dominate this newer form of weaving when palm-oil trading declined after 1900. Because of the decrease in

Figure 7.10 Akwete woman weaving a pattern inspired by imported
Indian madras traded to the coast of West Africa by the British
as early as the eighteenth century and introduced to the
Akwete women through trade with the Ijo.

trade, the Ijo visited Ndoki less frequently for the purchase of palm-oil
and cloths. And yet Ijo demands for Akwete cloths persisted. To meet
these demands, Akwete women began travelling south directly to the
Ijo patrons to sell their cloth and cloths from other Ndoki villages. As
marketeers, they were able to take economic control of weaving in
their clan, selling all cloths with the name *akwa akwete* (Akwete cloth).
This pattern continues today. Cloths woven in neighboring Ndoki
towns, such as the one illustrated in Fig. 7.11, are invariably sold to
Ijo patrons by Akwete traders, bearing the Akwete village name.

Weaving is now also a full-time activity for Akwete women, who are
less involved in farming than women elsewhere in Ndoki. As a full-
time activity, weaving has become an important aspect of their identity
both as women and as members of their own village. Rules to which
Akwete women adhere insure that this identity is reinforced. Young
Akwete boys may play at weaving and occasionally assist the mother
in winding the threads, but they will never be permitted to weave on
an adult loom for fear of impotency (*isi otiti*). More importantly, other
Ndoki women are denied the right to learn weaving in its newer form.
Akwete women will never reveal their secrets. If ever suspected of
doing so, they are severely reprimanded by other Akwete women,
for it is their belief that all weaving must be rooted in their own

Figure 7.11 Akwete cloth with *ikaki* (tortoise) design, women by women in the neighboring Ndoki village of Ohanso. It carries the Akwete label, however, because women from Akwete will very often purchase it from these weavers and trade it themselves to the Ijo.

village. Whatever weaving does exist elsewhere in Ndoki, Akwete women claim, had to have been introduced through an Akwete-born woman who married elsewhere.

Such claims were frequently denied by weavers of these other Ndoki villages, who often asserted that weaving had once been the prerogative of women throughout Ndoki, taught from generation to generation within their own villages. Such assertions are confirmed by oral histories and ceremonies recorded from these villages. During burial services honoring a senior woman from the Ndoki villages of Ohambele and Obunko, her eldest daughter danced with the deceased woman's beater stick (*otiti*) in praise of her weaving profession as a source of her sustenance in life.[7] While weaving is now only a minor occupation in those towns, the persistence of such ceremonies suggests that it was once economically significant to the women. Oral histories also cite the types of cloths these villagers were once weaving: narrow, handspun cloths of plain or striped designs.

Evidence that weaving had once existed elsewhere in the clan would then explain the very possessive behavior now characteristic of Akwete women. In essence women from Akwete have taken economic control of a new and improved craft, which caused the extinction of a simpler and once more prevalent form of weaving. In order to maintain ownership of the craft, Akwete women deny women outside the village the right to learn weaving. They justify this exclusive behavior by claiming that weaving was invented by their own village. This belief is legitimized by the legend of Dada Nwakwata continually told by the women, which states that no other women ever taught her to weave. Born in Akwete, Dada Nwakwata learned the art of weaving in her dreams.

Notes

1. For a more detailed survey and critique of the literature on African women in the visual arts see Aronson (1991).
2. There are exceptions, such as among the Hausa of northern Nigeria and the Baganda in East Africa, where both men and women are potters.
3. The *emir* is the supreme Muslim leader in Hausa society. His walking stick, along with other items in his possession, are important emblems of his power.
4. For two general texts on women's wall painting in sub-Saharan Africa, see Courtney-Clarke (1986, 1991).
5. Berns notes a similar dynamic with the pottery Ga'anda women make for use as burial pots. The women apply their own body scarification markings to the surfaces of the pots to ensure that the male or female soul contained within is properly nurtured on its journey to the spiritual realm (Berns 1988: 57–76).
6. This section is based on the author's own research in Nigeria (Aronson 1989a, 1989b, 1980); similar occupational associations are discussed in Chapter 9.
7. Akwete women informed me that this ceremony was once also practiced in Akwete. However, the impact of Christianity in Akwete has brought about the end of ceremonies, such as this one, that focussed on communication with the ancestors.

CHAPTER 8

Women in African literature

Deirdre LaPin

It is no surprise that the decade of the 1980s has ballooned with writing by and about African women. Moreover, critical perspectives on this work have increasingly assumed a feminist point of view. Worldwide inquiry into the experience, discourse, and psychology of the female 'other' has gained ground in many disciplines, and literature has granted generous space to the trend (Dobie 1990). Admittedly, not all African women writers – or Africans who write about women – are apologists for feminism. Indeed the notion in itself resists simple definition. Hilde Hein (1990: 281) observes that the project of feminism 'fixes upon the perspective that women bring to experience as subjects, a perspective whose existence has heretofore been ignored'. And yet any 'ism' in an African context rarely stands alone. Considerations of gender interface with such ideological categories as imperialism, nationalism, communalism, or individualism. A woman is 'other' in ways that extend beyond her sex because the female experience is inevitably nuanced by influences of culture, race, and class.

An assessment of the African woman's experience through literature is complicated further when treatment of 'isms' undergoes the scrutiny of critical interpretation. Processed though structuralism, postmodernism, or one or another mode of feminism, each work of literature fosters an interplay between real life experience, creation, and interpretation. Here is a shifting ideological ground that gives rise to searching questions about the condition of women in African society and women's relationship to literary art.

Consider the most recurrent of these questions: How does the experience of African women differ from that of men? What is uniquely African about African women's literature? When can the portrayal of the African female experience be considered an expression of feminism? The interrogation serves up a range of answers. In response to the first question, Katherine Frank ascribes a universal social experience to African women, grounded in 'the inherent sexism of traditional African culture' (1982: 478). Elsewhere Brown (1981), Davies (1986), Jones (1987), Little (1980), Miller (1986), and

Ward (1990) posit an African social reality that is multivalent and evolutionary, arguing that women are shaped by many sources. Fredric Jameson (1986) answers the second question by situating African literature in the class of all Third World literatures. Their common project, he suggests, is to create national allegories in which they portray themselves as 'other' in relation to dominant capitalist nations. V. S. Mudimbe (1985) proposes that 'African literature' does not in fact exist but has been 'invented' in the process of organizing literary discourse. When African art is set apart in this way, its continuity with the cultural mainstream is obscured. To the third question some observers suggest that linking a feminist perspective and African literature is illogical because of 'an irremediable antagonism between the African woman's identity as an African and as a woman' (Frank 1982: 492), or because 'female characters are enclosed in the . . . stereotypes of a male tradition, their human potential buried in shallow definitions of their sex' (Stratton 1988: 147). Other critics prefer to examine 'the African feminist consciousness', which admits a whole range of cross-cultural concerns, including positive aspects of polygyny and the extended family, the common struggle with African men against foreign exploitation, the African woman's traditional self-reliance, and so on (Davies 1986, Cobham 1985).

What many commentators overlook is that in Africa the woman's voice – a 'sweeter' voice – has not lain dormant suddenly to be unleashed by the world of print. It has spoken for centuries in an unbroken chain of verbal creations, some of which were gradually transmuted into the written word. Because in traditional Africa woman reigned supreme as the giver and sustainer of life, she met the most urgent requirements of the family unit and underscored her concern in creations of verbal art. She soothed her newborn with rocking tunes, composed verses to praise a son, sang bride's laments at her daughter's marriage, and instructed children through traditional tales. In this way she became a medium for the words of tradition. By recreating ancient images on behalf of her loved ones, she moved them to a sense of well-being and promoted harmony in her domestic domain.

'Sweet' in many African languages connotes a cluster of ideas that embrace notions of happiness, harmony, pleasantness, grace, and charm. The application is broad, for 'sweet' refers less to the various qualities inherent in things than to the particular human response these qualities elicit. To say, 'This is sweet,' is to claim that a thing affects men and women in a positive, deeply personal, and wholly satisfying way. Sweet things thrive best in the nurturing intimacy of the household, where they feed directly on the pulse of human life. Good food is 'sweet'; so, too, a visit from a friend, a private moment with a lover, a soft affecting voice, a well-executed story or song.

In her literary representation the African woman evolves from a past stamped with a domestic sweetness. The image is harnessed to notions of collective harmony and well-being. Traditional Somali poet Raage Ugaas takes up this theme in a lament about his dead wife. Without her his life is without sense or direction, and he is 'left bereft of my house and shelter', 'taken from the chessboard [of life]', 'borne on a saddle to a distant and desolate place' (Okpewho 1985: 164). Modern authors continue to use sweetness as a touchstone in their presentation of the woman's image. The woman symbolizes a newly independent Africa, at times as a nurturing mother, at others as a vigorous partner who braves the world's dangers to soothe the weak. Throughout these characterizations, it is the woman's voice that bears direct witness to her condition. Occasionally it turns strident. Mocking verses, work songs, political ballads, satirical festival tunes, and women's society songs have given ample expression to the aches particular to the female sex. Modern Nigerian playwright Zulu Sofola entitled her domestic comedy *The Sweet Trap* (1977), using 'sweet' sardonically to describe four middle-class households dominated by husbands who create discord by ruling with an iron hand. Ghana's Ama Ata Aidoo named her collection of short stories *No Sweetness Here* (1970) to underscore the bitterness of a woman's life without choices. By employing a conscious aesthetic of the 'anti-sweet', women artists play on the expectation of sweetness to expose human error and restore social balance. Such expressions fall into the literary preserve of irony, which, for all its appearance of challenging the norm, casts words into a context where they hover ambiguously between sincerity and mockery; irony leaves the ideal sweetness intact.

And intact it remains. More than 60 women are currently recognized as serious authors across the African continent, and they have been joined by male writers in giving treatment to women-centred themes. In many of these works the women's condition serves as a barometer for measuring social health. Writers draw this equation in countless ways. A mother stands for traditional African society straining to uphold its standards against the corroding influence of the West. A wife reduced to servitude represents the cruelty of badly managed polygamy. A prostitute exhibits the aberrant individualism fostered by social exploitation. Behind the wrongs that women suffer looms the specter of social disruption. Often female protagonists deploy their energy, doing battle to restore life's sweetness, either head-on in the manner of Ousmane Sembène's revolutionaries or in the probing style of Bessie Head's psychic changelings.

The women's voice, then, tells the story of a sweet feminine image evolving in response to social change. This chapter will trace this image from its roots in traditional oral forms, through transitional expressions that bridge speech and writing, and conclude with the searching debate that engages modern voices in a reassessment of women's roles.

Women and the spoken arts

African audiences, as a general rule, think of recreations of traditional lore as 'beautiful' or 'good' to the degree in which they meet aesthetic expectations and persuade listeners of social truths. A good artist, one who is both affecting and clear, needs to have a thorough command of traditional techniques, themes, characters, and images. At the same time she (or he) must be sensitive to the make-up and interests of the audience; successful performances can shape individual minds, bring them into line with prevailing attitudes, and by their lessons prevent social disorder.

In the past, though somewhat less regularly in the present, prose forms such as legends and tales equipped young people with a basic education. Bamana-born Madame Aoua Kéita, once such a listener, recounts vivid memories of stories told during village evenings in her autobiography, *Femme d'Afrique*:

> Very often they involved good and bad children, courageous men and lackeys, liars and truth-tellers, miracle-workers and misers, domestic animals endowed with speech, ceremonies held by wild beasts, and so on. These tales always ended with the triumph of the good or courageous characters over the rest. They always ended with admonitory warnings in which goodness, generosity, courage, and straightforwardness were in all cases strongly emphasized (Kéita 1975: 16; my translation).

These were not idle lessons for the young Aoua, who later led a woman's resistance movement that called for the independence of French Equatorial Africa. She drew her followers from among the women she cared for as a midwife but took her moral strength from the stories she had heard years before.

These story images made a tangible impression on juvenile minds across the continent, attracting boys and girls equally. The performance of certain narrative types might be closely associated with one sex or the other. For example, women performers are widely linked with young people's fictional tales, while accounts told for truth might in custom – if not in practice – be reserved for men. Indeed, across and within cultures these divisions remain in reality quite fluid.

More important to Aoua than the sex of the storyteller was no doubt the courage and determination of certain women who peopled the tales. Heroines who restore balance, or sweetness, to society are a regular feature of many traditions. The Yoruba tell about Moremi, and the Nguni about Nongqause (Dhlomo 1935), who both made great personal sacrifices to save their people from foreign incursion. The power these heroines wield is rarely political. Absent is the bullish, warring spirit typical of such masculine heroes as Chaka or Sundiata. Rather, the heroine's force seems to emanate from a superior moral conscience aided by an extraordinary intelligence and zeal.

A fine example of this uniquely feminine style of heroism appears in a traditional saga created over 17 days by a Xhosa storyteller and diviner, Mrs Mazithathu Zenani. Her epic explores three generations of characters, each with a woman at the center (Scheub 1977). In it the girl Mityi, chief protagonist, fuses these parts into a single narrative thread.

The story opens with the young orphan Mityi being threatened by a hostile grandmother. Winning the protection of a magnificent ox, the girl in time escapes into the veld, taking with her the ox's magical, all-providing horns. One night she uses them to build a fine homestead. The people of a nearby village conclude that the act is a miracle and that the homestead must be God's residence. Their chief has died without a male heir, and they set out for the homestead to seek God's advice. Mityi announces that God has advised them to make his daughter Mityi their chief. It is unusual for a woman to take such a title, but they accept her because it is God's will. Mityi's horns supply the people with homes, cattle, social institutions – in short, a whole way of life. She becomes the founder of Xhosa civilization and, in a final act, she establishes a male chieftaincy by passing power slowly to her shy and awkward husband.

Myths across the continent credit women with the founding of civilizations long before men established their present administrative supremacy. Later on, when men take charge, it is still women – the force behind social order – who intervene when things go wrong to put them right again. The Ondo Yoruba create a fictional romance about one such heroine. A king has sired 12 sons, and fearing financial ruin from the brideprice he will pay for their future wives, he resolves to sacrifice the brothers to the newborn, if she is a girl. A daughter is born and the king's wife secretly helps her sons escape into the forest. Some years later the heroine learns the story of her birth and resolves to reunite the family. She undertakes a treacherous journey into the forest and sets up a household for the young men. Unwittingly she plucks the 12 flowers containing their souls and undergoes a seven-year ordeal of silence to save them. The joyful band is finally reunited and once again woman is the agent of harmony in a domestic world disrupted by a failure of masculine insight (LaPin 1977: II, 9–48).

Heroines are superordinary by definition, but the vast majority of female protagonists are more recognizably human. Story plots often turn on conflicts between co-wives, marital infidelities, courtship, child-rearing – anything in short that touches on everyday feminine experience in a traditional setting. 'Don't be jealous in your husband's house,' the performer will admonish. 'Treat your co-wife's children as if they were your own', 'Don't marry a man against the advice of your parents'. Women, the stories suggest, are more likely to achieve happiness if they follow the guidelines tradition hands down.

Routine perceptions of women enter oral tradition and harden into normative images that shape expectations of feminine behavior. Male storytelling among the Hausa, for example, offers few positive characterizations of women; owing perhaps to a religious or masculine bias, the tales are replete with female figures who pose a danger to the community (Skinner 1969: xv-xvii). Yet when these stories of nefarious females are compared with variants from nearby cultures, one often finds the women's places taken up by mischief-making men.

One good example of character switch is a Hausa tale depicting a girl who marries a young man against the wishes of her parents.

She resolves to murder her mother with the boy's knife, and over his objections accomplishes the deed. Together they escape into the bush. In a parallel sequence the girl dies, and an eagle comes to asks the boy's permission to feast on the flesh. When the boy refuses, the eagle gives him some magic feathers to revive the girl but warns, 'Do not put your trust in women'. Once revived, the girl takes a slave as a lover and compounds her evil by passing the feathers on to him (Tremearne 1913: 326–33). In a Yoruba version of the same tale, the plot turns on jealousy and betrayal between two male friends, not on the unreliable nature of women.

As carriers of oral tradition, then, women do more than participate in the transmission of their images, they also exercise their prerogatives as oral artists to control audience attitudes toward their sex. Feminine personalities come alive in skilled impersonations by women performers. A gifted storyteller learns to assume the roles of her characters by achieving subtle changes in her voice, posture, or the expression on her face. In a performance about two rival co-wives, for example, the artist may deftly shift back and forth between the humble, solicitous junior wife and her arrogant, imperious senior. One speaks with downcast eyes and a tremulous voice, the other in a booming, strident tone. At a passionate moment the dramatized 'face' of the senior wife may contort into an angry rictus of hate, while the body of the storyteller swells with the force of her anger.

Women performers further embellish, enliven, and invent to bring fresh light on characters and themes. Mrs Mazithathu Zenani, who created Mityi's adventure, is a feminist storyteller who, by peopling her narratives with large numbers of 'rudderless' men, tips the balance in favor of women (Scheub 1977: 69). In a similar vein, a powerful Yoruba market trader, Alice Oyedola, once gave a feminist interpretation to a female character from a story a man in her village had told weeks before. The man's account presented an elder so staggered by the beauty of a young, passive woman that he begins a relentless campaign to win the girl. He fails, but only because the girl's passive and witless indifference dilutes his flagging desire. Alice Oyedola's version developed the same plot, but she portrayed the girl as a shrewd, independent trader who had made a handsome profit at a young age. In this account, she refuses the elder's proposal outright, preferring a businesswoman's freedom to the dull life of an elder's 'parlor' wife.

Women use verse – chanted or sung – in addition to prose to become spokespeople for their own sex by shaping literary materials to fit feminine-centered themes. Such poetic performances range from private ruminations to full-blown public displays. Several generations ago unmarried Zulu girls mastered the *umakhweyana*, a bow instrument, as a means of sharing their deeply felt stirrings of love with female relatives and friends:

I am burning with the long grass! . . .
I do not see the sun. . . .

Love is playing with me.
Love is hurling me onto the cliffs.

(Joseph 1987: 107)

Certain poetic genres have a demanding technique that often requires additional training and study. Poetry is specialized and thus grants women more opportunity to achieve status as experts in verbal art. Bound up with occupational or special interest groups, songs mark life transitions and important events and so define biological and social roles. At Limba memorial ceremonies in Sierra Leone, women instruct and entertain with a variety of dancing songs (Finnegan 1970: 98). At Hausa marriage dances young girls were famed for singing verses filled with sexual innuendo, to the accompaniment of erotic mime. Sarcastic 'reed' songs permit Khoisan women to criticize the errant ways of others (Finnegan 1970: 98). The wives of Fon chiefs practiced group performances in praise of their husbands (Herskovits 1938: II, 322), while female eulogists among the Hausa were specially trained in the praises of kings (Smith 1957: 27). Even in modern times, fresh poetic expressions embellish new contexts. Zinc roofing parties, school sporting events, and political rallies are natural occasions for the celebration and commentary that flow from the sweet words of women's songs.

Sometimes a woman will distinguish herself in one of these poetic genres and gain fame for her expertise. Anyone who spends time in an African village is likely to hear such remarks as 'Fatima is an excellent singer of wedding songs,' or 'Mama Tunde chants praise poetry (*oriki*) more sweetly than anyone else'. In some communities these stars are elevated to a near-professional status. Among the Ila and Tonga of Zambia, for example, *impango* song performances are the work of a semi-professional hand. At one time every woman was expected to develop a personal repertoire of these songs, but it was understood that only a few singers were also gifted composers. Typically a woman would first air her ideas with her friends, and then they would all together call on an expert *impango* artist and sing their oral 'rough draft'. For several days this expert would privately embellish and prune. Her 'editing' done, she would call the group back and organize several after-dinner rehearsals. Once it was learned, the song would revert to its original owner. Thereafter, whenever she forgot an important line, her friends were able to assist her (Finnegan 1970: 269–70).

An *impango* composer might receive a sixpence or a bit of tobacco for her service, but in the western Sudan women working as professional praise-singers and historians command a higher price. *Maroka*, or praise singers among the Hausa, include women performers who specialize in poetry honoring women. Malinke, Bamana, and Wolof griot traditions embrace a variety of women artists. Elsewhere, women may practice these arts professionally by virtue of occupation or status. Cult priestesses, herbalists, diviners, and midwives become performers whenever their role requires training in a body of verse.

149

In general, however, women are unspecialized, domestic poets. Their songs and verses are learned and reproduced informally at home as part of daily life. Any time women congregate around a grinding stone, delight in a new child, welcome a new wife into the household, or gather children beside an evening fire, they may embellish the event with the spontaneous sweetness of song. Poetic forms most frequently associated with women center naturally on the household. Lullabies, praise poems, courting songs, bride's laments, and dirges are examples of oral genres that validate and give meaning to important moments in the human life cycle. From infancy, a child is soothed with his praise name when he cries, nursed to the cadence of incantations, bounced to catchy tunes during play on his mother's lap. In the Dogon country of Mali a rhythmic lullaby entertains a child whose busy mother has left him tied to a minder's back. There, his little oval bottom sits perched, like a chicken egg:

Where has the little one's mother gone?
Gone to draw water
Not yet back from drawing water
Gone to pound baobab leaves
Not yet back from pounding leaves
Gone to prepare a meal
Not yet back from preparing the meal
On the cliff, on the cliff, hangs a chicken egg!
(Griaule 1938: 226; my translation)

In some parts of Africa the transmission of praises for family members is a feminine duty. Praise poems are society's way of giving a person definition. Verses link the subject to an ancestral history and at the same time draw attention to distinguishing traits. Here, in a Dinka praise poem from the Sudan, a bride exhibits a joyful absorption in the child she has made. She sings for herself as much as for the child, for he has granted her a new status, that of 'Mother-of-one':

O son, you will have a warrior's name and be a leader of men.
And your sons, and your son's sons, will remember you long
after you have slipped into darkness. . . .
O my child, now indeed I am happy.
Now indeed I am a wife –
No more a bride, but a Mother-of-one.
[My man's] soul is safe in your keeping, my child,
and it was I, I who have made you.
(Brooks 1974: 234–35)

Poetry is also an integral part of courtship. Forty years ago among the Luo of Kenya, girls of marriageable age still courted their young men in groups by visiting the youths' meeting houses at night. En route to the rendezvous, their insistent, bird-like voices could be heard across the fields as they sang special love songs called *oigo*. On arrival the singing continued to the accompaniment of men's reed flutes. The songs, which the girls composed out of traditional motifs, anticipate marriage by making subtle references to physical love. The following example takes as its central image a bell, 'probably,' explained Mr Owuor who collected the songs, 'a ceremonial bell hanging on the reed walls of the grain store, which the young would be forbidden to touch' (Owuor 1967: 51). Yet in a second sense the bell becomes a sexual image, an avenue for procreation and harvest among men and women:

> The *ree* for Ameli, daughter of Omolo,
> She is the Achichi who goads the encircling crowd . . .
> Shaking the bell
> The one who dares to shake the bell,
> It's the naughty one who loves to tickle the bell;
> Tickling the bell.
> I dare you to tickle the bell,
> The forbidden bell. . . .

(Owuor 1967: 53)

Marriage follows courtship in the life cycle, and harvest time is a preferred moment in many African communities for taking marriage partners. The romantic spirit, brought on by the expectation of leisure and plenty, spills into the entire region. Among the Kikuyu of Kenya, the sweet voice gives way to jovial satire as men and women assemble in the fields to assail one another in turn with mocking verses filled with erotic abuse (Ngugi 1977: 148). In Mali the Dogon enliven the fonio harvest with a similar jocular exchange. Women tease men about the painful ordeal of circumcision and ridicule male sexual desire (Calame-Griaule 1965: 303–5).

Death closes the life cycle, and at funeral ceremonies women are the most frequent singers (Finnegan 1970: 148). At Akan burials, women soloists chant dirges to mourn and eulogize the dead. Every woman is expected to achieve competence in this literary mode as part of her social upbringing. Here, a mourner laments the loss of her mother by portraying a home robbed of sweetness through the absence of her nurturing presence:

> O mother, I am struggling; all is not well as it appears. . . .
> The god *opem* has failed; the gourd of charms has won.
> O mother, there is no branch above which I could grasp.
> Mother, if you would send me something, I would like parched corn
> So that I could eat it raw if there were no fire to cook it.

(Nketia 1969: 196)

Transition: traditional heroines in print

The heroines of tradition, reshaped for generations by the bodies and minds of successive performers, in time became material for the medium of print. A continuity of spirit informed the transition. Often, these writers viewed their task as that of an oral artist recreating old images in a written mode. And yet, because the new medium encouraged individuality of expression, authors learned to experiment with traditional forms and themes. In his episodic novel *The Brave African Huntress* (1958), Amos Tutuola transformed the romantic Yoruba saga of the girl rescuing her 12 brothers into a highly charged adventure story about Adebisi, who saves her four brothers vanished on a hunting trip. By discovering the cause of their disappearance, she will preserve others from the same fate. More important, as her father's only remaining child, she must prove her mettle so that 'hunters will not die out in the family' (p. 14). Adebisi's bellicose spirit contrasts boldly with the patient suffering of the traditional heroine who inspired her. The 'huntress' confronts the monsters of the forest world with lusty, masculine drive. She drinks alcohol, enjoys the male prerogative of administrative power, and, like certain men, abuses both. In her zeal for dangerous living, this superwoman is only minimally community-conscious. Rather, she is a metaphor for the self-willed female who exercises her personality to the furthest limits. The outrageous product of a fancy gone riot, she adds a new dimension to the literary exploration of traditional sweetness.

It would be fair to say that among the heroines of early African literature must figure the women writers themselves. Evidence suggests that a tradition of women's poetry flourished in the western Sudan from the eighteenth century onward. Hauwa, mother of the famed Usman dan Fodio, won a wide literary reputation among the scholars and teachers (*mallams*) of Sokoto, and her son argued for women's education.

'One of the root causes of the misfortunes of this country,' he wrote, 'is the attitude taken by Malams who neglect the welfare of their womenfolk . . . How can these Malams allow their wives, daughters, and slave women to remain lost in ignorance . . .' (Dan Fodio, *Nur-al-albab*, unpublished, cited in Boyd 1986: 128). Dan Fodio's three wives similarly fashioned intricate verse forms in Hausa, Fula, and Arabic in order to defend the caliphate and promote the importance of education. Fadima, his granddaughter, committed some of her poems to the theme of women's rights:

> Listen to me, Evil doers. . . .
> Husbands should treat their wives
> properly and give them their entitlements
> otherwise they will be punished.
>
> (cited in Boyd 1986: 138)

For women writers of the West African coast old tales furnished a natural starting point for rethinking the woman's role. Flora Nwapa's novels *Efuru* (1969) and *Idu* (1970), for example, retain the flavor of Igbo imagery by putting it literally into English. Nwapa's lively dialogues recall the dramatized interactions of characters in oral tales. Her real attention, however, is centered on characters and themes, and most especially on nonconforming heroines who seek happiness despite their failure to bear children or behave in prescribed feminine ways. Nwapa the storyteller leaps beyond the old saws about a woman's proper conduct and anticipates the feminist literature of the next decade.

Ghana's women authors Efua Sutherland and Ama Ata Aidoo similarly undertook the earnest appraisal of feminine potential in a masculine-oriented world. Their common vehicle was a popular narrative about the proud virgin who spurned her village suitors and chose a stranger who ruined her life. Of her play *Anowa* (1970), set in the nineteenth century, Aidoo says, 'It's more or less my own rendering of a kind of . . . legend, because, according to my mother who told me the story, it is supposed to have happened. The ending is my own and the interpretations I give to the events that happen are mine' (Duerden and Pieterse 1974: 23).

Anowa is marked from girlhood by an uncommon destiny. Six years after puberty, she at last chooses a feckless husband against her parents' advice. Her years of toil and self-sacrifice make her husband a rich trader, but she is conscience-stricken by his trade in slaves. Anowa assumes the guilt for their ill-gotten wealth, and her 'restless soul' (Aidoo 1970: 28) leaves her barren. Worse, her husband is challenged by her competence, and she laments: 'Someone should have taught me how to grow up like a woman . . . here, they let a girl grow up as she pleases until she is married. And then she is like any woman anywhere: in order for her man to be a man, she must not think, she must not talk . . .' (p. 52). In what Aidoo calls a 'Freudian ending', Adowa's husband sends her away and in so doing knocks out the only prop that supports him. He shoots himself, and Anowa, alone and without choices, commits suicide by drowning.

In Sutherland's play *Foriwa* (1967) the same heroine returns, but in a happier mode. The drama unfolds in a backward village, whose progressive queen mother is spurned by reactionary elders. 'When you restricted women with taboos,' says one to the ancestors, 'you damned well knew what you were doing' (1967: 38). Against this background Foriwa, the queen's daughter, refuses to marry her suitors, who stand for the selfish interests that flourish in the old structure. She joins the cause of Labaran, a stranger, who proposes to build a school. The emboldened queen blasts the elders' refusal '[Are we] unwilling to open new paths ourselves because it demands of us thought, and goodwill, and action?' (p. 50). Foriwa achieves what Anowa could not. A harmonious conjunction of old and new restores sweetness to a tired, embattled society.

Transitional literature also includes Okot p'Bitek's *Songs*. Adapted from Acholi (Ugandan) women's laments and mocking verses, the songs comprise a series of poetic works that turn on the theme of domestic change. 'I found the [traditional] poetry was rich, the oral literature was full-blooded,' the writer said (Duerden and Pieterse 1974: 150). *Song of Lawino*, first in his series, records the voice of a traditional woman fighting for her husband's affection against the corroding influences of his Western education and modern mistress.

The robust dignity of the traditional form is perfectly suited to the ardent message that bursts out from her wounded heart. Lawino is ashamed of her husband's strange behavior, not for herself, but for him:

> All I ask
> Is that you give me a chance
> Let me praise you
> Son of a chief!

> (p'Bitek 1966: 215)

Lawino is a woman; she is also the personification of traditional Africa. Indignant, she mocks her rival Clementine, the embodiment of foreign sophistication. Powdered, lipsticked, and bewigged, she 'looks like a Guinea fowl' (p. 22), 'head huge like that of the owl' (p. 24), so slim 'You can hear the bones rattling' (p. 26). Against Tina's grotesque sterility, Lawino sings the virtue of Acholi womanhood: erect breasts, a bright mind, shining skin, body tattoos gleaming 'like stars on a black night' (p. 34).

But change, whatever its ills, must come for women and for society's view of them. If Tina is artificial, Lawino – unable to imagine herself in any role other than in the service of her 'master and husband' (p. 205) – is enslaved by the tradition she extols. And so the husband lifts his voice, and his song (*Song of Ocol* 1970) calls for her self-liberation: 'Sister/Woman of Acoliland/Throw down the pot/With its water' (p. 38). Ocol longs for a wife who is free and at ease with her personhood: 'Woman of Africa/Whatever you call yourself/Whatever the bush poets/Call you/You are not/A wife!' (p. 43).

Modern expressions: women seek a new place

With the advent of a literature wholly conceived and composed for the press, the African heroine underwent further examination. Traditional images of sweetness survived in echoes of old songs and tales. They filled many early novels and poems as complements to nostalgic accounts of precolonial life. Yet close upon the heels of this 'golden age' literature followed a wave of feminist rebellion. Its credo was the 'antisweet'. As women began to enter the ranks of published authors, they took the old images, pried them apart, examined them critically, and frequently denied them outright. Wives, mothers, young girls, and courtesans moved through a world charged with fresh possibilities and awakened to inner powers that would forever alter their sense of self. A new 'sweetness' was coming into being, one that would readjust the inequalities perceived in the old. In Hegelian fashion, the old synthesis would give way to antithesis before engendering a vision of the woman's new place.

Men in the early years were usually the first educated and hence the first authors. They populated their literature with women, but in an idealized mode. Woman was mother-nurturer and, by extension, symbol of a sweeter, more secure Africa which the educated man left behind. Camara Laye of Guinea, for example, opens his lyric, autobiographical novel *The African Child* (1959) with a praise poem to his mother:

O Daman. O my mother, you who bore me upon your back, you who gave me suck, you who watched over my first faltering steps . . . how I should love to be beside you once again, to be a little child beside you!

Black woman, woman of Africa, O my mother, let me thank you; thank you for all that you have done for me, your son, who, though so far away, is still so close to you!

(Laye 1959: 1)

The Malinke woman, says Laye, enjoyed 'fundamental independence' and 'personal pride' (p. 58). Daman's presence anchored each passage in his life. 'My mother, by the mere fact of her presence . . . saw to it that everything was done according to her own set of rules' (p. 56). She protested about his departure for France: 'Any excuse is good enough for you to run away from your mother!' (p. 155).

Meanwhile, the few woman writers of the early period fit their art to the same idealized view of Africa in its physical, cultural, and philosophical dimensions. Pioneer poet Gladys Casely-Hayford Africanized her style by turning to Krio language and themes and composed eulogistic poetry for an African continent built to meet divine requirements: 'Freetown, when God made thee, He made thy soil alone/Then threw the rich remainder in the sea . . .' ('Freetown' in Casely-Hayford 1967: 6).

Soon the political conflicts of independence and its aftermath began to tarnish the ideal. If woman equalled Africa in her literary persona, she was recast as the symbol of an ailing continent. Mozambique's Noémia de Sousa created a tortured characterization of woman to portray her country's long struggle for political freedom: Her poem 'If You Want to Know Me' (1972) echoes a recurrent theme of *négritude* poets who read the marks of an anguished, paralyzed continent in the iconography of an African mask:

This is what I am
empty sockets despairing of possessing life
a mouth torn open in an anguished wound
huge hands outspread and raised in imprecation and in threat
a body tattooed with wounds seen and unseen
from the harsh whipstrokes of slavery. . . .

(de Sousa 1975: 85–86)

In a similar way, Mother undergoes distortion and reappears as traitor in the dislocated world of Congolese poet Tchicaya U'Tamsi. In his verse woman is a surrealist symbol that attracts a constantly shifting set of values. She is Africa, the fertilizing waters, the moon. Yet running like a cross-current through these idealizations is the image of a treacherous and diminished being. Dehumanized by colonial disruption, woman becomes the sterile temptress, the agonized mother, the abandoned wife. 'I can console,' she says, 'I can betray' (U'Tamsi 1970: 82).

Playwright Athol Fugard, always searing in his criticism of South African apartheid, added a woman to his list of political victims in his grimly humorous play *Boesman and Lena* (1969). Lena, an 'angular, gaunt cipher of poverty' (p. 1), is locked into a marriage that mirrors the fruitless victimization characteristic of apartheid rule. Boesman tortures Lena. He beats her. He is bitterly contemptuous of her appearance and speech. He wilfully deprives her of sympathy and compassion. Lena's counter-weapon in the battle is her stubborn refusal to give in. She bombards Boesman with hard questions: 'Why must you hurt me so much? What have I really done?' Desperate for human warmth, she seizes on an old Xhosa man and gives up her food, wine, and place in their temporary shelter in exchange for permission to house him overnight. The man manages, despite barriers of language and culture, to recognize and repeat her name. This opened channel of human solidarity and exchange is a challenge to Boesman's private claim to Lena; it undermines his whole reality. For Lena the victim is the 'only real thing in his life' (p. 44), and that is why he hits her.

The erosion of feminine well-being was also a popular subject for women writers, and they initially saw it from the vantage point of their domain, the home. If the world was changing, so too was marriage, the family, and notions of women's work. Curiously, romantic love became a focal point in the budding feminist debate; it challenged family authority in marriage and extolled the virtues of individual freedom. The idea was new to African literature. Traditional folktales had argued that private desire, fulfilled without public sanction, isolated young people, made them vulnerable, and thereby posed a threat to social cohesion. Like the transitional women writers on the West African coast, East African women took issue with this notion. Charity Waciumba, Jane Bakaluba, and Hazel Mugot would follow Kenya's Grace Ogot, whose early short story, 'The Rain Came' (1964) reversed the old view by adapting the style of the traditional storyteller to a narrative in which a girl's defiant love is equated with courage and free will.

Early examples of self-willed romantic heroines also filled the pages of popular chapbooks sold in Nigeria's Onitsha Market. Their exploits often provoked disapproving clucks from their narrators, but old-fashioned moralizing could not dull their vibrant charm. With Cyprian Ekwensi's novel *Jagua Nana* (1961) the Onitsha heroine was transformed into a brassy, good-hearted, but heart-breaking prostitute who hurtles through dangerous encounters with picaresque abandon. At 45, Jagua is still sure that 'she could outclass any girl who did not know what to do with her God-given female talent' (1975 ed.: 6). A hard-loving woman, Jagua forsakes romantic security for the freedom of the street, feeding her sense of sexual power as much as sapping her clients of their wealth. In her trade, she finds an equality with men unthinkable in any sanctioned feminine role (p. 101).

Jagua is a complex character. Her dizzying array of traits ranges from amorality to political activism to altruism. Yet tragedies mark her life. She grieves for the children she cannot bear, for the murder of her young lover Freddie by her older lover Uncle Taiwo, for the disappointment she brings to her churchman father. And when she returns home to her village Ogabu, she grieves for her newborn who stays a mere two days before he dies. Transformed by this sweet moment of motherhood, Jagua resolves to stay at home and become a trader. 'I don' wan' to be me ol' self who suffer too much,' she says (p. 192), and awakens to the knowledge that the 'equality' she sought was of the wrong kind.

Elsewhere, male authors chose 'free' women to realize images of feminine potential unlocked by social change. The personal inde-pendence of prostitutes and courtesans often propelled them to politically significant acts. Penda's appearance in Ousemane Sembène's *God's Bits of Wood* (1970) serves to express the growing political consciousness of women in French West Africa during the 1947–48 railroad strike. Faced with shortages of money, food, and water, the women are spurred on to a series of revolutionary acts. Fifty-year-old Ramatoulaye, for example, finds new strength 'born beside a cold fireplace in an empty kitchen' (1970: 74), and openly defies her collaborator brother by murdering his fat and thieving ram. Street battles break out between the women and the colonial police. In Thiès the feminine revolt is organized into a mass march that gives dramatic shape to the 'different countenance' women have assumed (p. 33).

It is Penda the prostitute who leads the women on the march, passes out their rations, settles their quarrels, and urges them on. In her new role she forces even the men to respect her. She and her women have done more than their men could do. Penda is killed by the police as the women enter Dakar and dies a hero of the revolution. Strike leader Bakayoko tells a dreamy schoolgirl admirer: 'You will probably never be worth as much as Penda, and I know what she was worth . . . There are many ways of prostituting yourself, you know. . . . what about you?' (p. 221).

From the 1970s onward the wrenching battle between private choice and social limits would undergo hard scrutiny as writers – notably women writers – studied its effect on women's lives. It was clear that, while grand revolutionary gestures could address big issues, fine tuning was required to meet individual needs. Noémia de Sousa describes one sister weary of the double burden of family and war: 'Who has strangled the tired voice/of my forest sister?/. . . leashed with children and submission . . ./One child on her back, another in her womb/-always, always, always!' (de Sousa 1984: 161). Women would retire from the national battlefront to rearm morally and mentally for the fight behind domestic lines. The struggle would in time assume a greater purpose, 'pointing out to society where some of the inequities lie and thereby . . . involved in a struggle to reshape society' (Davies 1986: 13).

Undergirding this fledgling movement was a redefinition of the 'sweeter' voice. Woman, a concrete product of biology, society, and culture, became the stuff of a new 'African female aesthetic'. The new art was born from the most visceral and honest of genres: the autobiography. Three autobiographical traditions merit attention, one from Senegal, one from South Africa, and a third from the prolific pen of a single Nigerian writer – Buchi Emecheta. Nearly all of these works focus on a common theme, namely, the interplay between women's destinies and the exercise of individual will.

Senegalese autobiographies are inevitably stamped by the way women respond to Islamic prescription. While Mariama Bâ was composing her exposé of women's inequality in *So Long a Letter* (1980, trans. 1981), 30-year-old Nafissatou Diallo was filling idle hours at work penning a pious, self-effacing account of an old-style Muslim upbringing. Her memoir, *A Dakar Childhood* (1979, trans. 1982), blends didacticism and humor to impress a young audience with the lost wisdom of the time when a woman's status and importance were assured by the Islamic ethic of mutual personal respect. This morality tale describes the gentleness of an adored patriarch who demands strict obedience from the headstrong tomboy writer Nafisi in order to unlock the girl's intellectual skills. In uncritical and nostalgic tones Diallo presents a young girl's perception of polygyny (her father's wife in another town is calmly accepted but never seen), courtship (she is thrashed for meeting a young man alone), marriage (for the nonworking woman an escape from boredom), and education (a solemn obligation).

This dutiful portrayal contrasts with the polemic of Bâ's indignant semi-autobiography featuring the widowed Ramatoulaye. Rama confesses in letters to her friend, Aissatou, that her married life – and indeed that of all Senegalese women – began with a wedding in which a woman 'gives up her personality, her dignity, becoming a thing in the service of the man who has married her . . .' (1981: 4). Her loneliness and poverty following her husband's death are eased by the generosity of Aissatou, for her friend has already resolved the injustice of polygyny by divorcing her husband rather than sharing him with a second wife.

Such personal freedom is joyless for women without friendship. In *Le Baobab fou* (1984) Ken Bugul (née Mariétou M'Baye) offers a deeply psychological account of her exile as a Senegalese student in Belgium. Her story parallels that of the young Camara Laye, but Ken loses her Senegalese mother's care at the age of five and eventually goes adrift without maternal love. She leaves her studies, has an abortion, and turns to a life of prostitution and drugs. Having failed at her attempt to create a new identity in a promised land, her writing is a therapy that permits her to reorder her life: 'I could not confide in anyone and so I put it all down on paper' (cited in Mortimer 1990: 167).

South African autobiography is shaped by apartheid. Miriam Tlali, for example, finds writing the sole battlefield available against the color bar. Her first book, *Muriel at Metropolitan* (1979), tells the tale of a gifted Coloured woman quickly promoted from clerk-typist at Metropolitan Radio to become a writer of hire purchase contracts for nonwhite customers. Her loyalty is stretched between her employer's self-interest and the welfare of poor Africans. More often than not, her customers forfeit their goods and payments because they cannot meet contract terms. Tlali's account transcends naive racial caricature by focussing on detailed vignettes of routine office encounters between members of various classes, races, and religions. Muriel's resignation from her good job at Metropolitan shows a singular act of will, but one underlain by the forgiving notion that even the oppressors are victims in a system grounded in social injustice.

A more political account is read in Emma Mashinini's autobiography, *Strikes Have Followed Me All My Life* (1991). Formerly the black female secretary of the South African Catering and Commercial Allied Workers Union, Mashinini describes the struggle for equality in the working class.

For most South African women writers, however, it has been on the psychological battleground that freedom from external limits is won. When society does not grant women the power to make choices, women must summon the courage to claim that right for themselves. The late Bessie Head, one of Africa's most gifted authors, traces one such struggle in her personal study, *A Question of Power* (1974). Elizabeth, Head's alter ego, is driven by the painful contradictions of race, sex, and power into a private world marked by a hallucinatory contest with two psychic figures. One is Dan, a very dark, sensual, and attractive man who overwhelms the insecure and self-doubting woman with a destructive masculine egotism. In her anguished psyche Dan vies for control against his male opposite, Sello, who holds the promise of compassion, love, and personal growth. Elizabeth's cure from madness rests on the choices she makes concerning these two kinds of masculine power. Either she will submit to the old cycle of oppressor–victim, or she will find happiness in Sello's scheme of universal harmony. She chooses harmony, not with Sello, but in a private alliance with her African home. In the end Elizabeth makes 'a final gesture of belonging', and places 'one soft hand over her land' (1974: 206).

Meanwhile, in Anglophone West Africa, Buchi Emecheta's maiden autobiographical work, *In the Ditch* (1972), would unleash a flow of feminist writings unrivalled elsewhere south of the Sahara. A true spokeswoman for her sex, Emecheta draws her images from the raw experience of her own life. Her recurrent theme is the fulfillment of individual destiny, a notion rooted in the traditional Igbo concept of *chi* or personal spirit. Her autobiographical novel *Second-Class Citizen* (1975), explores this theme in a story of feminine resilience. Here, Adah, a resolutely independent girl, acts with awesome determination when blocked from an important goal. Her husband Francis stereotypically wants – and receives – sex on demand, his wife's pay, minimal responsibility for his children, sexual freedom for himself, absolute fidelity from his wife, no feminine competition, and uncompromised obedience. Adah, who resolved at a tender age 'never in her life . . . to serve [her husband's] food on bended knee' (1977: 20), finds that she must serve him in ways that humiliate her far more. In London, her second-class status is compounded by her race. Life becomes an endless list of battles against prejudice, unwanted pregnancies, and her husband's increasing physical abuse. When Francis destroys the manuscript of her first book, she rents a separate apartment and sets about the task of building an individual life.

With *The Bride Price* (1976), Emecheta's conflict against an unwanted social destiny escalates to a struggle between reason and a conditioned female unconscious. In this novel, the girl Aku-nna ('Father's Wealth') uncritically accepts that the brideprice is the sole measure of her worth, and her elopement to Chike, her schoolmaster, deepens her crippled sense of duty. Chike has not paid the brideprice, and Aku-nna's life ebbs away, sapped, she believes, by her uncle's vengeful spirit.

The Slave Girl (1977) was followed in 1979 by *The Joys of Motherhood*. Here, with dogged irony, Emecheta tracks her theme through the entwined lives of two Lagos co-wives. Rivals for their husband's affection, both discover in the end that maternity is a destiny synonymous with servitude. Submissive and illiterate Nnu Ego proves to be a direct reincarnation of a certain Ojebeta, a slave woman who embodied the same spiritual destiny (*chi*). Nnu Ego eventually bears sons to her second husband; yet they do not offer the happiness or security she expected but rather abandon their country and condemn their mother to an impoverished old age. Meanwhile, her co-wife Adaku must address her own failure to perform her maternal duty and turns to prostitution and petty trade as alternate sources of livelihood.

Together with other women writers, Buchi Emecheta continues in her recent works to brandish a literary sword against the poverty of women's social destinies. *Double Yoke* (1982), *Naira Power* (1982), *Destination Biafra* (1982), and *The Family* (1989) broaden the drama against the backcloth of a larger and more modern context, which includes the damaging effects of misguided political and economic policy.

Recently many writers have similarly stepped beyond the private borders of autobiography to explore feminist themes against a national and international backcloth. Somalia's Nurrudin Farah offers an early example of psychological realism in the adventures of the young, pensive Ebla, who asserts her independence to escape an arranged Islamic marriage. Says Farah of the novel *From a Crooked Rib* (1970), 'I'm interested in an individual who has been denied what are his or her rights . . . in the struggle and in the relationships which form after that struggle' (Farah 1981: 81). Because such relationships are key to changing roles, works throughout the decade explore feminist stirrings in several ways: in the complex ties between heroines and their mothers, fathers, or powerful social figures; in the broad structures of inequality; and in the force of female solidarity within and across cultural frontiers. Here, the theme of marriage returns, not from the viewpoint of the bride but from that of mothers, aunts, friends, and mothers-in-law. Bessie Head's short story, 'Snapshots of a Wedding' (1977) studies the ambiguous status of the modern, educated wife sought after because of her earning power by a husband whose true affection rests with a traditional girl. Will this new kind of mate succeed in forging a path to happiness? Her aunt's exhortation '"Be a good wife! Be a good wife!"' leaves the future in doubt. Miriam Tlali examines modern polygyny within the conflicting values of two female generations in her tale 'Masechaba's Erring "Child"' (1989). Tholoana uprightly repels the advances of Ntate ('Father') Sam, husband to her friend Masechaba, only to be accused by the widow after his death: 'How could you be so cruel anyway? Ntate loved you so much. . . . He was nearly sobbing like a child when he told me' (p. 150). Here is a structure that scrambles the roles of mother, wife, father, and child.

Elsewhere mothers are viewed as social victims who exploit daughters by forcing them into unwanted marriages, sexual liaisons, or prostitution. In *Tu t'appelleras Tanga* [Tanga will be your name] (1988), Cameroon's Calixth Beyala weaves a chilling tale in which preteenage Tanga is sent to sell herself in the street by her impecunious, childlike mother. The girl is subjected to unspeakable suffering, and she describes her life as that of a 'beast of burden,' 'a hated black-skinned thing,' 'a child widowed of her childhood'. Stolen by a child-slaver as his unwilling bride, she escapes, falls ill, and is promptly arrested. The deranged French Jewish teacher Anna-Claude, with whom she shares her prison cell, assumes the dying girl's identity. 'Give me your story. I am your deliverance,' she says to the girl (p. 17); and to Tanga's mother who visits too late, she makes a solemn declaration of feminine solidarity, 'You have killed *us*, Madame' (p. 200; my translation and emphasis).

Marriage further serves as a metaphor for social decay brought about by forces of economic exploitation. The charged political play *I Will Marry When I Want* (1982) by Kenya's Ngugi wa Thiong'o and Ngugi wa Mirii draws an analogy between a marriage built on false hopes and unhealthy international alliances based on greed. Cameroon's Werewere Liking in *Orphée Dafric* (1981) combines the Orpheus myth with Bassa rituals of passage to explore the self-transformation of a weak and timorous groom (Orpheus), condemned to an underworld of poverty and bad government, into a disciplined suitor worthy of the resources symbolized by Madame Nyango, the African Eurydice.

Today, with increasing tempo, women authors demand social and political reform. In 'You Can't Get Lost in Cape Town' (1987), Zoe Wicomb weaves the tale of Sally Smit, who undergoes a back street abortion. As a black woman, she cannot choose to marry her English lover and is denied access to safe health care. Ama Ata Aidoo challenges policy priorities for family health in her poem about an infant's death: 'Now/we look out/ for/ homicidal governments/ who/ plan/ our death/ with concern/ with care/ and/ mercenary medicals . . ./ too busy doing nothing' ('Of "Maami Aba Okese": Born 1977, Died 1977,' in *Someone Talking to Sometime*, 1985: 100). Amina Sow Fall in *The Beggar's Strike* (1981) satirizes an ambitious health minister who clears begging cripples from city streets in order to encourage tourism and thereby secure a promotion. The beggars go on strike and scotch the plan by rejecting the pious gifts on which the minister's promotion depends.

If women authors seek increasingly to expose social ills, it is also women characters who inspire the fight. V. S. Mudimbe creates Ya or 'Sister' as an African everysister for his novel *Before the Birth of the Moon* (1976, trans. 1989). Calloused by injustice and war, Ya unwittingly inspires in men an authentic love which she reserves for her own sex: 'She couldn't see why all these men gave themselves the right to brutalize her every time they felt like it' (p. 146). Ya spies without guilt on her politician lover, supplants his wife, and serves his enemies. In a darkened world unlit by the sweet rhythms of the moon, her calculated and hardened submission proves her ultimate means to survive; for she wins by turning systems of repression inside out, out-brutalizing – by not caring – the very men who have brutalized her.

Elsewhere heroines choose a path to social reform that is more positive and direct, becoming forces that shape Africa's destiny. Revolutionary Estina Bronzario presides over the multicultural world of Sony Labou Tansi's *Les Sept Solitudes de Lorsa Lopez* (1985). The novel scrambles fact and fiction by transforming Congolese history into deconstructed ribald and farcical cartoon. Against a background of social, political, and cultural upheaval, Estina emerges as a 'Lady of Bronze', 'Toughest Among the Tough', and centers her battle on a single idea: only the dignity of woman will preserve the African spirit against the falsehood of received historical truths. Women are sources of life, creation, and bearers of tradition. They are responsible for maintaining the honor, well-being, stability, and harmony of the race. To make her point Bronzario rallies her women to launch a 'sexual strike'. She renames the town piazza after a woman brutally murdered by her lover. She has her tombstone inscribed with the words 'Prepared to live'. The lesson is that women must use new weapons beside their femininity to preserve society, for 'women are also men' (p. 120).

If Estina Bronzario's banner is unmistakably feminist, Hillela, the liberal Jewish girl from South Africa, inspires a revolt against the broad injustice of apartheid in *A Sport of Nature* (1987). Her creator, Nadine Gordimer, describes her as a 'spontaneous mutant' who is unconscious of the risks she runs by ignoring society's limits on sex and race. For Hillela, 'cause' is another word for 'love': 'Without a cause is without a home . . . without a reason to be' (p. 162). Undomesticated and unstoppable in the service of her cause, she becomes a valuable ally to the ANC and to the two African freedom fighters she weds. Hillela makes a personal destiny (a *chi*) of her quest for love and racial justice, and as the regal wife of an African head of state, she assumes the Igbo name Chimeka, 'God has made a good destiny'.

Hillela's story is about a white African woman. In these times the destinies of all women and all societies are intertwined. The new literature from Africa suggests that justice for women and justice for society are in many ways one and the same. Today the struggle has crossed national boundaries. Hillela joins the struggle for black equality; Werewere Liking chooses a French woman as her artistic collaborator; Tanga imparts her story and identity to the French Anna-Claude; Mariama Bâ studies with sympathy the injury of interracial marriage; Nadine Gordimer crosses cultures to apply the Igbo notion of *chi* to the life story of her protagonist. A new generation of women authors urge their women characters to be pilots of whole nations as well as their own lives. The successes of Estina Bronzario, Hillela, and Aissatou are literary creations made by women who demand the fulfillment of feminine potential. Their work anticipates the renewed sweetness that will come with a society shaped equally by men and women of all nations. Until that new 'golden age', it should be expected that the sweeter voice will for some time to come take on a sharper edge with repeated honing against the grindstone of modern life.

CHAPTER 9

Women's voluntary associations

Audrey Wipper

This chapter describes some bases of association among African women today outside their immediate domestic or family groups. Different traditional groups will be discussed in order to provide some background. The main aim, however, is to examine several types of present-day women's associations. Among these groups are (1) rural cooperatives and self-help groups, (2) occupational associations, (3) urban business enterprises, and (4) social welfare, church, and entertainment groups. Finally, the chapter looks at the rapid growth of women's organizations in the 1980s, and the increased attention paid to these groups by their own governments and by foreign donors.

I will concentrate on indigenous associations, many of which have their roots in traditional groups, and will exclude such Western-sponsored organizations as the YWCA, the Girl Guides, the Red Cross, and the University Women's Association. One main difference between traditional and present-day associations is that in the former, membership was largely ascribed; women automatically became members of a particular group because of birth, age, sex, or adoption into a kin or territorial unit. In contrast, membership in today's associations is largely voluntary; a woman chooses to join a particular group. A voluntary association is thus an organized, corporate group, in which a person chooses membership. Examples are drawn from various African countries but because of the author's work in Kenya, examples from there predominate.

Voluntary associations are important for a variety of reasons. Traditionally, women came together to promote their common economic, political, and social interests. Colonialism and urbanization, however, undermined many of these associations, leaving women in a much less powerful position than men (Ardener 1975, Boserup 1970: 53–60, Van Allen 1972, 1976). In the modern context, these associations help women adjust to urban life. They regulate and promote trade, extend credit, teach new social and occupational skills, and provide monetary and psychological support (Little 1973: 49–60). Furthermore, the persistence, variety, and number of these associations illustrate the reality of female bonding, and suggest that if anthropologists such as Lionel Tiger are to be consistent, they must argue that women, as well as men, are biologically programmed for bonding (Tiger 1969).

Some traditional groups

In traditional African societies, the bases of women's associations included kinship (membership in lineages), age (age-sets), gender (society-wide puberty rites, secret societies, and women's interest groups), and village-level dance or work groups. Because of the limitations of space, I will comment on only three kinds of groups that have particular interest for the modern era: work groups, women's interest groups, and secret societies. Traditional dance groups will be briefly discussed in the last section on Muslim women's associations.

Work groups

Women have traditionally engaged in cooperative efforts for the efficient cultivation and harvesting of their crops (Boserup 1970). Since women do most of the day-to-day farming, it is less onerous and more sociable for neighboring women to get together and share the time-consuming tasks. Work groups of perhaps a dozen women would farm one member's field one day and move on the next day to another member's. These groups often served wider political and social functions, providing women with organizational and affiliative bases for nonagricultural pursuits (Lambert 1956: 67, Stamp 1975–76).

Among the Kikuyu, *ngwatio* was the custom whereby women jointly cultivated each other's farms. This cooperative spirit was carried over into other aspects of their lives. *Matega* was the custom in which women would bring enough firewood to a woman who had just given birth to last until she was capable of collecting it again herself. The other women in the new mother's compound would provide food for the assisting group.

These cooperative work groups may decline as opportunities open up for wage employment (Bledsoe 1980: 121). The more isolated people are, the more involvement there is in these traditional groups. A decrease in group involvement occurred among the Kpelle of Liberia when work for cash became available. In Gban-su, an isolated village in northern Liberia, four hours from the nearest road and far from wage labor opportunities, work groups of 30 to 40 women planted rice. In Digei, equally distant from a road but closer to a labor center, it was common to see smaller groups of six to ten women, while in Haindii, near a road and to Bong Mine, women often planted rice individually, with the occasional help of friends and kin but not of large groups. Liberian women prefer wage work because it gives them more autonomy. They do not have to rely on the labor of others and commit themselves to a group for a whole season of planting or

165

harvesting. In Haindii people tended to join work groups as a last resort when they had no other viable alternative (Bledsoe 1980).

Interest groups

In some traditional societies women had considerable autonomy in such areas as farming, trading, markets, and female rites of passage. In these areas, women's groups made and enforced rules and regulations. This section will look at how the Igbo women of Nigeria and Kom women of Cameroon protected their interests, wielding effective sanctions not only over their own membership but over the entire community. Interestingly, their sanctioning procedures were transformed into political weapons that led to riots and rebellions against colonial rule.

'Sitting on' or 'making war'

In precolonial Nigeria, Igbo women's base of political power lay in their own gatherings, of which there were many kinds. These gatherings performed a wide range of social, economic, and political functions. The gatherings that performed the major role in women's self-rule, and which articulated their interests as opposed to those of men, were the village-wide meetings of all adult women based on common residence, which under colonialism came to be called *mikiri* or *mitiri* (from 'meeting') (Van Allen 1972: 169–70). *Mikiri* played an important role in women's daily self-rule, serving as a forum where they could air complaints about people breaking the rules. Women were used to protecting their own interests as farmers, traders, wives, and mothers, and if their requests for compliance with the rules were ignored, the offender was first warned and asked to mend his or her ways. If compliance was not forthcoming, then other tactics such as strikes, boycotts, force, and 'making war' were used.

For instance, if a man had mistreated his wife, she might employ the collective sanction, 'sitting on a man' or 'making war' against him. She would give a shrill cry, which brought other women to her compound. If they agreed with her complaint, the other women would settle on a time to meet at her husband's compound. The women dressed in the same attire: their heads were bound with ferns, symbolizing war, and their faces were smeared with ashes; they wore short loincloths, and carried sticks wreathed with young palm fronds. The sticks supposedly invoked the power of the female ancestors. They gathered at the offender's compound, usually at night, where they danced, sang derisive songs outlining their complaints, banged on his hut with their pestles, covered it with mud, and in extreme cases, destroyed it and 'roughed him up'. This raucous behavior was kept up until the man repented and promised to mend his ways. 'Making war' was the strongest sanction women had for punishing wrongdoers and for enforcing compliance with their rules and judgements. It was regarded by the community as a legitimate institution.

Anlu

Like the Igbo, Kom women of Cameroon had spheres of activity that fell under their jurisdiction. They, too, had a punishment that bore a strong similarity to 'sitting on' a man. *Anlu* was employed to punish men who committed certain offenses such as beating or insulting a parent, beating a pregnant woman, incest, causing the pregnancy of a nursing mother within two years of a previous birth, abusing old women, or seizing a person's genitals in a fight. An offended woman would summon other women with a high-pitched call. Upon hearing the call, other women would echo it, leave whatever they were doing, and go to her aid. A crowd would gather quickly, followed by a wild dance during which the offended woman would tell the gathering about the offense. The accused would state his case to the head woman of the compound, who would discuss the matter with the older women; they would decide on a course of action. If they decided he was guilty, they might accept his apologies and payment of a goat and fowl, and this would settle the case. If he were an habitual offender, a more drastic sanction was meted out.

On a set day, the women, dressed in pieces of men's clothing, painted their faces, covered themselves in leafy vines, and paraded to the offender's home around 5:00 a.m. There they danced, sang obscene and mocking songs, and defiled his compound by defecating and urinating in the water storage vessels. 'Vulgar parts' of the body were exhibited. If the man was present, he was pelted with stones or a type of wild fruit called 'garden eggs'. Then the women shed their vines and garden eggs in his compound, leaving some of each on the threshold as the *anlu* sign that its use had been banned. Sometimes they would prohibit the offender from visiting other compounds as well as forbidding people to visit him. If he fled to another compound or even to another village, *anlu* activity continued (Ardener 1975).

An offender could seldom endure this kind of treatment for more than two months. When he capitulated, he put the *anlu* vines around his neck and went to the women to plead for their pardon. If his pleas and the offered compensatory goods were accepted, the women took him naked to a stream and bathed him in a purification ritual. If his cooking pots had been contaminated with garden eggs (contact with this fruit was believed to cause one to become sick and thin), they too were washed in the stream. Then the man went back to his compound, was rubbed with powdered camwood and palm oil, and given food. After this the incident was never mentioned again.

Anlu was greatly feared, for there was no appeal against its rulings. If pardon was refused, the culprit was forced to leave the country. Since the invoking of *anlu* was such a serious affair, it was used sparingly. One informant about 35 years of age said he had seen it used only four times in his lifetime (Ritzenthaler 1974: 151–56).

Both 'sitting on a man' and *anlu* became vehicles for wider political protest during the colonial period. The Women's War or Aba Riots in 1929 among the Igbo and the Anlu Uprising in 1958 among the Kom are both described more fully in Chapter 10. These two rebellions illustrate the strength of women's collective institutions when they felt their interests had been jeopardized.

Secret societies

Secret societies are another type of traditional group; some of them are still functioning. They exist under various names in West Africa, especially in Sierra Leone, the Ivory Coast, Guinea and Liberia. This section looks at the functions of the Sande society among the Kpelle of Liberia. Although there are similar societies throughout much of Africa, Sande is regarded as characteristic of West Africa. The parallel male secret society is known as Poro.

The functions of female secret societies are several: the education of young girls, the creation of cohesion among women, the provision of cross-cutting mechanisms to balance secular political power, and the strengthening of patterns of stratification in the larger society. In particular, these societies provide vehicles through which older, aristocratic women control younger women's sexual and labor services, thereby consolidating and increasing both their own power and social status and that of their lineage and age group.

Girls usually attend Sande from the ages of six to sixteen unless they are enrolled in some far-off mission or government school. For different periods of time, ranging from several days to several years, initiates live in secluded bush schools, isolated from their everyday activities. During this time they undergo clitoridectomies, labiadectomies, and scarification. (See the further discussion of female circumcision in Chapter 13.) They are instructed in household and family tasks, farming, medicine, dancing, and singing, acquiring knowledge and skills that prepare them to be wives and mothers. The major purpose of Sande rituals is to confer fertility on them (Bledsoe 1980: 59–80).

The girls learn that absolute obedience to their leaders is expected of them both in the bush school and later in life. The breaking of the rules of obedience and respect may bring threats of infertility, even death. The initiates are expected to obey the husbands their leaders give them, but they know that their ultimate loyalty lies with their leaders, who could order them to poison a husband who had violated higher tribal authority. Initiates swear to keep these cultural secrets. When their training is over, they return to their families.

The Sande society is internally ranked. The initiates have the lowest status, but they enjoy more prestige than the few Kpelle women who are not members of Sande. Generally, older women have the greatest status in Sande.

Sande and similar societies foster unity among women and loyalty to tribal institutions. The elders of secret societies make important decisions for the community in secret and wear masks when publicly announcing their decisions, in order to appear unanimous. 'The common bonds [of such secret societies] unite men with men, and women with women, as fellow members over a wide area, and to an extent which transcends all barriers of family, class, tribe and religion' (Little 1949: 202).

Sande leaders use their connections with land-owning lineages and their control over their initiates' productive and reproductive capacities to solidify the existing patterns of stratification and power. This is accomplished in several ways. The leaders are closely linked to the elite land-owning lineages. Only certain older women from these lineages who obtain religious and secular office get an opportunity to learn the society's most important secrets. These older women use their positions as leaders in the secret societies to expose the ancestry of newcomers who are challenging the elites' power and to select and approve secular leaders. In the name of social unity, older members call upon those beneath them for duty and self-sacrifice. Hence secret societies exist primarily not to eliminate factional lineage interests, but to preserve their differences and to protect the aristocratic lineages from threats to their position by aspiring newcomers (Bledsoe 1980: 70). Sande leaders and secular politicians obviously have overlapping interests.

In peaceful times, patrons are needed to protect low-status Kpelle from unfair fines, taxes, and legal suits. One way to secure this kind of protection as well as upward mobility is to enroll daughters in the secret societies of these powerful women (Hoffer 1972). Parents sometimes competed with each other to get their daughters into these bush schools. If patron–client relationships are crucial in stable periods, they are even more so in times of instability. Then alliances are formed with the more powerful to protect the weaker from the lawless factions searching for captives and booty (Bledsoe 1980: 70). It stands to reason that Sande activity would increase during political and military unrest as allegiances with the more powerful were even more crucial when people are faced with uncertainty.

Leaders of the secret societies profit from their initiates in several other ways. Parents pay entrance and exit fees, as well as providing food and other favors during their daughters' training period. In Sierra Leone, the leaders also benefit from the initiates' labor on their farms (Hoffer 1972). Young Sande dancers turn over the money they collect from spectators to the older leaders.

Sande leaders' power over the initiates' sexual services can be used to acquire the support of young men or those from outside lineages whom the leaders wish to control. The husbands-elect often vie with each other for the best singers and dancers, or for the most beautiful girls, and bestow goods on the leaders hoping to be successful in their quest (Bledsoe 1980: 74). The girls are carefully allocated to young men, powerful men, and rival families. In this way, aristocrats gain followers and allies and fortify their control over potentially dissident individuals and families.

Furthermore, it is the older women from the land-owning lineages in Sande who are the most important midwives. Women prefer to patronize midwives of powerful lineages and those who occupy important leadership positions in the Sande society, because they believe these women possess the most powerful medicine to protect both their own and their baby's lives. Women are highly dependent on the midwives' knowledge of obstetrics and gynaecology and this knowledge is jealously guarded. Midwives are well paid for their services. They wield considerable power and sometimes resort to threat and blackmail, having extracted private secrets from a woman during childbirth. Women who become powerful secular or secret society leaders 'achieve their status mainly by playing the "male" game of trading rights in the women they control for political support' (Bledsoe 1980: 78).

Rural cooperatives and self-help projects

From traditional work groups and the spirit of helping each other have evolved many of today's independent cooperatives where the members carry out projects and business ventures. These cooperative endeavors permit women to engage in undertakings far larger than their own limited resources would permit. Kikuyu women in Kenya often pool efforts to build better housing, for example, to add a roof of corrugated iron sheets, considered an improvement over the traditional thatched roofs. Such work groups are known as *mabati*, referring to the iron sheets used for roofing.

In the community of Mitero in the Kikuyu Highlands the women are committed, full-time agriculturalists (Stamp 1975–76). An expanding population has reduced the amount of land farmed per family to two acres or less, with the result that adult men migrate to the towns or large farms to secure wage employment and are away a good part of the year. The women, who number around one thousand, engage in subsistence agriculture; corn (usually called maize in Africa), beans, and potatoes are the main crops grown for consumption. Coffee, the chief cash crop, is cultivated on a family basis on a scale ranging from a few hundred bushes to plots of several acres.

In 1975–76 there were 10 women's groups in Mitero. The women pooled their meager resources in order to buy farms and businesses, with the profits being divided equally among the contributors according to the number of shares held. Profits were reinvested, used for children's school fees (traditionally the father's obligation), or for farm purchases. These groups sometimes bought collectively and thus more cheaply for their members and assisted them with loans. Poor women could join, since work gangs hired themselves out for farm work, and the women used part of their earnings to buy shares in cooperative ventures.

One of these contemporary groups, the Riakarime Women's Group, included 22 women and was founded for the purpose of cooperative farming. The women found that they could not manage single-handedly, because one woman did not have sufficient money to employ laborers. They decided to cultivate for each other, to build houses for themselves, and to work for wages. They purchased manure, fertilizer, and water tanks jointly for their own use, and bought farms and shares in other businesses. As of 1976, they had purchased shares in four companies (Stamp 1975–76: 41).

Although some literature maintains that it is the better-off women who join such associations, among Kikuyu women it seems to be the poorest women who join. Data for Mbiri Location (Kenya) shows that a disproportionately high percentage (62 per cent) of women from the poorest households belong to women's groups, compared to 34 per cent from the entire adult female population, and 14 per cent from the more affluent households (in nearby Weithaga location) (Thomas 1988a: 417).

What is striking about these women is their entrepreneurial spirit, and their drive to succeed against insuperable odds. They obviously realize that, if their husbands cannot be counted on to help improve their standard of living and to educate their children, then they must do it themselves. Many appear committed to a hard-working ethic that values a life of unrelenting toil, saving, and investing for the future. Though faced with pressing needs and a chronic shortage of money, they still reinvest their small earnings (Wachtel 1975–76, Stamp 1975–76). Growing coffee is seen as an investment that provides security, 'like putting your money in a bank', as one woman put it.

Corn mill societies

Governments often organize women's associations. Corn mill societies in Cameroon were at first government-initiated projects. Rural development officers decided to organize African women into societies that would meet monthly and help to raise the living standards of rural Africans (O'Kelly 1973: 108–21). In an attempt to reduce the heavy workload of women and to attract them to these societies, the Department of Education bought 15 corn mills in 1959 and made them available on loan to several villages. Corn mill societies were formed whose members paid a monthly fee for the use of the mill. By the end of the first year, 30 villages had repaid their loans and more mills were purchased for distribution to newly formed societies. The mill societies spread until they totalled 200, with a membership of some 18,000.

From the social gatherings that took place around the corn mills came the idea of holding classes in cooking, soap-making, child care, hygiene, and nutrition. The women then set about making bricks and cutting bamboo in order to construct a meeting hall. As the societies' strength increased, the women began to handle long-standing problems. They bought barbed wire on loan and put up fences to protect their gardens from stray cattle. The loan was repaid by putting more land under cultivation. Department of Agriculture assistants introduced a new and better strain of corn, which yielded an abundant harvest. The women began to understand the need for contour farming. Poultry schemes were begun, village plots reforested, and water storage facilities built. The societies' most ambitious scheme was the establishment of a cooperative store to allow women to import articles unavailable locally. Five thousand women raised the initial capital and several stores were soon in operation.

Harambee self-help projects

Kenya's Harambee projects, in contrast to the government-initiated corn mill societies and to the independent women's groups, illustrate grass-roots efforts that are later followed by government support. The Kenyan government has successfully cultivated local development by emphasizing that it helps those who help themselves. Harambee (Swahili for 'Let us pull together') puts the accent on people coming together in their communities and carrying out projects without waiting for the government to take the initiative. The rural populace decides what new programs and projects it wants, and only after these projects are underway will the government step in with aid. Schools, dispensaries, and roads have been built in this way. The people build a school and the government later staffs it. Although these projects are not exclusively women's, they are discussed here because women provide the bulk of labor and funds. In the northern division of Machakos District, the administrators pointed out that women constituted 80–90 per cent of the unskilled labor involved in self-help projects (Mutiso n.d.: 42–43). The work ranged from making bricks to whitewashing classrooms.

The traditional spirit of independence and self-help is largely responsible for the success of Harambee projects. The following figures provide an idea of what this mobilization entails. From 1965 to 1970, Harambee projects worth 3,197,966 shillings were carried out in the northern division of Machakos District. Of this sum the central government contributed only 44,061 shillings and the local government 8,301 shillings. The bulk of the money, more than 98 per cent, came from the rural people (Mutiso n.d.: 41–42). It is clear that these projects make an important contribution to economic and social development.

The persistence of traditional forms of cooperative work in Kenya and the proliferation of new cooperative forms appear to be in marked contrast to the situation in the 'labor reserve' areas of southern Africa. There agriculture is not flourishing and rural women depend on their husbands' wage from migrant labor for subsistence. Cooperative work arrangements and village development efforts, while sometimes attempted, produce little enthusiasm and are not particularly successful (Mueller 1977: 156–9).

Self-help groups face the persistent problem of being used for personal goals by both men and women. The more successful the groups are, the more desirable they are for this purpose. For instance, as the role of Third World women became recognized, politically aspiring women found it advantageous to be able to 'speak for' so many thousand rural women at international meetings, academic seminars, or political caucuses. The following examples are both drawn from Kenya.

Mbai sya Eitu ('clans of girls') groups were originally organized among the Kamba by the local member of parliament (MP) for electoral purposes in 1961. They were active in vote-getting in the 1963 and 1969 elections and raised money for many Harambee projects. The Swynnerton Plan, produced in 1953 to combat the growing threat of the 'Mau Mau' rebellion, was designed quickly to expand African economic development. With British aid, a rapid increase in cash cropping took place over the next few years. Coffee production in particular was emphasized. The land, however, had to be terraced before coffee could be planted. Communal labor was used under the aegis of the chiefs and sub-chiefs. The villages were organized into the traditional *mwethya* work groups, which went from farm to farm and terraced the land. Since more women than men were in the *mwethya*, the informal leaders were mostly women; these were younger women and not the grandmothers who had traditionally occupied the public roles. Later, most of these women turned up in the Mbai sya Eitu. Thus it was through the experience of terracing that Kamba women learned of the status to be gained through public matters. The mobilization of women into modern politics had begun (Mutiso n.d.: 7–8). An MP's electoral strategy was simply to control the votes of the biggest clans and thereby assure victory in the 1963 and 1969 elections. Women were sent to organize their clans of origin into a matrilocal clan organization led by a woman, and in this way voting could be controlled. It was this practice that gave rise to the Mbai sya Eitu, in which traditional organizations play modern political roles (Mutiso n.d.: 16–17).

Maendeleo ya Wanawake

The largest women's association in Kenya is Maendeleo ya Wanawake ('progress for women'), which at its height in the early 1980s involved some 8,000 rural clubs and a membership of 300,000. Organized by European women in the early 1950s under the auspices of the colonial government's Department of Community Development and Rehabilitation, Maendeleo was patterned after the Women's Institutes of rural England. Its objectives were to promote the advancement of African women and to raise their living standards through self-help. Maendeleo's activities ranged from instruction in farming methods to child care. Day care centers were opened, and new ideas about diet and hygiene were presented. Traditional handicrafts were encouraged, including basketwork, pottery, palm leaf, and woodwork. Traditional dancing and singing were cultivated, and competitions in various skills instituted. Homecraft centers were built, financed by central government funds with some help from district councils. Literacy classes were held and a monthly newspaper started that was translated into the Swahili, Kikuyu, Luo, and Kamba languages. And for the first time women participated in team sports (Wipper 1975–1976).

In its early years the leaders of Maendeleo were militant, dedicated women who continually campaigned for women's rights and prodded the government for more financial support. These women, a 'thorn in the government's side', called attention to the discrepancy between the government's verbal support for Maendeleo and its meager financial support. In the 1970s, however, the movement's national leadership changed, and a number of the new leaders were related to the political elite. With fathers, brothers, and husbands occupying some of the most powerful positions in the country, they had too much self-interest involved to query, let alone oppose, government practices. Charity balls, 'first nights', embassy receptions, donations to charities (when Maendeleo's own impoverished rural endeavours were floundering), and trips overseas to UN agencies to talk about the problems of Third World women, suggest that the national executive was out of touch with rural women, and developing a lifestyle far closer to that of the European elite than to the rural people. Tired of unfulfilled promises and fed up with what they saw as hypocrisy, the rural members were alienated in many ways from both the government and its own national executive (Wipper 1975–1976: 99–119).

During the 1970s and 1980s, Maendeleo became the preeminent women's organization in Kenya. At the 1985 Decade for Women Conference in Naibori, it assumed a leadership role both at the NGO Forum and at the governmental conference (Nzomo 1989: 11). It was given a great boost by the increasing attention of overseas aid agencies to women's projects. Maendeleo was seen by foreign donors as a viable vehicle through which to channel resources to women at the grassroots level. For example, a Kenya news magazine reported that Maendeleo received several million dollars over a three-year period in the mid-1980s (*The Weekly Review*, 1 Dec. 1989: 14). Any organization with that kind of money would be immensely attractive to a regime increasingly strapped for funds. The opportunity came in 1985–86 when Maendeleo became embroiled in a financial scandal. The government intervened, ostensibly to straighten out the mess, and in 1987 formally affiliated Maendeleo to the Kenya African National Union (KANU). President Daniel arap Moi announced that henceforth the organization would be known as KANU-Maendeleo and it would become the channel for all foreign donations for women's development projects (*The Weekly Review*, 1 Dec. 1989: 15). Since that time, all money for women's projects in Kenya has been controlled by men.

Occupational associations

Under the colonial system, education and training were primarily available to men, as were the new jobs in industry and government. As described in Chapter 3, there were few formal positions for illiterate women in the urban areas. Consequently many women became petty traders, prostitutes, and beer-brewers, the latter two occupations being illegal in many places.

Prostitutes' associations

The preponderance of single men in the urban areas, described in Chapter 3 above, provided a ready market for female sexual and domestic services in the later years of colonial rule and the early years of independence. Prostitutes were often estranged from their relatives in the countryside. Faced with considerable competition from other women, they were in insecure social and economic positions. In some cases these women had exchanged family and other traditional forms of security for personal liberty (Little 1966: 122); in specific areas of East Africa, some prostitutes maintained close connections with their kin groups and used their earnings to help support family members (White 1990). In any case, after migrating to urban centers, these women had to depend on their own limited resources for survival. In many areas of West Africa, prostitutes' associations acted as mutual aid organizations, providing the protective functions that were formerly performed within the rural kinship structure.

The most prestigious of these organizations was composed of the very successful 'courtesans' who sold their companionship and sexual services to successful businessmen, high-level civil servants, and professionals. In Zaire such women set up professional associations with a president, vice-president, treasurer, and other officials, for the purpose of providing aid to members in difficulty and organizing festivals and funerals (Balandier 1956). Similar professional unions existed in Nigeria and Ghana in the 1950s and 1960s (Boserup 1970: 100). Of Igbo women in colonial Nigeria it was said that 'prostitution is merely a new calling like any other; they become prostitutes as reasonably and as self-righteously as they would have become typists or telephone girls' (Leith-Ross 1965: 267–68). In Benin (formerly Dahomey), Senegal, and Togoland these women were known as *femmes libres* (or free women), and some fraternized with an elite clientele, sometimes deputizing at presidential balls and other diplomatic affairs; they were highly rewarded for their company (Little 1972: 287).

The associations formed by successful prostitutes and courtesans aimed at high standards in deportment and dress, discouraged 'unprofitable' business contacts, and helped the members advertise their best features, functioning like finishing schools. In Brazzaville, these associations provided musical and other kinds of public entertainment, where the experienced members taught the newcomers about elegance and deportment. Societies such as La Rose, Violette et Elegance, and Dollar tried to maintain their good reputation by limiting their membership to carefully selected young women. A mutual aid fund was maintained to help the members financially. The members also functioned as a substitute family. Should a member die, her funeral expenses would be paid by the association and her fellow prostitutes went into mourning for six months, during which time they did not wear their fine clothes or jewelry. At the end of the mourning period they held an all-night celebration (Balandier 1956: 145–8).

Such voluntary associations can be seen as assisting the socially mobile prostitutes and courtesans who did well financially and had no difficulty in retirement. They might own a house or two, or have saved enough money to open a hotel or start a business, or they might become wealthy traders. Irrespective of how they earned their money, they were usually able to assume a relatively prestigious position in society (Little 1972: 287).

In contrast, the associations formed by ordinary prostitutes, the streetwalkers and bar girls, emphasized bread-and-butter issues: no prostitute was allowed to charge a customer less than the price fixed by the president of her society, for example (Rouch and Bernus 1959: 237). These associations protected streetwalkers who were preyed upon by criminal gangs, and intervened on their behalf when they were arrested by the police. For lower-class women, many of whom were unmarried or who had lost contact with their families in the countryside, these associations provided not only monetary but psychological support. A recent study of prostitution in colonial Kenya found many examples of such cooperation among prostitutes, but no similar patterns of formal organization (White 1990). A more somber account of contemporary African prostitutes in the context of AIDS can be found below in Chapter 13 (see also Schoepf *et al.* 1991).

Market associations

Trading is the main occupation of urban women in West Africa. Its popularity rests on the fact that women can combine trade with domestic duties, it is lighter and more pleasant than farm work, and the market, the focal point of such activity, is seen as a congenial place. Some 80 per cent of all traders are women in southern Ghana and among the Yoruba, about 50 per cent in eastern Nigeria, and 60 per cent in the Dakar region of Senegal. The majority operate in the internal market system, trading in food and portable imported goods. They participate at the lower levels of trade where profits are small, while the higher and more profitable levels are dominated by men and large European firms.

Women traders have established associations that perform a variety of functions. They assist their members in starting or in expanding a business by lending them capital. They train women, new to the urban milieu, in business methods, and they put traders in contact with potential customers. At times they have become politically influential; this aspect is described in Chapter 10. Another important function of these associations is the enforcing of rules concerning prices and competition. In Lagos market, for example, each commodity has its own section – cloth, fish, vegetables, and so on – and the women sit according to the commodity they sell. Each section has its own association, or *egbe*, which discourages competition among women dealing with that particular article. The unity among the women, who spend many hours together each day gossiping and eating, is so strong that it is said no trader would think of disobeying her *egbe*. However, should one attempt to undercut the others in price, she would be ostracized by her fellows, who might report her offense to the leader of the *egbe* and if need be to the *iyalode*, the 'queen of the markets'. The queen is recognized as a chief and is second only to the *oba* or king at official functions. The *egbe* also makes certain that commodities designated as the exclusive concern of women traders are not sold by men (Little 1973: 50).

Sometimes, in the absence of a formal association, there are informal arrangements among the vendors as to who is allowed to sell what in a particular area. In a Kampala market, the sellers refer to each other by kinship names such as 'sister' or 'daughter'. This pseudo-kinship system, loosely organized, apparently works to prevent too many women from selling *matoke* (cooking bananas) in the same place. The object is to disperse sellers and to prevent intense competition (Southall and Gutkind 1957: 138).

Some market associations buy in bulk, thus acquiring the goods more cheaply than a single vendor could. Other associations make sure there is an adequate supply of the commodities that their members sell. A few associations have even gone into the production of goods for themselves. In southern Nigeria these societies have run such projects as a bakery, a laundry, and a calabash factory (Little 1973: 51).

There are many variations of these mutual aid societies. In Abidjan, market women join associations that help with occasions requiring money. For instance, if a trader had a daughter of marriageable age, she would join a marriage association to cover the costs of the wedding. If a baby were expected, she might join a birth association to help defray the financial obligations. The association joined reflects the economic position of its members, for the required contribution varies from 25 cents to 10 to 15 dollars (Lewis 1976: 147). Many efforts at forming mutual aid societies fail shortly after their creation. (See the discussion of potential problems in Lewis 1976.)

A final type of mutual aid society is the rotating-credit association, whose prime function is to provide its membership with capital. For example, among the Society of Friends (Nanamei Akpee) in Ghana, the members agree to make regular contributions to a fund which becomes the property of each contributor in turn. It provides each member with a lump sum, more than she could save on her own, given the constant demands for money. The system is fairly flexible, and if one member urgently needs some money, she may be permitted to jump the queue and receive the collection before she is entitled to do so (Little 1973: 52). (Rotating credit associations are also discussed in Geertz 1966: 420–22, and Ardener 1964: 201–29.)

Beer-brewers' associations

It should be borne in mind that while the occupations of trading, prostitution, and beer-brewing are carried on by separate groups, there is much overlapping with women who engage in long-distance trading or who operate bars, often selling their sexual services. Not infrequently women engage in all three activities. Hence market traders' and prostitutes' societies may also serve beer-brewers. In Nairobi, beer-brewers formed cooperative societies that spread the risks over a wide base and divided up the labor and the profits. One such association, called Tazamu Lako (or 'Mind Your Own Business') had a membership of 150. Premises for brewing were rented and the women were divided into three two-week shifts. Each shift shared in the brewing and in the profits.

Urban business enterprises

Women's involvement in the modern economy is still generally weak, especially in the business sector. Yet in the last 25 years urban women in Kenya, like the rural women in Mitero described above, have formed associations in which they pool their meager funds in order to invest in some business enterprise. Through such endeavors, sometimes built on traditional bases, poor women are able to carve out a small stake for themselves in the modern economy.

In Nakuru, a medium-size town in modern Kenya, women's corporate activity is composed of formal and informal groups that mobilize resources and channel them into various businesses (Wachtel 1976, 1975–76). Membership criteria vary and may include ethnicity, religion, neighborhood, and place of work or occupation. One group, for example, was recruited from a dance group that entertained visiting dignitaries. The following section briefly considers two of these ventures.

Kangei na Nyakinyua ('Mothers and Children') consumers' cooperative society

In mid-1969 an emergency meeting was called to discuss the plight of a destitute woman who had given birth in the Nakuru railway station. The gathering of around 50 women from different ethnic groups took up a collection for the woman, then discussed the need for women's unity in the face of urban insecurity. The group decided to collect money to buy a large building to rent; the money earned from it would provide some income for unemployed women.

The membership grew to 250, but the women had several setbacks before they found a building large enough on Nakuru's main commercial street. They had accumulated about $7,000 from the sale of shares and they gave that for an option on the property. Some influential men decided that they would bid against them, and the women almost lost their $7,000. In a spontaneous expression of solidarity, around 1,000 women (many more nonmembers than members) marched to State House and secured the intervention of President Jomo Kenyatta. The women concentrated on developing this property and have acquired a few smaller plots on which they hope eventually to build. The membership increased to 400.

Although Kangei na Nyakinyua had its start in welfare activity, as it evolved the economic side came to dominate. The original welfare fund was misused so it had to be reorganized, but considerable money has been dispensed in helping women, not necessarily members.

Ikobe farmers' cooperative society

Nakuru's first large-scale economic enterprise was started in 1964 by a core of market women with the support of the rural women with whom they traded. The society's goal was to buy a large farm. Each member paid a registration fee of 20 shillings on joining and purchased individual shares of 500 shillings. Money was raised by work groups hired out to local farms. A woman could apply all or part of her wage towards buying shares.

After the women demonstrated their seriousness by accumulating funds, they successfully negotiated a loan and purchased a 511–acre farm that grows wheat, barley, and pyrethrum, and grazes 300 sheep. The society employs a farm manager and hired labor to run the farm. Profits are applied towards repayment of the loan, and money over and above that has been set aside for the purchase of another farm. Though other women's groups in Nakuru had attempted to buy a farm, this was the only group that succeeded. The ownership of land, especially a farm, represents the ultimate security in the opinion of most town dwellers.

Urban insecurity and corporate activity

The cost of urban living is high. For the average family, there is never enough money to meet all the demands. Group ventures, if properly managed, can be a satisfactory solution. Savings increase, emergency loans can be made against paid-up shares, and through participating in such group activities, a woman can become part of an enterprise far beyond her own resources and capabilities.

These advantages cannot be gained, however, without considerable risk. The attrition rate of these enterprises is high. The goals of many projects are unrealistic and the projects are sometimes poorly organized. Unsophisticated in the ways of business, women suffer from severe handicaps that are only partially alleviated by their collective efforts: they usually lack literacy and bookkeeping skills and are unaware of such formal requirements as registering a company. (These are problems faced by predominantly men's groups, such as agricultural cooperatives, as well.) Lacking capital and business know-how, women's groups are sometimes easy prey for unscrupulous managers who abscond with the groups' money (Wachtel 1975–76). And while their entrepreneurial spirit, boldness, and willingness to sacrifice present rewards for investment in the future is laudable, if many projects are doomed to failure at the outset, it may be that the energy and money of poor people might better be used elsewhere. Since this is the very spirit that governments wish to cultivate, it might behove them to assist the women by providing the needed expertise to assure more success in these cooperative efforts. For example, a particularly successful cloth-dyeing cooperative in Mali depended greatly on the involvement of both the Malian government and international agencies (Caughman 1981).

Social welfare, church, and entertainment associations

This section looks at some voluntary associations among Protestant and Muslim women in East and West Africa. These groups are mainly concerned with fund-raising, social welfare projects, and entertainment. Church associations in Sierra Leone support traditional Christian values, while women's issues were only one concern among many that Muslim associations in Kenya worked on. None of these groups made women's issues its sole focus.

Protestant church associations in Sierra Leone and Zaire

Creole women of Freetown, the capital of Sierra Leone, belong to a number of Protestant church associations similar to the women's associations in the parent churches, such as the Mothers' Union, the Women's Guild, and prayer groups (Steady 1976: 220–37). Women work to preserve Christian values and to support their particular church by means of fund-raising endeavors – teas, bazaars, and luncheon sales. The proceeds go towards the maintenance of the church or the purchase of some special item, such as a stained glass window or a silver chalice. The members of the Ladies Working Band (Anglican) undertake to keep the church and its premises clean and to decorate it for religious ceremonies. In keeping with Christian teaching on philanthropy, part of their funds are donated to charities, and members visit hospitals, orphanages, and homes for the handicapped to present gifts and to sing on special occasions.

These groups provide women with avenues for religious leadership, at the same time supporting the status quo in which men occupy most prestigious and official church roles. Leadership of women's groups commands considerable respect both inside and outside the churches, and this largely accounts for their importance among women. Being a leader not only makes a woman an 'exceptionally good Christian', it adds to her status in the community at large (Steady 1976: 228–29).

Women's traditional and contemporary religious roles are further discussed in Chapter 6.

A Protestant Mothers Club in Zaire has become involved in the battle against AIDS. Aware of the work being done by the CONNAISSIDA ('Know AIDS') project in their city, the club asked project members to stage a workshop for women, including prostitutes, at their church. The workshop emphasized male peer group pressures as a key obstacle to behavioral changes that might slow the spread of AIDS, and helped women improve their communication skills and self-confidence in attempts to combat male attitudes. Participants talked about how to persuade their husbands and partners to avoid bars and prostitutes in order to protect the health of other members of their families. The women also requested that separate workshops be held for their husbands and younger members of their household, as many were reluctant to talk with their spouses or children about AIDS and about using condoms.

Role-playing and workshop discussions highlighted for the CONNAISSIDA researchers the fact that 'prostitutes', 'mothers', and 'church members' were not mutually exclusive categories for these Zairean women. Club members emphasized the relative lack of alternative income-generating activities for divorced, deserted, or widowed women in their congregation. The Mothers' Club was trying to provide some help for these women, but feared that some would have to take up prostitution as a survival strategy when all else failed.

Muslim women's associations in Kenya

Associations for Muslim women in Mombasa have evolved over the past 60 years from *lelemama* dance groups to associations concerned with current problems facing women (Strobel 1976). This evolution signifies important value and role changes for women in the Arab-Swahili community as these associations mobilize women in pursuit of values deemed important by the community.

The Ibinaal Watan and Banu Saada were only two of many associations that danced the *lelemama*, a dance brought from Zanzibar in the late nineteenth century. The popularity of these groups was greatest during the 1920s and 1930s, although there are still a few dance groups. *Lelemama* groups competed with each other, the idea being for one group to outspend and outperform another in dance competitions. They had sets of titles that reflected the social hierarchy of the Arab-Swahili and colonial communities. A woman rose in rank, securing more prestigious titles by spending lavishly. Thus the associations enforced status distinctions in a society concerned with hierarchy.

Lelemama groups often provided entertainment at weddings. Several hundred women attended, displayed their new clothes, and cheered the dancers on. The dancers sang songs, some of which shamed or ridiculed members of the community for various offenses, or challenged rival groups by impugning their dancing abilities. (The use of song as an instrument of social criticism, revenge, and the enforcing of norms, already mentioned above, is discussed further in Chapter 8.) Members helped each other out by contributing money and helping to prepare the food during weddings and funerals.

By the 1950s, dance groups had begun to decline, as fewer young women were interested. Rising prices prevented the members from continuing the lavish celebrations. Alarmed at their costs, the government had limited the competition between rival groups, eventually banning them, and hence a major reason for dancing had been removed. At the same time, a new consciousness was evolving about the status of coastal women. Arab leaders and the colonial government strongly encouraged secular education for Muslim girls. Debates raged about the seclusion of women, gender equality, and the great costs of weddings and funerals. Questions were asked as to whether Muslim women should go to the movies or be allowed in mosques for communal prayers. New political and social issues had arisen that *lelemama* failed to address, and these issues contributed to the emergence of new associations like the Muslim Women's Institute and the Muslim Women's Cultural Association, formed in 1957 and 1958 respectively.

These new associations concerned themselves with issues of social welfare and education by establishing adult classes in literacy, sewing, child welfare, and religion, and by fund-raising for philanthropic causes. The Muslim Women's Cultural Association has concentrated on the building and running of a nursery school since 1960. The Muslim Women's Institute has had a more varied program, including providing relief funds for Zanzibari refugees and Lamu fire victims, aid to mosques, religious classes for children, and scholarships for students abroad. Both organizations have tried to equip their members with an array of skills needed in a broader, more open society. Hence their concern for literacy, education, health and hygiene, poise in public gatherings, and economic independence through sewing and handicrafts. The members also participated in the campaign for female voting rights, visiting women in their homes to explain the importance of voting, and they condemned the forced marriages of Zanzibari girls.

This concern for modern education is shared by Muslim women's associations in Freetown as well. The All-Muslim Women's Association, the Amalgamated Muslim Women's Movement, and Tariku Fil Islam raise funds to provide secondary school scholarships for Muslim girls, in addition to giving religious instruction to their members and providing mutual aid services. The fact that many Muslim women in Freetown have always had a great deal of mobility and earning power as traders may have contributed to an independent outlook and a wish to secure modern education for their daughters (Steady 1976: 223).

Foreign aid, dependency, and male control

A number of factors came together in the 1980s to give a boost to African women and their associations. The shortcomings in development plans that neglected the role of women, who provide 60 to 80 per cent of the agricultural labor, grow an estimated 80 per cent of Africa's food, and form the majority in the commercial sector of many towns and cities, have been recognized. Research on women's self-help projects, cooperatives, and business enterprises has, in the main, emphasized their positive functions, especially for women who are among their country's poorest people and are the single heads of large families.

The United Nations Decade for Women, 1975–85, publicized women's social and economic contributions, highlighted their unequal status, especially in the Third World, and urged national governments to set up 'machineries' to enhance women's status and involve them in development on an equal basis with men. The impact of the UN Decade for Women and the ineffectiveness of much government machinery is further discussed in Chapter 10 (see also Wipper 1988). These national women's groups, with their emphasis upon the provision of clean water, education, food, and shelter, and their civic contributions such as the building of a community center, had goals clearly compatible with government development plans. Hence many African governments, under pressure from the UN, adopted policies favorable to women's groups and to their involvement in development. They established women's bureaus, advisory commissions, and even ministries to facilitate women's advancement, and instructed government departments to pay particular attention to women. Community development officials, for example, encouraged women to form groups and undertake all kinds of projects from tie-dyeing, soap-making, and tailoring to running a poultry farm and a bus service. At the same time, international aid agencies seeking new ways to reach the poorest in the rural sector turned to women's groups as vehicles through which to distribute aid.

The new prominence of women's organizations had several unforeseen consequences. Government encouragement and foreign funding led to a dramatic proliferation of groups. For instance, in Kenya's Coast Province, in four years the number of groups grew more than five times from 151 in 1980 to 802 in 1984, and membership increased almost eight times, from 5,208 in 1980 to 40,232 in 1984 (Maas 1991: 10). This expansion led to strong competition for aid, with only one in ten groups getting any assistance. It became apparent that groups with good political connections had the best chance of being funded (Maas 1991: 58).

There is a growing literature on the problems faced by these enterprises, problems ranging from poor organization and leadership to lack of capital, insufficient expertise, and internal strife (Feldman 1983, Mwaniki 1986, Monsted 1978). When foreign assistance is withdrawn, projects often collapse. For example, women in Mombasa decided to start a bakery from which they hoped to generate income. Their product, however, was not reliable enough to compete with bread from professional bakeries. Although initially funded with outside money, the members could not make it productive and the bakery failed to provide them with any income (Maas 1991: 46–49).

The Kenyan Women's Bureau is a good example of government-supported agencies designed to improve women's lives. Yet the effectiveness of Bureau-funded projects has been severely criticized:

> If the Women's Bureau is seriously interested in women gaining greater access to income-generating opportunities, it needs to question whether handicrafts projects without markets, consumer shops without wares to sell, buildings constructed with government grants to set women up as landlords for cheap housing, exotic poultry projects, and other uncompetitive enterprises – all affecting only a tiny proportion of Kenya's women – are really the solution. It needs also to examine whether the heavy financial commitment to individual women participating in such undertakings, and the consequent exclusion of women who cannot afford contributions, does not actually serve to destroy the important mutual welfare contribution which women's groups have the potential to make. (Feldman 1983: 83)

As a result of foreign funding, women's groups that had survived for years on meager resources may suddenly find their budgets vastly expanded. Giving large sums of money to inexperienced groups simply invites malfeasance, and as seen with Maendeleo, it may also attract the intervention of powerful male elites. Foreign funding and government control may well discourage genuine grass-roots initiatives and weaken the very traditions of independence and self-help among African women described in this chapter. If that spirit is killed, a vital component of development will be lost.

Yet there are success stories as well: poor women have demonstrated that they can utilize outside resources, yet maintain their autonomy. Illiterate women in Mali formed the Markala Cooperative to learn marketable skills and acquire an income. The cooperative produced and sold dyed cloth and laundry soap. The members were helped by grants from voluntary organizations, yet they financed their own lengthy job training, in order to remain as independent as possible. This meant their salaries remained low for years and met only a part of their monthly expenses. Many women obtained additional income at night using skills learned through the cooperative. After several years, working out of temporary quarters, the cooperative acquired a cement building with shaded porches on the sides so that during the hot months the workers could move outside. The Markala Cooperative stands as an example of how rural women can establish a successful cooperative and it has inspired other cooperatives in Mali (Caughman and N'diaye Thiam 1989). Other organizations with few assets have also effectively utilized the resources of public and private agencies to help achieve their goals while remaining self-reliant.

The Mraru Women's Group started a much-needed bus service in central Kenya, then built a retail shop with the profits. Later they developed a goat herd, and provided sewing lessons. Despite some temporary setbacks, the shop and goat-raising project continue to operate successfully (Kneerim 1989).

Women's groups and family planning

Now that women's groups are on the development agenda, and at long last getting the attention they so rightly deserve, demographers see them as ideal vehicles for introducing ideas about family planning. In these groups women can learn about their neighbors' experiences and acquire new information from women they know and trust. Voluntary associations have a particular strength in that they can cut across lineage- or clan-based organizations to draw on knowledge and practices from a wider network of contacts. In one study of voluntary associations and the use of contraceptives in rural Kenya, group members were found to be 33 per cent more likely to be current contraceptive users (controlling for age, education, and urban–rural residence), were more likely to have discussed family planning with their husbands, and to know more about methods and sources of supply than nonmembers. In addition, women's groups appear to affect contraceptive use indirectly. Nonmembers who live in areas with strong economically oriented women's groups were more likely to use them than women in areas without these groups (Hammerslough 1991). See Chapter 14 for a case study of contraceptive use in southern Nigeria.

Conclusions

The many women's groups amply demonstrate that present-day African women take collective action to tackle their various problems, as they did in the past. Work groups are still used to lighten the farm chores of individual women. They have also been put to new uses, such as working together for wages. With the money they earn, poor women can buy shares in businesses and farms, thus acquiring a stake in the modern economy. Other types of rural self-help groups have made important contributions to development projects.

New groups such as occupational associations have arisen with women's migration to urban areas and engagement in work other than farming. These groups provide financial and psychological support and training, and establish standards. In urban areas these associations take on a number of functions traditionally performed by the rural family. Church groups and Muslim women's associations perform social welfare activities, support particular religious organizations, and provide an avenue for women's leadership.

An area where women have lost considerable power and significant political roles is in the decline of such institutions as *mikiri* and *anlu*, which specifically protected their interests and provided them with considerable self-government. This loss in autonomy and power has not been regained with independence. An ever-present danger is that women's groups, particularly if they are externally funded, will be diverted from serving women's interests to serving the interests of men.

Part Three

Women in Politics and Policy

CHAPTER 10

African women in politics

Jean O'Barr and Kathryn Firmin-Sellers

Elements of the story

The emergence of Western feminist scholarship in the late 1960s focussed attention on African women, a topic first investigated under the auspices of colonial governments and now researched primarily by Western scholars to understand the ways in which women's status is socially and culturally constructed. Africa has proved to be a particularly rich laboratory for the study of women because of the wide variation in women's status and the relative prominence of the public aspects of women's lives as farmers and mothers, traders and wives, spiritual figures and daughters. The political dimensions of these social and cultural positions present intriguing issues for analysis.

In indigenous African societies, before the advent of colonial powers, women's political positions varied extensively across Africa's multiple ethnic and tribal groups; in some societies women exercised extensive authority. During the colonial period, however, European administrators imposed a legal and cultural apparatus that undermined women's traditional bases of power; women became politically and economically subordinated and marginalized. This marginalization was not reversed by postcolonial, independence governments, even where women had been active participants in nationalist and liberation movements. Thus, today, women in Africa remain politically underrepresented and economically disadvantaged.

Much of the research about African women has been grounded in a series of questions posed by outsiders, from colonial times to the present. It is well understood that colonialism altered the status of women and reduced their power through the imposition of Western conceptions of state and society, women, family, and gender. Less obvious, however, are the ways in which contemporary scholars and policy-makers reinscribe this same pattern through the unself-critical application of Western paradigms and categories. African women's perspectives on their own lives remain largely on the margins.

In this chapter, we will engage two interrelated tasks. First, we will present in greater detail what is known about the political positions of African women. What has been learned about African women in politics historically? What is being learned currently? Second, we will explore the analytical process that has generated these ideas and information. What questions have been asked – or not asked – about African women in politics? What assumptions underlie the research that has been done? How have these questions and assumptions shaped both the understandings of African women and the positions these women occupy in their societies?

Before undertaking these tasks, we need to spell out some of our own assumptions about African women in politics. The first assumption is that commonalities in African women's experiences are the most useful focus for this analysis. Africa exhibits enormous diversity among women on the basis of ethnicity, region, nationality, race, and class as well as historical experiences. Across all of this diversity, however, run certain common themes that we have selected to pursue here.

Our second assumption is that the historical legacy of African women in politics continues to shape their present circumstances, however dimly. Records of African societies before Western influence are scant, but we know that women generally exercised more political power then than they do now. Although we do not know how the political culture of the past continues to influence the present, we assume some connections, as we will argue later in the chapter.

Our third assumption is that all of the social and cultural institutions that originated in the West and were imposed on Africa carried with them specific ideas about gender. Nowhere is this clearer than in the Western idea that there is a public–private dichotomy in politics and that women's affairs belong in the private realm. We will explore this axis throughout the analysis.

Fourth, we have organized our comments around political processes rather than historical periods that reflect predominantly male experiences. Emphasizing process as opposed to chronology has proved more useful in gaining insight into what has happened to women, why and how. Thus, we do not talk strictly in terms of precolonial, colonial, and postcolonial time frames, but rather in terms of the questions being posed about African women. How different were African women from their European counterparts according to the first observers? Could colonial governments and missionaries effectively 'understand' and thereby control them? What accounted for the differences in authority and status among women in African societies and between African and non-African women?

Finally, as will become apparent, colonial governments, contemporary elites, and international experts have all created social institutions that rest on particular gender ideologies. We have been struck by the fact that the leaders who transferred these institutions to African societies with alternative gender ideologies have not yet learned about these differences in ideology or their importance. This ignorance may well be the reason why many reform programs and development policies have not worked in Africa.

Understanding the position of women in indigenous societies

The position of women in indigenous societies intrigued Western observers, primarily travellers, traders, and missionaries, who first journeyed to Africa in the nineteenth century (see Callaway 1987, Strobel 1991). Sometimes they noted the independence of African women. Other times they stressed their abject state of dependence. They talked about how hard women worked in the fields and contrasted their work with the apparent laziness of men. They marvelled at the ability of African women to maintain households and to raise children while appearing to lack sufficient material resources. They suggested that women were sexually lax because they did not dress modestly and did not appear to be under the control of men. Above all, whether they thought African women were tyrants or chattels or something in between, they registered alarm that women tended to inhabit their own worlds of work, family, and friendship with little regard for men. Their observations, which served as the first Western written records of African women, emphasized difference, the gap between what the observers saw and what they understood about middle-class European women.

Colonial governments employed anthropologists and other social observers to assist them in 'understanding' native peoples. The goal of that understanding, in the language of the time, was to help 'bridge the gap that lies between Africans and the ever-shifting administrative officers who represent to them the British government', rendering government administration more effective (Perham in Leith-Ross 1965: 39); today, we would talk in terms of achieving greater political control. Viewed in retrospect, these colonial-era research reports contain important information about what was and was not understood about women in Africa.

Only since the 1960s has there been a sustained and explicitly scholarly focus on women. But here, too, the emphasis has been on answering Western questions with African data. Michelle Rosaldo and Louise Lamphere put forward a central concern for Western feminists: 'Why, if our social worlds are so different from those of our ancestors, has the relation of the sexes continued to be asymmetrical, and how is it that social groups, which change radically through time, continue to produce and reproduce a social order dominated by men?' (1974: 7).

A major question for Western observers has been how African women fared under different types of precolonial political systems. Prior to the systematic penetration of European colonial systems, African women had a much broader role in decision-making than they did under colonialism, or than they have had since independence. As described in Chapter 1, the hunting and gathering societies of Central and southern Africa were characterized by relative political equity between women and men. There was no continuous formal political leadership, and each sex had its own sphere of activity, over which its leaders exercised control. Women organized the hunting of small animals, the gathering of roots and berries, the provision of water, and the care of small children; men were involved in the hunting of larger animals and the division and storage of the kill. Both participated in the ritual and communal activities of their societies (Collier and Rosaldo 1981).

In the agricultural societies of most of black Africa, where the majority of African women lived, women derived their political status from the key role they played in production. Whether the society was matrilineal or patrilineal, women usually (1) had political control over some area of activity, be it farming, marketing, trading, or household and family affairs; (2) had political institutions (usually councils) to decide how to rule their own affairs or to influence the affairs of men; and (3) were not subject to general control by men as much as they were autonomous in their own areas of responsibility (Hafkin and Bay 1976, Rosaldo and Lamphere 1974). Women's solidarity groups (based on kinship, age, culture, or economic production tasks) played a critical role in providing formal relationships for women in the community as well as in endowing women with a psychological sense of self-esteem. African women were bound to other women through a complex set of associations; that sense of belonging provided the base from which they carried on their day-to-day affairs.

Some African societies had even more economic stratification and political hierarchy. Women's economic roles in one such system, the precolonial kingdom of Burundi, are described in Chapter 1. The work compiled by Denise Paulme and her colleagues (1971) contrasted the position of women in centralized and non-centralized states. Weaving an analysis of class into considerations of women's status, they suggested that in states with elaborate hierarchical structures, a few women of the ruling class often held political offices and exercised authority over men and women of lower classes. In contrast, in decentralized agricultural and hunting and gathering societies, women appeared to exercise considerable control over their own affairs, in a collective manner and parallel to men but not separate from them. In these societies, the number of political offices was few, and women rarely held authority over men (Paulme 1971).

A major conclusion of research on precolonial African women is that, unlike women in Western societies, African women were not confined to a 'private' sphere and excluded from a 'public' sphere (Rosaldo and Lamphere 1974). Authors in the Rosaldo and Lamphere collection were the first anthropologists working in Africa to be trained in feminist scholarship. Making gender the primary lens through which the lives of African women were investigated, their contribution was to show that the public–private distinction thought of as natural in the West was in fact an artifact of Western history and was not a useful way to describe African gender systems.

In the process of contrasting women's status in different political systems and exploring the social and cultural correlates of status, researchers documented the many and varied positions of authority held by African women in the past. Some authors focussed on cases in which women exercised religious or spiritual power. Among the Igbo of Nigeria, for example, the *omu* assured the safe operation of the marketplace through her medicine and rituals (Okonjo 1976). In South Africa, the Lovedu queen was responsible for the fertility of both land and people (see Chapter 6 above). Other researchers studied women who exercised political authority or acted autonomously, and they found societies in which women were leaders, councillors, and/or spiritual figures. Western researchers were particularly impressed by societies in which women had their own institutions for conducting female affairs (in areas such as marketing, farming, and age group societies) especially where those institutions appeared to be parallel rather than subordinate to men's institutions. The Asante *ohemaa*, or queen mother, ruled jointly with a male chief; she operated her own court and could rule in the chief's absence (Aidoo 1981). In Yorubaland, the *iyalode* had jurisdiction over all Yoruba women and defended their concerns in the male king's council (Awe 1977).

Working with this kind of evidence, one author emphasizes the difference between the roles of sister and wife, showing that women as individuals and as a group had more control over their lives in some systems than in others. A *sister* in this sense is one who has economic control and is in a social system that is neither patriarchal nor excessively hierarchical, while a *wife* is one whose position derives from her husband and whose cultural system is patriarchal. Sisters fare better than wives politically; the cultural situations in which sisters flourish tend to be those without patriarchy and without a capitalist base. This argument, while clearly subject to debate, provides a clear distinction between conditions favoring political power and those that do not (Sacks 1979).

The economic basis of women's political position also concerned researchers, and it formed another cluster of findings. Led by the pioneering work of Ester Boserup (1970), this research demonstrated historically that African women had been economically productive and independent. In the West African nations of Ghana, Nigeria, Senegal, and Guinea-Bissau, many women had achieved financial success as market traders (Brooks 1976, 1983, Johnson 1981). Elsewhere, women's economic activities had been tied to agriculture. In southern Zambia, Tonga women's access to land and the labor of their sons and sons-in-law had helped them manage large, lucrative farms (Wright 1983). Throughout the Congo region and in parts of southeast, east, and western Africa, women had been responsible for nearly all subsistence cultivation (Boserup 1970: 17).

Recognizing the amount of work performed by African women in their subsistence economies, some planners and observers urged the inclusion of women in economic development schemes. The fact that women were responsible for anywhere between 30 and 79 per cent of the agricultural labor in Africa (Boserup 1970: 17) came as news to Western observers, however; it was news that was difficult to comprehend since it contradicted their assumptions about the relationship between women and economics.

Thus the range of powers and responsibilities held by women in precolonial Africa was wide and impressive. What happened to those positions under colonial rule was confining and problematic.

Challenging African women's ways of living

The administrative and economic systems introduced by colonial officials throughout Africa embodied a Western conception of state and society, with its distinction between public and private spheres and its complementary ideas about women, family, and gender. There are, of course, important variations in the experiences of African women under different colonial systems. Yet from the contemporary vantage point, the differences appear less important than the similarities.

Colonial officials (who were almost exclusively male), traders, and missionaries all set out to make African women more like their European counterparts. Through schooling and special projects, African women were taught to use modern medicine, prepare European meals, bear and raise children according to European experts' standards, engage in clubs and organizations that complemented those of men, and undertake decorative arts as a leisure activity. Nancy Hunt's account of the *foyer social* in the 1950s Belgian Congo presents a vivid picture of the African women who encountered these ideals of Western womanhood. The *foyers* were founded by missionaries and later run by the government, in order to give 'immoral Africans' a 'normal social life'. To this end, women were taught to be 'prudent ladies of the house, model wives and mothers of the family'. Building on women's 'natural feminine psychological propensity for motherhood and domesticity', the foyers worked to instill in a wife 'devotion, unselfishness, and discreet and intelligent collaboration in the profession of the husband' (Hunt 1990: 454–56).

Colonial administrative systems allowed European officials to govern through indigenous male authorities, formalizing male institutions while ignoring their female equivalents. The British system of indirect rule was most explicit in its reliance on indigenous authorities, but all systems attempted to create new administrative structures. In every case, simple expediency forced the very few European officials who were present to rely on informal systems and networks, and those systems they sought were exclusively male. In Igboland, the government transformed the traditional male office of the *obi* into a salaried position but ignored the *obi*'s female counterpart, the *omu* (Okonjo, 1976). Among the Asante, the British worked through the Asantehene and his male chiefs and councilors. When asked why

Asante men had not described the active role of women to European anthropologists, one Asante male remarked, 'The white men never asked us this; you have dealings with and recognized only the men; we supposed the European considered women of no account, and we know you do not recognize them as we have always done' (Rattray 1923: 84). Colonial administrators simply never considered the possibility that there were female political structures that should be incorporated into the colonial political system.

The Aba riots, or women's war, is a case in point. The Igbo women's institution of 'sitting on a man' is described above in Chapter 9. It was a well-developed political process for shaming men who violated women's rights. Women gathered in groups to sing songs of shame until offenders ceased their actions, and used this collective political mechanism against British colonial authorities as well. British officials saw the women's actions as random and irrational. Ignoring women while building up men's political sphere led to the loss of institutional authority for women during the colonial period (Van Allen 1976).

The legal system was another arena in which colonialism had a direct negative impact on women's lives. Customary law was written down and formalized without the participation of women. Previously fluid principles were codified to secure the status of a few privileged males (Chanock 1985). The two subjects most frequently codified were land law and marriage law. As described in Chapter 1, in many indigenous societies, land had been controlled by extended family members, both male and female, who gained use rights through family ties. When colonial authorities began to create a system of private property rights, they extended those rights only to men because ownership in the West was historically a male privilege. Thus, women both lost traditional access to land and failed to gain new property rights (see, for example, Hay 1982, Mikell 1989, Urdang 1989).

A similar process developed in the area of marriage law. Bridewealth or brideprice, inheritance, and even the legal recognition of marriage came under scrutiny. The process of codifying these practices, either through British common law or the establishment of legal codes under the colonial powers, altered the meaning of marriage as it had been understood in African society. Although there were as many marriage systems in Africa as there were different societies, in every system the value of women's labor was recognized in the marriage transaction, ancestral ties were maintained, and marriage was an arrangement made between social groups and not the result of a romantic attraction between individuals. As described in Chapter 4 on the family, the new processes imposed by colonial powers made individual women dependent upon individual men and thus helped to create a social dependency among women that has had lasting effects (see for example Callaway and Schildkrout 1986, Chanock 1985, Mann 1985).

The creation of cash economies based on the control of indigenous labor further contributed to the economical and political marginalization of African women. Many colonial policies were motivated by a desire to create an African labor force to operate European economic ventures. The central position of men in this cash economy was assured by an array of policy decisions. Men were given greater educational opportunities and access to government agricultural training; after the First World War, government-run marketing boards purchased crops almost exclusively from male farmers (Mikell 1989, Staudt 1978), and tight restrictions on the construction of urban housing made it nearly impossible for both husbands and wives to migrate to urban areas (White 1986). By denying women education, training, and access to urban employment, colonial legislation assured that women would play only a secondary role in the emerging cash economy, 'contributing to the support of male wage laborers and their dependents [and] lowering the cost of this labor' (MacGaffey 1988: 163).

The strategic use of legislation by the government of South Africa represents an extreme illustration of the colonizers' efforts to control wage labor. The South African government wanted a labor force comprising only migrant males, a labor force that 'would not be burdened with superfluous appendages such as wives, children, and dependents who cannot provide service' (cited in Bernstein 1985: 14). To this end, the Nationalist Party in 1948 introduced a program designating each black African a resident of a government-created tribal homeland. All urban wage earners were officially designated as foreign, migrant laborers. Women were denied access to urban areas, first by artificially maintained housing shortages and then, in 1964, by a formal ban on migration. The restrictions continue to be felt, even in the face of current legal reform.

The impact of these policies on South African women has been devastating. Left alone in rural areas, women have seen their workload double. As the productivity of the land has diminished, women have become increasingly impoverished. The ban on migration has condemned those women who have moved illegally to inhabit squatter camps and shanty towns on the outskirts of the cities. The resulting destruction of nuclear and extended family ties has isolated women from their traditional sources of support (Bernstein 1985).

One way to appreciate the vast impact of the new social institutions imposed by colonial governments is to listen to the voices of African women whose lives were changed. Colonial officials did not hear these voices, but they were there, trying to make themselves heard. The works of African women novelists are helpful here. Buchi Emecheta's novel, *The Joys of Motherhood*, (1979) looks at African society through the eyes of Nnu Ego, a poor and illiterate woman whose story illustrates the dangers of living by traditional values in an urban environment that no longer holds to those values. Emecheta's novel describes how women are entrapped by a world that demands motherhood but no longer venerates it. (Emecheta's work is described more fully in Chapter 8.)

Reacting to changing circumstances

In spite of the burdens imposed by colonial policy, African women have been active agents, responding to their changing circumstances. African women actively participated in many early anticolonial protests, as well as in the nationalist and liberation movements that swept the continent after the Second World War. As these events unfolded on an international scale, Western observers asked a series of questions: Were women aware of their distinctive position as women? Did women issue political demands based on their position as women? Did women participate in these movements with a feminist consciousness? (See Geiger 1987, Schuster 1983.) Although there was great variation in the ways in which women participated in these movements, it is accurate to say that they acted primarily as nationalists rather than as feminists. If we understand 'feminist' to mean those who look at social situations in terms of equality between women and men and who seek to rectify the imbalance of power between the sexes, it is clear that African women acted out their past; they pursued nationalist goals by utilizing female political structures rather than conceptualizing nationalism as a means of altering power relations between the sexes.

Accounts of women's participation in anticolonial protests in Tanzania, Kenya, Nigeria, and Cameroon, for example, are remarkably similar. In Tanzania and Kenya, women assumed public roles in response to threats to their community even though there were no indigenous precedents for their action. The tax riots in Pare District, Tanzania, in the 1940s precipitated the first active roles for many Pare women in modern politics. The riots grew out of a Pare District Council decision to levy a graduated income tax. In 1942–43, the colonially instituted council, composed of the nine male chiefs or 'native authorities', decided to institute the tax, in addition to the poll tax already in force. The new revenue was to be used solely for development projects in the district.

The direct cause of the riots was confusion arising out of imprecise and unclear procedures for tax assessment and collection. People demanded more information about the basis of assessment and objected to the use of the traditional name and form for the tax. Pare men became indignant, taking the position that people had a legitimate right to question the governing authorities. The chiefs, sensing that people were attacking their position and not simply their stand on the tax, became determined to impose the tax without any modifications as evidence of their authority. Thwarted by their discussions with the chiefs, people chose a more direct course of action. Early in 1945, thousands of men representing the various parts of Pare District marched on the district headquarters at Same, and announced their intention to remain there until the tax was abolished.

After the demonstrators set up camp, the chiefs and their assistants moved to the district headquarters as well. Several meetings were held among the people's representatives, the native authorities, and the officers of the colonial government, but little progress was made. After several months, women in one subdivision began to mobilize. The wives, mothers, sisters, and daughters of the demonstrators marched 25 miles to the district headquarters in order to show their support for the stand the men had taken. The women presented themselves as a delegation to the district officer and demanded that he either effect a settlement and allow the men to return to their homes, farms, and jobs or impregnate all of them himself. The women claimed that the controversy had so disrupted the normal life cycle that, if Pare society were to continue, they would have to follow their husbands to Same. Since the British officer had forced the men to abandon their wives and their work, he should assume their roles as husbands. For the women, the British officer symbolized the deadlock between their husbands and the native authorities.

The local officer, unable to see an easy resolution to the tax controversy, requested assistance from both the provincial and territorial governments. When the national officials arrived in Pare in 1946, they were stoned by crowds of angry women. Sensing that the situation had taken on new and uncontrollable dimensions, the chiefs relented. They remained firm that a tax should be levied but consented to a new form of assessment. Still dissatisfied, more than 2,000 Pare taxpayers (about one-fourth of the total) paid their 1946 tax in the neighboring district of Kilimanjaro, even though the rate there was slightly higher than in Pare District. Informants, later recalling this event, claimed that the taxpayers believed their actions demonstrated to the colonial government that they were indeed willing to pay the tax but were protesting about its form and the manner in which it had been levied. The idea of a graduated tax was dropped the following year, and the existing poll tax was raised. Other reforms in local government increased popular representation in district decision making, although none guaranteed direct involvement for women.

The involvement of the Pare women was essentially a conservative reaction. During the tax riots, women asked that the order of their lives be restored. They wanted their men home and the dispute settled. By asking to be impregnated, they vocalized their demand for a continuation of life as it was. Pare women were mobilized into this new form of political activity by the new circumstances in which they found themselves, not because of any pre-existing structures (O'Barr 1976).

In Nigeria and Cameroon women's indigenous political structures already existed and were redirected in response to new circumstances. The 'Aba Riots' among the Igbo in eastern Nigeria in 1929 are one example; they made use of the tradition of 'sitting on a man' described in Chapter 9. The Anlu Rebellion of 1958–61 in Cameroon illustrates a similar pattern (Shanklin 1990). On 4 July 1958, the Kom women of Cameroon launched a three-year period of rebellion, known as Anlu, in which they seized political power from Kom men. Their protest was provoked by rumours that Kom land would be sold to Nigerian

Igbos and by the colonial government's demand that women switch from horizontal to vertical contour farming.

Scholars have assigned multiple interpretations to the Anlu Rebellion. Some have suggested that, although it was a women's movement, Anlu was used by men to further their own political agenda (Ritzenthaler 1974, Konde 1992). Others have contended that Anlu was a valid women's movement that advanced uniquely female concerns (Ardener 1975). What is important here is that the Anlu rebellion was a modern adaptation of indigenous institutions in an effort to preserve the rights of the Kom community at large, not simply the rights of Kom women. In indigenous society, as described in the preceding chapter, *anlu* referred to the practice in which women would *lu* an offender until he or she repented for the alleged grievance. Through public singing, verbal insults, dancing and demonstrating in public, and by generally seizing control of resources and directing political outcomes, women attempted to get the offending party to change his or her behavior (Shanklin 1990: 159).

Shanklin has argued that modern Anlu is most accurately understood as an 'extension of women's right to protect the kingdom' (1990: 160). In the Anlu Rebellion, women acted in defense of Kom territory, not the female sex. They invoked symbols which signified their power over nature, not symbols of their own sexuality. Their right to take over the rule of the kingdom was unquestioned. The women who participated in Anlu cooperated with the male counterpart, *mukum*, 'to uphold and enforce' community values (Shanklin 1990: 168); they did not address women's issues per se. Thus, Anlu formed part of the continuum of women's anticolonial protest.

Since the colonial period came to a close in the 1950s and 1960s, additional evidence of the political roles played by African women has been collected. Various kinds of nationalist movements, as well as the periods in which they occurred, have created new contexts within which women acted. The earliest, relatively nonviolent and non-Marxist revolutions of West Africa were followed by similar movements in East and Central Africa. A second set of nationalist movements occurred in the entrenched settler economies of Kenya and Rhodesia/Zimbabwe, where violent struggle was necessary. A later wave of more self-consciously socialist and Marxist-Leninist movements led to intense fighting in Guinea-Bissau, Angola, and Mozambique. Finally, in South Africa, nationalist activity continues, originally in the face of strong repression and now in the process of transition.

In this section, we will discuss examples from Nigeria, Tanzania, Sierra Leone, and Guinea, all of which attest to the fact that women helped bring about the expulsion of colonial authorities, although the forms of participation differed in each case. We will also consider the ways in which women did or did not build on this power in the years after independence. The role of women in armed national liberation movements in Guinea-Bissau, Angola, Mozambique, Zimbabwe, and Namibia is discussed in Chapter 11 of this volume.

In Nigeria, where the nationalist movement was less violent and was centered on electoral struggles, organizations of market women were key supporters of the political parties during elections. In fact, the support of market women often became the leading factor in a party's ability to control an area. The women themselves were active in endorsing and financing potential candidates, extracting promises, and generally participating in the political process (Johnson 1981, Mba 1982). However, they limited their politicking to demands related to market activities and continually underestimated their own political strength. Thus, as time went on, the political clout they once exercised tended to decline.

The mobilization of urban women – beer brewers, market traders, and prostitutes – was key to the success of nationalist movements elsewhere. In Tanzania, the nationalist political organization, TANU, relied upon its women's section to conduct its grass roots campaign. Women conveyed information between branches, raised money, and mobilized local supporters. These urban women were able political activists. Most were older, divorced, and were engaged in their own income-earning activities. They had therefore achieved a degree of independence from their husbands and families that rural women did not enjoy (Geiger 1987). In addition, urban women could draw upon social organizations, such as the popular *ngoma* dance groups, and their own network of business relations, to reach a broad audience (Mbilinyi 1990: 123).

In other West African cases, such as Sierra Leone, women's political participation was institutionalized both during and after the nationalist period. The career of Constance Cummings-John is an excellent example of how some women became effective political leaders.

> Mrs Cummings-John's early career demonstrates how an elite woman became politically aware through family participation in local politics, reinforced by radical contacts she made while studying in Britain. . . . Her ideas developed partly as the result of discussions with West Africans and other black colonials about the colonial situation, and partly because of her own upbringing in a home in which politics was an important concern. Cummings-John's early success was due to her connection with Wallace-Johnson, one of the most astute politicians of the interwar period. From him, she learned the techniques of mass organization, protest demonstrations, and the necessity of keeping in touch with the people. The people in her constituency noticed that she listened to their complaints, took note of their needs, and helped them obtain what redress was possible. In the process, she became conscious of the power residing in the market women, although she did not seek to harness that power for political purposes until much later. For her the lesson of the inter-war years was that the parochial concerns of the established elite inhibited self-determination and limited development for the masses. In the 1950s she utilized her insights about the colonial situation to create a dynamic

new movement, the Sierra Leone Women's Movement. The association united Creole and Protectorate women in a fight against colonial policies inimical to their economic and political interest. She aligned the women's movement with the Sierra Leone People's Party, the Protectorate-based party which was much more in tune with the interests of the masses than the other, elitist colony-based parties. Thus Cummings-John became one of the most important women politicians in West Africa in the fight for independence (Denzer 1981: 31–32).

In Guinea, in former French West Africa, the nationalist movement assumed a more socialist ideology and had a greater commitment to political roles for women. Here women played a direct role in the rise to power of Sékou Touré, the principal nationalist leader, and they maintained that power thereafter. Touré appealed early to women as active participants. They responded with active involvement – they gave money, they provided communication links among the revolutionaries, and their leaders participated in policy formation. After independence, women stayed in the party and in power (Dobert 1970). In comparison to other regimes of that period, Guinean women exercised extensive political power, both as a result of recognizing and building on the support they had given Sékou Touré and as a result of his eagerness to use them. Like the leaders of the nationalist movements in Angola and Mozambique, Touré worked from a dual base vis-à-vis women. On the one hand, he had an ideological basis for his socialism, which demanded the equal participation of women. His view of the body politic required equal involvement of all citizens, male and female. On the other hand, he was an astute judge of his limited resources and was well aware of his need to mobilize all of them. Guinean women were key resources, by tradition and through modern market involvement, and he reached out to them.

A survey of the highlights of women's participation in the African nationalist movements would be incomplete without mentioning the experiences of South African women, black and white, in that country's protracted political struggle. The nature of South African politics makes it difficult to compile a full picture of how women have aided the as yet-unfinished anticolonial struggle. Accounts of earlier history demonstrate how white women's roles were interrelated with national politics during the Anglo-Boer War, which lasted from 1889 to 1902 (Spies 1980). The Black Sash, since 1963 a multiracial, liberal organization of women opposed to apartheid laws, has stood as an important example of how South African women have found ways of resisting the dominant political culture (Michelmann 1975). The fundamental link between apartheid policies and the intersection of gender, race, and class in the South African system has been described by Hilda Bernstein in *For Their Triumphs and for Their Tears* (1985). Bernstein demonstrated how the sex-gender system of white South Africa has been essential to the policies of apartheid, policies that systematically manipulated black family life and the place of women in society. In South Africa as elsewhere, women have been active in political movements, in this case the African National Congress and the United Democratic Front. Our knowledge of women's participation in the resistance is limited, but growing (Russell 1989). It appears that women, black and white, have resisted intolerable situations, usually by finding ways around the constraints, sometimes by initiating protest, often by joining with men in opposing repressive conditions. One area in which black women continue to be active is in labor organization (Berger 1986).

These brief accounts of African women's involvement in politics during the colonial period and in nationalist struggles suggest that women, by using ideas and tactics derived from traditional political experience, have been able to exercise some clout in spite of the negative impact of Western colonialism. In the years since independence, however, the situation has been much less conducive to women's political power.

Contemporary politics and women

Ignored by European administrators who insisted that women should occupy the private sphere, and manipulated by independent African governments that assigned secondary importance to women's issues, women in contemporary Africa are both politically underrepresented and economically marginalized. Women are underrepresented in the sense that few of them hold political office or participate in formal political organizations. Their invisibility can be documented at all levels of government. According to a 1986 UN survey, women occupied an average of 6 per cent of all national legislative seats in African governments. Only half of the 40 African states had women serving in the executive as cabinet members. All 29 of those cabinet officers were assigned to special women's issues – community development, health, nutrition, and social development – and were not directly involved with the policies that male government officials deemed essential. The sole exception was in Botswana, where a woman was serving as foreign minister (Africa Rights Monitor 1990).

Women may be better represented at the local level, but too little evidence exists to confidently describe the nature or extent of their participation. Women are generally inactive in the military, a politically salient fact given the number of military regimes that have been a controlling influence in African governance. Finally, few women are present at the supranational level. In 1986, for example, among the thousands of Africans at the United Nations, 47 were women, only two of whom occupied the positions of director or higher (Africa Rights Monitor 1990).

Two interrelated factors explain the political underrepresentation of African women. First, politics is viewed by most men and women as the quintessential male sphere of action, one in which women are both unwelcome and ineffective. Potential female candidates are often harassed, deterring their activism. According to one Zambian professional, a 'progressive and intelligent woman who participates in politics is regarded as a hooligan, she is said to have any possible fault, bad behavior. . . . [S]he isn't worth anything, she's finished' (Geisler 1987: 57). The individual women who are politically active succeed by adopting a masculine political stance: they ally with male party officials, they accept the party's agenda, they campaign on party issues. Under these circumstances, few women have the opportunity or desire to broach those issues that a female constituency would find compelling (Schuster 1983).

Second, most politically active women are members of the African elite. Better educated and wealthier, these women often pursue a political agenda that reflects their class rather than their gender interests (House-Midamba 1990). Sometimes their activities are irrelevant to the vast majority of African women. In Uganda and Kenya, for example, the leading women's groups campaigned for changes in the divorce laws; in Ghana, the National Council of Ghanaian Women called on the government to create a nursery school system. Both reforms would have affected only a small minority of elite urban women (Staudt 1986: 203). In other cases, elite women have become active participants in the creation of ideologies that preserve their elite status but undermine and subordinate them as women (Staudt 1986). Where women's auxiliaries to national ruling parties are dominated by elite women, the members allow themselves to be co-opted by the government. Zambia's UNIP Women's League acts, at the government's behest, as the guardian of Zambian moral and ethical code. Members exhort women to accept their domestic roles as mothers and wives and willingly police their communities to identify prostitutes, black market traders, and other women who encourage 'moral decay' (Geisler 1987). In Mali the National Union of Malian Women (UNFM) cannot engage any issues that the government does not endorse, and in Kenya the party expressly prohibits its women's auxiliary from addressing any political issues (Staudt 1986: 208, Africa Rights Monitor 1990: 51).

Western academics know little about the lives of individual African politicians or about the ways in which class and gender divisions interact in Africa. This ignorance is significant, for the two factors seem directly related to the average woman's alienation from politics. Under existing conditions, most African women feel ignored, persecuted, and powerless (Schuster 1983). They have no interest in politics or politicians because no government officials – male or female – address issues relevant to their daily experience. In this sense they are also misrepresented.

Unfortunately, there is little to suggest that these conditions will change in the near future. First, educational systems are not adequately training future political leaders. Education provides a bridge to political influence, largely because literacy is a prerequisite to holding office. Thus, policies enacted today will greatly influence whether or not the next generation of women will be prepared to hold political office, engage in political activity, or even follow political debate.

Throughout Africa educational attainment by women has improved over the past decade. Nations with poor educational records have extended primary education to increasing numbers of girls. Other countries have narrowed the gap between the percentage of male and female children enrolled in school. (See Appendix for additional data on women's education.)

Nevertheless, women's achievements have been limited, which suggests that the future pool of female activists and leaders will be small. In many countries the differential between the rates of males and females receiving an education is still large, reaching 20 per cent in Togo and climbing even higher in Kenya, Mauritius, Sao Tome, and Zambia. Even where girls receive primary education, the rate of secondary education is lower, dipping below 30 per cent in most nations. Women enrolled at the postsecondary level are channelled into 'female fields', such as the humanities and teaching. Women are most poorly represented in engineering, law, and science, those disciplines that lead to well-paid, influential professions (Africa Rights Monitor 1990: 53). International efforts to alter these trends have proved inadequate in scope and impact.

Second, many women have responded to their underrepresentation by withdrawing from the arena of formal state control (Parpart 1988). Rather than confront the institutions and ideologies that subordinate them, African women have adopted strategies that allow them to evade state authority. The willingness of African women to rely on their own institutions may have its roots in a women's political legacy. Whatever their origin and contemporary forms, the political manifestation of these strategies is clear: women do not advance themselves (or other women) as political candidates, and many of them abstain from political parties and women's auxiliaries.

Much recent research on African women and politics has focussed on the patriarchal composition of the state and its resultant policies. Women's experience is portrayed as one of exclusion from state resources, inequality of access, neglect, and outright oppression (Parpart and Staudt 1989; the impact of state policies on women is further discussed in Chapter 12). There are variations on this general pattern ranging from the less common extreme of state domination and coercion of women, to the more common situation in which women are 'uncaptured' by the regime and consciously dissociate themselves from it (Chazan 1989). In between are patterns of weak and inconsistent domination, exemplified by Zambia's ineffectual attempts to regulate women's marketing (Hansen 1989), and patterns of unequal vertical exchange, exemplified in the active but often ineffective involvement of Nigerian women under military rule (Mba 1989).

Interestingly, many women's activities seem to lie beyond the reach of the formal state apparatus. The best example is women's widespread participation in the informal economy, through which they demonstrate their ability to create positions of power and autonomy. A study of rural Kenya found that many women, denied access to the economic resources of their villages and excluded from political office, had turned to prostitution as an '"institutional weapon" forged . . . to enlarge their freedom of social manoeuvre' (Bujra 1977: 13). In Nairobi, prostitution allowed women to become socially respected members of the 'petty bourgeoisie who owned profit making enterprises – the sale of sexuality, the sale of domestic services, the rental of rooms . . . for which they provided the labor' (White 1986: 273). In Zaire, some women built upon prostitution and other small-scale activities to become prominent members of an emerging capitalist class (MacGaffey 1988: 170).

In the short term, withdrawing from the formal sector can be a viable strategy for coping with the challenges that confront women daily. Withdrawal is an individual strategy that does not require collective mobilization in order to confront institutionalized practices. Participation in the informal sector can also give women some degree of economic autonomy. In the long run, however, the strategy leaves African women vulnerable. First, the sexual division of labor present in the formal sector is recreated in the informal sector. In both, women work in low-paid, low-skilled, labor-intensive positions; they shoulder the double burden of domestic work and participation in the cash economy; and they are at a disadvantage when competing against their male counterparts because men can draw upon the labor of their extended family, wives, and children, resources that are unavailable to women. Thus, while some women find wealth in the informal sector, the majority live at the subsistence level and remain economically vulnerable.

In addition, the voluntary departure of women from politics only perpetuates their misrepresentation. This short-run, reactive stance forestalls any proactive efforts to secure resources or reform from the government (Parpart 1988a: 221). Even where reforms are envisioned, planners proceed without any direct knowledge of women's needs and interests. This void has been acutely felt during the past decade of international and national reform.

The UN Decade and international reform

Over the past 15 years international and national policy-makers have launched many programs designed to strengthen women's position by integrating them more fully into existing economic and political institutions. Progress has been slow, however. Lacking input from the very women they have sought to help, development specialists have not been forced to examine the assumptions they bring to policy-making. Thus, most development programs have been established without an awareness of the precolonial political structures that served women; instead, Western notions of family and the division between public and private life have been incorporated in development programs, notions that are manifestly inappropriate in Africa.

The challenge of women in development gained international prominence during the United Nations Decade for Women launched in 1975. Inspired by recent scholarship arguing that women had been systematically disempowered by the processes of economic growth, international agencies and individual donor nations determined to assess the way in which their aid programs affected women (Fraser 1987). At the 1975 Women's Decade conference, delegates adopted a threefold strategy for change. First, they agitated for the creation of national women and development institutions to monitor the status of women and make governments more accountable to women's needs. Second, they campaigned for changes in family law that would guarantee women equal status. Third, they lobbied for the creation and implementation of new economic policies targeting women.

Each of these goals has been partially attained. The United Nations Decade for Women inspired institutional and legal reforms throughout Africa and elsewhere. By 1985, the governments of seven African countries had created full ministries for women's affairs: Cameroon, Burundi, Gabon, the Ivory Coast, Zaire, Mauritius, and Zimbabwe (Fraser 1987: 163). By 1990 mechanisms existed in 40 nations to monitor the impact of development policy on women (Africa Rights Monitor 1990: 57). African women supplemented these government agencies with their own organizations devoted to research on African women conducted by African women: the Association of African Women for Research and Development (AAWORD), which they founded, for example, and Development Alternatives for Women in a New Era (DAWN), an international organization in which they actively participated (Parpart 1986, Keller 1989).

The Decade for Women helped inspire a series of legal reforms in the area of family law. These reforms were intended to give single women greater autonomy and economic security, especially in cases of divorce, desertion, or widowhood. In Zimbabwe, for example, the 1982 Legal Age of Majority Act gave unmarried women majority status at the age of 18, allowing them to enter contracts, to arrange their own marriages, and to own property; the 1985 Matrimonial Causes Act gave divorced women a legal claim to property that the woman and her husband had owned jointly (Made and Whande 1989). In Senegal, legal changes enacted in 1988 extended existing family laws to women. A woman was allowed to act as executor of her husband's estate if the husband were absent for an extended period; husbands were required to give wives child support in the case of divorce; and women were granted the right to have their marriages annulled if they had wed while under age (Fatou 1989: 34). Chapter 5 of this volume discusses the ways recent changes in Zambia's inheritance laws will affect women.

Unfortunately, institutional and legal changes have not always improved the status of women in Africa. The existence of institutions does not necessarily indicate that a government is committed to ameliorating the position of women. Women's bureaus may exist, but they are often poorly funded and staffed. Government officials may ignore the bureaus because they see them as peripheral to essential policy concerns, or because they deny the reality of women's subordination. The Kenyan government, for example, maintains that women have already made significant progress and now occupy positions of importance in both the public and the private sector (Nzomo 1989: 10). In Zambia, the government's official ideology of humanism denies that women are affected by growth or policy initiatives any differently from men (Keller 1984: 5). Because institutions are often directly tied to the ruling party, they lack the leverage to challenge the government's complacency and demand changes in the status quo.

The Zambian government's approach to women in development is illustrative of the way in which women's bureaus can be rendered politically and economically ineffective. Multiple institutions exist in Zambia to integrate women into development. The ruling party's Women's League has written a Program for Action, which parallels the program written during the UN Decade; the Planning Unit of the Agricultural Department employs a women's program advisor at the national level and female extension service agents at the provincial level; and the National Commission for Development Planning works with a women's project officer. In spite of these bureaucratic positions, the Zambian government rarely initiates policy reforms for women; instead, policies typically are conceived by international agents who then try to market the program to Zambian officials (Keller 1984: 12–14). The process, repeated throughout Africa, results in 'small, isolated projects of foreign inception which are appended to and do not become an integral part of Zambia's development efforts' (Keller 1984: 15). Policy successes are rare and consist of small victories, granted by men, that are largely irrelevant to the vast majority of women (Keller 1989: 20).

Similarly, legal changes promoted during the UN Decade have not strengthened women's status. Where legal reforms have been enacted, their impact has been diluted by the absence of enforcement mechanisms and by the reluctance of women to demand their legal rights in court (Parpart 1988a: 219). Both phenomena suggest an essential weakness in the strategy of pursuing change through legal reform: such reforms do not necessarily alter prevailing social attitudes about women. Throughout Africa, men have resisted legal changes because they threaten the patriarchal cultural system under which men have profited. In Mozambique heavy opposition forced the government to withdraw a legislative package that would have granted women greater rights in marriage and divorce (Urdang 1989). In Kenya amended marriage and divorce laws were twice defeated in 1987 (Nzomo 1989). In Nigeria tension between the strategy of legal change and the power of social attitudes was actually written into the constitution. The 1979 constitution formally guaranteed women equality, stating that 'every citizen shall have equality of rights, obligations, and opportunities before the law'. At the same time, the document preserved elements of Muslim law, the *shari'a*, that subordinate women. In cases where the two principles clashed, the Nigerian courts demonstrated a willingness to defer to arguments based on tradition and morality (Callaway and Schildkrout 1986).

The third leg of the UN strategy, the use of development policy to give women greater economic security, has received the greatest support from the international donor community. These programs have attempted to integrate African women in development by giving them greater access to existing resources and institutions and by ensuring that they will control the profits of their labor. Most of the resulting policy initiatives have targeted special groups of women – the rural poor or urban out-of-school-girls, for example – and organized them into special development projects for women. As described in Chapter 9 on women's associations, these programs have emphasized self-help and self-reliance, ostensibly in an effort to give women control of their own economic lives. Women are organized most often into small cooperatives, which then engage in income-generating activities: farming, roof thatching, raising pigs or poultry, weaving, or knitting. The participation rate in these programs has been high. In 1986 alone, Kenya's self-help program encompassed 15,000 groups and more than 550,000 persons (Chitere 1988: 50). In 1985, more than 125,000 Zimbabwean women participated in some 8,000 different development projects (Batezat and Mwala 1989: 62). Such projects and women's groups are discussed more fully in Chapters 9 and 12.

One project that has been relatively successful is Green Belt in Kenya, a movement in which women were paid small amounts to work at bettering the environment and strengthening community resources. Wangari Maathai, a biologist and the first Kenya woman appointed as professor at the University of Nairobi, was a founding member of a community tree-planting campaign set up by the National Council of Women in 1977. This campaign later became the Green Belt Movement. For her work in taking the environmental message to African women farmers, Dr Maathai has gained international recognition, winning the first Better World Award in 1986, as well as the UN Environment Program's Global 500 award. Despite this international recognition, in recent years Dr Maathai herself has come under pressure from the Kenyan government for her actions.

The Green Belt movement has established more than 1,000 tree nurseries and helped organize as many local groups, involving some 50,000 households. In addition, some 3,000 schools, with a total of one million students, are also involved in tree planting. 'Women are by far our greatest target,' said Dr Maathai, 'because they are the people who work the land in Africa'. The women give tree seedlings raised in the nurseries to other farmers and neighbors free of charge. If the seedlings survive more than three months outside the nursery, the women get paid, money that may well represent their only income.

The Movement has encountered some difficult problems in organizing women, however. Most are illiterate and speak different languages, making communications difficult. In addition, many of the women are so poor they are preoccupied with matters of everyday survival; unless they see quick results, they may abandon the project. Nevertheless, progress is being made, not only in spreading environmental aware-ness, but also in strengthening rural women's self-confidence. 'You can actually see change,' Dr Maathai said. 'You can see people being empowered and realizing their self-worth' (Topouzis 1990: 44).

Such success is not often replicated. In spite of the high participation rates, many women's development projects are widely viewed as failures. Irrigated rice projects in Gambia and agricultural extension reforms in Kenya, neither of which benefitted women, are discussed in Chapter 12. And although a few successful projects are mentioned in Chapter 9, that chapter too stresses the many failed efforts. Few projects have actually generated income for their participants, and those that have succeeded have been taken over by male community leaders and bureaucrats anxious to claim credit for their success (Feldman 1983, Thomas 1988b).

Explaining failure

What explains the marginal impact that all of the UN strategies – institutional, legal, and economic – have had on African women's lives? Several seemingly unrelated factors have combined to under-mine reform efforts. First, in spite of a new public awareness of the problems faced by Third World women, the international community has devoted only sporadic attention to development policy focussing on women. International donors still channel only a fraction of their development assistance to women. According to the 1990 Africa Rights Monitor, only 0.05 per cent of UN agricultural sector allocations were devoted to women's programs; only 4 per cent of U.S. AID funds benefitted women; and 3.5 per cent of UN agency projects (0.2 per cent of the overall UN budget) were for women (1990: 62). Agencies thus appear to be doing something new as opposed to responding to the economic roles women have long played.

Second, the legal campaign for equality has not extended to the area of land law, in spite of the fact that African women grow an estimated 80 per cent of Africa's food (Minority Rights Group 1988: 7). In Zimbabwe a government resettlement scheme has not altered customary land rights, and in Mozambique the government has undermined the operation of its own state farms by failing to relieve women's burden in subsistence farming (Jacobs 1984, Urdang 1989). Consequently, women have been left in a position of economic dependence and impoverishment. This stands in contrast to their traditional positions from which they could appeal to kin groups for redress.

Third, development programs created for women have been poorly planned and managed. In most cases women participants have not received the training or education they need to manage an income-generating project. In addition, development agencies themselves have often failed to plan the projects effectively. Projects have begun without prior feasibility studies to determine start-up or operating costs. Thus, for example, textile industries have been established with little thought to how factor inputs would be received or how the finished product would be transported; poultry raising was introduced and crops were cultivated without consideration for how the goods could be marketed. As long as a donor agency has sponsored the project, the resulting expenses have been surmountable, but rural women have not been able to sustain the projects themselves (Mwaniki 1986). The failures of such development projects are discussed more fully in Chapter 12.

A more fundamental problem underlies each of these disparate concerns, that of women's political invisibility. Women are excluded from policy-making at every stage – local, national, and international. At the local level, male elders control and disburse development funds received from the government (Thomas 1988a). At the national and international levels, male bureaucrats gain political capital from managing successful programs. Consequently, African women are rarely in a position to voice their needs and concerns. They are not present to pressure either international donors or national politicians to place women's issues at the center of development planning; they are not present to demand changes in land law; they are not present to give input into the design of effective development programs.

As a result of the exclusion of women, many reform efforts are conceptually flawed. For example, contemporary development policies are based on the assumption that women have been left out of economic development and that they need to be integrated into the economic system. If women can be made to participate in existing economic institutions, the thinking goes, then they too will benefit fully from development. What this assumption fails to recognize is that women already are integrated; they already play vital economic roles in subsistence agriculture and in the informal economy. Without so-called women's work, formal (male) economic institutions would not function. Thus, women will not be empowered by integration. Their position can be strengthened only when existing institutions, those economic and social structures that devalue women's work, are both understood and reformed (Feldman 1983).

The theoretical confusion embedded in African development policy is vividly illustrated by the conception held by most policy-makers that the central economic institution is the family. Most economic initiatives implicitly accept a Western view of the family, in which the father is the primary wage earner and the wife works only to supplement family income. In Zambia, for example, the government's retraining program teaches carpentry to urban males while it teaches tailoring to urban women. Tailoring, a lower paid skill, is deemed suitable for women because the work can be done at home on a part-time basis (Keller 1984). Throughout Africa self-help programs draw heavily on women's domestic skills such as cooking and sewing. In South Africa policy-makers are most concerned with apartheid's destruction of the family unit. And in Mozambique, Angola, Ethiopia, and the Sudan, the first priority of refugee relief efforts is to reunite husbands with their wives and children (Reflections on Forum '85 1986: 593–94).

By adopting this image of the nuclear family, policy-makers have accepted the myth that the father acts as a benevolent patriarch who allocates family resources for the mutual benefit of all family members. Few programs help women gain independent access to the cash or credit necessary to pay membership fees to cooperatives or training courses or to purchase raw materials for production. Similarly, initiatives do not give women control over any profits generated; these revert to their husbands, who control family finances (Parpart 1986). Thus, women's ability to participate in and benefit from development programs is left under the control of their husbands or fathers.

By design, then, these programs encourage women to treat development projects as secondary and peripheral. Women are to engage in special projects only when their other tasks have been completed. They are given the means of increasing their economic production but are not given independent control over such production or the profits earned (Parpart 1986).

In the final analysis, current reform efforts have not altered women's status because they have not addressed the core causes of women's subordination. Almost uniformly these programs have created new, labor-intensive tasks for women, each of which supplements or supports male economic activity. This structure mirrors and duplicates the phenomenon of the colonial period, when women's economic and political positions were originally undermined.

The Western ideology of a male, public sphere and a female, private sphere, imposed on indigenous societies during the colonial era, has placed African women on the economic periphery. Yet male migration, primary school education, and cash-crop cultivation have forced women to adopt multiple economic roles. Women's workload has increased, but the cultural value assigned to such work has diminished, and women have lost the economic security once generated by extended family ties. Policy-makers continue to perpetuate the Western dichotomy between male and female spheres of action and, with it, the mechanisms of women's subordination.

Conclusion

The existing body of research on women in Africa reveals the processes by which Western conceptions of gender and family, state and society have been imposed on African societies, first by missionaries and travellers, later by colonial administrators, and finally by scholars and policy-makers, both African and international. The cumulative impact of this activity has been devastating for African women. Western ideology has created a private, domestic

211

sphere for women in which they are expected to be both silent and subordinate. At the same time, traditional sources of female power have been devalued or eliminated. Left without public mechanisms for expression, most women have withdrawn from the national political arena. The challenge for African women is to find a base of power for continued political expression. Inevitably their efforts will consciously assess and challenge the Western ideologies that have disempowered them. As Stella Graham, Ghanaian member of the Foundation for Women's Health, Research and Development, explained, 'The feminist struggle in the West is to get women together, to get the bonding, and already in Africa we have the bonding, we have the structures, all we need to do is direct the power of these structures' (cited in Davies 1987: 248). And, we might add, assure that the power of those structures is recognized.

CHAPTER 11

Women in national liberation movements

Stephanie Urdang

The map of Africa changed radically in the 1950s and early 1960s. In the many colonies of France and Britain, the colonial flags – symbols of the oppression and exploitation suffered for decades – were lowered to be replaced by the bright new flags of independent Africa. For the most part, these victories were won at negotiating tables, though often only after nationalist movements had organized intensive protest. Certain countries, however, were conspicuously absent from the independence celebrations. Portugal refused steadfastly to relinquish its rule over Angola, Guinea-Bissau, and Mozambique. The white settlers in Rhodesia, fearing Britain's threat to grant independence to the African majority, declared their own unilateral independence with little response from London. South Africa continued to strengthen its hold on Namibia (then known as South West Africa), in defiance of United Nations condemnation and the World Court's ruling that their occupation was illegal. And in South Africa itself, the white government, technically independent since 1910, continued to impose its brutal minority rule over the considerable black majority.

This then was the African stage by the late 1960s and early 1970s when wars of national liberation were launched in the last colonial territories as the only way out. Ultimately there were successes here too. As a direct result of the wars in Portugal's African colonies, the fascist Caetano regime in Portugal was overthrown in 1974, and Angola, Mozambique, and Guinea-Bissau won their independence, led respectively by the Popular Movement for the Liberation of Angola (MPLA), the Front for the Liberation of Mozambique (FRELIMO), and the African Party for the Independence of Guinea and Cape Verde (PAIGC). A five-year armed struggle in Zimbabwe eventually forced the settler regime to the negotiating table, and majority rule became a reality in that country in 1980. In Namibia a similar war of independence forced the apartheid regime to relinquish its hold, and Namibia became the last of the African colonies to achieve independence in 1989. And now the final piece has fallen into place. The most intransigent government of all, the apartheid regime with its repressive laws and active brutality against the majority of the South African population, has now accepted democratic majority rule. South Africans have fought long and hard for these changes.

Ideology is perhaps the most striking difference between these liberation movements and the earlier independence movements, which achieved generally peaceful transfers of power. In many of the latter cases, power was taken while inequalities remained intact. Black faces supplanted white faces, while independence made little impact on the material conditions of life for the majority of people. In contrast, the liberation movements had a vision and a mission. They insisted that their fight stretched beyond victory on the battlefield to the more fundamental question of building a new and just society in each of their countries, ending all forms of exploitation. They saw their ideology as a basis for a new government and a new country to be constructed on firm democratic and socialist principles that would transform their societies: equity, development for all the people, justice, no discrimination on the basis of gender. And to achieve this last goal, the active liberation of women was key.

These were more than noble ideals. In the years that followed independence, countries like Mozambique tried valiantly to put these principles into practice. The second half of the 1970s and the early 1980s were heady ones, filled with hope and bright images of the future.

By the 1990s, the economies of Mozambique and Angola were in tatters. The countries were torn by strife, reflecting the activities of antigovernment movements fostered and encouraged by the apartheid regime to the south. Hundreds of thousands died from bloodshed and from the ensuing famine. Mozambique and Angola had become victims to a wider political scenario over which they had little control. Ultimately a totally free, democratic South Africa would have to be in place before the killings and misery could be halted, and before a point of no return had been reached.

In Zimbabwe and Namibia the people fared somewhat better under their own flags. But while these countries were not torn apart by postindependence conflicts, the realities of developing their economies and providing for the people were sobering prospects. Less and less development aid was heading for Africa in the 1990s, as the global political scene changed course at almost dizzying speed, and the economies of the industrial nations stood on shakier ground than had been the case in earlier decades. In South Africa itself, perched on the brink of change, political and criminal violence reached new heights, egged on by a dying apartheid regime. But hope still remained that when all the people of South Africa were finally able to elect a popular government, the southern African region would develop to its full potential. Only then could peace and democracy have a chance.

And so we sketch a sober picture of southern Africa in the early 1990s, less than 20 years after the wars of liberation achieved independence. It was not only the people of southern Africa who had rejoiced so fervently at independence, filled with hope for a new future. Those who had supported the liberation struggles were inspired by a possibility that these nations could show a new way, particularly with regard to women. This hope was born out of the positive steps taken during the fight for independence and soon after independence. The region was looked towards as an example of what might be achieved when national liberation movements fought battles armed with more than guns: with a commitment to deep and positive change. It is a period of history that held great promise, especially for women.

Phase one: the wars of national liberation and the commitment to women

President Samora Machel articulated this commitment clearly at the founding conference of the Organization of Mozambican Women (OMM): 'The liberation of women is a fundamental necessity for the revolution, a guarantee for its continuity and a precondition for its victory' (Machel 1973). Machel's statement was a compelling one. But what did the 'liberation of women' mean to FRELIMO and the other movements? Why did they view it as so important? How successful were their efforts?

One reason for a guerilla movement's commitment to involving women is sheer need: every man, woman, and child had to be called upon to participate in some way to overthrow repressive regimes. The ideology of these movements, however, provided a basis on which women's involvement could flower into something far more profound and become a 'precondition for victory'.

While all movements made strong statements about the need for the liberation of women, those who fought over a longer period (and thus had more time to win the trust of the population) were the most effective in establishing programs and mechanisms to put theory into practice. Movements such as FRELIMO in Mozambique, MPLA in Angola, and PAIGC in Guinea-Bissau were able to set up the elements of new societies in the areas they liberated and to begin to implement programs that were positive for women. Hence it appeared to be that the longer the war, the stronger the commitment.

That women suffered grave discrimination was acknowledged in different ways by the movements' leaders. The words themselves were fine. Samora Machel asserted that 'generally speaking women are the most oppressed, humiliated and exploited beings in society' (Machel 1973). Similarly, Robert Mugabe, president of ZANU during the fight against the settler regime in Rhodesia (as Zimbabwe was called before independence), and later president of Zimbabwe, explained that:

> Custom and tradition have tended more to favor men than women, to promote men and their status and demote women in status, to erect men as masters of the home, village, clan and nation. Admittedly, women

have . . . been allowed sometimes a significant, but at other times a deplorably insignificant role to play. The general principle governing relationships between men and women has, in our traditional society, always been that of superiors and inferiors. Our society has consistently stood on the principle of masculine dominance – the principle that the man is the ruler and the woman his dependant and subject (Mugabe 1979).

Indeed the words of the leaders are fine. And they were supported by the women who spoke out during the wars when interviewed by visitors about their experiences. Netumbo Nandi, a SWAPO militant, recalled her feelings when she first decided to join SWAPO:

SWAPO came into existence in Namibia in 1960. Even though I was young, I could still not fail to be impressed by SWAPO's militant activities. . . . Seeing what SWAPO was doing and realizing what SWAPO said about the exploitative conditions existing in Namibia, I felt the urge to join. I found out that it's only through SWAPO that all the Namibia people could be united to face the colonizers. So that's why, in 1966, I joined SWAPO. I was just 15 years old at the time (Collins 1977).

Other women militants spoke of their consciousness of the subordinate position of women and the added level of political consciousness that they derived from being able to join the movement as equals. Teodora Gomes, a political worker in the liberated zones of Guinea-Bissau and a ranking member of PAIGC, was one such:

I saw how women lived in misery, struggling to survive. They had to contend with a lot of problems from their husbands. But what could we do at the time? What the men wanted was for the women to stay home. They had control over all the money. If they chose to give some to their wives they gave it. If not, they didn't. We could do nothing because we were oppressed. To me [the thought of marriage] meant that I would enter a life of hardship, but one that could be avoided.

Her father joined PAIGC and although he did not tell his family, she suspected that something was afoot:

Knowing that my father would refuse to answer my questions, I began to plague one of his workers. Eventually he agreed to talk about PAIGC and took me to visit a camp (one night when my father was asleep). I was welcomed as a friend and for two hours they talked about the struggle and the mobilization. It changed my life.

A while later Portuguese soldiers rounded up 10 well-known people in her town, all supporters of PAIGC, and shot them to death in full view of the townspeople. That day her whole family decided to join the guerrillas. From that time she became an active and responsible militant in the movement. She added, 'We [women] did not know how to fight together to change our lives as women. This we have now learned through PAIGC' (Urdang 1979: 207–08).

At the other end of the continent, Sarudzia Churucheminzwa spoke of her experience in growing up in Zimbabwe and joining ZANU:

> As I grew up I strongly resented the attitude of my society which deliberately underrated and underestimated women's capabilities to mould society. Such an attitude deprived many women of giving assistance where they could and all incentives to cultivate their talents as human beings.

After she finished school, she could not find a job. Her family was destitute so she and her mother went to work on the land of a settler farmer. The land was so vast that much of it was left idle. 'From this inhuman treatment we were getting, it was easy for me to see how it was possible for the Boer to own a big luxurious house, several cars and a huge store. My experience at this farm increased my hatred against the rapacious Boers' (Churucheminzwa 1974). When Churucheminzwa heard of ZANLA, the armed wing of ZANU, she decided to find them. She and a friend eventually did, and were admitted to a base, where they joined the movement. They were the only two women in the military base. 'After political education, the comrades introduced us to the rigors of the strategy and tactics of guerilla warfare. . . . As women we felt pride in being able to tackle tasks which at home [were] regarded as men's tasks.'

But their pride grew to exaggerated self-importance, until one of the commissars rebuked them. 'A gun is not an object for you to use as an instrument of showing off; neither is it a certificate that you are equal to men comrades. A gun is only for killing the fascist soldiers of Ian Smith and the eradication of . . . exploitation in Zimbabwe.' The two young women grasped this point more fully when they were sent with others to set an ambush; they exchanged fire with the enemy and bullets whizzed past their ears. 'Then I learned more of the use of my submachine gun. It's either you kill the Boer or the Boer kills you. With more of such experiences in ZANLA we became more enlightened about our convictions and our freedom-bound duty' (Churucheminzwa 1974).

But what about those women – the considerable majority – who did not seek to join the movements from their own initiative? It was here that political education played a critical role in mobilizing women. It was often found that women were particularly adept in undertaking such mobilization. Josina Machel, one of FRELIMO's top women cadres until her untimely death from illness at the age of 25, explained: 'Firstly, it is easier for us to approach other women, and secondly, the men are more easily convinced of the important role of women when confronted with the unusual sight of confident and capable women militants who are themselves the best examples of what they are propounding' (Machel n.d.: 5).

Sometimes women responded more readily to political mobilization than did the men, because of their understanding of their double oppression. They had more to fight for and more to gain, and once in motion they often surpassed the commitment of their male comrades. Francisca Pereira, a senior member of PAIGC, made this point:

> [Women] realized that this was a great opportunity for their liberation. They knew the attitude of the party, and understood that, for the first

time in the history of the country, they would be able to count on political institutions to safeguard their interests. This was important because they also knew that the burden of colonization had rested more heavily on their shoulders. In this respect, we can talk about various forms of colonization – by the colonizers themselves, by the men, and by the customs practiced by different ethnic groups (Urdang 1979: 212).

But generally, women were hesitant to come forward, and special measures were sometimes taken to ensure that women participated more fully. For instance in Guinea-Bissau, few women attended when the early mobilizers began calling village meetings. So they would insist that at least a few women be chosen by the other women to attend. These women would then return home and tell the others what had been discussed. Then the next time, a few more women would attend, and slowly the numbers increased until the majority of the village would set off for the secret gathering place.

In Guinea-Bissau's liberated areas, five-member councils were established. The only women members of the councils were those responsible for provision of rice for the guerrilla camps. Even though this was an extension of their reproductive labor, it did provide an opportunity for women to take part in discussions and contribute to the making of decisions. And so there were councils on which these women played an active role and were assigned tasks previously regarded as 'men's'. Bwetna N'dubi was a member of such a council:

Today I work together with men, having more responsibility than many men. This is not only true for me. I understand that I have to fight together with other women against the domination of women by men. But we have to fight *twice* – once to convince women, and the second time to convince men that women have to have the same rights as men. . . . The party has brought new ways and a new life for women. But we must continue to defend our rights ourselves (Urdang 1979: 131–32).

When I met Bwetna N'dubi again after independence, she was a shadow of the strong, forceful woman I had met in the war. She was no longer on the council and complained that men no longer took women seriously.

Perhaps the most dramatic visual evidence of a change in the social roles of some women was the sight of women carrying guns. Each movement trained some women soldiers, though few fought in combat. Their role was often one of logistical support. In Mozambique the sight of women bearing arms became more of a daily reality than in the other territories. With it came considerable resistance from the population. As one member of FRELIMO's women's detachment recalled:

When we started to work there was strong opposition to our participation. Because that was against our traditions. We then started a big campaign to explain why we also had to fight, that the Frelimo war was a people's war in which the whole population must participate, that we women were even more oppressed than men and that we therefore had the right as well as the will and the strength to fight (Liberation Support Movement, n.d.: 11).

FRELIMO's experience appears to show that the women's detachment was able to provide impetus for the mobilization of women, although women's military actions tended more often to take the form of defense of the liberated zones rather than combat on the front. As Josina Machel reported:

> As in the case of military units composed of men, one of the principal functions of the Women's Detachment is naturally, participation in combat. In Mozambique, the military activities of the women are generally concentrated, together with the militia, in defense of the liberated zones. In this way, the men are partly freed from the task of defense and can concentrate on the offensive in the advance zones. Nevertheless there are women who prefer to participate in more active combat and fight side by side with men in ambushes, mining operations, etc. They have proved to be as capable and courageous as their male comrades (Machel n.d.: 5).

Phase two: the struggle continues

Then came the end of the wars, one by one. First the Portuguese flag was lowered in its three colonies. Then the Rhodesian flag was replaced by the Zimbabwe national one. Then Namibia. And finally, democratic elections in South Africa established a new government, with Nelson Mandela as president.

With such a strong commitment to overthrowing not only the colonial oppressors, but also the oppression of women, the stage seemed to be set for gender-responsive development planning that would integrate women in all facets of political, economic, and social life. This was not to be. Perhaps the most vivid examples of hopes and dreams gone awry can be seen from the Mozambican experience. FRELIMO made the strongest statements during the war and probably engaged in the most far-reaching practices to include women. As independence was won, the statements initially became even stronger, such as the one made at the first congress of the national women's organization shortly after independence, referring to women's key role in food production:

> Mozambican women not only cannot remain outside [the process of transforming subsistence agriculture], but they must be its principal agents and beneficiaries. The Mozambican peasant woman has to be assured equal opportunities to learn new techniques, to have access to the use of machines, to the acquisition of theoretical knowledge and above all to participating in the political organs, in the direction of and management to the same extent as her participation in the work (Isaacman and Stephen 1980: 71).

Soon after independence, as a central thrust of the rural development program, communal villages and state farms were established throughout the country, and in many of them women became active in diverse aspects of village life. And for the first time in many of their lives, women emerged as leaders and took on productive roles not known to them before.

Mama Leia didn't know the year of her birth but when interviewed five years after independence in 1980 she was already a grandmother many times over. Mama Leia was born in the south of the country. Her family were peasants. Her mother and her father's three other wives worked the land. Her father went to South Africa to the mines. She hardly knew him and he died when she was still young. Her mother died soon after. Treated unkindly by her mother's co-wives, she was raised by her older sister. Then, soon after she had reached puberty, it was time to marry. Her sister had recently died and she was married to her brother-in-law, a man many years her senior. Her husband worked on the mines and died from lung disease, leaving her with five young children to raise. She lived in reasonable harmony for a while until her nephew/stepson married and she was treated badly by the new wife. Her stepson built her another house and she continued to work the fields.

One day Portuguese men arrived unexpectedly at her house, asking to see her fields. They looked at her field and pointed. From here to here, they instructed, she would grow cotton, only cotton, and sell it to the Portuguese. 'Here to here' was half the field. What was left was not enough to grow food for her family; not enough for a surplus to sell so that she could buy goods such as soap, candles, and matches. And producing cotton was intensive work, leaving little time for growing the food crops anyway. She would carry heavy bags of raw cotton to the store. But Mama Leia never got the fixed price, which was low enough. She couldn't read and the buyers lied shamelessly about the weight of her sacks. When people complained, their sacks were confiscated and they got nothing. 'Heh!' she exclaims, remembering those days, 'We certainly knew hunger'. Gradually news of FRELIMO began to filter down from the north and out of the underground in the cities, to the people living in Mama Leia's locality. The rumors meant little to her: her horizons stretched no further than her immediate community. And then came 25 April 1974, the day of the coup that overthrew the fascist regime in Portugal, the beginning of the end of the colonial brutality. On independence day, Mama Leia recalls, 'We danced and danced. Hai! We never stopped dancing. We could begin to put our suffering behind us.'

She immediately became active in the community. She was given responsibilities on local committees and joined the thousands of Mozambicans who took on the task of politically mobilizing the population in the countryside. Her village, Três de Fevereiro, was established on 3 February 1977, eight years after the assassination of FRELIMO's founding president.

When Mama Leia moved into the communal village, she had little else to go on than the dreams promised by a new and still inexperienced government. But in the following years schools were established, water pumps brought clean water close to central locations in the villages (women used to walk for miles a day or scoop unsanitary water from the nearby Limpopo River), literacy and adult education were introduced. Clinics were built within reach and an ambulance would come for the really ill. There was a crude but usable soccer field. A community center was built. Radio news was piped through a public address system. Electricity was brought to the main street through the village. For the first time in their lives, villagers voted for their own local assemblies and for the justice tribunals. Mama Leia was one of the 22 women members of the 32-member assembly. When the executive council of five was elected, however, all were men, although the majority of people living in the village were women, the majority of the voters were women, and the majority of those elected for the people's assembly were women. 'No,' intervened the provincial representatives overseeing the election, 'This isn't right. It is important to elect women on the executive council as well'. In the end, the council had two women members and three men. Mama Leia became president of the women's organization and her personality, dedication, and hard work made her a central figure in the village (Urdang 1989: 120–21).

* * * *

It was January 1982. Four heavy tractors, dwarfing their drivers, maintained a steady pace as they traversed the vast open field, leaving neat rows behind them, ready for sowing the corn. The leader of the team wore a dust-impregnated floppy hat, and perky yellow sneakers. Only when the tractors reached the edge of the field did the length of cloth wound around her waist come into view. When the third driver made a U-turn, it became clear that this tractor, too, was driven by a woman.

Over one-quarter of the tractor drivers at Moamba State Farm were women. The farm was taken over by the state after the owner had fled Mozambique, leaving behind a farm that was run down and poorly paid workers now without any income at all. On the state farm, working conditions were improved; shifts were shortened and wages increased. Relationships between managers and workers were transformed, and women were hired for the first time.

Rosalina Ndimande, one of the field workers hired during a two-week period set aside for women applicants only, remembered those early days well.

> The men kept telling us we wouldn't be able to do the same work as they and left the worst jobs for us – like spreading manure. They were sure we shouldn't earn the same salary and were angry when they found out we were. We ignored them and went about the work as if nothing was the matter. And showed them we could do the work as well as they. They gradually learned to accept us and now we have no problems with the men (Urdang 1989: 91).

Maria Madonsela was one of the tractor drivers. At a very young age, her parents arranged for her to marry a man she did not know. From the beginning he beat her. Her two children died in the same month, aged six and four. The abuses increased until she finally left her husband. She fell in love with another man whom her parents accepted and once more the bride price was paid. At first everything was fine, and she soon bore a child. But however much she wanted another, she could not get pregnant again. Her second husband then became abusive. He refused to provide food for her. 'Why should I feed you if you don't have children? It's like living with another man.' Then one day he simply came home with a new wife, a young woman already pregnant, and told Maria to get out.

Maria went to live with her parents and built her own house alongside theirs. She fell in love again, but this time she was cautious.

> He has his house. I have mine. Sometimes he visits me, sometimes I visit him. I am tired of suffering. If I leave my own home to go and live with him, how do I know he won't get tired of me because I don't get pregnant and beat me just like the others did? He can get tired of me if he wants and he can leave me. I can continue living in my own home. Before I was just doing the work of women in the fields and in the home. I was always crying. I cried because I had no husband. I cried because I lost my children. I cried because I had no money. But now I can support myself. I'm so happy. I have put an end to my tears (Urdang 1989: 94).

* * * *

Now it's 1989. In a district in the south, an old woman cultivates a dry plot of land. She is alone. The land is unyielding after years of drought. Her thin wiry body bends low as she expertly handles her hoe. Her clothes are worn sheer, and the cloth wound around her waist has lost any color it might have once had. Her eyes are deep in her thin face and a look of pain is imprinted in them. She is trying to grow food for her grandchildren. She shakes her head. 'Life was better under the Portuguese,' she says, 'At least we had enough food to eat then. The government does not look after us. We can't survive' (interview with author).

* * * *

In the years in between the hope of Mama Leia and the despair of this woman of the same generation, hopes swelled and hopes died. In the intervening years it was not just drought that brought about widespread death. It was a war, sponsored by South Africa, Mozambique's apartheid neighbor, who was determined to ruin the economy and ensure the failure of a dream. Ill-conceived decisions were made, and government policies were established at a time when only peace could be envisioned over the horizon. In the end Mozambique enjoyed perhaps three years of development in a peaceful setting, from 1980 (when Zimbabwe finally became independent, and the Rhodesian forces ceased their armed campaign against Mozambique) until 1983, when the first attacks by RENAMO, the South African-bred and -sponsored movement, began. Hundreds of thousands of people died from the ensuing famine and from brutal killings. It was a war fought with a brutality that was echoed in the killing fields of Cambodia and the destruction in Bosnia.

> It happened at night, as it always does. Like owls or hyenas, the bandits [RENAMO rebels] swooped down on a village in the area of Taninga. . . . Among the kidnapped were pregnant women and little children. Among the little ones was a small girl of nearly eight. . . . They put down their loads and the bandits selected who could return home and who had to carry on. Of those who had to keep going, many were boys between twelve and fifteen. . . . Others were girls between ten and fourteen, who would become women after being raped by the bandits. . . (Magaia 1988: 107).

And with the many dreams that were dashed went the hopes for women's equality and empowerment. But more than the war is to blame here. Words that sounded so fine on paper were not actualized. The policy towards women's equality was confused. Men continued to dominate the political and economic spheres of the new countries. And when women, given some space, pushed for more, they were seen as a threat. In the end, the process is a highly complex one, and one that can only be fought for by the women themselves. Freedom is never given, as history has taught us. Participation in a war of independence is not sufficient to change the future. It is a struggle that must continue. But dreams of equality are hard to sustain when hunger is the daily reality, when conditions of poverty are so pervasive. And when another war, with more atrocities than could ever be imagined, replaced the hard-earned independence, it was hard not to despair.

But part of the blame lies outside the particular circumstances of southern Africa, Mozambique, and the international political scene. Development policies and practices have been gender-blind, whether found in Asia, Latin America, or Africa. Development that addresses women has resembled welfare in approach: to help the impoverished women make more of their lives. Development funds have gone to small income-generating projects, to small credit schemes, to alleviating the burden of women's reproductive labor in the form of grain mills, clean water, and sanitation, health clinics, and small animal raising. Women have been treated as passive recipients, not as actors in decisions that so fundamentally impinge on their lives. Important as it might be to improve the conditions of women's existence, development aid has, for the most part, ignored the needs of both men and women for an equal place on the political, social, and economic spectrum. All development should be gender-responsive. Every single program or project funded by international donor agencies should be examined to check for its impact on

223

women's lives, to see whether it will enhance equality between the sexes and empowerment for women. This has been done as seldom in Mozambique as elsewhere. And until there is a new approach to development practices, until governments demand a new approach, much may change for a country's economy while little may change for its women. Questions of development assistance are examined in greater detail in the next chapter.

Yet as the independence fighters found so starkly, freedom cannot be given. It must be fought for and won. This is as true for a nation as a whole as it is for its women. But the women's quest for survival and for better lives is strong. In the end, perhaps it is with the women themselves that long-lasting, sustainable change will be the key to the future – to all our futures.

CHAPTER 12

The Impact of Development Policies on Women

Kathleen Staudt

. . . for African women the subject of women's advancement is highly political because it is an integral part of our quest for justice not only at the household level but all the way within the local, national and world economic order (Johnson-Odim 1991: 317–18).

For several decades, voluminous research has made visible African women's extensive economic involvement in agriculture, trade, and services. Research tied to practice, known as 'Women in Development' (WID), focussed on the consequences of economic development strategies (Boserup 1970), of public policies (Staudt and Jaquette 1983), and of development projects (Lewis 1984), on relations between men and women. New frameworks address the *political* questions asked by Achola Pala Okeyo in the quotation above.

The development mainstream was slow to understand the centrality of women in the development process. Harboring assumptions that women's work was irrelevant or that gains for women meant losses for men, development theorists and practitioners blindly viewed men as the motor for development. Gender-blind thinking was difficult to sustain when analysis linked population growth to economic growth and equity, although approaches that viewed women primarily as mothers (or 'at risk' for motherhood, as enthusiastic population advocates would term it) still ignored women's economic activities and opportunities. Early WID analysts concluded generally that development policies increased women's dependency on men and aggravated gender gaps.

With the advent of the International Women's Decade in 1975 and an explosion of female organizational voices and of feminist academic research, attention became focussed on women's work across the African continent. Still, analysis was grounded in either a technical policy/project focus, or in economic determinism. Technical policy analysts assumed that if one got the data, planning, or language right, then rational people would include women in development efforts. Development agencies typically skirted overt discussion of

225

politics and power, shrouding their actions in seeming technical competence. Economic determinists, on the other hand, whether from the ideological right or left, assumed that if the appropriate economic structure was in place, women's lives would improve from 'modernization' or 'revolution'.

While these shifts in analytic focus took place, economic crises relentlessly gripped the African continent. Agricultural productivity has decreased in per capita terms. Women's labor force participation fell, and their unemployment rose (Appendix, Tables A.1 and A.2). Population growth continues at high rates, and health problems are rampant as measured in such terms as infant and maternal mortality rates, undernutrition and starvation, and HIV infection rates (see Chapter 13 and Appendix, Table A.5). Faced with problems like these, even mainstream developmentalists have increasingly looked to women for involvement and solutions.

More recently, the WID framework has shifted to focus on state–society relations within the context of global economic structural readjustment. As such, the debate necessarily highlights the politics of government and international organizational machinery: Who controls the machinery? What gendered ideologies guide their behavior? And what leverage do people have to make the machinery accountable for the ways in which they are unequally burdened and benefitted? How do they make their livelihoods in spite of the machinery? In this chapter, answers are discussed as 'gendered development'.

The first section will outline women's needs as they relate to international and national policy agendas. The next section will clarify the various relationships embodied in gendered development, especially the state, policy formation, implementation, and people's everyday acquiescence or resistance thereto. Following that, three cases of gendered development interventions are examined in order to draw lessons for action and change. A central theme that runs through this work problematizes the lack of democracy for women in development.

Women's work: policy implications

By now a consensus exists that women are a majority of Africa's farmers. As farmers, women prepare the soil, plant, weed, harvest, and store food for consumption and crops for sale or export, as described in Chapters 1 and 2 of this volume. Staff at the Economic Commission for Africa estimate that women are responsible for 60 to 80 per cent of total agricultural labor (UN/ECA 1972: 359–60).

In cities and small towns, women frequently work as traders and also engage in a wide range of tasks in the 'informal sector', buying, selling, and transporting goods and services, as described in Chapter 3 (see also Appendix). In many parts of West Africa, women have long sustained a tradition of staffing trading networks. They buy crops, fish, and other goods and resell under highly competitive circumstances. In such work, they earn personal incomes that·go far in meeting household expenditures and school and health fees. As will be addressed later, however, women's control over household income is questionable.

Various studies of urban agriculture find significant subsistence farming in African cities, primarily an income-substituting rather than income-generating activity. In Nairobi, for example, one-third of households cultivate and one-fifth raise some livestock in open spaces, rented/borrowed plots, and near their homes. It is no surprise, given Africa's characterization as a female-farming continent, that women represent more than two-thirds of cultivators (Freeman 1991: 50, 56, 92). The job of 'feeding African cities,' as Jane Guyer's (1987) illuminating collection of case studies shows, is often handled by women.

As for reproduction, the rearing and sustenance of Africa's children is largely in women's hands. Africa leads all world regions in population growth rates, which have in recent decades reached 3 per cent per year, leading to the doubling of national populations in 23 years (World Bank 1992); total fertility rates average 6.2 children per woman (Appendix, Table A.5). Given historically high rates of male-outmigration from rural areas, sizeable numbers of women head households (Due 1991: 103 estimates a quarter of households) and depend on their own incomes and irregular contributions from men to rear families.

Women's extensive activities in production and reproduction reveal both their stakes in government policies and government stakes in their female populace. Policy areas of particular significance for women include agriculture, land, and trade. Women farmers need secure access to property as their means of production. Land title would also give them access to credit to improve and expand their agricultural activities. Women need agricultural inputs, such as new technology, implements, and seeds. Women also need information about technology use, markets, prices, and agricultural innovations. Such information is typically delivered through agricultural and community development field staff. Finally, women need to be able to trade their goods and produce for a fair price, free from appropriation by government officials, husbands, and relatives.

However, policies are implemented in bureaucratic machinery within the state apparatus. Beyond that, international machinery envelops state action and intervention, supplying or restricting capital movements and markets. It is this complex of policies and institutions that results in what is here called 'gendered development'.

Gendered development

When sub-Saharan African nations began achieving political independence more than three decades ago, many shared high hopes of a proactive state that would amass resources to accomplish the structural transformations of colonial economies in equitable ways. After all, the rhetoric stressed development with equity, even socialism in some cases. Women found an institutional home in the 'women's wing' of many political parties. In cases where independence was achieved through violent struggle, many people assumed that women's visible participation would give them leverage in state policy-making (see Chapter 10). At independence, international agencies affiliated with the United Nations seemed poised to provide loans and grants in ways not tied to the foreign policy and export agendas of rich countries and their bilateral aid programs. Sovereign nations anticipated an ability to foster competition among bilateral donors to maximize their advantage. In the 1960s, development 'experts' shared an ideology that relied on active state intervention to promote economic development and rational planning. Although seemingly gender-blind, this ideology only continued the preferential bias toward men in existence from colonial times.

State institutions and policies

Crawford Young has eloquently described the 'ephemeral . . . graft of cuttings of parliamentary democracy upon the robust trunk of colonial autocracy' (1982: 57). We must acknowledge that the trunk had virtually institutionalized male preference in most of its programs. Men dominate the political machinery in Africa; this is the essence of gendered development.

The other side of women's exclusion is women's withdrawal from and resistance to male political machinery under colonialism and independence (see Chapter 10). Examples of what James Scott calls 'everyday peasant resistance' can be found in women's refusal to work on cash crops without compensation, documented from Tanzania (Meena 1989) to Kenya and Senegal (summarized in Staudt 1987) and poignantly focused in Zambian women's question: 'Why should we grow maize for the government?' (Keller 1989). When women divert produce from official to informal marketing channels and flee highly controlled settlement schemes such as Mwea, the Volta Valley Authority, or rural areas, they express their political voice.

Many studies document what gendered development has meant in terms of 'who gets what' from public revenue. In the area of agriculture, women have limited access to agricultural credit and training, documented in many areas. (See, for example, Bukh 1979, Elabor-Idemudia 1991: 136, Fortmann 1982, and many others.) Land reform programs created commercially valuable titles that officially consolidated property overwhelmingly in men's names (see selections in Davison 1988, Jacobs 1989), leaving women without surety for credit or a secure property base. The overwhelming majority of agricultural field agents are male, and their numbers have increased tenfold in some countries since independence (Staudt 1991: 75). Such staffing patterns create the appearance of a job subsidies program for men. With the cover of officialdom and technical development language, men made and implemented policies and programs in ways that subsidized their interests and solidified their patron–client ties with state agencies.

One basic axiom in agricultural development thinking is that farmers need returns for their labor. Women with incentives contribute energy to production, as an empirical test of conflict within households in Cameroon reveals: women's remuneration levels are related to their labor contributions to rice production (Jones 1983, see also Staudt 1988). While in some African cultural groups women are entitled to control their own incomes (a corollary is often extensive obligations for household expenditures), in other groups husbands control incomes (see selections in Guyer and Peters 1984 and in Dwyer and Bruce 1988). But many development policies have consistently ignored the gender division of control over income.

Male control over female labor and its remuneration may preclude resistance and literally force acquiescence. An old Zambian woman farmer told historian Maud Muntemba: 'Now a woman is like a slave. She works hard. . . . At the end of the year, the family sells one hundred bags of maize. The man gives her K20 (about $25). Following year the family sells three hundred bags. He still gives her K20. What is that but slavery?' (1982: 99). Commercial farmers in Zimbabwe expand cultivation through marrying multiple wives. As one said: 'Before a man becomes a polygamist, he works hard with his first wife in order to get money. When he has enough, he will marry another. The two wives will work hard and make enough money to marry another wife. . . . A polygamist should always remember that the junior wives were paid for with the money made by the first wife' (Cheater 1981: 362). A particularly invidious feature of political machinery in gendered development involves the official designation of husbands ('heads' of household) as payees in cooperatives and state marketing boards. As such, men mediate incomes and appropriate surplus (see Kenya cases in Nzomo and Staudt 1994). Does integration into gendered development institutions bring benefits or losses for women?

Those women who work at the periphery of state control have traditionally had to cope more with the vagaries of the market than with patronage. But increasingly, political machinery ensnarls them as well. Officials too often viewed informal sector activities as an uneconomic phase of underdevelopment, to be licensed, squeezed, and controlled until larger-scale industrialization and centralized marketing took hold. Market women maneuver within these constraints, working amid accusations that they cause shortages, fix prices, and hoard during economic crisis (Robertson 1983 on Ghana, Schuster 1979 and Hansen 1989 on Zambia, Elwert 1984 on Togo). Urban agriculture is officially discouraged as a health hazard; growers face many problems, among them eviction and crop destruction by authorities (Freeman 1991, Rakodi 1988). Some of independent Africa's gravest human rights abuses, similar to those of apartheid South Africa, have to do with bulldozing squatter settlements and ridding cities of illegal traders. Such was the case with the 1990 Muoroto demolition and subsequent campaigns in Nairobi, which left 30,000 homeless.

African states are widely characterized as arbitrary, personalistic, corrupt, and ineffective, and their current development crisis is partly the product of what Thomas Callaghy calls 'crony statism', where political rather than economic logic prevails (1990: 260). This political logic builds a base of support among mostly men in authoritarian structures, dispensing patronage among key players. Women have only a limited influence among key political players in and around the state (Parpart and Staudt 1989; see also Chapter 10 of this volume on women in politics). Women's representation is miniscule in cabinets and legislatures; the latter are virtually impotent in most authoritarian regimes. Women's representation in political parties is designed to control rather than empower them, and to reward a few women associated with the dominant class and separate them from the rest, as examples from Zambia and Kenya illustrate (Geisler 1987, Nzomo 1989; see also Chapter 9 in this volume). Unfortunately, the ability of women's nongovernmental organizations to influence the state is practically nil. In between military coups in Nigeria, for example, women's voice in democratic transition has been weak, despite the existence of many women's organizations and groups (see Mba 1989).

We should be wary, however, of treating the African state as a monolith. Multiple ministries and parastatal organizations make up the machinery of the state, each pursuing special agendas that may compete with or contradict one another (Hansen 1989). Within these diverse ministries, different organizational cultures prevail, yet these organizational cultures are also gendered: their male founders incorporated and infused gender ideologies into operating procedures, recruitment, and incentive structures that minimize accountability and responsiveness to women.

How do gendered ideologies persist in state institutions? The bureaucratic machinery of Malawi is a grim example. The most powerful ministries and agencies (Treasury or Statistics, for example) contain little or nothing on women in planning documents that could guide or justify policies. Few professional women work in decision-making, and those who do are engulfed in control-oriented bureaucratic machinery that puts them at a distance from peasant women (Hirschmann 1990). In many African countries, women's bureaus within ministries or whole ministries are devoted to women's affairs. Typically, women's advocacy units are assigned the huge responsibility of making government more responsive to women through providing more data for planning, staff knowledgeable about women's activities, monies for women's development projects, and a voice (often the lone female voice) for women in cabinet decision making. Perhaps predictably, such huge mandates receive budgets that amount to only around 1 per cent of government spending (Kriger 1992: 235, Nzomo 1989, Ooko-Ombaka 1980). From the outside, these 'official' women appear to avoid threatening male interests (Rogers

1983, Seidman 1984), though Zimbabwean Minister Joyce Mujuru, former guerrilla fighter, has said she faces more obstacles in bureaucracy than in the war (cited in Staudt 1990: 21).

Women's advocacy offices have made limited gains. They manage small set-aside funds for women's projects; they use policies as leverage to document discrimination and to retrain bureaucratic staff; they invent innovative pilot projects that capture international resources. Considerable space exists in public agencies to do more, given political will and accountability. However, as Chapter 10 also points out, even women's advocacy units can be co-opted by the ruling (male) coalition (Lewis 1990; the co-optation of nongovernmental women's associations is described in Chapter 9).

The global economic context: structural adjustment

Until the world recession around 1980 and thereafter, donor machinery supported existing programs in ways that strengthened the states' hands in development. National planning, parastatal marketing bodies, and state-owned enterprises were viewed as rational ways to modernize economies. Belated attention was given to agriculture, long neglected in favor of industry. When agriculture received external support, money generally supported growth in (male) extension staff, credit for larger (landowner) farmers, and export agriculture rather than food self-sufficiency.

By 1981, the World Bank began making an influential case for limiting the size of states, cutting back civil service spending, and giving freer rein to market forces, particularly to encourage export-oriented production (see World Bank 1981). The official African statist response, the Lagos Plan of Action, emphasized self-reliance and gave token space to women. The Bank's ideology endured, however, and permeated development thinking thereafter. State officials were encouraged to undergo 'structural adjustment' and 'stabilization' to strengthen the hand of markets. These changes involve deficit reduction, currency devaluation, and personnel cuts among other reforms, all with the aim of increasing economic efficiency, trade, and exports. Bankers preferred loans, to be disbursed only on condition that specific reforms were instituted. Such conditionality can infringe on national sovereignty, although bankers frequently join forces with ideologically like-minded officials in ministries of finance and treasury (see selections in Nelson 1990).

Such reforms *could* work to the advantage of women farmers and those generally excluded from the state's network of preference and privilege. In the area of agriculture, for example, parastatal marketing boards frequently compensate farmers at less than international price levels to pay for operating costs and to generate budgetary revenue. If prices are allowed to rise, women farmers would receive higher prices for their crops, and if they share or control proceeds, they stand to gain. Under this scenario, however, women consumers in urban areas, where food prices have often been subsidized, will lose.

Strapped for resources due to rising oil costs, indebtedness, and stagnant or declining international prices for their products, many African states have partially or completely acquiesced to the Bank's terms. Budget and civil service cuts frequently occurred in programs with marginal political constituency support, so that less well-connected citizens suffered the costs. A two-volume UNICEF study found that military programs were generally spared but health programs most severely damaged in Africa compared to other world regions (selections in Cornia *et al*. 1987, also see Due 1991). Since health care was already a low priority in many central government budgets, the resulting cuts translated into fewer services, shortages of pharmaceuticals, and increases in user fees. Women who care for children suffer the most from such cuts.

Is structural adjustment working in Africa? The Bank says yes, documenting its answer through tenuous, macro-level, but narrow indicators of success (evaluated in Staudt 1991: Ch. 8). It claims to recognize the 'human face' of adjustment with its 1990 *World Development Report* that stresses poverty alleviation and conditionality based on such targeted programs. Although the current scenario is unsatisfactory, even tragic, Uma Lele argues that the consequences of not adjusting are even worse (1991: 48). Meanwhile, food crises continue and more are likely through the 1990s (Gladwin 1991: 8–9).

Gendered development, as currently experienced, is development failure. While policies symbolically support women, the institutional practice is quite different. As Chapter 10 also argues, the performance gap is the product of gender ideologies that permeate organizational cultures, and of state and political machinery that excludes women and women's voices in decision-making. Outside that machinery, women's organizational activities flourish and their informal sector livelihood strategies sustain households.

Case studies of gendered development

In choosing case studies, I have sought to provide a broad representation of African societies and of development intervention strategies. Intervention frequently takes the form of discrete projects, budgeted for fixed numbers of years; of programs, ongoing operations in government; and of policy change. In the context of global structural adjustment, policy change has represented a shift in relations between government and the market, frequently strengthening market forces and those who are active, privileged, and skilled in that context. Policy change usually requires shifts in the political coalitions that support existing states, and thus mandates paying attention to changing political forces and women's involvement therein. The Gambia case below illustrates project interventions; the Kenya case, program interventions; and the case of Ghana, policy change. Following the cases, diagnoses are profferred and solutions proposed.

The Gambia: project interventions

When 'women in development' research and advocacy began, the debate was often centered on whether support for women ought to occur in 'separate' or 'integrated' projects. Separate projects had the potential merit of being under female leadership and the possible consequence of empowerment if group members became a political force. Separate projects, however, were often funded at miniscule levels, representing a cheap way for governments and donor organizations to claim that their programs responded to women.

While separate projects should have a place in development, particularly as they mesh with indigenous women's work and organizational traditions, they should not serve as an excuse for maintaining male preference in the better endowed mainstream projects. Such projects are funded through government pilot efforts, through international nongovernmental organizations, and/or with international loans and grants.

The Gambia, a tiny country in West Africa, has become famous in women in development studies for the consistent ways in which government officials, working with outside donors of various ideological stripes (Peoples Republic of China, Taiwan, World Bank, US, and Britain) have ignored women farmers and/or stripped them of indigenous resources. The ignorance also produced project failure.

Jennie Dey's research (1981) analyzes the intricate and complex division of labor among Mandinka people in The Gambia. Men and women grow different crops, on different plots of land, for either household consumption or disposal at the cultivator's discretion. Even collective work arrangements are gendered. Land comes in different types, and is based on the notion of 'ownership for use'. In colonial times and thereafter, outside planners frequently asked men alone about customary land rights and got answers that gave men leverage to expand their authority and property rights.

Rice irrigation schemes were designed on the assumption that unified household units were directed by single male heads. A variety of inputs provided (male) farmers with pumps for canal irrigation and credit provided through cooperatives. Women were excluded from irrigated land ownership and credit, but planners were counting on women's labor for men's rice production. Customary rights gave women the option to refuse, though some women did provide labor and secured wages from husbands or other men. Men's cash-crop operations competed with the time women needed for their own crops and plots.

Judith Carney's more recent research (1988) reveals continuing intra-household conflicts in irrigated rice projects. Earlier projects had successfully introduced a Green Revolution in rice technology, but had not resulted in the kind of marketable surplus that would reduce The Gambia's dependence on imported rice, its basic foodstuff. New donors, wary of the international infamy of past efforts, claimed determination to learn lessons from past failure and build women's

233

ownership and gender equity into new operations. The Gambian government agreed, as did the women. As one put it: 'It seems this project is just like the Chinese one when we suffered before. We aren't going to put up with that again. . . . I have to say to you men, We women aren't going to accept the way we have been treated in the past. We were asleep then. But now we are awake' (quoted in Carney 1988: 69). Women used a BBC film to gain leverage and to make their claims more visible.

The policy of equity broke down in procedures and day-to-day management. While irrigated land distribution during this phase showed a majority of plots in women's names, this ownership was only cosmetic. Men felt threatened by the new arrangements, and project managers responded by listing the names of male heads of household next to those of female 'owners', and plots were thereby designated for household use with control over female labor. As Carney concludes, the 'economic benefits of irrigated rice are centralized under control of the male household head' (1988: 72).

Kenya: program interventions

Kenyan women participate in many tasks associated with agricultural production. High rates of male outmigration during the colonial period and thereafter left sizeable numbers of women as *de facto* household heads and farm managers. Ongoing agricultural and livestock programs supply technical assistance and credit through a large staff of field extension officers. Ongoing programs, as opposed to projects, have the value of routine, institutionalized public action. However, male preference has frequently been built into the institutionalization process. The paragraphs below are summarized from Nzomo and Staudt (1994).

Studies in the mid-1970s documented bias in the delivery of extension advice, training, and credit to women farm managers, especially those in lower-income households. Extension officers (usually men) viewed women farmers as backward, yet studies reveal the relatively poor job extension officers did of communicating research recommendations even to the surprisingly few farmers on whom they concentrated. Extension staff in coffee and tea parastatal organizations that served registered (mostly male) farmers did a better job. Home economists, a miniscule fraction of all extension staff, served women with a domesticated view of women's responsibilities as homemakers, cooks, and only partially as 'gardeners'.

Women's advocacy certainly had some impact on the government of Kenya. A Women's Bureau was established in 1975 in the Ministry of Social Affairs. Donor institutions armed with internal studies and vigorous advocacy offices themselves recognized women's importance in agriculture. Agricultural colleges used affirmative action tactics in recruitment to increase the number of female extension staff. Women's organizations gained visibility as development actors (see also Chapter 9). The second largest United Nations conference ever was held in Nairobi in 1985, to close the international Women's Decade. And finally, government documents made women's work more visible with more gender-disaggregated data.

Reforms were proposed in the early 1980s to improve the quality of extension staff and embrace more women farmers. Besides recruiting more women, agricultural colleges softened the sharp lines between agriculture and home economics curricula. Male extension workers were encouraged to work with women's groups to avoid the bias of individualist extension and to increase numbers served. The major reform, instigated with World Bank funding, implanted a 'Training and Visit' extension model. In this model, closely supervised and trained officers meet regularly with 'contact farmers', the latter of whom are to work with 'follower farmers'. Although Bank reports applauded the reform for its supposed outreach to women, the consequences for women have been limited, as both Bank and government studies have documented. The more certain outcome is that agricultural production has been intensified, and increased labor burdens fall on women's shoulders. Government agencies that market specialized crops typically pay proceeds to husbands, so that women's gains are dependent on their husbands' goodwill.

Ghana: policy reform

Ghana has been the World Bank's major success story in Africa. Under authoritarian but charismatic military rule, Ghana underwent severe austerity programs in 1983 and thereafter, known as structural adjustment. Currency was devaluated, thousands of civil service positions were eliminated annually, state-owned enterprises were privatized, tax revenue collection improved, and prices for agricultural commodities began to match market prices. Corruption was targeted; 25,000 'ghost workers' were eliminated from the Cocoa Marketing Board alone (Callaghy 1990: 276). Such policy shifts changed the political coalitions on which the regime was based, creating new winners and losers in the process. Women were part of both groups, but were primarily losers.

Nearly 10 years of structural adjustment have produced substantial policy and spending shifts. Cocoa prices rose, thus benefitting wealthier export-oriented farmers. Military spending declined; and spending on education, health, and welfare increased as a percentage of central government revenue (World Bank 1991: 224). With increased education and health fees and few formal sector jobs, the consensus seems to be that people's standards of living declined. Per capita caloric intake even dropped. Many were forced to seek informal income-generating work (summarized in Kraus 1991; also see Callaghy 1990).

Before and after structural adjustment, the Ghanaian state had uneasy relationships with market women, whom it was never able to control fully. These women are a highly differentiated group, with a small fraction of 'commodity queens' who have controlled extensive capital and contacts to do business on a large scale (Dumor 1982), versus the vast majority of small traders. High prices and shortages were blamed on women traders rather than on misguided policies and corruption. Careful studies show that economic crisis has continued or intensified for the majority of women traders (Clark and Manuh 1991). Structural adjustment has not worked for this important group of women.

As more and more people turn to informal work, income-substitution work, and self-help strategies to survive in these austere settings, it is important that they be able to establish accountability for public policies and their effects. In recognition of the social damage that structural adjustment produced, Ghana adopted a Programme of Action to Mitigate the Social Costs of Adjustment (PAMSCAD). While it is a belated, tacked-on effort (Loxley 1990), women's organizational activities, affiliations, and coalitions have demanded change within this limited political space. Yet women also affiliate with the dominant class, members of which sometimes use these grassroots organizations for other political agendas (Mikell 1991). Through political struggle, women's larger voice should bring some accountability to policy shifts. However, international donors and banks have rarely sought to reinforce democratic process.

Diagnoses and change: closing thoughts on gendered development

Some analysts have urged the insulation of development logic from politics and a reliance on economic logic instead (see Callaghy 1990, for example). On the contrary, this discussion has emphasized the importance of democratic logic for making development work for more people, including women. A political logic must be created that responds to both men and women and that recognizes patronage and subsidies for what they are. Women must be consulted, they must be involved in and benefit from development so that the surplus from growth can improve living conditions for the largest number of people. Should women work with or against the state? Answers vary from one country to another, according to whether a particular state's development agenda impairs or benefits the majority of people. Beneficial development necessarily involves more democratic process within and between institutions, thus changing ideologies of development.

Women's voice was limited in all three cases discussed in this chapter; women had little leverage or authority. Such silence allowed day-to-day program and project managers to assume that men's position ought to be strengthened in the property, payments, and resources associated with development. In the intriguing project shift in The Gambia, managers publicly appeased active women, but later responded to perceived threats to men's status through intricate procedures that only later revealed continuing male preference. This case makes it clear that project participants, especially women who are routinely excluded, must either share authority with managers or hold leverage to make managers accountable.

Managers are also part of the problem, both in specific projects and in the bureaucratic machinery generally. Officials with their own ideologies, biases, and personal frailties make important and mundane decisions that have crucial effects on the public. Whether affiliated with international or state machinery, mostly male managers work in response to past precedent, which privileged men and responded to ideological, political, and structural incentives that devalued female labor. Some analysts believe that 'gender training' is in order, so that development managers can confront assumptions about the gender division of labor and responsibilities, learn about work realities, and apply that knowledge to their work settings (Rao et al. 1991). At the Eastern and Southern African Management Institute in Arusha, Tanzania, the Women in Development/Women in Management Program under the able leadership of Hilda Tadria is a fine example of such gender training for women and men (discussed in Rao et al. 1991). For fuller institutionalization of needed changes, such trainees also need resources, leadership, and constituency pressure to assure that new knowledge is really used in the work world.

More women officials and managers, working with women's advocacy offices, should also improve data collection and responsiveness to women. This insider strategy may be viewed as a form of infiltration from within. Sometimes seemingly minor procedural leverage, such as the requirement for gender-disaggregated data, can give committed women staff the ability to make preferential patterns transparent and public so that political constituencies can press for change (see Keller and Mbewe 1991 for a Zambian example). Under current conditions, the number of such women managers is far below the kinds of 'critical mass' that could make much impact on implementation. Moreover, the women's units have too few staff, resources, or authority to provoke change. Even with larger numbers and resources, however, we should be cautious about how much change insiders can make without support from outside political forces. Women's bureaus and ministries sometimes reproduce the larger (male) patronage machinery in which they are enmeshed, focussing on selective or unrepresentative female constituents. Class and cultural divisions among women are real (Lewis 1990; selections in Staudt 1990), and a fine line exists between infiltration and co-optation.

Under structural adjustment, women have no voice during negotiations and subsequent policy reform. Yet they often bear the brunt of cuts in health and social services, limited as those services have been in the past. Women and the wider public must organize to respond to shifting policy and revenue commitments. The consequences of those shifts must be made more transparent. Here, women's networks can be of service in disseminating data and research findings.[1]

Market reforms that eliminate male patronage and control from the public agenda could enhance women's access to resources. Yet relics of practices that allow men to mediate women's relationship with the market still exist, such as husbands being designated as payees in cooperatives. Women must secure the right to control their own incomes in law and in practice, and they must obtain support from husbands for their children and household expenses. Ultimately, such legal foundations are vested in the state.

Through informal sector work, women have been able to secure a livelihood for themselves and their children, sometimes at more profitable levels than the formal sector in the most disaster-stricken African economies, as the Tanzanian case shows. As Aili Tripp has warned about renewed government enthusiasm to license those workers and thus extract more revenue, this amounts to 'making the poorest members of society pay for the right to subsist' (1989: 620). Women's relative autonomy from the state and solidarity in self-help networks make some sense in these transitional times.

It has become all too easy for state and international agencies to 'recognize' women in development through policy rhetoric. In practice, male control over women and their labor continues. Africa's future ability to survive its economic and food crises depends on women's empowerment. If those who staff gendered development institutions do not act on this reality soon, it may be too late.

Note

1. At the annual meeting of the US African Studies Association, a group of 30 African and 30 North American women scholars met for two days to discuss 'The Status of Women's Studies in Africa, 1991' with support from the MacArthur and Ford Foundations. That meeting was coordinated by Claire Robertson. A useful summary is included in the ASA Women's Caucus Newsletter of March 1992, 'Reports,' pp. 5–13. That Caucus and their newsletter represent one of the worthy attempts at networking; contact Cora Ann Presley, History Department, Tulane University, New Orleans, LA 70118–5698. Other important examples include the newsletter of the Women's Research and Documentation Centre in Nigeria (contact: WORDOC Editor, Institute of African Studies, University of Ibadan, Ibadan, Nigeria), and the African Training and Research Centre for Women Update (contact: ATRCW, Economic Commission for Africa, P.O. Box 3001, Addis Ababa, Ethiopia). For a list of the many women's studies and women in development units in Africa (and the world), see Rao *et al.* 1991.

CHAPTER 13

African women and health issues

Meredeth Turshen

Women's health issues arise from women's productive and reproductive work, which on the one hand determines the value society
places on women and consequently the claims they can make on
national and household resources. Women who are highly valued
for the wages they earn outside the home can make legitimate,
recognized claims on household assistance with their tasks or, to
give another example, on expert care for their health needs. On the
other hand, women's productive and reproductive work also creates
health problems and needs for health care.

Women's productive work in the African countryside is mainly
agricultural, and whereas farm work is considered one of the most
hazardous occupations in the United States, it is rarely regarded as
such by African authorities if the work is done in the subsistence
sector, in which most women work, rather than on plantations that
pay wages to their employees. Nigerian market women, forced by
economic change to plant yams, recognize that farm work is harder,
demands more energy, and is more tiring than trading (Mebrahtu
1991). If they could command household help or hire casual labor,
they could reduce their workload. Otherwise, 'When women cannot
mobilize the labor of others they may work themselves to exhaustion'
(Roberts 1988: 112).

Women's reproductive work is narrowly considered to be childbearing, in the eyes of health authorities, and fertility control is
the focus of most public health programs (see Chapter 14 below).
Recently, several international agencies mounted 'safe motherhood'
campaigns, which advocate better obstetrical assistance in childbirth
to reduce the very high maternal death rates registered in Third World
countries (Herz and Measham 1987). African maternal mortality rates
at the end of the 1980s were 2,000 per 100,000 live births in Ethiopia,
1,680 per 100,000 in Benin, and 1,500 in Nigeria; in contrast, rates
in industrialized countries are 13 per 100,000 live births in France
and 2 per 100,000 in Canada (Turshen 1991: 108–109; see Appendix,
Table A.5, for rates in other African countries). Many health service

workers appear to pay little attention to the physical and mental stresses of child-rearing, other than to lecture women on the need to space and limit their pregnancies.

Chronic diseases

Although in industrial countries we think of infections as acute and short-lived, in Africa many communicable diseases, such as malaria, tuberculosis, diarrhea, sleeping sickness, and river blindness, are chronic – that is, they last for a long time or recur often. Until 1992, the World Health Organization paid little attention to the way these diseases affect women, and there was little research on how sex and gender determine their transmission and distribution.[1] For example, the sexual division of labor assigns laundry and water-hauling duties to women and girls; these tasks bring them into frequent contact with contaminated rivers and expose them to water-borne diseases like schistosomiasis (sometimes called snail fever, or bilharzia).

The common chronic infections in Africa are diseases of poverty such as leprosy, which is prevalent among people with no routine health care, no safe water supplies, and no sanitation services. Women who contract leprosy are more disadvantaged than men because they have less education, fewer resources, and poorer access to health services, and because their subordinate status renders them more vulnerable to the social stigma attached to this disease.

Medical and public health services are highly concentrated in urban zones, although 70 per cent of Africans live in rural areas. Historical patterns of labor migration have left more women in the countryside than men, so the lack of rural health care affects more women than men. In Zambia, for example, nearly 100 per cent of the urban and 50 per cent of the rural population have access to health services; in Somalia, some 50 per cent of the urban and 15 per cent of the rural population have access to these services. The maldistribution of doctors and nurses is well documented. Typically, almost all of Senegal's dentists, 70 per cent of its physicians and pharmacists, 60 per cent of its midwives, and over 40 per cent of its nurses are concentrated in the Dakar–CapVert region, where less than 30 per cent of the population lives.

Nutrition and famine

Repeated, closely spaced pregnancies are known to take a toll on women's nutrition. A developing fetus will draw upon a woman's nutritional stores, depleting her reserves of iron and calcium, and leaving her with less energy to respond to the demands of a newborn baby. Many programs for nutritional supplements and health education focus on the foods consumed during pregnancy and breast feeding, but consumption is the end stage of a long chain of events, few of which are under women's control. African women themselves were the first to draw attention to the importance of food systems in determining the availability of food and, in conditions of scarcity, to the importance of distribution within households in determining who eats what and when (FAO 1979, United Nations 1974). Food systems encompass women's rights to land, the proximity of water, access to farm technology, credit arrangements, and labor to help cultivate, harvest, transport, process, store, cook, and serve food.

Nutritional problems and infectious disease are markedly seasonal in Africa, as in other parts of the Third World that have two main seasons, wet and dry (Scofield 1974). In rural areas, food is always in shortest supply just before the long rainy season, which marks the beginning of the agricultural cycle. The demand for women's work is greatest when crops are being sown and, at the same time, infections are more common and resistance to infection is lower in the wet season. The short-term effects are reduced stores of body fat, weight loss, depletion of muscle tissue (especially if meals contain less protein), and increased susceptibility to infection. Infection, in turn, interferes with food absorption, creating a synergistic interaction between infection and malnutrition. If a woman is pregnant during this period, she may become anemic, and severe anemia can lead to heart failure and death (Royston and Armstrong 1989: 85–89).

Interpretations of famine and drought, and policies for famine relief and safe water supplies are critical women's issues, because African women play central roles in agriculture, in tending small livestock, in food preparation, in the provision of food for themselves and their children, in obtaining firewood for cooking, heating, and lighting, and in ensuring water supplies for household and some farm uses.

For decades, policy-makers thought that famine was the result mainly of drought-induced food shortages, and they regarded drought as a natural calamity over which people had no control. Recent scholarship suggests that this analysis is wrong in four respects. First, famine is not the necessary consequence of food shortages: the outcome depends in part on the redistributive mechanisms of society (Turshen 1986). Second, drought is not a natural calamity: research on the occurrence of large-scale disasters in this century shows no major geological or climatological changes that could account for the increased loss of life per disaster in the Third World (O'Keefe et al. 1976: 565), and studies of desertification (the encroachment of deserts) reveal how ecologically irresponsible economic development policies create drought (Franke and Chasin 1981, Toure 1988). Third, peasants do exert some control when they call upon their large repertoire of effective responses to drought; these include exchanges with unaffected groups, eating grasses and other food substitutes, farm dispersal, wage labor, and migration (Turshen 1984: 100–105, Wisner, 1973).

The fourth and most important respect in which this analysis is wrong is that it attributes famine to food shortages. The pioneering studies of A. K. Sen (1981, 1990), who analyzed a number of modern famines, revealed that the total availability of food per person was no less (and was sometimes more) than in previous years. Sen (1990: 141) showed that famines result from the decline or loss of the resources that enable people to procure food – for example, the alienation of land, the loss of grazing rights, the loss of employment, the failure of money wages to keep up with food prices, and the failure of prices of animal products or crafts or services to keep up with food prices.

The groups likely to be most affected in a famine include widows and other lone women with children, who 'are often especially vulnerable, not only because they tend to have smaller plots and more limited access to labour and credit, but because in many societies they are regarded as food providers, not to be provided for' (Raikes 1988: 239, see also Vaughan 1987).

Famine relief and food security

Famine relief programs, which offer basic rations, often in return for work on public projects, are usually out of step with local African responses to food shortage. Food distribution programs, for example, can undermine market women's and farm women's ability to sell farm surpluses, and the effects may last beyond the emergency if the imported foods to which people become accustomed cannot be produced locally (Andrae and Beckman 1985).

Far more millions of people are malnourished or undernourished than are affected by outright famine. The World Bank estimates that 50 per cent of Africa's population is malnourished and 25 per cent seriously so (but see Raikes 1988: 69, for a critique of these figures). Poor peasants account for most of Africa's hungry people; others are the poorest urban families and landless rural laborers. Women suffer more from food shortage than men.

> [Women's] access to sources of income from farming, wage labour, and petty trading is poorer, as is their access to means of production and credit. They have very much weaker . . . rights in land, most especially where private property in land has been registered. This all relates to their generally subordinate social situation and to a specifically subordinate relation to men as fathers and husbands (Raikes 1988: 261).

The guarantee of food security requires far more than food aid or increased food production, which may only push peasants and pastoralists off their land and reduce its fertility. One critical issue is income, because real income levels fell during the decade of the 1980s in Africa. Another is war and the refugees created by wars. As many as 70 or 80 per cent of refugees are women and their children, and one-third of the world's 14 million refugees are to be found in Africa (United Nations 1991: 74). Effective food strategies at the local level require greater equity: gender equity within families, gender equity in society, equity for ethnic minorities, rural–urban equity, and economic justice in class relationships; they also require reform measures to reduce market discrimination against women.

Environmental degradation and ecofeminism

Some writers on the environmental degradation that is central to the food crisis in Africa blame rapid population increases and the growing number of poor people for pollution, for denuding the countryside of its protective wood cover, and for such land abuse as overgrazing and overcultivation (Eckholm and Brown 1977, World Bank 1979). The inference is that women, who are the majority of Africa's poor, are responsible for these problems. Other researchers fault these analysts for blaming the victims and for ignoring the pressures of external and macrolevel policies, such as unfavorable terms of trade and the debt crisis, which dictate increased export production and force farmers to expand into marginal areas (Juma and Ford 1992). Rather than blame women as the cause of Africa's food and energy crises, policy-makers should acknowledge the added burdens that environmental deterioration imposes on women's workloads and health, and they should credit women for their contributions to the solution of these problems.

Land, water, and trees are critical resources to rural people. Exhausted soils yield less, with direct consequences for nutrition and income. Thinning forests and dwindling or polluted water supplies force women – the traditional haulers of water and wood – to range farther afield and spend more time on these chores. Longer forays mean carrying heavier loads over greater distances; if this work continues during the last trimester of pregnancy, depriving women of needed rest, childbirth may be more difficult and the chances of mother and child surviving may be reduced (Royston and Armstrong 1989: 67–70).

Far from being passive victims, women respond to ecological challenges in a variety of creative ways that have been collectively labeled 'ecofeminism'. For example, Kenyan women are in the forefront of forest management, with many women's groups involved in tree planting and soil conservation (Dankelman and Davidson 1989: 63–65). The best known is the Green Belt Movement founded by Wangari Maathai (see Maathai 1985; see also the discussion in Chapter 10 above). Kenyan women are also involved in a Maendeleo ya Wanawake project to reduce the demand for fuelwood and charcoal by promoting the use of improved cooking stoves. The project trains women to build stoves that consume less fuelwood more efficiently and result in a cleaner kitchen in a healthier environment (Dankelman and Davidson 1989: 85–86).

Birth control and population policy

Environmental deterioration is but one of the problems that some analysts attribute to rapid population growth. The Population Crisis Committee (1989), one of a number of nongovernmental organizations in this field, describes demographic pressure as a menace to democracy and a potentially destabilizing force on governments and national political institutions. The Committee also blames rapid population growth for problems of massive urbanization, an unbalanced age pyramid (too many children under 15 years of age), and an expansion of the working-age population that cannot find jobs. Of the 60 countries with high rates of population growth identified by the Committee as most at risk of destabilization, 25 are African. Uganda is at the top of the Committee's list of 60.

African populations are growing fast. (Total fertility rates, or the total number of children that would be born to an average woman, are shown in the Appendix, Table A.5; they average about 6.2). The debate over population growth is polarized between neo-Malthusian groups like the Population Crisis Committee, which hold that the 'population explosion' is the cause of poverty, and anti-Malthusians who believe that African underdevelopment is the result of underpopulation (Amin 1972, see Cordell and Gregory 1994). The debate is important to women because the policy outcomes of the neo-Malthusians are radically different from those of women-centered positions. In general, neo-Malthusians support population control programs that aim to slow rates of natural increase, whereas the goal of women-centered family planning programs is improved maternal and child health. Malika Ladjali of Algeria clarifies this distinction:

> Family planning entails individual counselling; population control employs mass media campaigns, in which the health rationale is no longer primary. The difference between family planning and population control lies in the huge difference between contraceptive use and fertility control (Ladjali 1991: 134–35).

Women's individual wishes and needs are sometimes subservient to the goals of population control programs; this is illustrated by government policies that regulate women's fertility in order to control ethnic and racial diversity. At least one government has employed natalist and antinatalist policies selectively in order to remain in power. The apartheid government in South Africa worked to promote an increase in the white population but to limit fertility among blacks (Brown 1987). The South African government's policy in Namibia was similar in the 1970s, when contraception was the only free health service provided for blacks (Lindsay 1991). In these situations, black women bear the burdens of forced contraception and sterilization abuse.

When abortion and contraception are not legal and accessible and modern contraceptive technology is not widely available, many women resort to illegal or self-induced abortion to interrupt unwanted pregnancies. Unsafe abortion is identified as the leading cause of maternal mortality in some African urban areas; in Lusaka, it accounts for 25 per cent of maternal deaths; in Tanzania it is the direct cause of 17 per cent of maternal mortality (Defense for Children International – USA, 1991: 122).

Some people interpret high abortion rates as indicators of unmet needs for family planning, but studies show that abortion rates rise with the introduction of contraception (Royston and Armstrong 1989: 129–34). The relationship is complex because women who are subordinate to their husbands do not control their fertility and, without the consent and cooperation of their men, cannot use contraception successfully even when it is available (see Ladjali 1991, for a discussion of attitudes in Algeria). A Zimbabwean research study found:

> In respect of family planning, women's attitudes proved to be extremely complex. . . . Attitudes were influenced by a combination of traditional, 'Westernized', and religious beliefs, together with financial considerations. At the same time, health education and family planning were perceived by women to be inadequate, not always addressed to the right people, and often delivered in a cultural vacuum. Women were often ignorant of the way their reproductive systems functioned and were thus unable to exploit the limited information they might receive, in order to control their own fertility, particularly in the face of extreme pressure from most husbands and extended families to produce quantities of children (Chinemana 1988: 101–102).

Some population programs try to control women's fertility through legislation, in addition to the use of modern contraceptive technology. One way is by raising the legal age of first marriage for girls, especially in societies that do not condone teenage pregnancy out of wedlock; policy-makers thus try to shorten the biological period of childbearing. Also, a broad range of government policies can act as economic incentives or disincentives to childbearing – tax and housing policies and entitlements to social benefits that depend on family size. The next chapter discusses recent attempts by the Nigerian government to limit population growth through contraceptive technology.

For many African women, as for women everywhere, family planning is a personal issue and not a matter of national policy: their concern is to be able to exercise control over their own bodies. For these women, men's attempts to control their sexuality is the core issue of contraceptive use, as it is in the circumcision controversy.

Female circumcision

An increasing number of African and Arab women are writing and speaking out about female circumcision (see, for example, Asma El Dareer 1982, Nawal El Saadawi 1980, Olayinka Koso-Thomas 1987, and Awa Thiam 1986; see also Chapters 6 and 10 of this volume). They ask Western feminists to place the issue in context – as one among many traditional practices, some of which are positive, others negative; as one health issue in countries where other health problems claim many more lives; and as a changing problem within a dynamic society, one that African women and their leaders are working to solve. In Naawal el-Saadawi's words:

> I am against female circumcision and other similar retrograde and cruel practices. I was the first Arab woman to denounce it publicly and to write about it in my book, *Woman and Sex*. I linked it to the other aspects of female oppression. But I disagree with those women in America and Europe who concentrate on issues such as female circumcision and depict them as proof of the unusual and barbaric oppression to which women are exposed only in African or Arab countries. I oppose all attempts to deal with such problems in isolation, or to sever their links with the general economic and social pressures to which women everywhere are exposed, and with the oppression which is the daily bread fed to the female sex in developed and developing countries, in both of which a patriarchal class system still prevails (El Saadawi, 1980: xiv).

There are three main types of female circumcision: in the first, part or all of the clitoris is removed (clitoridectomy); in the second, part or all of the clitoris and labia minora is removed (excision); and in the third, the clitoris, labia minora, and parts of the labia majora are removed, the two sides of the vulva are joined, and only a small opening is left through which urine and menstrual fluids pass (infibulation). The medical complications of all three operations are immediate, including the dangers of blood loss and infection, while the third operation also entails long-term complications – obstruction during urination, menstruation, and childbirth, and chronic pelvic and urinary tract infections.

Female circumcision is not required by any religion; it is not a Muslim custom. The importance of circumcision for both men and women in many traditional African rituals is recounted in Chapter 6 of this volume. Today, female circumcision is widely practiced in 24 countries of sub-Saharan Africa, and there are reports of some cases in seven others. Infibulation, the most extensive operation, is widely practiced in five African countries and in parts of four others, including Ethiopia and Eritrea, where a majority of the population is Christian (Paquot 1983: 341). In North Africa, female circumcision is limited to Egypt. The United Nations estimated in 1986 that 30 to 74 million women had undergone the operation (Royston and Armstrong 1989: 149). African and Arab women writing about circumcision seem to agree that it has lost its ritual significance in the context of sexual initiation, now that it is performed on infants and young children, and that it represents men's attempt to control women's sexuality, even though older women perform the operation.

AIDS: Acquired Immune Deficiency Syndrome

Like female circumcision, AIDS should be set in context, as one among many diseases that claim lives in Africa. Numerically, AIDS is a minor cause of mortality and morbidity among African women. Countries report cases of AIDS, rather than deaths from AIDS, to the World Health Organization: in 1992, 42 African countries reported a total of 45,000 cases (WHO 1993). This figure should be compared to a yearly estimate of 80 million cases of malaria (a leading cause of death) and 1.2 million cases of tuberculosis. A very large number of women contract sexually transmitted diseases, which can cause infertility, cervical cancer, pelvic inflammatory disease, and ectopic pregnancy. Most of the sexually transmitted diseases could be prevented or cured but are not because health services are not adequate, accessible, or affordable.

African women are bearing the brunt of the AIDS epidemic, as the majority of the afflicted population (women and children account for more than 60 per cent of the AIDS cases in Africa) and as caretakers of afflicted family members. They also suffer from being accused of spreading HIV, the human immunodeficiency virus that causes AIDS, although there is no clinical documentation of the transmission of HIV from women to men. Many members of the scientific community and the press who blame women focus on the sexual transmission of HIV, although the virus can be transmitted with greater efficiency through blood transfusions, contaminated medical instruments, and from mother to fetus.

African women wrote very little about AIDS before 1990. In recent articles, their collective voice rejects victim-blaming and calls for increased investment in supportive health and welfare services and in income-generating projects. One report remonstrates that African women are being stigmatized as prostitutes, blamed for transmitting HIV to their clients, for having 'unprotected' sex, for getting pregnant, and for passing HIV to their infants (Bassett and Mhloyi 1991). Another article signals the growing distress of African women with health policies that do not address the issues that most preoccupy them – care of the sick and dying and support of survivors and dependents (Ankrah 1991).

There are divergent views on the cause of the AIDS epidemic. One group of demographers (Caldwell *et al.* 1989, Van de Walle 1990) alleges widespread sexual promiscuity in Africa and blames these mores for the spread of HIV. Other analysts (Hunt 1988, Sanders and Sambo 1991) maintain that the population at risk is increased directly by urban migration, poverty, women's powerlessness and prostitution, and indirectly through a decrease in health care provision. The current recession, the debt crisis, and certain development policies – notably structural adjustment programs, which have led to broad cutbacks in health services (see Chapter 12) – all affect the transmission, spread, and control of HIV infection; poor health care and high rates of migration, especially of single men and men without their families, have intensified the impact of poverty and contributed to the spread of AIDS.

Disease epidemics generally erupt in times of crisis, and the spread of HIV in a country like Zaire is clearly related to the economic turmoil, widespread unemployment, intense economic competition in the crowded informal sector, the feminization of poverty, and women's low status in that nation, one reporting many cases of AIDS (Schoepf *et al*. 1991: 201).

The migrant labor system, discussed in Chapter 1 and still dominant in many parts of Africa, creates a market for prostitution as male workers are away from home and alone for months at a time. Urban prostitution is one factor in the spread of AIDS. The difficulties faced by migrant workers are particularly acute in South African mining towns:

> In a lonely and hostile environment and separated for long periods from their wives, some migrants may seek sexual relationships with women in nearby towns. Migrancy also subjects marriages to great strain, and divorce or abandonment deprives women of economic support. With access to few opportunities on the labor market, some women may choose prostitution as the only means of economic survival (Jochelson *et al*. 1991: 157).

Other possible sources of AIDS are foreign military bases and the tourist industry, both of which also promote prostitution. International agencies encourage tourism as a solution to underdevelopment, and in some parts of the Third World, sex tours are sponsored by national governments. Sex tourism is clearly linked with AIDS in Thailand, for example (Enloe 1989: 37–39), while the introduction of AIDS to the Philippines has been attributed to visits by the US military (*New York Times* 23 April 1988). The same may be true of Kenya, because the bases at Mombasa regularly received British and American troops (Turshen 1991: 232–36). As yet there is little research on these questions in Africa.

Health policies based on the assumption that AIDS is primarily a sexually transmitted disease are skewed towards prevention, and they do not provide for the treatment of people with AIDS. The classic public health responses to sexually transmitted diseases – education, contact tracing, and condom distribution – have little relevance to women who do not have control over their sexuality (Carovano 1991).

Health services for African women in the age of AIDS

If preventive health policies were reoriented and based on the classification of AIDS as a blood-borne disease, they would emphasize the reequipment of laboratories, hospitals, blood banks, health centers, and clinics, and the retraining in aseptic techniques of all personnel who handle medical equipment. The needs for this sort of investment are massive in Africa, where health services have been seriously underfunded for the past decade as a byproduct of structural adjustment programs (*Lancet* 1990). Women are the majority users of these services, especially of blood transfusions after unsafe abortions or hemorrhage in childbirth.

Although WHO and some bilateral aid programs are promoting separate services for AIDS, African analysts are calling for a different health policy, one that entails an investment in the prevention and treatment of common infections, including malaria, tuberculosis, and sexually transmitted diseases. They feel priority should be accorded to caring for persons with AIDS, taking their social as well as their physical health needs into consideration (Ankrah 1991). There is also a call for new solutions to malnutrition that address the entire food system, beginning with issues of landlessness, and are not limited to attempts to improve distribution and increase consumption.

A broad environmental approach to health would address the underlying determinants of the spread of many diseases, including AIDS. The ultimate causes of disease are to be found in the structures of underdevelopment that created the need for men to migrate in search of work, and in the process destroyed the social and familial networks that had protected people from some types of disease experience. Although women do not advocate a return to traditional institutions of patriarchal domination, there is widespread recognition of the failure of alternative networks in urban areas to protect young girls, in particular, from the sexual exploitation that is the stigma of sexually transmitted disease and AIDS.

Note

1. See the special issue of *Social Science and Medicine* **37**, 4 (1993), which is devoted to women and tropical diseases.

CHAPTER 14

Case study: monitoring the impact of contraceptive technology on women in Nigeria

Tola Olu Pearce

While in the West, the new reproductive technologies have given rise to serious political, legal, moral, and emotional problems associated with surrogate motherhood, the commercialization of childbearing, and experimentation in fertility research, in Africa and other Third World nations, the impact of new, efficient contraceptive devices remains the main concern. A great deal of attention has been focussed on possible causes for the economic crisis of the past 20 years, and for Africa's general failure to 'develop'. All too readily, the high fertility rates characteristic of many African nations (see Appendix, Table A.5) were targeted and population control was perceived as mandatory to stop the growth of consumers of resources needed for sustained development.

In Nigeria, although private organizations, foreign donors, and local physicians had been involved since the late 1950s with the distribution of 'modern' contraceptives (Farooq and Adeokun 1976, Adeokun 1979, Ebigbola 1985), the government intentionally stayed in the background until the mid-1980s. By that time, a national fertility survey had been conducted (National Population Bureau 1984), the economic crisis was now undeniable, and a connection had been made, in official circles, between the population burden and the lack of headway in development. In 1984, the total fertility rate (TFR) stood at 6.34, and the natural rate of increase was estimated to be 3.2 per cent, while the population was believed to be 100 million. Numerous studies revealed a rise in nutritional disorders and preventable diseases (over which a measure of control had been gained earlier), as well as the stubborn persistence of low values for the standard health indicators such as life expectancy, infant mortality, and maternal mortality rates. Official aversion to involvement in the controversial issue of birth control was then set aside, and by 1988 a National Population Policy was developed. To date, this policy is voluntary.

One major aspect of this National Population Policy is the stipulation that women should strive to bear only four children each. With this development came increased attention to the reproductive activities of rural populations, which comprise about 65 per cent of the nation, and the growth of numerous experimental programs of contraceptive distribution. Attempts are being made to flood the population with efficient contraceptive methods in the hope that a high degree of acceptance would follow and the runaway population rate would be controlled. Nonetheless, the 1990 national Demographic and Health Survey revealed that the total fertility rate remained high at 6.1, contraceptive usage among married women was only 6 per cent (as compared to 4.5 per cent in 1982) and the majority of women still desired more than four children. In addition, attitudes towards the new contraceptives remain mixed (Pearce 1991). One growing concern has been the health dimension of widespread distribution programs (Ogbuagu 1985). While it is important to safeguard the health of women by stemming continuous and late childbearing (a common feature of married life), it is also necessary to watch closely the health of those who use contraceptives.

Under ideal conditions, women using contraceptives should receive a thorough examination and counselling prior to choosing any method. In addition, monitoring the health impact of particular methods of contraception should be an integral part of any distribution program. However, there are indications that this aspect of family planning programs has received minimal attention, even though family planning is advertised as a health enhancement program aimed at reducing maternal mortality (which stands at 1,500 per 100,000 live births) and pregnancy-related health complications. My interest in this dimension of reproductive activities led to a small study of family planning clinics in 1987. The clinics were located within the rural areas of two states in Yorubaland, the southwestern region of Nigeria. In both locations, it soon became clear that examinations and check-ups were not given priority. The problems encountered by both the users and providers of imported contraceptives are illustrated below by the data gathered at one rural Basic Health Center in Ondo State.

Monitoring the health of contraceptive users

The data reported here were collected as part of a larger three-year study, in which the present author was involved during the final two years. The ongoing project sought to obtain information on the availability of health facilities, the attitudes of health care providers, and the service utilization patterns of consumers in a rural Local Government Area (LGA) in Ondo State. The LGA had been selected by the government, in 1983, as one of 52 in the nation to develop 'model' primary health care programs. This LGA is situated in the eastern part of the state, and the population in 1987 was estimated at 367,020 inhabitants. The community in which the study was conducted had about 10,000 people. As part of the primary health care program, a family planning clinic was opened in November 1985. Clinic day was each Friday, between 8:00 a.m. and 3:30 p.m.

251

This family planning clinic was just one of the many clinics developed in the Basic Health Center under the 'model' Primary Health Care Program. The Center was headed by a health sister, assisted by a nurse/midwife, a community health assistant, two community health aides, and two community health orderlies. Each staff member, except the orderlies, was expected to conduct home visits and to reach out into the surrounding community. Tuesdays and Thursdays were set aside for home visits. At the time of the study (1987), there was still strong opposition from men in the area to the use of modern contraceptives. Some Yoruba men worried that effective contraception would encourage female promiscuity (Olusanya 1969).

Data were collected between July and October 1987 by the trained interviewer residing in the community for the larger study. Information was gathered from the clinic records of all who had attended the family planning clinic between November 1985 and August 1987, from discussions with staff, and with those active clients who agreed to be interviewed. The sample was therefore composed of persons who were willing to be interviewed either at home or in the clinic. Altogether, 22 clients agreed to be interviewed.

Between November 1985 and August 1987, a total of 63 women had used the services of the clinic. Nine new clients had registered in 1985, 25 in 1986, and 29 in 1987 respectively. The clinic staff indicated that response was initially slow, but had started to gain some momentum. For instance, between August (when client interviews were completed) and October (when follow-up discussions were scheduled with the health sister), an additional 17 new clients had approached the clinic for contraceptives. During the two months of client interviews, 31 of the 63 clients attended clinic regularly. Thirty did not show up, and the records of one could not be located. The other client had died. Thus it would appear that the clinic has lost about half of the original 'acceptors'. Three reasons were given by the staff for their clients' defaulting: the intervention of irate husbands, health side-effects of the particular method used, and the wish to have more children.

Data collected on the demographic characteristics of defaulters and active clients showed that the former tend to be younger, slightly better educated, and to have fewer children than the latter. Thus 41 per cent of defaulters compared to 27 per cent of the active clients were under 30 years of age. About one-quarter of the defaulters had no formal education at all, compared to one-third of the active contraceptive users, while 52 per cent had primary education, compared with 45 per cent of the active users. Finally, 58 per cent and 23 per cent of each group respectively had four children or fewer, while 23 per cent of the regular clients compared to 14 per cent of the defaulters had seven or more children.

For both defaulters and active clients, the pill was the most common method used. It must be stated, however, that a client's ability to choose was rather restricted. The health sister usually made the choice for newcomers after taking a health history and examining the patient. Exceptions were made, however, when a client appeared to be well-educated (having attended secondary school) or when a change of method was indicated because of health side-effects. In addition, intrauterine devices (IUDs) were not issued within the clinic, and clients needed to be referred to facilities in a nearby larger town if they were to be fitted. Thus 90 per cent of the defaulters and 82 per cent of those still attending the clinic were on the pill. The rest of both groups were given the controversial three-monthly injection of Depo Provera.

Information was sought on three related aspects of the health-monitoring efforts. These included the type of medical examination received by new clients, what 'acceptors' were told about possible health problems, and whether examinations were conducted during subsequent clinic visits. On the first issue it was obvious that tests and examinations were hampered by the lack of adequate equipment. The temperature, blood pressure, and weight of new clients was taken. In addition, the breast was examined by manual palpitation for possible lumps. No provision was made for any form of pelvic examination before the pill was issued or injections given. There was also no equipment for blood or urine tests. However, there was extensive (medical) history taking. When asked if they were aware of possible side-effects of the contraceptive issued to them, only four clients said yes. Nonetheless, in her own interview, the health sister insisted that all contraceptive users are normally briefed on potential health problems.

The monthly visits scheduled for each client seemed to be a problematic dimension of the program. Of the 22 respondents, only three indicated that any form of physical check-up had been conducted since the original examination. Two of these reported that the check-up consisted of only verbal questioning. All the other respondents, including one client who had been on the pill for five years, said that no tests or reexamination had been performed. Three-quarters of the sample said that this was because they had not complained of side-effects. The remaining respondents did not give any reasons. While four of the respondents had been on the contraceptive for less than two months before the study, nine had been on it for up to six months and eight between seven months and a year. Given the possibilities of changes in these women's health status resulting from either the use of the pill or injections, a closer monitoring of the women should have occurred. The monitoring system relied only on gross indicators such as unexpected bleeding or vomiting which a client is expected to report.

The study thus revealed important shortcomings in the monitoring of clients. There was a high drop-out rate, and the staff were unable to visit clients as regularly as expected, since the Center has not yet been furnished with a bus, ambulance, or car. Women from the smaller adjacent villages could therefore not be easily reached. The home visits were thus restricted by the lack of transportation. Furthermore, it was obvious that equipment for physical examinations

253

was rudimentary and physical reexaminations appear not to be conducted on contraceptive users.

Data collected by the author in 1987 at another clinic in a community-based distribution project in rural Oyo State (adjacent to Ondo State) confirmed the above findings. Monitoring was also minimal at the clinic where in fact, contraceptive users were not even given initial examinations before the pill was issued. Six-monthly check-ups were supposed to occur, but during the year before the study (1986), only two of 165 women on the pill (or 1.2 per cent) had come back to the clinic for check-ups. The staff complained of difficulties in tracking down the clients, as mentioned in the Ondo State clinic.

Conclusion

Although it is recognized that the high rate of maternal mortality in Nigeria is related to early and persistent childbearing, programs aimed at the large-scale distribution of contraceptives will increasingly become controversial unless accompanied by other activities. These include the development of services and programs to monitor the health of contraceptive users. Successful and humane family planning clinics require many supporting services, including a range (and a choice) of contraceptive devices, testing equipment, coordinated hospital referral schemes, and an adequate health education package. In Nigeria, much of this remains superficial and, in the face of the deepening economic crisis, increasingly difficult to supply.

The wholesale distribution of contraceptives as the main focus of population control must also be reconsidered. A broader perspective on population dynamics must be at the heart of activities. The history of Western nations has revealed the force of such factors as education, improvement in the quality of life, and political participation in leading to reduced birth rates.

In addition, studies have revealed that women are increasingly becoming concerned about their reproductive health (Olukoya 1986). Data on teenagers also indicate the fear of health side-effects as a deterrent in contraceptive usage (Oronsaye and Odiase 1983). In a recently concluded health care study among market women in Ile-Ife, it was discovered that the same health concerns existed among a group of older, married food vendors. These women complained of a variety of side-effects from contraceptive use, including weight gain, weight loss, headaches, bleeding, and mood changes (Kujore and Pearce 1988–91). There was particular concern over any impediment to work. The women carry heavy financial responsibilities with regard to child care. Food vending is labor-intensive, and the working hours are long. Thus feeling unwell or weak poses real problems. In addition, many neighborhoods in Ile-Ife do not have a reliable flow of piped water. Households tend to depend on unreliable sources, which include rain water collected in buckets or large containers, water vendors or tankers, and shallow, contaminated wells. Therefore, intermittent or heavy bleeding becomes both a sanitation and financial burden.

Poorly organized and sparsely equipped clinics can themselves become a health hazard. One Nigerian researcher pointed to the rejection of contraceptives by former users in a sample of single, educated urban women. Her own 1988 survey revealed that among the sexually active urban women, those who had used contraceptives in the past were less likely than nonusers to indicate future use (Makinwa-Adebusoye 1991); these findings were confirmed by the national Demographic and Health Survey. Thus, in 1988, only 20.4 per cent of former contraceptive users and 64 per cent of nonusers gave positive responses about future use. In 1991, the figures were 23 per cent, as compared to 53 per cent; Makinwa-Adebusoye concluded that 'these figures are indicative of some profound defects existing in family planning programmes' (1991: 11).

Insofar as the use of modern contraceptives is expected to be the trend for the future, it is necessary at this juncture to draw attention to the critical issue of health monitoring for women who accept the new technologies. Alongside short-term side-effects, long-term health problems must also be investigated, especially since the efficient devices were developed with the generally well-nourished Western body in mind. When these devices are used on poor and often malnourished rural women, other complications may arise (Pearce 1988).

Some selected statistics on African women

Sharon Stichter

The national-level statistics on women in Africa offer one important guide to what women do for a living and to the differences in women's economic and social situation from country to country. Often they are the only means to approximate cross-national comparisons in these areas. Yet the indices must be used carefully, for they have important limitations.

Tables A.1 to A.5 in this Appendix present data on women's economic participation, occupations, fertility, and educational levels. The data are based on the latest national population censuses or sample surveys. Comparability between nations is assured only to the extent that each country follows the conceptual and procedural guidelines recommended by the coordinating international agencies. In some cases, where recent censuses are lacking, agencies such as the World Bank or the International Labor Organization have made estimates and projections based on earlier data.

Table A.1 shows the rates of economic activity for African women and their changes over the past two decades. The *economically active population*, or *labor force*, in this table comprises all adults who furnish the supply of labor for the production of economic goods and services as defined by the United Nations systems of national accounts, during a specified short time-reference period, such as the preceding day or week. The *economic activity rate*, or *labor force participation rate*, is the proportion of the population over the age of 15 classified as economically active.

According to the United Nations, economic goods and services should include all production and processing of primary products, whether for own consumption, for barter, or for sale in the market, plus the production of all other goods and services for the market. This recently adopted definition is intended to include the subsistence production that is a main role of women in many developing areas, especially Africa. Before 1982, such production was not included (see Beneria 1981). Nonmarketed domestic services are still excluded, so that women who are solely housewives are not counted. Nor are students, retired, or wholly dependent persons. The way in which the concept of economically active population is actually applied during census counts varies greatly from country to country; practices that underestimate the work of women are still common.

1. *Subsistence production*. The distinction between domestic production and unpaid housework is very difficult to draw in developing nations. African women spend great amounts of time in household food preparation, child care, gathering firewood, carrying water, and looking after domestic livestock, as well as planting, weeding, and harvesting. The first two activities are generally not included in national accounts, but there is a great deal of uncertainty and variation as to how much of the rest of this work is included.

2. *Unpaid family workers*. There are great variations among national statistical departments as to how unpaid workers in small family enterprises are counted. Most of these workers are women and children. Some countries use a reference period to distinguish nonworkers from part-time workers, others do not. In general, part-time work presents difficulties for census takers unless the frequency of the work is clearly specified. Many women who work only seasonally or intermittently may not be counted.

3. *Informal sector activities*. Large numbers of rural and urban African women engage in small-scale trade and industry – crafts, food selling, beer-brewing, hawking, prostitution, and so forth. These activities are on the periphery of the formal wage-labor sector; the women involved are free-lance or perhaps partly employed, for example on a commission basis. Conceptually these workers are supposed to be included in the economically active population, but frequently they are not, because their activities are done irregularly or in conjunction with other economic roles or because they are shifting in locale and perhaps quasi-legal.

4. *Unemployment*. Those who have no job or economic activity but are actively seeking work are classified as in the labor force but 'unemployed'. In the case of women, however, there is a tendency for census-takers automatically to relegate a married woman who is not working to the status of 'economically inactive', or 'housewife', rather than 'unemployed', without probing whether or not she is looking for work or would accept a job if one were offered. For this reason, the unemployment figures given in Table A.3 may well be underestimates.

Despite these difficulties with the concept of 'economically active population' and its measurement, Table A.1 does reveal some interesting information. Compared to other regions of the world, sub-Saharan Africa ranks high in the percentage of women engaged in economic activity other than unpaid housework. Most West, East, and southern African nations report at least 40 per cent of all women over age 15 as economically active, with women forming over 30 per cent of

257

Table A.1 African women's economic activity, 1970–1990

| | Estimated Economic Activity Rate* | | Women as a Percentage of Economically Active Population Age 15 and Over |
	1970	1990	1990
North Africa			
Algeria	4	8	9
Egypt	6	9	10
Libya	6	9	9
Morocco	12	19	20
Tunisia	11	26	25
West Africa			
Benin	83	77	48
Burkina Faso	85	77	46
Cameroon	51	41	33
Central African Rep.	80	68	46
Chad	27	23	21
Côte d'Ivoire	64	48	34
Equatorial Guinea	60	52	40
Gabon	54	47	37
Gambia	65	58	40
Ghana	59	51	40
Guinea	65	57	40
Guinea-Bissau	63	57	41
Liberia	42	37	30
Mali	17	16	16
Mauritania	24	24	22
Niger	87	79	47
Nigeria	52	46	35
Senegal	60	53	39
Sierra Leone	44	38	32
Togo	53	47	36
Zaire	58	45	35
East Africa			
Ethiopia	59	52	37
Burundi	86	78	48
Kenya	65	58	40
Rwanda	86	79	47
Somalia	60	53	39
Sudan	22	24	22
Uganda	68	62	41
United Rep. Tanzania	89	77	48
Central & South Africa			
Angola	59	52	39
Botswana	55	42	36
Lesotho	76	65	44
Madagascar	63	55	39

Table A.1   (Continued)

	Estimated Economic Activity Rate*		Women as a Percentage of Economically Active Population Age 15 and Over
	1970	1990	1990
Malawi	68	57	41
Mozambique	89	79	48
Namibia	24	24	23
South Africa	40	40	36
Swaziland	63	53	39
Zambia	31	33	28
Zimbabwe	51	44	34

*Economically active female population aged 15 years and over as a percentage of total female population aged 15 years and over.

Source: United Nations, The World's Women 1970–1990, Table 8. Based on ILO, Economically Active Population Estimates 1950–1980, Projections, 1985–2025; ILO, Yearbook of Labour Statistics, various years.

the total labor force (Table A.1). This picture reflects African women's traditionally important roles in food production and trade in most areas. In a few countries, such as Mozambique, Tanzania, and Benin, women make up close to half the total labor force. Interestingly, African women's labor force participation does not show any sharp drop during adult childbearing and child-rearing years, in contrast to Latin America, east and southeast Asia, the Middle East, and most industrialized countries (UN, World's Women, 1991: Tables 6.6 and 6.8). African women generally either combine child care with agricultural work, or depend on family, friends or hired help for child care while they continue at their jobs.

There is a marked contrast between the high rates of female economic activity in most of sub-Saharan Africa and the low rates for North Africa and other Islamized areas. Where sub-Saharan women's activity rates fell below 30 per cent in 1990, these were areas of strong Arab and Islamic influence, such as Mali, Mauritania, Chad and the Sudan. Interestingly, women's economic participation in North Africa and the Sudan is increasing, or at least becoming more recognized, whereas that in most of the rest of Africa is decreasing.

The economic crises of the past two decades have hit African women particularly hard. Estimated economic activity rates for women actually fell between 1970 and 1990 for nearly every major African nation (Table A.1). By contrast, women's labor force participation over this period rose in Latin America, the Middle East, and East Asia, and declined only slightly in south and southeast Asia; Africa is the only region showing a sharp decline (UN 1991: Chart 6.6).

Within Africa, the only areas where the proportion of women in economic activity grew are either the Islamized areas mentioned above, which are reporting a slow growth in women's participation from a previously low level, or mining economies such as South Africa, Namibia, or Zambia, where women's productive roles seem to be gaining importance as male employment decreases. In the rest of Africa, total population levels rose sharply, and the absolute numbers of economically active people of both sexes rose as well, but ultimately could not keep pace with total population growth. Therefore, both men's and women's activity rates dropped over the past 20 years, and in nearly every case women's rates dropped more than men's.

Similarly, women's share in the total labor force increased or stayed steady between 1970 and 1990 in all major regions of the developing world except sub-Saharan Africa (UN 1991: Table 6.5). Africa is the only major region where the male labor force is expected to increase faster than the female as development proceeds (UNESCO, *World Survey*, 1986: 13). In agriculture and the urban informal sector, many women may find themselves squeezed out of income-producing work as agriculture modernizes and population pressure increases on the land and in cities.

The percentage of economically active African women who have formal-sector wage or salaried employment is about 30 per cent on average, varying from lows of about 10 per cent in countries with few paid employment opportunities to much higher levels in southern Africa. Africa is now the only major world region where this percentage is markedly lower for women than for men, since women's employment has been increasing worldwide (UN 1991: Table 6.12, Stichter 1990). Although the general level of wage and salaried employment has grown in most African countries over the last two decades, it has not kept pace with the growth in population. Employment for women has in fact been growing somewhat faster than for men, so that in a number of nations women increased their share of wage employment during the decade of the 1980s. Table A.2 shows that this is the case for Botswana, Kenya, Malawi, Mauritius, Niger, and Swaziland. Available numbers do not allow us to confirm whether this is the case elsewhere in Africa, but it is apparently not so in Tanzania or Zimbabwe. Table A.2 shows that, among countries with available statistics, the percentage of wage and salaried jobs held by women varies from a low of 5.3 per cent in Islamized Chad, to a high of 35.7 per cent on the island of Mauritius, where many multinational companies have invested and have instituted policies of hiring mostly women.

The lag of employment behind population growth has led to an increase in reported unemployment in many African countries during the 1980s, as well as much unreported under-employment. This has affected both sexes, but women disproportionately. Table A.3 shows that women's share of unemployment increased during this time in several major African nations, including Ivory Coast, Senegal, Angola, Niger, Sudan, Chad, and Mauritius. This occurred in part because

Table A.2 African women in wage and salaried employment

	Year	Female Employment	Total Employment	Women as a Percentage of Total Employment
Angola	1989	73.43	367.63	20.0
Botswana	1980	19.4	83.4	23.3
Botswana	1991	76.1	222.8	34.2
Chad	1989	0.599	11.27	5.3
Gambia	1987	4.98	26.09	19.1
Kenya	1980	176.8	1005.8	17.6
Kenya	1990	308.5	1409.0	21.9
Malawi	1980	42.19	370.4	11.4
Malawi	1989	62.6	441.5	14.2
Mauritius	1980	51.32	197.1	26.0
Mauritius	1991	100.6	281.4	35.7
Niger	1980	0.865	26.0	3.3
Niger	1989	2.554	28.0	9.1
Swaziland	1980	18.999	75.12	25.3
Swaziland	1988	26.041	85.87	30.3
Tanzania*	1984	86.19	633.38	13.6
Zimbabwe	1984	172.0	1036.4	16.6

*excluding Zanzibar

Source: International Labor Organization, *Yearbook of Labour Statistics*, 1989–90, 1991, 1992, Tables 2B and 3A.

in times of economic hardship and recession, women workers are more vulnerable than men as employers discriminate in workforce reductions. But in addition the number of women seeking paid work as opposed to self-employment may well have increased (UNESCO, *World Survey*, 1986: 30).

Table A.4 shows the concentration of women in certain occupations in three representative areas of Africa and the ratio of women to men in occupations. The categories used here do not reflect a detailed occupational breakdown based on skill levels. Only the first three categories are occupational ones, and correspond roughly to 'white-collar' jobs. The rest are sectoral divisions, and include all skilled and unskilled workers below the clerical level. The background to this present-day occupational distribution among African women is discussed more fully in Chapter 3 of this volume.

In most African countries, the great majority of working women and men, but especially women, are employed in agriculture. The situation illustrated by Zimbabwe, where there are 128 economically active women in agriculture for every 100 men, is very common. Nigeria is somewhat unusual in this respect, having a greater percentage of working women in sales than in agriculture. This reflects a traditional division of labor in Yoruba communities, where men do the bulk of

Table A.3   African women's
unemployment as a percentage
of total unemployment,
Available statistics, 1980–1991

	Year	Percentage
Angola	1984	33.2
	1986	37.1
Burundi	1983	10.6
(Bujumbura)	1989	11.7
Chad	1983	0.4
	1989	0.8
Ivory Coast	1984	24.1
	1990	29.4
Ethiopia	1981	37.9
	1991	43.8
Ghana	1980	29.5
	1989	10.0
Centr Afr. Rep.	1980	11.9
(Bangui)	1988	9.3
Mauritius	1980	30.9
	1991	50.6
Niger	1980	3.7
	1989	5.1
Senegal	1983	11.0
	1988	13.7
South Africa	1980	53.4
(blacks only)	1989	52.2
Sudan	1980	17.7
	1991	48.6

Source: ILO, *Yearbook of Labour Statistics,*
1989–90, 1992, Table 9A.

the farm work. If one looked at waged work in agriculture, however, men would predominate in most countries.

African women are greatly underrepresented compared to men in the production, mining, and transport sectors. Women's participation in factory production work is growing, however. Whereas in the countries shown in Table A.4, only 3 to 6 per cent of working women are in non-agricultural production, compared to 13 to 16 per cent of the men, the proportion in countries such as South Africa or Mauritius is much greater.

As one might expect, the most serious area of underrepresentation for women in Africa, as for women everywhere, is in administration and management. Even in the best case shown, Zimbabwe, managerial employees constitute only 0.3 per cent of the female labor force but 1.3 per cent of the male. Women do somewhat better in the professional and technical occupations, which include nursing and teaching. In the countries shown there are 35–67 women for every

Table A.4 Occupational distribution of the economically active population (selected cases)

	Women (%)	*Men (%)*	*f/100m*
Nigeria Sept. 1986[1]			
Professional & technical	5.2	7.3	35
Administrative and managerial	0.0	0.3	6
Clerical workers	2.1	4.6	23
Sales workers	46.4	13.1	177
Service workers	1.1	4.4	13
Agriculture	33.7	47.3	36
Production, mine and transport	5.8	16.4	18
Not classified	5.7	6.6	
Total	100.0	100.0	
Sudan 1983[2]			
Professional & technical	2.5	2.6	40
Administrative & managerial	0.0	0.2	2
Clerical workers	1.3	2.3	23
Sales workers	1.2	5.5	9
Service workers	2.5	5.8	18
Agriculture	74.6	57.5	53
Production, mine, transport	4.0	12.6	13
Not classified	13.9	13.5	
Total	100.0	100.0	
Zimbabwe, 1986–87[1]			
Professional & technical	3.6	4.9	67
Administrative & managerial	0.3	1.3	18
Clerical workers	1.9	4.8	37
Sales workers	2.4	2.9	78
Service workers	4.4	9.6	42
Agriculture	75.1	53.7	128
Production, mine, transport	3.1	14.8	20
Not classified	9.1	7.9	
Total	99.9*	99.9*	

*rounding
[1]Labor Force Sample Survey
[2]Census

Source: ILO, *Yearbook of Labor Statistics*, 1992, Table 2B.

100 men in these occupations. In all countries, the two occupations of nursing and primary school teaching account for a very large proportion of all African professional women, the occupations having become feminized since the colonial era (for examples, see Bujra 1986 and Schuster 1981).

Table A.4 reveals the striking contrast across Africa in women's roles in trade and commerce. West African women's traditional and persisting dominance in this area is evident in the case of Nigeria, where an incredible 46 per cent of the female labor force work in sales, and there are 177 women for every 100 men in this form of employment. But this phenomenon is not found to nearly the same extent in southern Africa, where only 2.4 per cent of Zimbabwean women work in sales and the numbers of men and women in trade are roughly comparable. Islamic nations such as the Sudan are at the other extreme from Nigeria: only 1.2 per cent of working women are in trade, and there are only 9 women for every 100 men. Most women working in trade are self-employed; there are usually greater numbers of men holding waged and salaried jobs in larger commercial enterprises. Thus, the business skills of the famous market women of West Africa are not yet being translated into modern employment (Akerele 1979: 39–40, Boserup 1970: 99, ILO 1975: Table 2B). On the other hand, self-employment in trade has in many cases been an important channel of economic success for African women (MacGaffey 1988, Robertson 1984).

Women's participation in clerical work has been growing in Africa, although the occupation has not become so completely feminized as it is in Western industrial societies. As described in Chapter 3, clerks and white-collar workers were almost wholly male during the colonial period. Table A.4 shows that men still predominate. However, a closer look at the categories of typist and stenographer would probably reveal female predominance. In Kenya in 1978, for example, 90 per cent of all secretarial workers were women (Bujra 1986: 133).

One reason for the difficulties African women face in the labor market compared to men is their relative lack of access to education. In sub-Saharan Africa as a whole, three-quarters of women aged 25 and over are still illiterate. Most of these are in rural rather than urban areas. Illiteracy rates are falling for young women, but are still much higher for young women than young men (UN 1991: Chart 3.1 and 3.2). In some quite populous African countries, such as Ivory Coast, Ethiopia, Liberia, Senegal and Sierra Leone, the ratio of female to male enrolment in primary school was still less than 75 per cent in 1985/86. Out of 39 African nations, 16 were in this category, including Benin, Burundi, Chad, Guinea-Bissau, Mali, Somalia and Sudan. On the other hand, in thirteen countries female primary school enrolment equalled or exceeded male enrolment, including Zimbabwe, Zambia, Tanzania, Swaziland, Mauritius, Kenya, and Botswana. In Nigeria there were 79 women per 100 men; in Ghana 78, in Zaire 75. In nearly all countries, the percentage of women among secondary-school enrollees was lower than that among primary enrollees (UN 1991: Table 4). (For the growth of women's education in Africa, see Robertson 1986).

A major part of the work women do in Africa today is the bearing and rearing of children. As economies modernize, it becomes

Table A.5 African women: fertility and maternal mortality

Country	Total Fertility Rate, 1990	Approximate maternal mortality per 100,000 live births, 1980/90*
Angola	6.5	n.a.
Benin	6.3	1,680 (1980)
Botswana	4.7	200–300
Burkina Faso	6.5	810
Burundi	6.8	n.a.
Cameroon	5.8	300
Cape Verde	5.2	107
Central African Republic	5.8	600
Chad	6.0	860
Congo	6.6	1,000
Côte d'Ivoire	6.7	n.a.
Equatorial Guinea	5.7	n.a.
Ethiopia	7.5	2,000 (1980)
Gabon	5.7	n.a.
Gambia	6.4	n.a.
Ghana	6.2	1,000
Guinea	6.5	n.a.
Guinea-Bissau	5.4	n.a.
Kenya	6.5	510 (1980)
Lesotho	5.6	n.a.
Liberia	6.3	173 (1980)
Madagascar	6.3	240
Malawi	7.6	100
Mali	7.1	n.a.
Mauritania	6.8	119 (1980)
Mauritius	1.9	126
Mozambique	6.4	479 (1980)
Namibia	5.9	n.a.
Niger	7.2	420
Nigeria	6.0	800
Rwanda	8.3	210
Senegal	6.5	600
Sierra Leone	6.5	450
Somalia	6.8	1,100 (1980)
South Africa	4.3	83**
Sudan	6.3	660
Swaziland	6.5	n.a.
Togo	6.6	476 (1980)
Uganda	7.3	300
Tanzania	6.6	340
Zaire	6.2	800
Zambia	6.7	151
Zimbabwe	4.9	480

*maternal mortality in hospitals and other medical institutions only
**rural areas, 1980–550

Sources: World Bank, *World Development Report 1992*, Tables 27, 32, United Nations 1991 *World's Women 1970–1990*: Table 5.

increasingly difficult to combine labor force participation with high levels of childbearing, as many African women are able to do today. Table A.5 shows the *total fertility rate* for each African nation. This measure gives the number of children that would be born to a woman if she were to live to the end of her childbearing years and bear children at each age according to the prevailing age-specific fertility rates. Thus it gives the total number of children an average woman will bear in a society.

By comparison with most other areas of the developing world, sub-Saharan African fertility remains high. The regional average of 6.2 births per woman compares to 5.4 for the Middle East and North Africa, 5.4 for southern Asia, 3.6 for Latin America and the Caribbean, and 3.0 for East Asia. Some parts of the developing world, such as China, have experienced steep declines in fertility between 1970 and 1990, while other areas had moderate declines, but sub-Saharan Africa had only a very small decline in average fertility over the two decades (UN 1991: Table 4.8).

Until greater economic and social development takes place in Africa, until larger numbers of people experience larger incomes, longer life expectancy, old-age security, and a decline in infant mortality, birth rates will remain high in Africa. Mortality rates, especially for infants and children, are also comparatively high. The fertility transition now taking place in many parts of the Third World is only beginning in Africa.

African women still bear the heavy physical burdens of childbearing, and multiple pregnancies take a toll on health. The risks are often very high, as indicated by the maternal mortality rates shown in Table A.5. Estimated maternal mortality per 100,000 live births in Africa as a whole in the mid-1980s was about 630, in contrast to about 50 for developed regions and about 300–400 in Latin America and the Middle East. Only South Asia equalled Africa's rates (UN 1991: Table 4.4). Maternal mortality is one good indicator of the general quality of health services provided to women. The need for more well-funded health services for women is discussed more fully in Chapters 13 and 14 of this volume.

References

Note: *items marked with an asterisk (*) are important books and articles that will be particularly useful for nonspecialist readers:*

Abu, Katherine (1983) 'The separateness of spouses: conjugal resources in Ashanti Town', in Christine Oppong (ed.) *Female and Male in West Africa*, London, pp. 156–69.

Adams, M. J. (1978) 'Kuba embroidered cloth', *African Arts*, **12:** 24–39.

Adams, M. J. (1980) 'Spheres of men's and women's creativity', *Ethnologische Zeitschrift Zurich*, **I:** 163–67.

Adeokun, L. (1979) 'Family planning in southwestern Nigeria: levels and determinants of KAP', in L. Adeokun (ed.) *National Survey of Fertility, Family and Family Planning*, Ile-Ife, pp. 62–104.

Afonja, Simi (1989) 'Toward the creation of a new order for Nigerian women: recent trends in politics and policies', *Issue: A Journal of Opinion*, Summer, **17**(2): 7–8.

Africa Rights Monitor No. 16 (1990) 'A woman's right to political participation in Africa', *Africa Today*, **27**(1): 49–64.

Aidoo, Ama Ata (1970) *Anowa*, London.

Aidoo, Ama Ata (1970) *No Sweetness Here*, New York.

Aidoo, Ama Ata (1985) *Someone Talking to Sometime*, Harare.

Aidoo, Agnes Akosua (1981) 'The Asante queen mother in government and politics in the nineteenth century', in Filomina Chioma Steady (ed.) *The Black Woman Cross-Culturally*, Cambridge, pp. 65–78.

Akerele, Olubanke (1979) *Women Workers in Ghana, Kenya, Zambia*, Addis Ababa.

Akeroyd, Anne V. (1991) 'Gender, food production and property rights: constraints on women farmers in southern Africa', in Haleh Afshar (ed.) *Women, Development, and Survival in the Third World*, New York, pp. 139–73.

Al-Amin bin Aly Mazrui (1932) *Wajibu Wetu kwa Wanawake* ('Our Duty Toward Women') and *Uwongozi* ('Guidance'), Mombasa reprint, 1955.

Albert, Ethel M. (1971) 'Women of Burundi: a study of social values', in Denise Paulme (ed.) *Women of Tropical Africa*, Berkeley, California, pp. 179–216.

Allot, A. N. *et al.* (1969) 'Legal personality in African law', in M. Gluckman (ed.) *Ideas and Procedures in African Customary Law*, Oxford, pp. 179–95.

Alpers, Edward, A. (1983) 'The story of Swema: a note on female vulnerability in nineteenth-century East Africa', in Martin Klein and Claire C. Robertson (eds) *Women and Slavery in Africa*, Madison, Wisconsin, pp. 185–219.

Alpers, Edward, A. (1984) '"Ordinary household chores": ritual and power in a 19th-century Swahili women's spirit possession cult', *International Journal of African Historical Studies*, **17**: 677–702.

Alverson, Hoyt (1978) *Mind in the Heart of Darkness: Value and Self-Identity Among the Tswana of Southern Africa*, New Haven, Connecticut.

*Amadiume, Ifi (1987) *Male Daughters, Female Husbands: Gender and Sex in an African Society*, Atlantic Highlands, N.J.

Amin, Samir (1972) 'L'Afrique sous-peuplée', *Développement et civilisations*, **47–48**: 59–67.

Anderson, Martha (1983) 'Central Ijo art: shrines and spirit images', Ph.D. thesis, Indiana University.

Andrae, Gunilla and Björn Beckman (1985) *The Wheat Trap: Bread and Underdevelopment in Nigeria*, London.

Aniakor, Chike (1979) 'Igbo architecture: a study of forms, functions, and typology', 2 vols., Ph.D. thesis, Indiana University.

Ankrah, E. Maxine (1991) 'AIDS and the social side of health', *Social Science and Medicine*, **32**(9): 967–80.

Ankrah, E. Maxine and Bizimana, Peninah D. (1991) 'Women's studies program for Uganda', *Signs*, **16**: 864–69.

Ardener, Shirley G. (1964) 'A comparative study of rotating credit associations', *Journal of the Royal Anthropological Institute*, **94**(2): 201–29.

Ardener, Shirley (1975) 'Sexual insult and female militancy', in Shirley Ardener (ed.) *Perceiving Women*, New York, pp. 29–54.

Armstrong, Alice (1990) *Women and Rape in Zimbabwe*, Maseru, Lesotho.

*Aronson, Lisa (1980) 'Akwete weaving and patronage', *African Arts*, **13**: 62–66.

Aronson, Lisa (1989a) 'Akwete weaving: tradition and change', in *Man Does Not Go Naked: Textilien und Handwerk aus Afrikanischen und Anderen Landern*, Basler Beitrage zur Ethnologie, Volume 30: 35–63.

Aronson, Lisa (1989b) 'To weave or not to weave: apprenticeship rules among the Akwete Igbo of Nigeria and the Baule of the Ivory Coast', in Michael Coy (ed.) *Apprenticeship From Theory to Practice and Back Again*, Albany N.Y.

*Aronson, Lisa (1991) 'African women in the visual arts', *Signs: Journal of Women in Culture and Society*, **16**(3): 550–74.

Association of African Women for Research and Development (1982)

'The experience of the Association of African Women for Research and Development (AAWORD)', *Development Dialogue*, **1**(2): 101–113.

Awe, Bolanle (1975) 'Asude: Yoruba jewelsmiths', *African Arts*, **9:** 60–70.

*Awe, Bolanle (1977) 'The Iyalode in the traditional Yoruba political system', in Alice Schlegel (ed.) *Sexual Stratification: A Cross-Cultural View*, New York, pp. 144–95.

Awe, Bolanle and Mba, Nina (1991) 'Women's Research and Documentation Centre (Nigeria)', *Signs,* **16:** 859–64.

Bâ, Mariama (1981) 'Interview' with Barbara Harrell-Bond, *The African Book Publishing Record*, **6**(3 and 4): 209–14.

Balandier, Georges (1956) *Sociologie des Brazzavilles Noires*, Paris.

Bandler, Jane and Donald Bandler (1977) 'The pottery of Oshafa', *African Arts*, **9:** 26–31.

Barker, Jonathan (1989) *Rural Communities under Stress: Peasant Farmers and the State in Africa*, Cambridge.

Bassett, M. T. and Mhloyi, M. (1991) 'Women and AIDS in Zimbabwe: the making of an epidemic', *International Journal of Health Services*, **21**(1): 143–56.

Batezat, Elinor and Mwala, Margaret (1989) *Women in Zimbabwe*, Harare.

Baumann, Hermann (1928) 'The division of work according to sex in African hoe culture', *Africa*, **I**(3): 289–319.

Bay, Edna G. (1982a) *Women and Work in Africa*, Boulder, Colorado.

Bay, Edna G. (1982b) 'Servitude and worldly succession in the palace of Dahomey', in Claire C. Robertson and Martin A. Klein (eds.) *Women and Slavery in Africa*, Madison, Wisconsin, pp. 340–69.

Beneria, Lourdes (1981) 'Conceptualizing the labor force: the underestimation of women's economic activities', in Nici Nelson (ed.) *African Women in the Development Process*, London, pp. 10–28.

Beneria, Lourdes and Sen, Gita (1981) 'Accumulation, reproduction, and women's role in economic development: Boserup revisited', *Signs,* **7**(2): 279–98.

Berger, Iris (1976) 'Rebels or status seekers? Women as spirit mediums in East Africa', in Nancy Hafkin and Edna Bay (eds) *Women in Africa: Studies in Social and Economic Change,* Stanford, California, pp. 157–82.

Berger, Iris (1986) 'Sources of class consciousness: South African women in recent labor struggles', in Claire Robertson and Iris Berger (eds) *Women and Class in Africa*, New York, pp. 216–36.

*Berger, Iris (1992) *Threads of Solidarity: Women in South African Industry, 1900–1980*, Bloomington, Indiana.

*Berns, Marla (1988) 'Ga'anda scarification: a model for art and identity', in Arnold Rubin (ed.) *Marks of Civilization: Artistic Transformations of the Human Body*, Los Angeles, pp. 57–76.

Berns, Marla and Barbara Rubin Hudson (1986) *The Essential Gourd: Art and History in Northeastern Nigeria*, Los Angeles.

Bernstein, Hilda (1985) *For Their Triumphs and for Their Tears: Women in Apartheid South Africa*, Cambridge, Massachusetts.

Beyala, Calixthe (1988) *Tu t'appelleras Tanga* [Tanga will be your name], Paris.

Bledsoe, Caroline (1980) *Women and Marriage in Kpelle Society*, Stanford, California.

Boddy, Janice (1989) *Wombs and Alien Spirits: Women, Men, and the Zar Cult in Northern Sudan*, Madison, Wisconsin.

Boone, Sylvia (1986) *Radiance from the Waters: Ideals of Feminine Beauty in Mende Art*, New Haven, Connecticut.

*Boserup, Ester (1970) *Woman's Role in Economic Development*, New York.

Boyd, Jean (1986) 'The Fulani women poets', in Madhi Adamu and A. H. M. Kirk-Greene (eds) *Pastoralists of the West African Savanna*, Manchester, pp. 127–42.

Breidenbach, Paul (1979) 'The woman on the beach and the man in the bush: leadership and adepthood in the Twelve Apostle Movement of Ghana', in Bennetta Jules-Rosette (ed.) *The New Religions of Africa*, Norwood, N.J., pp.99–125.

Broadhead, Susan Herlin (1983) 'Slave wives, free sisters: Bakongo women and slavery c. 1700–1850', in Claire C. Robertson and Martin A. Klein (eds) *Women and Slavery in Africa*, Madison, Wisconsin.

Brooks, Charlotte K. (1974) (ed.) *African Rhythms*, New York.

Brooks, George (1976) 'The Signares of Saint-Louis and Gorée: women entrepreneurs in eighteenth-century Senegal', in Nancy Hafkin and Edna Bay (eds) *Women in Africa: Studies in Social and Economic Change*, Stanford, California, pp. 19–44.

Brooks, George (1983) 'A Nhara of the Guinea-Bissau Region: Mae Arelia Correia', in Claire Robertson and Martin Klein (eds) *Women and Slavery in Africa*, Madison, Wisconsin, pp. 295–319.

Brown, Barbara (1980) 'Women, migrant labor, and social change in Botswana', Boston University, *African Studies Center Working Paper No. 41*, Boston, Massachusetts.

Brown, Barbara (1987) 'Facing the black peril: the politics of population control in South Africa', *Journal of African Studies*, **13**(2).

*Brown, Lloyd (1981) *Women Writers in Black Africa*, Westport, Connecticut.

Bryceson, Deborah (1980) 'Proletarianization of Tanzanian women', *Review of African Political Economy*, **17**: 4–17.

Brydon, Lynne (1979) 'Women at work: some changes in family structure at Amedzofe-Avatime, Ghana', *Africa*, **49**: 97–107.

Bugul, Ken [Mariétou M'Baye] (1984) *La Baobab fou*, Dakar, 1984.

*Bujra, Janet (1975) 'Women entrepreneurs of early Nairobi', *Canadian Journal of African Studies*, **9**: 213–34.

Bujra, Janet M. (1977) 'Production, property, prostitution: sexual politics in Atu', *Cahiers d'études africaines*, **65**: 13–39.

Bujra, Janet (1986) 'Urging women to redouble their efforts: class, gender, and capitalist transformation in Africa,' in Claire Robertson and Iris Berger (eds) *Women and Class in Africa*, New York, pp. 117–40.

270

Bunger, Robert L. (1973) *Islamization Among the Upper Pokomo*, Syracuse, N.Y.

Bukh, Jette (1979) *The Village Woman in Ghana*, Uppsala.

Cagatay, Nilufer, Grown, Caren and Santiago, Aida (1986) 'The Nairobi Women's Conference: toward a global feminism?', *Feminist Studies*, **12**: 401–12.

Calame-Griaule, Geneviève (1965) *Ethnologie et Langage: la parole chez les Dogon*, Paris.

Caldwell, J., Quiggin, P. and Caldwell, P. (1989) *Disaster in an Alternative Civilization: The Social Dimensions of AIDS in Sub-Saharan Africa*, Canberra.

Callaghy, Thomas (1990) 'Lost between state and market: the politics of economic adjustment in Ghana, Zambia, and Nigeria', in J. M. Nelson (ed.) *Economic Crisis and Policy Choice*, Princeton, pp. 257–320.

Callaway, Barbara and Schildkrout, Enid (1986) 'Law, education and social change: implications for Hausa Muslim women in Nigeria', in Lynne B. Igletzin and Ruth Ross (eds) *Women in the World 1975–1985: The Women's Decade*, Santa Barbara, California, pp. 181–207.

Callaway, Helen (1987) *Gender, Culture and Empire: European Women in Colonial Nigeria*, Urbana, Illinois.

Carney, Judith A. (1988) 'Struggles over land and crops in an irrigated rice scheme: the Gambia', in Jean Davison (ed.) *Agriculture, Women, and Land*, Boulder, Colorado, pp. 59–78.

Carney, Judith and Watts, Michael (1991) 'Disciplining women? Rice, mechanization, and the evolution of Mandinka gender relations in Senegambia', *Signs*, **16**(4): 651–81.

Carovano, K. (1991) 'More than mothers and whores: redefining the AIDS prevention needs of women', *International Journal of Health Services*, **21**(1): 131–42.

Casely-Hayford, Gladys (1967) 'Freetown', in Donatus Ibe Nwoga (ed.) *West African Verse*, London, p. 6.

Caughman, Susan (1981) 'Women at work in Mali: the case of the Markala cooperative', Boston University, *African Studies Center Working Paper No. 50*, Boston, Massachusetts.

Caughman, Susan and N'diaye Thiam, Mariam (1989) 'The Markala cooperative: a new approach to traditional economic roles', in Ann Leonard (ed.) *SEEDS: Supporting Women's Work in the Third World*, New York, pp. 31–48.

Chanock, Martin (1982) 'Making customary law: men, women and courts in colonial Northern Rhodesia', in Margaret Jean Hay and Marcia Wright (eds) *African Women and the Law: Historical Perspectives*, Boston, pp. 53–68.

Chanock, Martin (1985) *Law, Custom, and Social Order: The Colonial Experience in Malawi and Zambia*, Cambridge.

Chappel, T. J. H. (1977) *Decorated Gourds in North-Eastern Nigeria*, London.

Chazan, Naomi (1989) 'Gender perspectives on African states', in Jane Parpart and Kathleen Staudt (eds) *Women and the State in Africa*, Boulder, Colorado.

Cheater, Angela (1981) 'Women and their participation in commercial agricultural production: the case of medium-scale freehold in Zimbabwe', *Development and Change*, **12:** 349–77.

Cheater, Angela (1984) *Idioms of Accumulation: Rural Development and Class Formation among Freeholders in Zimbabwe*, Gweru, Zimbabwe.

Chinemana, Frances (1988) 'Liberated health in Zimbabwe? The experience of women 1981–1983', in Marcia Wright, Zena Stein and Jean Scandlyn (eds) *Women's Health and Apartheid: The Health of Women and Children and the Future of Progressive Primary Health Care in Southern Africa*, New York.

Chitere, Preston (1988) 'The women's self-help movement in Kenya: a historical perspective, 1940–1980', *Transafrican Journal of History*, **17:** 50–68.

Chona, Mainza (1976) in Law Development Commission, 'Working Paper on the Customary Law of Succession', Lusaka.

Clark, Gracia and Manuh, Takyiwaa (1991) 'Women traders in Ghana and the Structural Adjustment Program', in Christina H. Gladwin, (ed.) *Structural Adjustment and African Women Farmers*, Gainesville, Florida, 217–38.

*Cobham, Rhonda (1985) 'Introduction', in Rhonda Cobham and Chikwenye Okojno Ogunyemi (eds) *Research in African Literatures: Special Issue on Women's Writing*, **19:** 137–42.

*Cock, Jacklyn (1980) *Maids and Madams: A Study in the Politics of Exploitation*, Johannesburg.

*Cole, E. (1967) *House of Bondage*, New York.

Coles, Catherine and Mack, Beverly (1991) 'Women in twentieth-century Hausa society', in Catherine Coles and Beverly Mack (eds) *Hausa Women in the Twentieth Century*, Madison, Wisconsin, pp. 3–26.

Collier, Jane and Rosaldo, Michelle (1981) 'Politics and gender in simple societies', in Sherry Ortner and Harriet Whitehead (eds) *Sexual Meaning*, Cambridge, pp. 275–329.

*Collins, Carol (1977) *This is the Time: Interview with Two Namibian Women*, Chicago.

Cooper, Frederick (1977) *Plantation Slavery on the East Coast of Africa*, New Haven, Connecticut.

Copet-Rougier, Elisabeth (1987) 'Etude de la transformation du marriage chez les Mkako du Cameroun', in David Parkin and David Nyamwaya (eds) *Transformations of African Marriage*, Manchester, pp. 75–93.

Coquery-Vidrovitch, Catherine (1988) *Africa: Endurance and Change South of the Sahara*, Berkeley, California.

*Cordell, Dennis D. and Joel W. Gregory (eds) (1994) *African Population and Capitalism: Historical Perspectives*, Madison, Wisconsin.

Cornia, Giovanni Andrew *et al.* (1987) *Adjustment with a Human Face*, Vol. I, Oxford.

Courtney-Clarke, Margaret (1986) *Ndebele: The Art of an African Tribe*, New York.

Courtney-Clarke, Margaret (1991) *African Canvas: The Art of West African Women*, New York.

Cross-Upcott, A. R. W. (1955) 'Barikiwa Pottery', *Tanganyika Notes and Records*, **40:** 24–29.

Dankelman, Irene and Joan Davidson (1989) *Women and Environment in the Third World: Alliance for the Future*, London.

Darish, Patricia (1989) 'Dressing for the next life: raffia textile production and use among the Kuba of Zaire', in Annette B. Weiner and Jane Schneider (eds) *Cloth and Human Experience*, Washington and London, pp. 117–40.

Davies, Carol Boyce (1986) 'Introduction', in Carol Boyce Davies and Anne Adams Graves (eds) *Ngambika: Studies of Women in African Literature*, Trenton, N.J.

Davies, Miranda (1983) (ed.) *Third World: Second Sex*, London.

Davies, Miranda (1987) (ed.) *Third World: Second Sex, Vol. 2*, London.

*Davison, Jean (ed.) (1988) *Agriculture, Women, and Land: The African Experience*, Boulder, Colorado.

Defense for Children International – USA (1991) *The Effects of Maternal Mortality on Children in Africa: An Exploratory Report on Kenya, Namibia, Tanzania, Zambia, and Zimbabwe*, New York.

DeLancey, Virginia (1977) 'Women at the Cameroon Development Corporation: how their money works', Paper presented at the 1977 African Studies Association Annual Meeting, Houston, Texas.

Denzer, LaRay (1981) 'Constance A. Cummings-John of Sierra Leone: her early political career', *Tarikh*, **25:** 20–32.

de Sousa, Noémia (1984) 'Appeal,' in Gerald Moore and Ulli Beier (eds) *The Penguin Book of Modern African Poetry*, London.

Dey, Jennie (1981) 'Gambian women: unequal partners in rice development projects?' in N. Nelson (1981), pp. 108–22.

Dhlomo, Herbert I. E. (1935) *The Girl Who Killed to Save: Nongqase the Liberator*, Lovedale, South Africa.

Diallo, Nafissatou (1982) *A Dakar Childhood* (trans. Dorothy Blair), London.

Dobert, Margarita (1970) 'Liberation of the women of Guinea', *Africa Report*, **15**(7): 26–8.

Dobie, Elizabeth Ann (1990) 'Interweaving feminist frameworks', *The Journal of Aesthetics and Art Criticism*, **48:** 381–94.

Dolphyne, Florence Abena (1991) *The Emancipation of Women: An African Perspective*, Accra.

Draper, Patricia (1975) '!Kung women: contrasts in sexual egalitarianism in foraging and sedentary contexts', in Rayna Reiter (ed.) *Toward an Anthropology of Women*, New York, pp. 77–109.

Due, Jean M. (1991) 'Policies to overcome the negative effects of structural adjustment programs on African female-headed households', in C. H. Gladwin (ed.) *Structural Adjustment and African Women Farmers*, Gainsville, Florida, pp. 103–127.

Duerden, Dennis and Pieterse, Cosmo (eds) (1974) *African Writers Talking*, London.

Dumor, Ernest (1982) 'Commodity queens and the distributive trade in Ghana: a sociohistorical analysis', *African Urban Studies*, **12:** 27–45.

Dupire, Marguerite (1971) 'The position of women in a pastoral society', in Denise Paulme (ed.) *Women of Tropical Africa*, Berkeley, California, pp. 47–92.

Dwyer, Daisy and Judith Bruce (eds) (1988) *A Home Divided: Women and Income in the Third World*, Stanford, California.

Eades, J. S. (1980) *The Yoruba Today*, Cambridge.

Eames, Elizabeth A. (1988) 'Why the women went to war: women and wealth in Ondo Town, Southwestern Nigeria', in Gracia Clarke (ed.) *Traders Versus the State: Anthropological Approaches to Informal Economies*, Boulder, Colorado, pp. 81–97.

Ebigbola, J. (1985) 'Fertility level and change in South-Western Nigeria in the Decade of Rapid Development, 1971–1981', paper presented at National Conference on Human Behaviour and the Challenge of National Development in Nigeria, Ile-Ife.

Eckholm, Erik and Lester Brown (1977) *Spreading Deserts: The Hand of Man*, Worldwatch Paper 13, Washington, D.C.

*Ekwensi, Cyprian (1961) *Jagua Nana*, New York.

Elabor-Idemudia, Patience (1991) 'The impact of structural adjustment programs on women and their households in Bendel and Ogun States, Nigeria', in Christina H. Gladwin (ed.) *Structural Adjustment and African Women Farmers*, Gainesville, Florida, pp. 128–50.

El Dareer, Asma (1982) *Women, Why Do You Weep? Circumcision and Its Consequences*, London.

Eldredge, Elizabeth, A. (1991) 'Women in production: the economic role of women in nineteenth-century Lesotho', *Signs*, **16**(4): 707–731.

*El Saadawi, Nawal (1980) *The Hidden Face of Eve: Women in the Arab World*, London.

Elswert, Georg (1984) 'Conflicts inside and outside the household: a West African case study', in Jean Smith *et al.* *Households and the World Economy*, Beverly Hills, California, pp. 272–95.

Emecheta, Buchi (1972) *In The Ditch*, London.

Emecheta, Buchi (1975) *Second Class Citizen*, New York.

Emecheta, Buchi (1976) *The Bride Price*, London.

Emecheta, Buchi (1977) *The Slave Girl*, London.

*Emecheta, Buchi (1979) *The Joys of Motherhood*, London.

Emecheta, Buchi (1982a) *Destination Biafra*, London.

Emecheta, Buchi (1982b) *Double Yoke*, New York.

Emecheta, Buchi (1982c) *Naira Power*, London.

Emecheta, Buchi (1989) *The Family*, New York, (1990 edn.).

Enloe, Cynthia (1989) *Bananas, Beaches and Bases: Making Feminist Sense of International Politics*, Berkeley, California.

Etienne, Mona (1979) 'The case for social maternity: adoption of children by urban Baule women', *Dialectical Anthropology*, **4:** 237–43.

*Etienne, Mona (1980) 'Women and men, cloth and colonization: the transformation of production–distribution relations among the Baule (Ivory Coast)', in Mona Etienne and Eleanor Leacock (eds) *Women and Colonization*, New York, pp. 214–238.

Etienne, Mona (1986) 'Contradictions, constraints and choice: widow remarriage among the Baule of Ivory Coast', in Betty Potash (ed.) *Widows in African Societies*, Stanford, California, pp. 241–83.

Evans-Pritchard, E. E. (1965) *The Position of Women in Primitive Societies and Other Essays in Social Anthropology*, London.

Fall, Amina Sow (1981) *The Beggar's Strike, or The Dregs of Society* (trans. Dorothy S. Blair), London.

Fapohunda, Eleanor R. (1988) 'The nonpooling household: a challenge to theory', in Daisy Dwyer and Judith Bruce (eds) *A Home Divided*, Stanford, California, pp. 143–55.

Farah, Nurrudin (1970) *From a Crooked Rib*, London.

Farah, Nurrudin (1981) 'A view of home from the outside', *Africa*, (Dec. 1981), cited in J. I. Okonkwo, 'Nurrudin Farah and the changing roles of women', *World Literature Today: A Literary Quarterly of the University of Oklahoma*, **58:** 215–21.

Farooq, G. and Adeokun, L. (1976) 'Impact of rural family planning program in Ishan, Nigeria (1964–72)', *Studies in Family Planning*, **7**(6): 158–69.

Fatou, Sow (1989) 'Senegal: the Decade and its consequences', *Issue: A Journal of Opinion*, Summer, **17**(2): 32–36.

Feldman, Rayah (1983) 'Women's groups and women's subordination: an analysis of policies towards rural women in Kenya', *Review of African Political Economy*, 67–85.

Fikry, Mona and Ward, Mark (1992) *Economic Integration of Women in the Development Process of Burundi*, USAID, Washington, D.C.

Finnegan, Ruth (1970) *Oral Literature in Africa*, Oxford.

Fisher, Allan G. and Fisher, Humphrey J. (1971) *Slavery and Muslim Society in Africa*, New York.

Food and Agriculture Organization (FAO) (1979) 'Women in food production, food handling, and nutrition with special emphasis on Africa', A Report of the Protein Advisory Group of the United Nations, Rome.

Fortmann, Louise (1982) 'Women's work in a communal setting: the Tanzania policy of Ujamaa', in E. G. Bay (ed.) *Women and Work in Africa*, Boulder, pp. 191–206.

Frank, Katherine (1982) 'The death of the slave girl: African womanhood in the novels of Buchi Emecheta', *World Literature Written in English*, **21:** 476–97.

Franke, Richard W. and Barbara H. Chasin (1981) *Seeds of Famine: Ecological Destruction and the Development Dilemma in the West Africa Sahel*, Montclair, N.J.

Fraser, Arvonne (1987) *UN Decade for Women*, Boulder, Colorado.

Freeman, Donald B. (1991) *A City of Farmers: Informal Urban Agriculture in the Open Spaces of Nairobi, Kenya*, Montreal.

Fugard, Athol (1969) *Boesman and Lena*, Cape Town.

Gaitskell, Deborah (1983) 'Housewives, maids or mothers: some contradictions of domesticity for Christian women in Johannesburg, 1903–1939', *Journal of African History*, **57:** 234–58.

Geertz, Clifford (1966) 'The rotating credit association: a "middle rung" in development', in I. M. Wallerstein (ed.), *Social Change: The Colonial Situation*, New York, pp. 420–46.

*Geiger, Susan (1987) 'Women in nationalist struggle: TANU activists in Dar es Salaam', *International Journal of African Historical Studies*, **20**(1): 1–26.

Geisler, Gisela (1987) 'Sisters under the skin: women and the women's league in Zambia', *Journal of Modern African Studies*, **25**(1): 43–66.

Gessain, Monique (1963) 'Coniagui women', in Denise Paulme (ed.) *Women of Tropical Africa*, Berkeley, California, pp. 17–47.

Gill, Margot (1981) 'The potter's mark: contemporary and archaeological pottery of the Kenyan Southeastern Highlands', M.A. thesis, Boston University.

*Gladwin, Christina H. (ed.) (1991) *Structural Adjustment and African Women Farmers*, Gainesville, Florida.

*Glaze, Anita (1975) 'Women power and art in a Senufo village', *African Arts*, **3**: 25–29; 65–68.

*Glaze, Anita (1981) *Art and Death in a Senufo Village*, Bloomington, Indiana.

Goheen, Miriam (1988) 'Land and the household economy: women farmers of the grassfields today', in Jean Davison (ed.) *Agriculture, Women, and Land: The African Experience*, Boulder, Colorado.

Goody, Esther (1982) *Parenthood and Social Reproduction: Fosterage and Occupational Roles in West Africa*, Cambridge.

Goody, Jack and Buckley, Joan (1973) 'Inheritance and women's labor in Africa', *Africa*, **43**(2): 108–21.

*Gordimer, Nadine (1987) *A Sport of Nature*, New York.

Griaule, Marcel (1938) *Jeux Dogons* (Dogon Games), Paris.

Grier, Beverly (1992) 'Pawns, porters, and petty traders: women in the transition to cash crop agriculture in colonial Ghana', *Signs*, **17**(2): 304–328.

Guyer, Jane I. (1978) 'The food economy and French colonial rule in central Cameroon', *Journal of African History*, **29**(4): 577–97.

*Guyer, Jane I. (1981) 'Household and community in African studies', *African Studies Review*, **24**: 87–137.

Guyer, Jane (1984) *Family and Farm in Southern Cameroon*, Boston.

Guyer, Jane (1986) 'Beti widow inheritance and marriage law: a social history', in Betty Potash (ed.) *Widows in African Societies*, Stanford, California, pp. 193–220.

Guyer, Jane I. (ed.) (1987) *Feeding African Cities: Studies in Regional Social History*, Bloomington, Indiana.

Guyer, Jane I., with Olukemi Idowu (1991) 'Women's agricultural work in a multimodal rural economy: Ibarapa District, Oyo State, Nigeria', in Christina H. Gladwin (ed.) *Structural Adjustment and African Women Farmers*, Gainesville, Florida, pp. 257–80.

Guyer, Jane I. and Peters, Pauline (eds) (1984) *Conceptualizing the Household: Issues of Theory, Method and Application*, Charlottesville, Virginia.

*Hackett, Rosalind I. J. (1993) 'Women in African religions', in Arvind Sharma (ed.) *Religion and Women*, Albany, NY, pp. 61–92.

Hackett, Rosalind I. J. (1995) 'Women and new religious movements in Africa', in U. King (ed.) *Gender and Religion*, Oxford.

Hackett, Rosalind I. J. (forthcoming) 'Women church founders', in V. Y. Mudimbe (ed.) *African Religions and Philosophy*, New York.

*Hafkin, Nancy and Bay, Edna (eds) (1976) *Women in Africa: Studies in Social and Economic Change*, Stanford, California.

Hale, Sondra (1992) 'The rise of Islam and women of the National Islamic Front in Sudan', *Review of African Political Economy*, **54:** 27–41.

Hammerslough, Charles R. (1991) 'Women's groups and contraceptive use in rural Kenya', paper prepared for IUSSP Seminar on 'The Course of Fertility Transition in Sub-Saharan Africa', Harare, Zimbabwe, 19–22 November.

Hanger, Jane and Moris, Jon (1973) 'Women and the household economy', in Robert Chambers and Jon Moris (eds) *Mwea: An Irrigated Rice Settlement in Kenya*, Munich, 209–44.

Hansen, Karen Transberg (1989) 'The black market and women traders in Lusaka, Zambia', in Jane L. Parpart and Kathleen A. Staudt (eds) *Women and the State in Africa*, Boulder, Colorado, pp. 143–60.

Hansen, Karen Tranberg (1989) *Distant Companions: Servants and employers in Zambia, 1900–1985*, Ithaca, NY.

Hansen, Karen Tranberg (1992) *African Encounters with Domesticity*, New Brunswick, N.J.

Harms, Robert (1983) 'Sustaining the system: trading towns along the middle Zaire', in Claire C. Robertson and Martin A. Klein (eds) *Women and Slavery in Africa*, Madison, Wisconsin, pp. 95–111.

Haswell, Margaret (1975) *The Nature of Poverty*, London.

Hay, Margaret Jean (1976) 'Luo women and economic change during the colonial period', in Nancy Hafkin and Edna Bay (eds) *Women in Africa: Studies in Social and Economic Change*, Stanford, California, pp. 87–111.

Hay, Margaret Jean (1982) 'Women as owners, occupants, and managers of property in colonial Kenya', in Margaret J. Hay and Marcia Wright (eds) *African Women and the Law*, Boston.

Hay, Margaret Jean (1988) 'Queens, prostitutes and peasants: historical perspectives on African women', *Canadian Journal of African Studies*, **22**(3): 431–447.

*Hay, Margaret Jean and Wright, Marcia (1982) (eds) *African Women and the Law: Historical Perspectives*, Boston.

Head, Bessie (1974) *A Question of Power*, London.

Head, Bessie (1977) 'Snapshots of a wedding', in Charlotte Bruner (ed.) *Unwinding Threads: Writing by Women in Africa*, London, 1983, pp. 157–61.

Hedlund, Hans (1979) 'Contradictions in the peripheralization of a pastoral society: The Maasai', *Review of African Political Economy*, **15/16:** 15–34.

Hein, Hilde (1990) 'The role of feminist aesthetics in feminist theory', *The Journal of Aesthetics and Art Criticism*, **48:** 281–92.

Hemmings-Gapihan, Grace (1982) 'International development and the evolution of women's economic roles: a case study from northern Gulma, Upper Volta', in Edna G. Bay (ed.) *Women and Work in Africa*, Boulder, Colorado.

Herskovits, Melville J. (1938) *Dahomey: An Ancient West African Kingdom*, New York.

Herz, B. and Measham, A. R. (1987) *The Safe Motherhood Initiative: Proposals for Action*, Washington, D.C.

Hill, Polly (1969) 'Hidden trade in Hausaland', *Man*, **4**(3): 392–409.

Himonga, C. B. (1989) 'The law of succession and inheritance in Zambia and the proposed reform', *International Journal of Law and the Family*, **3:** 160–76.

Hirschmann, David (1990) 'The Malawi case: enclave politics, core resistance, and "Nkhoswe No. 1"' in K. Staudt (ed.) *Women, International Development and Politics: The Bureaucratic Mire*, Philadelphia, pp. 163–89.

Hoch-Smith, Judith (1978) 'Radical Yoruba female sexuality: the witch and the prostitute', in Judith Hoch-Smith and Anita Spring (eds) *Women in Ritual and Symbolic Roles*, New York, pp. 245–67.

Hoch-Smith, Judith and Anita Spring (eds) (1978) *Women in Ritual and Symbolic Roles*, New York.

Hoffer, Carol (1972) 'Mende and Sherbro women in high offices', *Canadian Journal of African Studies*, **6**(2): 151–64.

House-Midamba, Bessie (1990) 'The United Nations Decade: political empowerment or increased marginalization?', *Africa Today*, **37**(1): 37–48.

Hunt, C. W. (1988) 'Africa and AIDS: dependent development, sexism and racism', *Monthly Review*, **39**(9): 10–22.

*Hunt, Nancy Rose (1989) 'Placing African women's history and locating gender', *Social History*, **14:** 359–79.

Hunt, Nancy Rose (1990) 'Domesticity and colonialism in Belgian Africa: Usumbura's *Foyer Social*, 1946–1960', *Signs: Journal of Women in Culture and Society*, **15**(3): 447–474.

Huntington, Suellen (1975) 'Issues in woman's role in economic development: critique and alternatives', *Journal of Marriage and the Family*, **37:** 1001–12.

Idowu, Olukemi and Jane I. Guyer (1993) 'Commercialization and the harvest work of women, Ibarapa, Oyo State, Nigeria', *Boston University African Studies Center Working Paper*, No. 172.

International Labour Organization (ILO) (various years) *Yearbook of Labour Statistics*, 1945–89, 1975, 1989–90, 1991, 1992. Geneva.

International Labor Organization (ILO) (1978) 'Women, technology, and the development process', mimeo paper prepared for the African Regional Meeting of UNCSTD, Cairo, 24–29 July 1978.

*Isaacman, Barbara and Stephen, June (1980) *Mozambique: Women, the Law, and Agrarian Reform*, Addis Ababa.

Jacobs, Susie (1984) 'Women and land resettlement in Zimbabwe', *Review of African Political Economy*, **27/28**: 33–42.

Jacobs, Susan (1989) 'Zimbabwe: state, class, and gendered models of land resettlement', in J. L. Parpart and K. A. Staudt (eds) *Women and the State in Africa*, Boulder, pp. 161–84.

Jameson, Fredric (1986) 'Third world literature in the era of multinational capitalism', *Social Text*, **15**: 65–88.

Jochelson, K., Mothibeli, K. and Leger, J.-P. (1991) 'Human immuno-deficiency virus and migrant labor in South Africa', *International Journal of Health Services*, **21**(1): 157–73.

Johnson, Cheryl (1981) 'Madam Alimotu Pelewura and the Lagos market women', *Tarikh*, **25**: 1–10.

Johnson-Odim, Cheryl (1991) 'Common themes, different contexts: third world women and feminism', in Chandra Talpade Mohanty *et al.* (eds) *Third World Women and the Politics of Feminism*, Bloomington, Indiana, pp. 314–27.

Jones, Christine (1983) 'The mobilization of women's labor for cash crop production: a game theoretic approach', *American Journal of Agricultural Economics*, **65**(5): 1049–54.

*Jones, Eldred Durosimi (ed.) (1987) *Women in African Literature Today: A Review*, London.

Joseph, Rosemary M. F. (1987) 'Zulu women's bow songs: ruminations on love', *Bulletin of the School of Oriental and African Studies*, **50**: 90–119.

*Jules-Rosette, Bennetta (1979) 'Symbols of power and change: an introduction to new perspectives on contemporary and African religion', in Bennetta Jules-Rosette (ed.), *The New Religions of Africa*, Norwood, N.J., pp. 1–21.

Jules-Rosette, Bennetta (1984) *The Messages of Tourist Art: An African Semiotic System in Comparative Perspective*, New York.

Juma, Calestous and Richard Ford (1992) 'Facing Africa's ecological crisis', in Ann Seidman and Frederick Anang (eds) *Twenty-first Century Africa: Towards a New Vision of Self-sustainable Development*, Trenton, N.J., pp. 183–201.

Kaberry, Phyllis (1952) *Women of the Grassfields: A Study in the Economic Position of Women in Bamenda*, London.

Kapteijns, Lidwien (1991) 'Women and the Somali pastoral tradition', *Boston University, African Studies Center Working Paper*, No. 153.

Karanja, Wambui, Wa (1987) '"Outside wives" and "Inside wives" in Nigeria: A Study of Changing Perceptions in Marriage', in David Parkin and David Nyamwaya (eds) *Transformations of African Marriage*, Manchester, pp. 247–63.

Keim, Curtis A. (1983) 'Women in slavery among the Mangbetu c. 1800–1910', in Claire C. Robertson and Martin A. Klein (eds) *Women and Slavery in Africa*, Madison, Wisconsin.

Kéita, Aoua (1975) *Femme d'Afrique: La Vie d'Aoua Kéita racontée par elle-même* (African Woman: The Life of Aoua Keita as told by Herself), Paris.

Keller, Bonnie (1984) *The Integration of Zambian Women in Development*, Lusaka, Zambia.

Keller, Bonnie (1989) 'Struggling in hard times: the Zambian workers movement', *Issue: A Journal of Opinion*, Summer, **17**(2): 18–25.

Kenyatta, Jomo (1938) *Facing Mount Kenya: The Tribal Life of the Gikuyu*, London.

Kettel, Bonnie (1986) 'The commoditization of women in Tugen (Kenya) social organization', in Claire Robertson and Iris Berger (eds) *Women and Class in Africa*, New York, pp. 47–62.

Kneerim, Jill (1989) 'Village women organize: the Mraru, Kenya bus service', in Ann Leonard (ed.) *SEEDS: Supporting Women's Work in the Third World*, New York, pp. 15–30.

Koenig, Dolores B. (1977) 'Sex, work, and social class in Cameroon', Ph.D. thesis, Northwestern University.

Konde, Emmanuel (1992) 'Reconstructing the political roles of African women: a post-revisionist paradigm', Boston University African Studies Center Working Paper No. 161.

Koopman Henn, Jeanne (1978) 'Peasants, workers, and capital: the political economy of labor and incomes in Cameroon', Ph.D. thesis, Harvard University.

Koso-Thomas, Olayinka (1987) *The Circumcision of Women: A Strategy for Education*, London.

Kraus, Jon (1991) 'The struggle over structural adjustment in Ghana', *Africa Today*, **38**(4): 19–39.

Krige, Eileen Jensen (1974) 'Woman-marriage, with special reference to the Lovedu: its significance for the definition of marriage', *Africa*, **44**: 11–37.

Kriger, Norma J. (1992) *Zimbabwe's Guerrilla War: Peasant Voices*, Cambridge.

Kujore, O. and Pearce, T. (1988–91) 'The health care of families: the approach of market women in Ile-Ife', Ford Foundation sponsored study in Ile-Ife, Nigeria.

Kuria, Gibson Kamau (1987) 'The African or customary marriage in Kenyan law today', in David Parkin and David Nyamwaya (eds) *Transformations of African Marriage*, Manchester, pp. 283–307.

Ladjali, Malika (1991) 'Conception, contraception: do Algerian women really have a choice?' in Meredith Turshen (ed.) *Women and Health in Africa*, Trenton, N.J., pp. 125–41.

Lancet (1990) 'Structural adjustment and health in Africa', 35: p. 885.

Landberg, Pamela (1986) 'Widows and divorced women in Swahili society', in Betty Potash (ed.) *Widows in African Societies*, Stanford, California, pp. 107–31.

Lambert, H. E. (1956) *Kikuyu Social and Political Institutions*, London.

*Lapchick, Richard and Urdang, Stephanie (1982) *Oppression and Resistance: The Struggle of Women in Southern Africa*, Westport, Connecticut.

La Pin, Deirdre (1977) 'Story, medium and masque: the idea and art of Yoruba story-telling', Ph.D. thesis, University of Wisconsin.

Laye, Camara (1959) *The African Child*, Glasgow (first published as *L'Enfant Noir*, Paris, 1953).

Lebeuf, Annie M. D. (1971) 'The role of women in the political organization of African societies', in Denise Paulme (ed.) *Women of Tropical Africa*, Berkeley, California, pp. 93–120.

Leeuwenberg, Jef (1977) *Transkei: A Study in Economic Regression*, London.

Leith-Ross, Sylvia (1965) *African Women: A Study of the Ibo of Nigeria*, London.

Lele, Uma (1991) 'Women, structural adjustment, and transformation: some lessons and questions from the African experience', in C. H. Gladwin (ed.) *Structural Adjustment and African Women Farmers*, Gainesville, Florida, pp. 46–80.

Lewis, Barbara (1976) 'The limitations of group action among entrepreneurs: the market women of Abidjan, Ivory Coast', in Nancy Hafkin and Edna Bay (eds) *Women in Africa: Studies in Social and Economic Change*, Stanford, California, pp. 135–56.

*Lewis, Barbara (1977) 'Economic activities and marriage among Ivoirian urban women', in Alice Schlegel (ed.) *Sexual Stratification*, New York, pp. 161–92.

Lewis, Barbara (1984) 'The impact of development policies on women', in Margaret Jean Hay and Sharon Stichter (eds) *African Women South of the Sahara*, 1st edn., Longman, Harlow, Essex, pp. 170–97.

Lewis, Barbara (1990) 'Farming women, public policy, and the women's ministry: a case study from Cameroon', in K. Staudt (ed.) *Women, International Development and Politics: The Bureaucratic Mire*, Philadelphia, pp. 180–200.

Lewis, I. M. (1971) *Ecstatic Religion: An Anthropological Study of Spirit Possession and Shamanism*, Harmondsworth.

Lewis, I. M. (1986) *Religion in Context: Cults and Charisma*, Cambridge.

Liberation Support Movement (n.d.) *The Mozambican Woman in Revolution*, Richmond, B.C.

Liedholm, C. and Chuta, E. (1976) 'The economics of rural and urban small-scale industries in Sierra Leone', *African Rural Economy Paper No. 14*, Michigan State University.

Lindsay, Jenny (1991) 'The politics of population control in Namibia', in Meredeth Turshen (ed.) *Women and Health in Africa*, Trenton, N.J., pp. 143–67.

Linton, Ralph (1936) *The Study of Man*, New York.

Lipman, Beata (1980) *We Make Freedom: Women in South Africa*, London.

Little, Kenneth (1949) 'The role of the secret society in cultural specialization', *American Anthropologist*, **51**: 199–212.

Little, Kenneth (1966) *West African Urbanization: A Study of Voluntary Associations in Social Change*, Cambridge.

Little, Kenneth (1972) 'Voluntary Associations and Social Mobility Among West African Women', *Canadian Journal of African Studies*, **6**(2): 275–88.

*Little, Kenneth (1973) *African Women in Towns*, London.

Little, Kenneth (1980) *The Sociology of Urban Women's Image in African Literature*, Totowa, N.J.

Longwe, Sarah and Roy Clarke (1990) 'Perspectives on research methodology', *Women and Law in Southern Africa Research Project Working Paper* No. 2, Harare, pp. 183–204.

Lovett, Margot (1989) 'Gender relations, class formation, and the colonial state in Africa', in Jane L. Parpart and Kathleen A. Staudt (eds) *Women and the State in Africa*, Boulder, Colorado.

Loxley, John (1990) 'Structural adjustment in Africa: Ghana and Zambia', *Review of African Political Economy*, **47:** 8–27.

Lucas, Robert (1979) 'The distribution and efficiency of crop production in tribal areas of Botswana', *African Studies Center Working Paper* No. 20, Boston, Massachusetts.

Maas, Maria (1991) *Women's Social and Economic Projects*, Report No. 37, African Studies Centre, Leiden, Netherlands.

Maathai, Wangari (1985) 'Kenya: the Green Belt Movement', *IFDA Dossier*, September–October, **49:** 4–12.

McClain, W. T. (1970) 'The rights of widows under customary law', in *Women's Rights in Zambia*, Report of a consultation, Mindolo Ecumenical Foundation.

MacCormack, Carol P. (1982) 'Control of land, labor and capital in rural southern Sierra Leone', in Edna G. Bay (ed.) *Women and Work in Africa*, Boulder, Colorado, pp. 35–55.

McFadden, Patricia (1982) 'Women in wage-labour in Swaziland: a focus on agriculture', *South African Labour Bulletin*, **7**(6 and 7): 140–66.

MacGaffey, Janet (1988) 'Evading male control: women in the second economy in Zaire', in Sharon Stichter and Jane Parpart (eds) *Patriarchy and Class: African Women in the Home and the Workforce*, Boulder, Colorado, pp. 161–76.

MacGaffey, Janet (1986) 'Women and class formation in a dependent economy,' in Claire Robertson and Iris Berger (eds) *Women and Class in Africa*, New York, pp. 161–177.

Machel, Josina (n.d.) 'The role of women in the struggle', in Liberation Support Movement, *The Mozambican Women in Revolution*, Richmond, B.C.

Made, Patricia and Whande, Nyorovai (1989) 'Women in southern Africa: a note on the Zimbabwean success story', *Issue: A Journal of Opinion*, Summer, **17**(2): 26–28.

Magaia, Lina (1988) *Dumba Nengue: Run For Your Life: Peasant Tales of Tragedy in Mozambique*, Trenton, New Jersey.

Makinwa-Adebusoye, P. K. (1991) 'Contraception among urban youth in Nigeria', Paper presented at the DHS Conference, Washington, D.C.

Mann, Kristin (1982) 'Women's rights in law and practice: marriage and dispute settlement in colonial Lagos', in Margaret Jean Hay and Marcia Wright (eds) *African Women and the Law: Historical Perspectives*, Boston, pp. 151–71.

*Mann, Kristin (1985) *Marrying Well: Marriage, Status, and Social Change among the Educated Elite in Colonial Lagos*, Cambridge.

Manning, Patrick (1981) 'The enslavement of Africans: a demographic model', *Canadian Journal of African Studies*, **15**(3): 499–526.

Mashinini, Emma (1991) *Strikes Have Followed Me All my Life*, London.

Matthews, Thomas (1977) 'Mural printing in South Africa', *African Arts*, **10**: 28–33.

May, Joan (1982) *Zimbabwean Women in Colonial and Customary Law*, Gweru, Zimbabwe.

Mba, Nina (1982) *Nigerian Women Mobilized: Women's Political Activity in Southern Nigeria, 1900–1965*, Berkeley, California.

Mba, Nina (1989) 'Kaba and Khaki: women and the militarized state in Nigeria', in Jane L. Parpart and Kathleen A. Staudt (eds) *Women and the State in Africa*, Boulder, Colorado, pp. 69–90.

Mbilinyi, Marjorie (1986) 'Agribusiness and casual labor in Tanzania', *African Economic History*, **15**: 107–41.

Mbilinyi, Marjorie (1988) 'Agribusiness and women peasants in Tanzania', *Development and Change*, **19**: 549–83.

Mbilinyi, Marjorie (1990) '"This is an Unforgettable Business": Colonial State Intervention in Urban Tanzania', in Jane Parpart and Kathleen Staudt (eds) *Women and the State in Africa*, Boulder, Colorado, pp. 111–29.

Mebrahtu, Saba (1991) 'Women, work and nutrition in Nigeria', in Meredith Turshen (ed.) *Women and Health in Africa*, Trenton, N.J., pp. 89–105.

Meena, Ruth (1989) 'Crisis and structural adjustment: Tanzanian women's politics', *Issue: A Journal of Opinion*, **17**(2): 29–30.

Meena, Ruth and Mbilinyi, Marjorie (1991) 'Women's research and documentation project (Tanzania)', *Signs*, **16**: 852–59.

*Mernissi, Fatima (1975) *Beyond the Veil: Male-Female Dynamics in a Modern Muslim Society*, New York.

Michelmann, Cherry (1975) *The Black Sash of South Africa: A Case Study in Liberalism*, London.

Middleton, John (1981) 'Christianity', 'Islam', and 'Traditional Religion', in Roland Oliver and Michael Crowder (eds) *Cambridge Encyclopedia of Africa*, Cambridge, pp. 406–12.

Middleton-Keirn, Susan (1978) 'Convivial sisterhood: spirit mediumship and client-core networks among black South African women', in Judith Hoch-Smith and Anita Spring (eds) *Women in Ritual and Symbolic Roles*, New York, pp. 191–205.

Miers, Suzanne and Kopytoff, Igor (eds) (1977) *Slavery in Africa: Historical and Anthropological Perspectives*, Madison, Wisconsin.

Mikell, Gwendolyn (1989) *Cocoa and Chaos in Ghana*, New York.

Mikell, Gwendolyn (1991) 'Equity issues in Ghana's rural development', in Donald Rothchild (ed.) *Ghana: the Political Economy of Recovery*, Boulder, Colorado, pp. 85–100.

Miller, Christopher L. (1986) 'Theories of Africans: the question of literary anthropology', in Henry Louis Gates, Jr. (ed.) *Race, Writing, and Difference*, Chicago, pp. 281–300.

Minority Rights Group Report No. 77 (1988) 'Women in sub-Saharan Africa', London.

Mirza, Sarah and Strobel, Margaret (eds) (1989) *Three Swahili Women: Life Histories from Mombasa, Kenya*, Bloomington, Indiana.

Mitchell, J. Clyde (1956) *The Yao Village*, Manchester.

Molokomme, Athaliah (1991) 'Emang Basadi (Botswana)', *Signs*, **16:** 848–51.

Monsted, Mette (1978) *Women's Groups in Rural Kenya and Their Role in Development*, Copenhagen.

Morrow, Sean (1986) '"No girl leaves the school unmarried": Mabel Shaw and the education of girls at Mbereshi, Northern Rhodesia, 1915–1940', *International Journal of African Historical Studies*, **19:** 601–35.

Mortimer, Mildred (1990) *Journeys Through the French African Novel*, Portsmouth, N.H.

*Mudimbe, V. S. (1976, trans. 1989) *Before the Birth of the Moon* (translated Marjolijen de Jagar), New York.

Mudimbe, V. S. (1985) 'African literature: myth or reality?' in Stephen Arnold (ed.) *African Literature Studies: The Present State*, Washington, D.C.

Mueller, Martha (1977) 'Women and men, power and powerlessness in Lesotho', in Wellesley Editorial Committee (ed.) *Women and National Development*, Chicago, pp. 154–66.

Mugabe, Robert (1979) 'Opening speech to the first Zimbabwe women's seminar, May 1979', Zimbabwe News, Maputo.

Muller, Jean-Claude (1986) 'Where to live? Widows' choices among the Rukuba', in Betty Potash (ed.) *Widows in African Societies*, Stanford, California, pp. 175–93.

Mullings, Leith (1976) 'Women and economic change in Africa', in Nancy Hafkin and Edna Bay (eds) *Women in Africa: Studies in Social and Economic Change*, Stanford, California, pp. 239–64.

Munachonga, Monica (1988) 'Income allocation and marriage options in urban Zambia', in Daisy Dwyer and Judith Bruce (eds) *A Home Divided*, Stanford, California, pp. 173–95.

Muntemba, Maud Shimwaayi (1982) 'Women and agricultural change in the railway region of Zambia: dispossession and counter-strategies, 1930–1970', in Edna G. Bay (ed.) *Women and Work in Africa*, Boulder, Colorado, pp. 83–104.

Murray, Jocelyn (1974) 'The Kikuyu female circumcision controversy, with special reference to the Church Missionary Society's sphere of influence', Ph.D. thesis, University of California at Los Angeles.

Murray, Jocelyn (1976) 'The Church Missionary Society and the "female circumcision" issue in Kenya', *Journal of Religion in Africa*, **8:** 92–104.

Musisi, Nakanyike B. (1991) 'Women, "elite polygyny," and Buganda state formation', *Signs*, **16**(4): 757–786.

Musisi, Nakanyike B. (1992) 'Colonial and missionary education: women and domesticity in Uganda, 1900–1945', in Karen Tranberg

Hansen (ed.) *African Encounters with Domesticity*, New Brunswick, N.J., pp. 172–94.

Mutiso, Gideon (n.d.) 'Mbai sya Eitu: a low status group in centre-periphery relations', unpublished paper, University of Nairobi.

Mvunga, M. P. (1979) 'Law and social change: a case study in the customary law of inheritance in Zambia', *African Social Research*, University of Zambia, Institute for African Studies, No. 28.

Mwaniki, Nyaga (1986) 'Against many odds: the dilemmas of women's self-help groups in Mbeere, Kenya', *Africa*, 56(2): 210–27.

Ndulo, M. (1985) 'Widows under Zambian customary law and the response of the courts', *Comparative and International Law Journal of Southern Africa*, 18: 1.

Nelson, Joan M. (ed.) (1990) *Economic Crisis and Policy Choice: The Politics of Adjustment in the Third World*, Princeton, N.J.

Nelson, Nici (1979) 'Women must help each other: the operation of personal networks among Buzaa beer brewers in Mathare Valley, Kenya', in Patricia Caplan and Janet Bujra (eds) *Women United, Women Divided*, Bloomington, Indiana, pp. 77–98.

*Nelson, Nici (ed.) (1981) *African Women in the Development Process*, London.

Netting, Robert MaCormack (1969) 'Women's weapons: the politics of domesticity among the Kofyar', *American Anthropologist*, 71: 1037–46.

Ngugi wa Thiong'o (1977) *Petals of Blood*, London.

Ngugi wa Thiong'o and Ngugi wa Mirii (1982) *I Will Marry When I Want*, London.

Nketia, J. H. Kwabena (1969) *Funeral Dirges of the Akan People*, New York.

Ntarangwi, Mwenda Gideon (1993) '*Tarab* music and women's resistance among the Swahili of Mombasa, Kenya', unpublished paper.

Nwapa, Flora (1966) *Efuru*, London.

Nwapa, Flora (1970) *Idu*, London.

Nzomo, Maria (1989) 'The impact of the Women's Decade on policies, programs and empowerment of women in Kenya', *Issue: A Journal of Opinion*, 17(2): 9–17.

Nzomo, Maria and Staudt, Kathleen (1994) 'Man-made political machinery in Kenya: political space for women?' in Najma Chowdhury and Barbara Nelson (eds) *Women and Politics Worldwide*, New Haven, Connecticut.

O'Barr, Jean (1976) 'Pare women: a case of political involvement', *Rural Africana*, 29: 121–34.

Obbo, Christine (1976) 'Dominant male ideology and female options: three East African case studies', *Africa*, 46(4): 371–89.

*Obbo, Christine (1980) *African Women: Their Struggle for Economic Independence*, London: Zed Press.

Obbo, Christine (1987) 'The old and the new in East African elite marriages', in David Parkin and David Nyamwaya (eds) *Transformations of African Marriage*, Manchester, pp. 263–83.

285

*Oboler, Regina Smith (1985) *Women, Power and Economic Change: The Nandi of Kenya*, Stanford, California.

Oboler, Regina Smith (1986) 'Nandi widows', in Betty Potash (ed.) *Widows in African Societies*, Stanford, California, pp. 66–84.

Ochieng', William R. (1975) 'Editorial', *Kenya Historical Review*, 3(2): i–iv.

Ogbuagu, S. (1985) 'Women and Depo-Provera usage in Nigeria: chosen or imposed forms of birth control?', *Rural Africana*, **21**: 81–90.

Ogot, Grace (1964) 'The rain came', in Ellis Ajitey and Ezekiel Mphahlele (eds) *Modern African Stories*, London, pp. 180–9.

O'Keefe, Phil, Ken Westgate and Ben Wisner (1976) 'Taking the naturalness out of natural disasters', *Nature*, **260**: 565–66.

O'Kelly, Elizabeth (1973) *Aid and Self-Help*, London.

Okeyo, Achola Pala (1979) 'Women in the household economy: managing multiple roles', *Studies in Family Planning*, **10**: 337–43.

Okonjo, Kamene (1976) 'The dual-sex political system in operation: Igbo women and community politics in midwestern Nigeria', in Nancy Hafkin and Edna Bay (eds) *Women in Africa: Studies in Social and Economic Change*, Stanford, California, pp. 45–58.

Okpewho, Isidore (1985) *The Heritage of African Poetry: An Anthropology of Oral and Written Poetry*, London.

O'Laughlin, Bridget (1974) 'Mediation of contradiction: why Mbum women do not eat chicken', in Michelle Rosaldo and Louise Lamphere (eds) *Women, Culture, and Society*, Stanford, California, pp. 301–18.

Olukoya, A. (1986) 'Traditional child spacing practices of women: experiences from a primary care project in Lagos, Nigeria', *Social Science and Medicine*, **23**(3): 333–36.

Olusanya, P. (1969) 'Nigeria: cultural barriers to family planning among the Yorubas', *Studies in Family Planning*, **37**: 13–16.

Ooko-Ombaka, Ooki (1980) 'An assessment of national machinery for women', *Assignment Children*, **49/50**: 45–61.

Oppong, Christine (1974) *Marriage Among a Matrilineal Elite*, Cambridge.

Organization of African Unity (1981) *Lagos Plan of Action for the Economic Development of Africa*, Geneva.

Oronsaye, A. and Odiase, G. (1983) 'Attitudes towards abortion and contraception among Nigerian secondary school girls', *International Journal of Gynaecology and Obstetrics*, **21**(5): 423–26.

Owuor, Henry (1967) 'Luo songs', in Ulli Beier (ed.) *Introduction to African Literature*, London, pp. 50–56.

Palmer, Ingrid (1991) *Gender and Population in the Adjustment of African Economies: Planning for Change*, Geneva.

Paquot, E. (1983) 'Excision et infibulation, pourquoi mutiler le sexe des petites filles?' in Elisabeth Paquot (ed.) *Terre des Femmes*, Paris, pp. 338–40.

Parpart, Jane (1986) 'Women's rights and the Lagos Plan of Action', *Human Rights Quarterly*, **8**: 180–96.

Parpart, Jane (1988a) 'Women and the state in Africa' in Naomi Chazan and Donald Rothchild (eds) *The Precarious Balance*, Boulder, Colorado, pp. 208–230.

Parpart, Jane L. (1988b) 'Sexuality and power on the Zambian copper-belt: 1926–1964', in Sharon B. Stichter and Jane L. Parpart (eds) *Patriarchy and Class*, Boulder, Colorado, pp. 115–38.

*Parpart, Jane L. and Staudt, Kathleen A. (eds) (1989) *Women and the State in Africa*, Boulder, Colorado.

Paulme, Denise (1971) (ed.) *Women of Tropical Africa*, Berkeley, California.

*p'Bitek, Okot (1966) *Song of Lawino: An African Lament*, Nairobi.

p'Bitek, Okot (1970) *Song of Ocol*, Nairobi.

Pearce, Tola Olu (1988) 'Modern fertility regulation techniques in southwestern Nigeria', Paper submitted to UNESCO Working Group on New Reproductive Technologies and Women's Rights.

Pearce, Tola Olu (1991) 'Women's reproductive practices and bio-medicine: cultural conflicts and transformations', paper presented at the Wenner-Gren International Symposium on The Politics of Reproduction, Teresopolis, Brazil.

Pélissier, Paul (1966) *Les Paysans du Sénégal*, Saint-Yrieix.

Perham, Margery (1937) *Native Administration in Nigeria*, London.

Pons, V. (1969) *Stanleyville*, London.

Population Crisis Committee (1989) 'Population pressure is a menace to democracy', Washington, D.C.

Potash, Betty (1978) 'Some aspects of marital stability in a rural Luo community', *Africa* **48**: 380–97.

Potash, Betty (1985) 'Female farmers, mothers-in-law and extension agents: development planning and a rural Luo community', Michigan State University *Working Papers on Women in International Development*, **90**, East Lansing, Michigan.

Potash, Betty (1986) *Widows in African Societies: Choices and Constraints*, Stanford.

Potash, Betty (1989) 'Gender relations in sub-Saharan Africa', in Sandra Morgen (ed.) *Gender and Anthropology: Critical Reviews for Research and Teaching*, Washington, D.C., pp. 189–277.

Poyner, Robin (1980) 'Traditional textiles in Oyo, Nigeria', *African Arts*, **14**: 47–51.

Priebatsch, Suzanne and Natalie Knight (1978) 'Traditional Ndebele beadwork', *African Arts*, **11**: 24–27.

Quarcoo, A. K. and Marion Johnson (1968) 'Shai pots: the pottery tradition of the Shai people of southern Ghana', *Baessler-Archiv*, **16**: 47–88.

Quimby, Lucy (1979) 'Islam, sex roles, and modernization in Bobo-Dioulasso', in Bennetta Jules-Rosette (ed.) *The New Religions of Africa*, Norwood, N.J., pp. 203–18.

Raikes, Philip (1988) *Modernising Hunger: Famine, Food Surplus and Farm Policy in the EEC and Africa*, London.

Rakodi, C. (1988) 'Urban agriculture: research questions and Zambian evidence', *Journal of Modern African Studies*, **26**(3): 495–515.

Ranger, T. O. (1972) 'Missionary adaptation of African religious institutions: the Masasi case', in T. O. Ranger and Isaria Kimambo (eds) *The Historical Study of African Religion*, London, pp. 221–51.

Rao, Aruna *et al.* (1991) *Gender Training and Development Planning: Learning from Experience*, New York.

Rattray, R. S. (1923) *Ashanti*, Oxford.

Raum, O. F. (1973) *The Social Functions of Avoidance and Taboos Among the Zulu*, Berlin and New York.

'Reflections of Forum '85 in Nairobi, Kenya: voices from the International Women's Studies Community' (1986), *Signs: Journal of Women and Culture in Society*, Spring, **11**(3): 584–608.

Reisman, Paul (1980) 'The Fulani in a development context', in Stephen P. Reyna (ed.) *Sahelian Social Development*, Abidjan, pp. 71–186.

Republic of Kenya (1978) Ministry of Finance and Economic Planning, Central Bureau of Statistics, *Women in Kenya*, Nairobi.

*Richards, Audrey I. (1956) *Chisungu: A Girls' Initiation Ceremony Among the Bemba of Northern Rhodesia*, London.

Richards, Audrey I., Sturrock, Ford and Fortt, Jean M. (1973) *Subsistence to Commercial Farming in Present-Day Buganda: An Economic and Anthropological Survey*, Cambridge.

Ritzenthaler, Robert E. (1974) 'Anlu: a women's uprising in the British Cameroons', *African Studies*, **19**: 3.

Roberts, Penelope A. (1988) 'Rural women's access to labor in West Africa', in Sharon B. Stichter and Jane L. Parpart (eds) *Patriarchy and Class: African Women in the Home and the Workforce*, Boulder, Colorado, pp. 97–114.

Robertson, Claire C. (1983) 'The death of Makola and other tragedies, male strategies against a female-dominated system', *Canadian Journal of African Studies*, **17**(3): 674–95.

*Robertson, Claire (1984) *Sharing the Same Bowl: A Socioeconomic History of Women and Class Formation in Accra*, Bloomington, Indiana.

Robertson, Claire (1986) 'Women's Education and Class Formation in Africa, 1950–1980' in C. Robertson and I. Berger (eds) *Women and Class in Africa*, New York, pp. 92–113.

Robertson, Claire (forthcoming) *'Sharing Our Pain Gave Us Strength': Women, Men, and Trade in the Nairobi Area, 1890–1990*.

*Robertson, Claire C. and Klein, Martin A. (1983) *Women and Slavery in Africa*, Madison, Wisconsin.

Rogers, Susan G. (1983) 'Efforts toward women's development in Tanzania: gender rhetoric vs. gender realities', in Kathleen Staudt and Jane Jaquette (eds) *Women in Developing Countries: A Policy Focus*, New York, pp. 23–42.

Rohmann, G. F. (1974) 'Decoration in Southern Africa', *African Arts*, **7**: 18–21.

Rosaldo, Michelle and Lamphere, Louise (1974) 'Introduction', in Michelle Rosaldo and Louise Lamphere (eds) *Woman, Culture, and Society*, Stanford, California, pp. 1–16.

Rothchild, Donald and Chazan, Naomi (eds) (1988) *The Precarious Balance: State and Society in Africa*, Boulder, Colorado.

Rouch, Jean and Bernus, E. (1959) 'Notes sur les prostitués "toutous" de Treichville et d'Adjamé', *Etudes Eburnéenes*, **6**: 231–42.

Roy, Christopher (1975) 'West African pottery forming and firing techniques', M.A. thesis, Indiana University.

*Royston, Erica and Sue Armstrong (eds) (1989) *Preventing Maternal Deaths*, Geneva.

Rubin, Barbara (1970) 'Calabash decoration', *African Arts*, **4**: 20–25.

Russell, Diana E. H. (1989) *Lives of Courage: Women for a New South Africa*, New York.

*Sacks, Karen (1979) *Sisters and Wives: The Past and Future of Sexual Inequality*, Westport, Connecticut.

Sanders, D. and Sambo, A. (1991) 'AIDS in Africa: the implications of economic recession and structural adjustment', *Health Policy and Planning*, **6**(2): 157–65.

Scheub, Harold (1977) 'Performance of oral narrative', in William R. Bascom (ed.) *Frontiers of Folklore*, Boulder, Colorado, pp. 54–78.

Schildkrout, Enid (1978) 'Age and gender in Hausa societies: socio-economic roles of children in urban Kano', in J. S. LaFontaine (ed.) *Sex and Age as Principles of Social Organization*, New York, pp. 109–37.

Schmidt, Elizabeth (1991) 'Patriarchy, capitalism, and the colonial state in Zimbabwe', *Signs*, **16**(4): 732–56.

Schmidt, Elizabeth (1993) *Peasants, Traders, and Wives: Shona Women in the History of Zimbabwe, 1870–1939*, Portsmouth, NH.

Schoepf, Brooke G. *et al.* (1991) 'Gender, power, and risk of AIDS in Zaire', in Meredith Turshen (ed.) *Women and Health in Africa*, Trenton, N.J., pp. 187–203.

Schuster, Ilsa (1979) *New Women of Lusaka*, Palo Alto, California.

Schuster, Ilsa (1981) 'Perspectives in development: the problem of nurses and nursing in Zambia' in Nici Nelson (ed.) *African Women in the Development Process*, London, pp. 77–97.

Schuster, Ilsa (1982) 'Marginal lives: conflict and contradictions in the position of female traders in Lusaka, Zambia', in Edna G. Bay (ed.) *Women and Work in Africa*, Boulder, Colorado, pp. 105–27.

Schuster, Ilsa (1983) 'Constraints and opportunities in political participation: the case of Zambian women', *Genève-Afrique*, **21**(2): 7–37.

Scofield, Sue (1974) 'Seasonal factors affecting nutrition in different age groups and especially preschool children', *Journal of Development Studies*, **11**(1): 22–40.

Scott, James C. (1985) *Weapons of the Weak: Everyday Forms of Peasant Resistance*, New Haven, Connecticut.

Seidman, Ann and Frederick Anang (1992) *Twenty-first Century Africa: Towards a New Vision of Self-sustainable Development*, Trenton, N.J.

Seidman, Gay (1984) 'Women in Zimbabwe: post independence struggles', *Feminist Studies*, **10**(3): 419–40.

*Sembène, Ousmane (1970) *God's Bits of Wood* (trans. Francis Price),

London, 1979 (first published as *Les Bouts de bois de Dieu*, Paris, 1960).

Sen, Amartya K. (1981) *Poverty and Famine: An Essay on Entitlement and Deprivation*, Oxford.

Sen, Amartya K. (1990) 'Gender and cooperative conflicts', in Irene Tinker (ed.) *Persistent Inequalities: Women and World Development*, New York, pp. 123–49.

Shanklin, Eugenia (1990) 'ANLU remembered: the Kom Women's Rebellion of 1958–1961', *Dialectical Anthropology*, **15**: 159–81.

Shields, Nwanganga (1980) 'Women in the urban labor markets of Africa: the case of Tanzania', World Bank Staff Working Paper No. 380.

Sibisi, Harriet (1977) 'How African women cope with migrant labor in South Africa', *Signs*, **3**(1): 167–77.

Sieber, Roy (1972) 'Kwahu terracottas, oral traditions, and Ghanaian history', in Douglas Fraser and Herbert Cole (eds) *African Art and Leadership*, Madison, Wisconsin, pp. 173–83.

Skinner, Neil (ed. and trans.) (1969) *Hausa Tales and Traditions: An English Translation of 'Tatsuniyoyi na Hausa'* (originally compiled by Frank Edgar), London.

Smith, Fred (1978a) 'Gurensi basketry and pottery', *African Arts*, **12**(1): 78–81.

Smith, Fred (1978b) 'Gurensi wall painting', *African Arts*, **11**(4): 36–41.

Smith, Fred (1986) 'Compound entryway decoration: male space and female creativity', *African Arts*, **19**: 52–59.

*Smith, Mary (1981) *Baba of Karo: A Woman of the Muslim Hausa*, New Haven, Connecticut (first published 1955 with introduction by Michael G. Smith).

Smith, Michael G. (1957) 'The social functions and meaning of Hausa praise-singing', *Africa*, **27**: 26–43.

Société d'Etudes pour le Développement Economique et Sociale (SEDES) (1965) *Région de Korhogo*, 9 vols, Paris.

Sofola, Zulu (1977) *The Sweet Trap*, Ibadan.

Southall, A. W. (1961) (ed.) *Social Change in Modern Africa*, London.

Southall, A. W. and Gutkind, P. C. W. (1957) *Townsmen in the Making*, Kampala.

Spencer, Dunstan S. C. (1976) 'African women in agricultural development: a case study in Sierra Leone'. Overseas Liaison Committee, American Council on Education, Paper No. 9, Washington, D.C.

Spies, S. B. (1980) 'Women and the war' in Peter Warwick (ed.) *The South African War: The Anglo-Boer War, 1899–1902*, London, pp. 161–85.

Spindel, Carol (1989) 'Kpeenbele Senufo potters', *African Arts*, **22**(2): 66–73.

Spring, Anita (1978) 'Epidemiology of spirit possession among the Luvale of Zambia', in Judith Hoch-Smith and Anita Spring (eds) *Women in Ritual and Symbolic Roles*, New York, pp. 165–89.

Spring, Anita and Vicki Wilde (1991) 'Women farmers, structural adjustment, and FAO's plan of action for the integration of women in development', in Christina H. Gladwin (ed.) *Structural Adjustment and African Women Farmers*, Gainesville, Florida, pp. 387–408.

Stamp, Patricia (1975–1976) 'Perceptions of change and economic strategy among Kikuyu women of Mitero, Kenya', *Rural Africana*, **29:** 19–43.

Stamp, Patricia (1986) 'Kikuyu women's self-help groups', in Claire Robertson and Iris Berger (eds) *Women and Class in Africa*, New York, pp. 27–47.

Stamp, Patricia (1991) 'Burying Otieno: the politics of gender and ethnicity in Kenya', *Signs*, **16:** 808–45.

Staudt, Kathleen (1978) 'Agricultural productivity gaps: a case study of male preference in government policy implementation', *Development and Change*, July, **9**(3): 439–58.

Staudt, Kathleen (1986) 'Class stratification and its implication for women's politics', in Iris Berger and Claire Robertson (eds) *Women and Class in Africa*, New York, pp. 197–215.

Staudt, Kathleen (1987) 'Uncaptured or unmotivated? Women and the food crisis in Africa', *Rural Sociology*, **52**(1): 37–55.

Staudt, Kathleen (1988) 'Women farmers in Africa: research and institutional action, 1972–1987', *Canadian Journal of African Studies*, **22**(3): 567–82.

Staudt, Kathleen (1990) 'Gender politics in bureaucracy: theoretical issues in comparative perspective', in K. Staudt (ed.) *Women, International Development and Politics: The Bureaucratic Mire*, Philadelphia, pp. 3–38.

Staudt, Kathleen (1991) *Managing Development: State, Society, and International Contexts*, Newbury Park, California.

Staudt, Kathleen and Jaquette, Jane (eds) (1983) *Women in Developing Countries: A Policy Focus*, New York.

Steady, Filomina Chioma (1975) *Female Power in African Politics: The National Congress of Sierra Leone*, Munger Africana Notes No. 31, Pasadena, California.

*Steady, Filomina Chioma (1976) 'Protestant women's associations in Freetown, Sierra Leone', in Nancy Hafkin and Edna Bay (eds) *Women in Africa: Studies in Social and Economic Change*, Stanford, California, pp. 183–212.

Steady, Filomina Chioma (1987) 'Polygamy and the household economy in a fishing village in Sierra Leone', in David Parkin and David Nyamwaya (eds) *Transformations of African Marriage*, Manchester, pp. 211–33.

Stichter, Sharon (1985) *Migrant Laborers*, Cambridge.

Stichter, Sharon B. (1988) 'The middle-class family in Kenya: changes in gender relations', in S. Stichter and J. Parpart (eds) *Patriarchy and Class: African Women in the Home and the Workforce*, Boulder, Colorado, pp. 177–204.

Stichter, Sharon (1990) 'Women, employment and the family: current debates' in Sharon Stichter and Jane L. Parpart (eds) *Women, Employment and the Family in the International Division of Labour*, London, pp. 11–71.

*Stichter, Sharon B. and Parpart, Jane L. (eds) (1988) *Patriarchy and Class: African Women in the Home and the Workforce*, Boulder, Colorado.

Stratton, Florence (1988) 'The shallow grave: archetypes of female experience in African fiction', in Rhonda Cobham and Chikwenye Okojno Ogunyemi (eds) *Research in African Literatures: Special Issue on Women's Writing*, **19**: 143–69.

Strobel, Margaret (1976) 'From Lelemana to lobbying: women's associations in Mombasa', in Nancy Hafkin and Edna Bay, *Women in Africa: Studies in Social and Economic Change*, Stanford, California.

*Strobel, Margaret (1979) *Muslim Women in Mombasa, 1890–1975*, New Haven, Connecticut.

Strobel, Margaret (1991) *European Women and the Second British Empire*, Bloomington, Indiana.

Sudarkasa, Niara (1981) 'Female employment and family organization in West Africa', in Filomina Chioma Steady (ed.) *The Black Woman Cross-Culturally*, Cambridge, Massachusetts, pp. 49–65.

Sule, Balaraba B. M. and Starratt, Priscilla E. (1991) 'Islamic leadership positions for women in contemporary Kano society', in Catherine Coles and Beverly Mack (eds) *Hausa Women in the Twentieth Century*, Madison, Wisconsin, pp. 29–48.

Sundkler, B. G. M. (1961) *Bantu Prophets in South Africa* (first published 1948), London and New York.

Sutherland, Efua Theodora (1967) *Foriwa* (first published 1964) Accra-Tema.

Swindell, Ken (1985) *Farm Labour*, Cambridge.

*Tansi, Sony Labou (1985) *Les Sept Solitudes de Lorsa Lopez*, Paris.

Thiam, Awa (1986) *Black Sisters, Speak Out: Feminism and Oppression in Black Africa*, London.

Thomas, Barbara (1988a) 'Household strategies for adaptation and change: participation in Kenyan Rural Women's Associations', *Africa*, **58**: 401–22.

Thomas, Barbara (1988b) 'State formation, development, and the politics of self-help in Kenya', *Studies in Comparative International Development*, **23**(3): 5–27.

*Thompson, Robert (1969) 'Abatan: a master potter of the Egbado Yoruba', in Daniel Biebuyck (ed.) *Tradition and Creativity in Tribal Art*, Berkeley, California, pp. 120–82.

Tiffany, Sharon W. (1978) 'Models and the social anthropology of women: a preliminary assessment', *Man*, **13**: 34–51.

Tiger, Lionel (1969) *Men in Groups*, London.

Tlali, Miriam (1979) *Muriel at Metropolitan*, London.

Tlali, Miriam (1989) 'Masechaba's erring "child"', in *Soweto Stories*, London, pp. 138–62.

Topouzis, Daphne (1990) 'Kenya women fight deforestation', *Africa Recovery*, **4**(3–4): 44.

Toure, Oussouby (1988) 'The pastoralists of northern Senegal', *Review of African Political Economy*, **42**: 32–39.

Trager, Lillian and Clara Osinulu (1991) 'New women's organizations in Nigeria: one response to structural adjustment', in Christina H. Gladwin (ed.) *Structural Adjustment and African Women Farmers*, Gainesville, Florida, pp. 339–58.

Tremearne, A. J. N. (1913) *Hausa Superstitions and Customs*, London.

Tripp, Aili Mari (1989) 'Women and the changing urban household economy in Tanzania,' *Journal of Modern African Studies*, **27**(4): 601–623.

Turner, Victor (1957) *Schism and Continuity in An African Society*, Manchester.

Turshen, Meredith (1984) *The Political Ecology of Disease in Tanzania*, New Brunswick, N.J.

Turshen, Meredith (1986) 'Food and hunger in Ciskei', in Peter Lawrence (ed.) *World Recession and the Food Crisis in Africa*, London.

*Turshen, Meredith (ed.) (1991) *Women and Health in Africa*, Trenton, N.J.

Tutuola, Amos (1958) *The Brave African Huntress*, New York.

United Nations (1974) *The Role of Women in Population Dynamics Related to Food and Agriculture and Rural Development in Africa*, Economic Commission for Africa, Addis Ababa.

United Nations (1991) *The World's Women 1970–1990: Trends and Statistics*, New York.

United Nations Economic Commission for Africa (1972) 'Women: the neglected human resource for African development', *Canadian Journal of African Studies*, **6**(2): 359–70.

UNESCO (1986) *World Survey on the Role of Women in Development*, New York.

*Urdang, Stephanie (1979) *Fighting Two Colonialisms: Women in Guinea-Bissau*, New York.

*Urdang, Stephanie (1989) *And Still They Dance: Women, War, and the Struggle for Change in Mozambique*, New York.

U'Tamsi, Tchikaya (1970) *Selected Poems* (ed. and trans. Gerald Moore), London.

Van Allen, Judith (1972) 'Sitting on a Man: Colonialism and the Lost Political Institutions of Igbo Women', *Canadian Journal of African Studies*, **6**(2): 165–81.

Van Allen, Judith (1976) '"Aba riots" or Igbo women's war? Ideology, stratification, and the invisibility of women', in Nancy Hafkin and Edna Bay (eds) *Women in Africa: Studies in Social and Economic Change*, Stanford, California, pp. 59–86.

Van de Walle, E. (1990) 'The social impact of AIDS in sub-Saharan Africa', *Milbank Quarterly*, **68**(suppl. 1): 10–32.

*Vaughan, Megan (1987) *The Story of an African Famine: Gender and Famine in Twentieth-century Malawi*, Cambridge.

Vaughn, James (1973) 'Kyagu as artists in Marghi society', in Warren d'Azevedo (ed.) *The Traditional Artist in African Societies*, Bloomington, Indiana, pp. 62–93.

Vellenga, Dorothy Dee (1983) 'Who is a wife? Legal expressions of heterosexual conflict in Ghana', in Christine Oppong (ed.) *Female and Male in West Africa*, London, pp. 144–56.

Vellenga, Dorothy Dee (1986) 'The widow among the matrilineal Akan of southern Ghana', in Betty Potash (ed.) *Widows in African Societies*, Stanford, California, pp. 220–41.

Vincent, Jeanne-Françoise (1976) *Traditions et transition: Entretiens avec des femmes Beti du Sud Cameroun*, Paris.

Waane, S. A. C. (1977) 'Pottery-making traditions of the Ikombe Kisi, Mbeya Region, Tanzania', *Baessler-Archiv*, **25**: 251–317.

Wachtel, Eleanor (1975–1976) 'A farm of one's own: the rural orientation of women's group enterprises in Nakuru, Kenya', *Rural Africana*, **29**: 69–80.

*Wachtel, Eleanor (1976) 'Minding her own business: women shopkeepers in Nakuru', *African Urban Notes*, **2**(2): 27–42.

Wahlmann, Maude (1972) 'Yoruba pottery-making techniques', *Baessler-Archiv*, **20**: 313–46.

Wahlmann, Maude (1974) *Contemporary African Arts*, Chicago.

Walker, Sheila (1979) 'Women in the Harrist Movement', in Bennetta Jules-Rosette (ed.) *The New Religions of Africa*, Norwood, N.J., p. 87–97.

Ward, Cynthia (1990) 'What they told Buchi Emecheta: oral subjectivity and the joys of "Otherhood"', *PMLA: Publications of the Modern Language Association of America*, **105**: 83–97.

Weiss, Ruth (1986) *Women of Zimbabwe*, London.

Werner, Alice and Hichens, William (eds.) (1943) *Utendi wa Mwana Kupona* (Advice of Mwana Kupona upon the Wifely Duty), Medstead, Hampshire.

White, Luise (1986) 'Prostitution, identity, and class consciousness in Nairobi', *Signs: A Journal of Women in Culture and Society*, **11**(21): 255–73.

White, Luise (1988) 'Domestic labor in a colonial city: prostitution in Nairobi, 1900–1952', in Sharon B. Stichter and Jane L. Parpart (eds.) *Patriarchy and Class: African Women in the Home and the Workforce*, Boulder, Colorado, pp. 139–61.

*White, Luise (1990) *The Comforts of Home: Prostitution in Colonial Nairobi*, Chicago.

Wicomb, Zoe (1987) *You Can't Get Lost in Cape Town*, London.

Williams, Denis (1973) 'Art in metal', in S. O. Biobaku (ed.) *Sources of Yoruba History*, Oxford, pp. 140–64.

Wipper, Audrey (1972) 'African women, fashion, and scapegoating', *Canadian Journal of African Studies*, **6**(2): 329–49.

Wipper, Audrey (1975–1976) 'The Maendeleo ya Wanawake movement in the colonial period', *Rural Africana*, **29**: 195–214.

*Wipper, Audrey (ed.) (1988) special issue, *Canadian Journal of African Studies*, **22**(3).

Wisner, Ben (1973) 'Global interdependence, drought and the struggle for liberation', *Journal of the Geographical Association of Tanzania*, **8**: 86–112.

Wisner, Ben (1992) 'Health of the future/the future of health', in Ann Seidman and Frederick Anang (eds) *Twenty-first Century Africa:*

Towards a New Vision of Self-sustainable Development, Trenton, N.J., pp. 149–81.

Wolff, Norma (1986) 'A Hausa aluminium spoon industry', *African Arts*, **19**(3): 40–44, 82.

Women and Law in Southern Africa Research Trust Zambia Group, (WLSA Zambia) (forthcoming) 'Report of the law of inheritance in Zambia'.

World Bank (1979) *Environment and Development*, Washington, D.C.

World Bank (1981) *Accelerated Development in Sub-Saharan Africa*, Washington, D.C.

World Bank (1990) *World Development Report*, Washington, D.C.

World Bank (1992) *World Development Report*, Washington, D.C.

World Health Organization (WHO) (1993) 'Update: AIDS cases reported to surveillance, forecasting and impact assessment unit, Office of Research, global programme on AIDS, 1 July 1993', Geneva, mimeo.

Wright, Marcia (1983) 'Technology, marriage, and women's work in the history of maize-growers in Mazabuka, Zambia: a reconnaissance', *Journal of Southern African Studies*, October, **10**(1): 73–75.

Wright, Marcia (1984) *Women in Peril*, Lusaka, Zambia.

*Wright, Marcia (1993) *Strategies of Slaves and Women: Life Stories from East/Central Africa*, New York.

Yanagisako, Sylvia (1979) 'Family and household: the analysis of domestic groups', *Annual Review of Anthropology*, **8**: 16–205.

Young, Crawford (1982) *Ideology and Development in Africa*, New Haven, Connecticut.

Young, M. Crawford (1988) 'The colonial state and its connection to the current political crisis in Africa', in Rothchild and Chazan (1988), pp. 25–66.

Yusuf, Bilkisu (1991) 'Hausa-Fulani women: the state of the struggle', in Catherine Coles and Beverly Mack (eds) *Hausa Women in the Twentieth Century*, Madison, Wisconsin, pp. 90–106.

Notes on contributors

Lisa Aronson is associate professor of art history at Skidmore College in Saratoga Springs, New York. Her research focuses on two main areas of interest, the impact of trade on Nigerian textile production and issues of gender in African art. Her publications include 'African Women in the Visual Arts: Review Essay', *Signs: Journal of Women in Culture and Society* (1992); 'African Cloth as Language' (forthcoming); and a broad series of articles about weaving in Southeastern Nigeria.

Kathryn Firmin-Sellers is assistant professor of political science at Indiana University. A graduate of Carleton College, she earned her Ph.D. from Duke University in 1993. Her current research focuses on the transformation of customary land tenure regimes during the colonial and independence eras.

Jane I. Guyer is an economic anthropologist, trained at the London School of Economics and Political Science and the University of Rochester. She has carried out extensive field research in Nigeria and Cameroon and has published widely on changing rural economies, including *Family and Farm in Southern Cameroon* (Boston, 1984); two edited collections, *Feeding African Cities* (Bloomington, Indiana, 1987) and *Money Matters: Instability and Values in West African Community Life* (Porstmouth, New Hampshire, 1994); and numerous articles. Currently director of the Program of African Studies at Northwestern University, she has held regular faculty positions at Boston University and at Harvard University and has also taught in Cameroon.

Margaret Jean Hay is associate professor of history and publications editor at the African Studies Center, Boston University. Her principal interests include rural social and economic history and the changing roles of African women. Her publications include *African Women and the Law: Historical Perspectives* (co-edited with Marcia Wright, Boston, 1982); 'Queens, Prostitutes, and Peasants: Historical Perspectives on African Women, 1971–1986', *Canadian Journal of African Studies* 22, 3 (1988); 'Hoes and Clothes: Production and Consumption among the

Luo', in Mary Jo Arnoldi and Kris Hardin (eds) *New Perspectives on African Material Culture* (forthcoming, Indiana University Press); and the Africa section of the *American Historical Association Guide to Historical Literature* (1995, co-edited with Joseph C. Miller). In addition, she is the editor (with Allen Isaacman) of the Heinemann Social History of Africa series.

Jeanne Koopman, an economist and research fellow at Boston University's African Studies Center, has lived in Africa for ten years, teaching at the University of Dar es Salaam and conducting macroeconomic and village-level research on the economic lives of men and women in Cameroon and Tanzania. She currently consults for United Nations agencies on rural development policy, projects, and gender issues, work that has brought her the pleasure of collaborating with feminist colleagues throughout Africa.

Deirdre LaPin has taught African literature and folklore at the Universities of Ife and Arkansas. She lived and conducted field research in Nigeria from 1972 to 1977 and again in 1982. Since 1984 Dr. LaPin has worked in the field of international health and social development for Africa, managing the UNICEF program in the Benin Republic and serving as UNICEF planning officer in Somalia. She currently works as a senior advisor in the US Agency for International Development. Her publications reflect combined interests in African folklore, comparative literature, and anthropology; they include 'Narrative as Precedent in Yoruba Tradition', in *Oral Traditional Literatures*, ed. John M. Foley (Columbus, Ohio, 1981); 'Tale and Trickster in Yoruba Verbal Art', *Research in African Literatures* (1981); and *Words and the Dogon World*, a translation with introduction of Geneviève Calame-Griaule's *Ethnologie et language: la parole chez les Dogon* (Philadelphia, 1982).

Margaret Mulela Munalula is a lecturer in law at the University of Zambia. Her major research interests are sociology/anthropology of law and gender. She is a long-standing member of the Women and Law in Southern Africa Research Trust and is currently involved in research on the family.

Winnie Sithole Mwenda has a Master of Law degree from the University of Zambia. She is a lawyer in private practice and a researcher with the Women and Law in Southern Africa Research Trust. She has a great interest in promoting women's rights. She has published an article on 'The Commercial Laws of Zambia' in *Digest of the Commercial Laws of the World* (Dobbs Ferry, NY, 1990).

Jean O'Barr is director of women's studies at Duke University. A graduate of Indiana University, she earned her Ph.D. in political science from Northwestern University in 1970. Her most recent publications include *Engaging Feminism: Students Speak Up and Speak*

Out (1992); *Africa and the Disciplines* (1993); *Feminism in Action: Building Institutions and Community Through Women's Studies* (1994); and *Conversations on a Journey: Feminist Scholars on Experiences, Images, and Applications of Gender* (forthcoming).

Tola Olu Pearce has a Ph.D. in medical sociology from Brown University. She is an associate professor at the University of Missouri and holds a joint position in the Department of Sociology and the Women's Studies Program. Her research interests concern various aspects of women's health, particularly reproductive health. She is currently working on material collected on the health roles of market women in Ile-Ife, Nigeria. Her publications include 'Perceptions on the Availability of Social Supports for Child Care Among Women in Ile-Ife', in *Child Health in Nigeria* (1994); *Importing the New Reproductive Technologies* (forthcoming, co-edited with Toyin Falola) and *Women's Reproductive Practises and Biomedicine* (forthcoming).

Betty Potash is editor of *Widows in African Societies: Choices and Constraints* (Stanford, 1986) and author of 'Gender Relations in Africa', in Sandra Morgan (ed.) *Gender and Anthropology: Critical Reviews* (Washington, DC, 1989). She has done research in East and West Africa, consults for the Population Council, and teaches at New York University.

Claire Robertson received her Ph.D. from the University of Wisconsin in 1974, and is professor of history and women's studies at the Ohio State University. She is the author of several dozen articles and a book, *Sharing the Same Bowl: A Socioeconomic History of Women and Class in Accra, Ghana* (Bloomington, Indiana, 1984), which won the African Studies Association's Herskovits Award in 1985. She co-edited two books, *Women and Slavery in Africa* (with Martin Klein, Madison, 1983) and *Women and Class in Africa* (with Iris Berger, New York, 1986). She has recently completed her book, *Healing Together Gave Us Strength: Women, Men, and Trade in the Nairobi Area, 1890–1990*, which should appear in 1995.

Kathleen Staudt received her Ph.D. in political science and African studies from the University of Wisconsin. She is professor and chair of the Political Science Department, University of Texas at El Paso. She has published many articles on gender development and women in politics in such journals as *Development and Change, Comparative Politics*, and *Canadian Journal of African Studies, Rural Africana*, and *Mexican Studies*. Her most recent books include *Women, International Development and Politics: The Bureaucratic Mire* (Philadelphia, 1990) and *Managing Development: State, Society, and International Contexts* (Beverly Hills, 1991). She is currently working on the 'informal economy' at the U.S.–Mexico border. Her forthcoming book focuses on the uneasy relationship between plural feminisms and the political science discipline.

298

Sharon Stichter is professor of sociology at the University of Massachusetts, Boston. She is currently working on a study of economic and family roles among middle- and low-income women in Nairobi. Her publications include *Migrant Labour in Kenya: Capitalism and African Response, 1895–1975* (London, 1982); *Women, Employment, and the Family in the International Division of Labour* (London, 1989); *Patriarchy and Class: African Women in the Home and Workforce* (co-edited with Jane Parpart, Boulder, Colorado, 1988); and *Migrant Labourers in Africa* (Cambridge, 1985).

Margaret (Peg) Strobel is professor of women's studies and history at the University of Illinois at Chicago. Her first book, *Muslim Women in Mombasa, 1890–1975* (New Haven, 1979), was co-winner in 1980 of the African Studies Association Herskovits Prize. She has also published *Three Swahili Women: Life Histories from Mombasa, Kenya* (co-edited with Sarah Mirza, Bloomington, Indiana, 1989), *European Women and the Second British Empire* (Bloomington, Indiana, 1991), *Western Women and Imperialism: Complicity and Resistance* (co-edited with Nupur Chaudhuri, Bloomington, Indiana, 1992), and *Expanding the Boundaries of Women's History: Essays on Women in the Third World* (co-edited with Cheryl Johnson-Odim, Bloomington, Indiana, 1992). Her current research focuses on the Chicago Women's Liberation Union.

Meredeth Turshen is associate professor of urban studies and community health, and graduate director of women's studies at Rutgers, the State University of New Jersey. She is currently working on a study of the privatization of health services in Africa. Her publications include two books, *The Politics of Public Health* (New Brunswick, New Jersey, 1989) and *The Political Ecology of Disease in Tanzania* (New Brunswick, New Jersey, 1984), and two edited collections, *Women's Lives and Public Policy: The International Experience* (Westport, Connecticut, 1993) and *Women and Health in Africa* (Trenton, New Jersey, 1991).

Stephanie Urdang is a consultant for the United Nations Development Programme, specializing in gender and in human development issues. When she has time, she pursues her other life as a journalist/writer. She has written extensively on women and Africa. Her most recent book is *And Still They Dance: Women, War, and the Struggle for Change in Mozambique* (New York, 1989).

Audrey Wipper is professor of sociology at the University of Waterloo in Canada. Her research has focused on Kenya, and she has edited several key collections on African women, including *The Roles of African Women: Past, Present, and Future*, a special issue of the *Canadian Journal of African Studies* (1972), *Rural Women: Development or Underdevelopment?*, a special issue of *Rural Africana* (Winter, 1976), and *Current Research on African Women* (1988).

Index